AMERICAN RIFLE DESIGN AND PERFORMANCE

AMERICAN RIFLE DESIGN AND PERFORMANCE

L. R. Wallack

WINCHESTER PRESS

Library of Congress Cataloging in Publication Data

Wallack, Louis Robert, 1919–
American rifle design and performance.
Includes index.
1. Rifles. I. Title.
TS536.4.W34 683'.42 77-1410
ISBN 0-87691-194-7

Winchester Press
205 East 42nd Street
New York, N.Y. 10017

Printed in the United States of America

DEDICATION

To the Bill of Rights

The first ten amendments to the Constitution, known as "A Bill of Rights," were adopted by the first Congress, called to meet in New York City, March 4, 1789. They were later ratified by the various States, and on December 15, 1791, were made a part of the Constitution.

Amendment I

Freedom of Religion, Speech, and the Press; Right of Assembly and Petition

CONGRESS shall make no law respecting an establishment of religion, or prohibiting the free exercise thereof; or abridging the freedom of speech, or of the press, or the right of the people peaceably to assemble, and to petition the government for a redress of grievances.

Amendment II

Right to Keep and Bear Arms

A well regulated militia, being necessary to the security of a free state, the right of the people to keep and bear arms shall not be infringed.

Amendment III

Quartering of Soldiers

No soldier shall in time of peace be quartered in any house without the consent of the owner, nor in time of war, but in a manner to be prescribed by law.

Amendment IV

Regulation of Right of Search and Seizure

The right of the people to be secure in their persons, houses, papers, and effects, against unreasonable searches and seizures, shall not be violated, and no warrants shall issue but upon probable cause, supported by oath or affirmation, and particularly describing the place to be searched and the persons or things to be seized.

Amendment V

Protection for Persons and Their Property

No person shall be held to answer for a capital or otherwise infamous crime, unless on a presentment or indictment of a grand jury, except in cases arising in the land or naval forces, or in the militia, when in actual service in time of war or public danger; nor shall any person be subject for the same offense to be twice put in jeopardy of life or limb; nor shall be compelled in any criminal case to be a witness against himself, nor be deprived of life, liberty, or property, without due process of law; nor shall private property be taken for public use, without just compensation.

Amendment VI

Rights of Persons Accused of Crime

In all criminal prosecutions, the accused shall enjoy the right to a speedy and public trial by an impartial jury of the State and district wherein the crime shall have been committed, which district shall have been previously ascertained by law, and to be informed of the nature and cause of the accusation; to be confronted with the witnesses against him; to have compulsory process for obtaining witnesses in his favor, and to have the assistance of counsel for his defense.

Amendment VII

Right of Trial by Jury in Suits at Common Law

In suits at common law, where the value in controversy shall exceed twenty dollars, the right of trial by jury shall be preserved, and no fact tried by a jury shall be otherwise re-examined in any court of the United States, than according to the rules of the common law.

Amendment VIII

Protection Against Excessive Bail and Punishments

Excessive bail shall not be required, nor excessive fines imposed, nor cruel and unusual punishments inflicted.

Amendment IX

Constitution Does Not List All Individual Rights

The enumeration in the Constitution of certain rights shall not be construed to deny or disparage others retained by the people.

Amendment X

Powers Reserved to the States and the People

The powers not delegated to the United States by the Constitution, nor prohibited by it to the States, are reserved to the States respectively, or to the people.

CONTENTS

Part I The Rifle
ONE Basic Small Arms 3
TWO Manually Operated Breech Actions 7
THREE Semiautomatic Breech Actions 29
FOUR Breech-Action Locking Systems 37
FIVE Feeding Systems 45
SIX Extraction and Ejection Systems 51
SEVEN Triggers 57
EIGHT Firing Systems 65
NINE The Rifle Barrel 71
TEN The Gun Stock 89
ELEVEN Sights and Scopes 109

Part II Ammunition and Ballistics 123
TWELVE Ammunition 125
THIRTEEN Calibers 131
FOURTEEN Cases and Primers 139
FIFTEEN Propellants 147
SIXTEEN Bullet Design and Performance 153
SEVENTEEN The Bullet's Flight 165
EIGHTEEN Whims, Engraving, Craftsmanship 183
NINETEEN Accuracy 193
TWENTY Hits and Misses 199

Index 209

INTRODUCTION

There is an enormous amount of work involved in the design and development of a firearm. And the simpler that gun may seem to be, the more work went into it to make it that simple. This book is about the various types of guns and the whys and hows of their operation. It is written for the person who seeks to know more than just how to load and shoot his gun. It is a book about how the varied types work, whether they are a relatively simple single-shot or a more complicated semiautomatic. And it will tell why things that happen must happen.

There are a certain very few books on the subject of guns that I consider classics. One is *The Gun and Its Development,* originally written in 1881 by W. W. Greener, the great English gunmaker. This book was revised several times, the most famous revision being the Ninth, issued in 1910. Another classic is that by Major Sir Gerald Burrard, a great 3-volume work on English shotguns in 1932 entitled *The Modern Shotgun* with a revision and slight updating in 1950. The third is *Small Arms Design and Ballistics,* in two volumes, by Col. Townsend Whelen, published in 1945.

While I never met Greener, I did correspond briefly with Burrard and I got to know Townsend Whelen toward the end of his brilliant career as one of the world's leading gun authorities. In fact, I did some custom gun work for Whelen in the 1950's.

All these books are great works, but they are also out of date. Many of the principles remain the same, but the arms industry in America has made vast progress since 1945. Many of these advances have involved methods of manufacture; some represent the gradual evolvement of a type of gun; and others are the result of inventive genius. This has always been happening, but it is necessary to update from time to time and that is what I have sought to do in the following pages.

What I have attempted, in simple language, is to explain how and why today's guns work as they do. The knowledge should aid in an understanding of how a gun functions; and perhaps that knowledge will help you to enjoy your sport more and to more fully appreciate your guns. Also it will give you the basics to understand when something goes astray.

Note that the publisher of this book is *Winchester Press.* That's a division of the company that makes Winchester guns and ammunition. You should know at the outset that there has never been any pressure on me to push Winchester products or to diminish those of other manufacturers. On the opposite side of the coin, some of the best cooperation I've had is from Winchester's leading competitors. I should like to acknowledge that support, from the entire American gun industry, which includes major manufacturers, importers, custom gunmakers and many individuals.

This is a book that should remain basic and current for a long time. But who can forecast the future? Who can tell when another John Browning will come along, or what other innovations someone like Bill Ruger might have in his mind? The whole world of gundom might change in the next few years. These things aren't likely but they can happen and if you read history you will understand that man always thinks, wrongly, that today is the ultimate. Just look back over your shoulder.

L.R. Wallack
January, 1977

PART ONE

THE RIFLE

CHAPTER ONE

BASIC SMALL ARMS

Let's understand each other from the beginning. There are "guns" that squirt grease, ooze caulking, and bleed glue. But we're not talking about them; we're talking about basic firearms, more specifically about rifles — the kind that shoot a bullet propelled by a charge of gunpowder.

Ever since guns were invented several hundred years ago, man has consistently tried to improve them by increasing accuracy or velocity, rapidity of fire, size of projectile, and the effect that projectile has upon its arrival at the target. There have been dramatic developments in some of these areas. In others there has been no significant advance whatever in the past few hundred years simply because the laws of physics can't be repealed.

Wars have always stimulated small-arms development, usually to a degree that resulted in advantages to the civilian rifleman, although we now appear to have reached the point where further military developments in small arms will be of little value to sporting gundom. For example, World War II saw the basic infantryman of all major armies employ semiautomatic rifles almost exclusively. While sporting use of similar rifles and shotguns has expanded greatly since then, recent military development of semiautomatic guns has generally not been of a type that has much sporting use. On the other hand, the American Civil War produced a tremendous breakthrough because it began with muzzle loaders and ended with breechloading rifles. That statement is somewhat oversimplified, as Civil War buffs will understand, but is basically true.

The end of World War I sent American soldiers home with awe and respect for the Springfield .30/06, a bolt-action rifle. Up until that time, most hunters preferred the older lever-action types; but after 1918 there came a gradual, and grudging, approval of the "knob" action and, at the same time, a vast improvement in bolt-action sporting rifles as they evolved over the succeeding twenty to twenty-five years.

A rifle, no matter what its action, may be defined as a shoulder arm with spiral grooves in its bore to force the single projectile to rotate in flight. Other firearms have rifled bores, however, a few examples being pistols and revolvers, machine guns, submachine guns, and artillery. A battleship's 16-inch guns are really rifles, just as is the Springfield .30/06.

There is often some fast and loose employment of words and definitions in the gun game. It's common — and legitimate outside the U.S. Marine Corps — to call a rifle a gun. The word is generic for all firearms, even though the serious shooter prefers to be more specific. This book will confine itself primarily to sporting rifles, although an occasional example will be used to explain some points that will involve machine guns and even artillery.

Several other words will occasionally occur; one is carbine, which is a short-barreled rifle. The word comes from old horse-cavalry days when shorter barrels, which could fit in a scabbard, were required for mounted troops. The precise barrel length at which a rifle becomes a carbine, or the other way around, depends on who is rendering the definition. Since Winchester (and Marlin) offers 20-inch barrels in their traditional .30/30 lever-action carbines, we may as well adopt that. The exact measurement is of no importance today anyway. Technically, a carbine is a rifle because it has a rifled bore.

A musket is not a modern gun at all, but with the current interest in black-powder shooting, the musket is once again being produced. It describes a firearm of rifle size and outward resemblance but with a smooth, that is not rifled, bore. It shoots a round ball or sometimes an elongated slug. Muskets were held in high esteem by early European armies, especially those of England and France. Their advantage was that they were far easier to load during battle than a rifle. Black powder leaves an awful mess of dirt in the bore after firing a shot, and when you're muzzle loading, you have to drive the new projectile down the barrel with a ramrod. It's much easier to do if the bore is smooth instead of rifled. Muskets were used by the American colonists chiefly in New England, which was largely settled by the English. The rifle came to early America with German and Swiss emigrants, most of whom arrived in Pennsylvania while a few settled in upstate New York.

A machine gun is a military weapon that continues firing until its ammunition is exhausted or the trigger is released. Put another way, the machine gun is truly automatic in that every step of its operation is provided by the energy generated by the gun itself in the act of firing. A submachine gun is the same thing except that it's smaller and can be hand held. We will not be particularly concerned with machine guns in this book except to touch briefly on their method of operation.

The Gatling gun is not a machine gun in the strict sense of the definition. Invented by a Chicago dentist, Dr. Richard Gatling, the gun more closely resembles an artillery piece, in that it contains as many as ten barrels mounted on a large breech mechanism that, in turn, is supported by a big pair of wheels. The Gatling is gravity fed by means of a hopper on top of the breech; the gun is then operated by turning a crank that rotates the entire cluster of barrels much like a huge revolver cylinder. Each barrel is fired as it comes into firing position. The faster the crank is turned, the faster the Gatling will shoot.

A few Gatlings saw limited service in the Civil War, and many were used in Indian wars later; then the Gatling went into oblivion until a few years ago, when the principle was again adopted for the Vulcan, a .60-caliber, multibarreled aircraft cannon. Hydraulic power has replaced the soldier with the crank; otherwise, it operates on the same principle.

Two additional terms that are often confused are automatic and semiautomatic. An automatic gun is a machine gun. A semiautomatic, also called autoloading, gun requires a separate, deliberate pull of the trigger for each shot fired, but every other step in the operational sequence is performed by the energy developed by the gun in firing.

An example will help explain how the use of firearms dictates their design. This is an old example, but the same principle is true today. The German

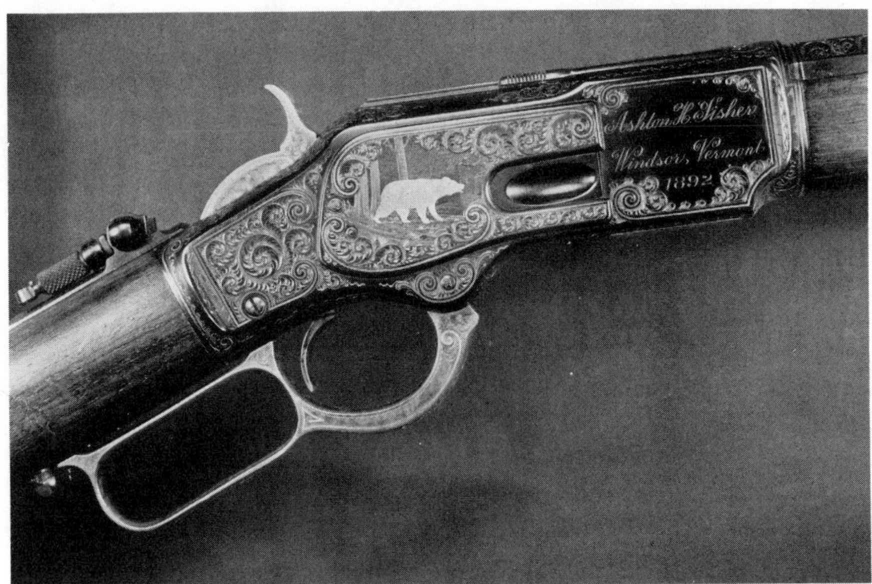

A fine example of the gunmaker's craft is this Winchester 1873 rifle engraved by Alvin White, who is probably the dean of American engravers at this writing.

and Palatine Swiss gunsmiths of Colonial days settled in two areas. One was Pennsylvania, near Lancaster, and the other was New York, near Palatine Bridge. These gunsmiths brought their traditional Jaeger rifles to the colonies, but the Jaeger was a heavy rifle, too cumbersome for use on the American frontier. Over a period of time, the Jaeger underwent drastic changes, doubtless as frontiersmen came back from such places as Kentucky and complained about such drawbacks as excess weight. What eventually emerged was the long, small-calibered, slim, and handsome Kentucky rifle. Some people still think it should be called the Pennsylvania rifle, because it was made there. But it's called the Kentucky because that's where it was used and the use dictated the design — and the name.

Some years later, when the frontier moved west of the Mississippi and St. Louis was the jumping-off place, other gunsmiths moved there. Game in the West was different from the East. Instead of deer, black bear, an occasional panther, and some Indians, the Western explorer had to contend with buffalo, grizzly bears, elk, and — some said — more hostile Indians. Moreover, the Western hunter or mountain man used a horse. The Kentucky rifle wasn't the gun for the West and again the gradual evolvement dictated by use began. The rifle became shorter, so it would be handier on horseback. The stock became thicker, so it wouldn't break in a fall with a horse. And the caliber became heavier, because the game was meaner, bigger, and tougher. Thus developed the Plains Rifle. Some think it uglier than the Kentucky, but I've always felt it was just as handsome. It was developed to do a job and it filled an important niche in our Western history from the early 1800s until the breechloaders replaced it after the Civil War.

THE SEVEN STEPS OF OPERATION

Every gun, no matter its type or method of operation, goes through seven steps of operation for every shot that it fires. This is true with everything from a single-shot rifle to the most modern machine gun. And a thorough understanding of these basics is essential to an understanding of how and why any gun works . . . or doesn't work. The steps do not necessarily work in the same order; sometimes two or more of them occur at the same time. But, in every gun, they all must be performed. In a single-shot rifle, for example, these steps work in the exact order given, and each step is performed by hand, or manually. In a lever- or pump-action repeater some of the steps occur simultaneously and they don't always correspond with the order given here. In an autoloading system, every one of the steps is performed by the gun's energy except pulling the trigger. And in a machine gun even that is automatic.

The important thing to remember is that every single one of the following steps must be performed for *every* shot fired with any firearm.

1. Firing: Pulling the trigger releases a mechanism, either a hammer or firing pin under spring tension, that strikes the primer of the cartridge in the barrel's chamber. The primer is activated by the blow and ignites the powder charge which, in turn, generates propellant gas to drive the bullet down the barrel.

*2. **Unlocking:*** The breech pressure required to drive a bullet must be contained until that bullet has left the bore. It is obvious that the magnitude of gas pressure we're talking about must only move the bullet, and it should be equally obvious that to open the breech prematurely would allow gas under enormous pressure to flow into the action. Consequently, the breech must be locked securely against this high pressure. Before any of the following steps can take place, the action must be unlocked. Unlocking is always performed by the very first part of the movement of operating lever, pump handle, bolt, or operating rod.

During unlocking, another completely automatic event occurs called primary extraction. In firing, the high pressure that is developed forces the brass cartridge case tightly against the chamber walls. The precise amount of loosening required depends upon several factors, including the amount of pressure, smoothness of chamber walls, and brittleness of the brass cartridge case among others. Before this empty case can be withdrawn, it must be loosened from the chamber. This is always accomplished by mechanical leverage during the first part of unlocking. Primary extraction is vital in a hot, modern cartridge — such as the .300 Winchester Magnum — and far less important in rifles developing much lower chamber pressures, such as the .30/30.

*3. **Extraction:*** The withdrawal of the fired, or empty, cartridge case from the chamber. Extraction is usually performed by a hook on the breechbolt that pulls the empty out as the bolt is withdrawn from the barrel.

*4. **Ejection:*** The removal of the empty case from the gun. Note the difference between extraction and ejection; the words are often confused but the distinction is important to an understanding of operating systems. Ejection is generally performed at the end of the rearward stroke of the breechbolt, when the empty is flipped out of the gun.

*5. **Cocking:*** Storage of energy in the firing-mechanism spring. It is accomplished by drawing and holding back either hammer or firing pin with a small part connected with the trigger, or by the trigger itself.

*6. **Feeding:*** Moving the fresh, unfired cartridge from the magazine into the chamber of the barrel, ready for firing. In a single-shot firearm, feeding is manually performed by simply placing the new cartridge directly into the chamber with the fingers.

*7. **Locking:*** The reverse of unlocking. Locking holds the breechblock securely against the gas pressure generated during firing. As a safety feature, most guns will not fire until they are fully and securely locked.

That's what every firearm must do to shoot and shoot again. A successful gun must perform every one of these steps logically, simply, and with as few parts as possible, and it must have the capability to perform them thousands of times without failure.

We can now break down the guns we're going to talk about into two groups: those that are manually operated and those of semiautomatic (or autoloading) type. The principal manually operated firearms in common use today are bolt, lever, pump, single shot, double barrel, and revolver. Those of semiautomatic action are operated either by gas, short recoil, long recoil, or blowback.

CHAPTER TWO

MANUALLY OPERATED BREECH ACTIONS

THE BOLT ACTION

Even though the bolt action has been popular in America only since World War I, it is one of the oldest of our current operating systems. The first bolt action is credited to a Prussian named Johann Nikolaus von Dreyse, who patented the Prussian needle gun in the early 1800s. Long before the days of metallic cartridges, the needle gun used a paper-wrapped load with the primer ahead of the powder charge – between it and the bullet. The term needle came from the abnormally long firing pin, long enough to penetrate the powder charge completely and reach the primer.

Basically, although it's a bit oversimplified, the principle of a bolt-action is the same as that of a sliding-bolt door lock, the kind you raise 90° and draw back to allow the door to open. There's only one real difference: the thrust against the locked door is sideways; the thrust against a rifle bolt is in a straight line with the bolt itself. Most .22 rimfire rifles indeed have a bolt almost exactly like the door-lock type. The surface used for locking the .22 bolt is the handle, where it turns down into the receiver. A high-power rifle bolt, however, has stout locking lugs that engage recesses in the receiver. (The receiver, a common word in any gun, is that part that houses the action. It's also known as the "major item" and that's why it is the part that bears the serial number.) There are departures from the original, but all turning-bolt locking systems are essentially similar.

One of the most important bolt-action developments to follow the needle gun was Peter Paul Mauser's 1872 rifle, which had a bolt that foreshadowed those of today's rifles. It was a single-shot rifle, but was soon followed by the repeating Model 71/84, a military arm that was used by Turkey, Germany, Serbia, and a number of other countries. At about the same time, Remington Arms in the U.S. was experimenting with a couple of bolt designs and actually marketed two of them. Neither gained appreciable fame or following, however, and they were soon dropped.

The first really modern bolt action was the Mauser Model 1893, which was built in Germany for Spain and has ever since been called the Spanish Mauser. The magazine was an especially important development; it replaced "under-the-barrel" and "inside-the-stock" tubular magazines with the "staggered-box" style that placed all five cartridges directly under the bolt and staggered them, rather than having one directly atop another. This gave the action a slimmer, shallower profile. The magazine also permitted the use of more efficient sharp-pointed bullets, known after the German as spitzers, which couldn't be used in tubular-type magazines because of the danger of a bullet tip hitting the primer of a cartridge ahead of it. This model also introduced the smokeless-powder-loaded 7mm Mauser cartridge.

American military experts and arms manufacturers were aware of the Mauser efforts, for Mauser had visited the United States and seen its major arms makers. But the American public was introduced to the Spanish Mauser in a brutal fashion. The Spanish-American War found the U.S. Army primarily armed with the old single-shot Springfield, chambered for the equally ancient .45/70 black-powder cartridge. Every time an American fired, a huge cloud of powder obscured his vision and disclosed his position to the enemy. Moreover, the old Springfield was given to sticky extraction problems that usually had to be solved by prying the stuck empty out with a knife.

Meanwhile the Spanish soldiers were shooting the 7mm small-bore, high-velocity cartridge with smokeless powder that did not obscure their targets and did not give away their positions. In the battle of San Juan Hill in 1898, 700 Spaniards inflicted 1,400 casualties on the Americans. (That, incidentally, is an excellent example of how war stimulates the development of firearms.)

Peter Paul Mauser had another couple of refinements in mind and they resulted in the Mauser Model 1898, which remains to this day one of the world's outstanding bolt actions. Like the earlier 93 action, it retained the two stout locking lugs at the front end of the bolt body, but it also added a safety lug near the back of the bolt, which was meant to work if the forward lugs should shear off. The 98 also included a cocking cam designed to cock the firing pin on the opening stroke of the bolt handle, and thereby smooth out the operation. (A cam is a surface whose purpose is to change the direction of a force; it can be a projection or an angled surface.) This cocking cam is cut into the rear surface of the bolt and connects with a mating surface on the firing pin. As the bolt handle is rotated open, this cam forces the firing pin back into cocked position by compressing the firing-pin spring. The principal benefit of a cock-on-opening bolt is better mechanical advantage. Cocking becomes easier, and it also makes chambering a dirty or sticky cartridge easier because this heavy spring does not also have to be cocked at the same time, as was required in the Model 93 rifle.

Any turning-bolt system is a direct descendant of Mauser's basic design. That even applies to many of today's guns that are operated by gas, levers, pump handles, and recoil. When the breechbolt turns into locked position and its lugs engage recesses in corresponding notches in the receiver, the action is partly Mauser.

Let's follow a typical bolt action, using the Mauser as an example, through the seven steps of operation:

*1. **Firing:*** Pulling the trigger releases the firing pin which has been under tension from the mainspring. This pin drives ahead smartly and its point crushes the primer of the chambered cartridge, causing it to fire.

*2. **Unlocking:*** Simply raising the bolt handle 90° (or less in some actions) turns the locking lugs out of engagement with their recesses in the front ring of the receiver. This initial movement also drives the bolt backwards a fraction of an inch, with the powerful mechanical advantage employed by an extracting cam, and the cartridge is broken loose from its seal in the chamber.

*3. **Extraction:*** Withdrawing the bolt extracts the fired cartridge from the chamber by holding it against the bolt face with the extractor hook.

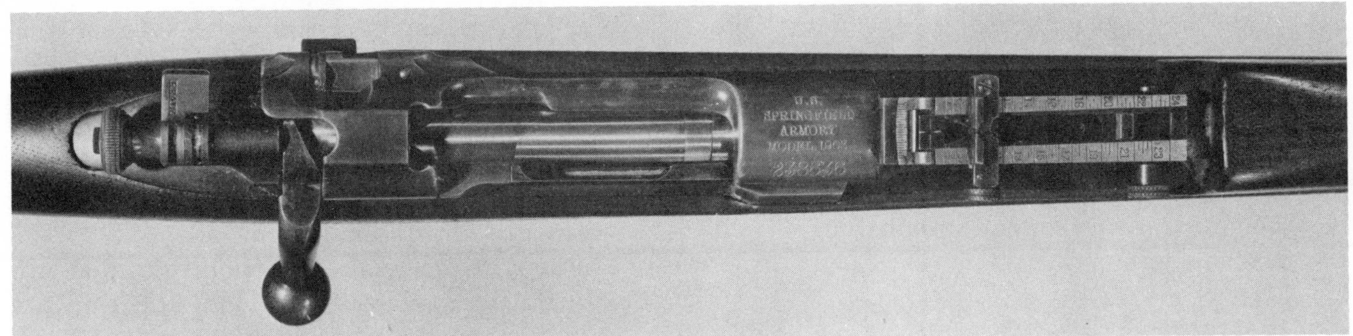

An early 1903 Springfield rifle, as determined by its serial number which is under a quarter million. These rifles were made by Springfield and Rock Island armories during peace time, and by Remington and Smith-Corona during World War II. The 1903 Springfield was the first modern bolt-action rifle made in America and it is still regarded as one of the finest.

4. Ejection: When the bolt reaches its rearmost point and just before it is stopped by the bolt stop, the left side of the cartridge is contacted by the ejector. With the extractor hook on the right side pulling, and the ejector on the left stopping further rearward movement, the cartridge is simply flipped clear of the action.

5. Cocking: This was accomplished during the initial lift of the bolt handle by means of the cocking cam forcing the firing pin back.

6. Feeding: The bolt is now thrust forward and the bottom edge of its face will engage the next cartridge lying in the magazine. The fresh cartridge is forced ahead, its nose is raised by a feeding ramp and it is guided into the chamber. Meanwhile, the base of this new cartridge is forced upward against the bolt face and its extracting groove engages the extractor hook.

7. Locking: Turning the handle back down causes the locking lugs to engage their recesses in the receiver ring and the cartridge to become fully seated in the chamber and ready to fire, and the final cocking is accomplished. (While moving back and forth in the bolt, the firing pin is resting against the rear of the bolt body.) During the final closing in the locking step, a notch in the firing pin contacts the sear (which in turn is connected to the trigger); at this point the sear holds the firing pin in cocked position while the bolt rotates closed and locked. The rifle is now ready to fire.

VARIATIONS

There are numerous variations in the locking systems of today's bolt actions. Some of them really are improvements on the basic Mauser, while others are simply alterations and are not necessarily better. Others are for convenience and/or appearance.

When Germany adopted the 1898 Mauser, the United States' service arm was the Krag-Jorgensen. Firing a .30-caliber rimmed cartridge with a 220-grain bullet, the Krag action was a turning bolt but with a single locking lug. The old Krag was a serviceable rifle, the chief advantage of which was that it boasted the smoothest bolt movement known to man. But the single locking lug limited its chamber-pressure capability and its magazine was an abomination. (The Krag had a magazine latch, nearly an inch square, on the right side of the action. To load, you flipped this down, inserted five cartridges individually and closed the latch. Cartridges were pushed across, under the bolt, and fed from the left side. Very awkward, very slow, and very ugly.)

Taking a good look at the Mauser, and remembering the Spanish-American War, American Ordnance developed the 1903 Springfield rifle for a 220-grain load that was originally called the .30/03 (the designation indicates it was a .30-caliber rifle, the cartridge dated 1903). But this heavy bullet had neither enough range nor flat enough trajectory and was changed in 1906 to a 150-grain pointed (spitzer) bullet. All the .30/03 rifles were recalled and rechambered for the new .30/06 cartridge.

The revamped 1903 Springfield was one great rifle, make no mistake about that. It was universally acclaimed by early gun writers as the greatest. What isn't often discussed about the Springfield is that it so closely resembled the Mauser that the U.S. paid Germany a royalty on it for years. In a few minor respects the Springfield was better than the Mauser; in a few others, it was inferior. But following World War I, before the American giants, Winchester and Remington, woke up to the bolt-action market, it was better than anything offered commercially for many years.

BOLT-ACTION SPORTERS

The development of the bolt-action sporting rifle as we know it today began through the efforts of a President of the United States, a writer with decided opinions and a loyal following, and several American custom gunsmiths. The President was Theodore Roosevelt, the writer Stewart Edward White, and the gunsmiths, first Louis Wundhammer, then Bob Owen, Jim Howe, and a very few others. In 1903, T.R. asked the Springfield Armory to remodel one of the newly issued Springfield military rifles for sporting purposes. This was accomplished by changing and shortening the stock and equipping the arm with a Lyman sporting sight. This was in all probability the first sporting bolt-action rifle produced. White, with the assistance of Wundhammer, adapted another Springfield, which he took to Africa with him.

By the 1920s, Springfield Armory made a rifle called the NRA Springfield Sporter, which was available to civilian members of the National Rifle Association. Its distinguishing features included a sporter stock, Lyman 48 receiver sight, and a superb metal finish. It was a high-class rifle, and was rated above any commercial offering by contemporary gun writers. In fact, the writers of today have never quarreled with that judgment.

The first commercial bolt-action rifles that can be called "modern" were the Model 30 Remington and its slick counterpart, the 30S Express. These were first marketed in 1921 and they were excellent rifles for their times. Remington's problem was that they were kept in the line until 1940, by which time they were well out of date. Remington's Model 30 was a remodeled, sporterized 1917 Enfield. Which brings us back to military history.

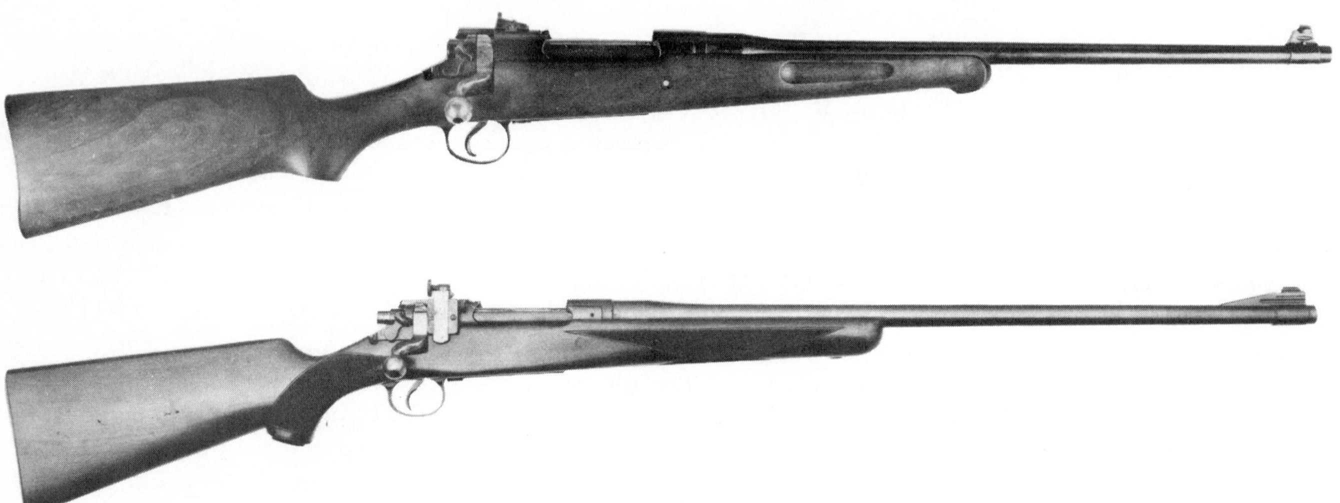

The first modern sporting bolt-action rifle was the Remington Model 30 (above) introduced in 1921, and (below) the Model 30S, a refined and improved version that came with a Lyman 48 receiver sight.

During World War I, Remington had vast contracts to manufacture a rifle for England. It was a new Enfield rifle, never before manufactured in quantity, chambered for the .303 British military cartridge. These rifles were to be produced both in the company's main plant in Ilion, New York, and in a plant leased from the Baldwin Locomotive Works in Eddystone, Pennsylvania. By the time the U.S. entered the war in 1917, production had been underway for about two years. It was imperative that America have rifles — there was a deficit of 3,000,000 rifles that had to be filled within two years. For such companies as Winchester and Remington to tool up for the Springfield (which was difficult to manufacture) would have been impossible, so the more easily made Enfield was altered to accommodate the U.S. .30/06 cartridge and was made in vast quantities by both companies. (One million of these old rifles were said to have been stored in government arsenals and then sent to England for the home guard during the early days of World War II.)

In any event, at the war's end, Remington found itself with parts, tooling, and a market for a high-powered bolt-action rifle. The early Model 30 wasn't a bad rifle, but it retained the 1917 Enfield's cock-on-closing motion, which wasn't very pleasant for a sporter, and it was stocked badly. The Model 30S was stocked much better. These rifles had two great features, however: The bolt handle was pitched at such an angle that you could mount a scope without alteration (which you had to do with Mauser and Springfield rifles) and it had one of the best safeties ever developed. Remington still uses basically the same safety today.

The Europeans never learned how to stock a bolt-action sporter until they began copying American stocks. Early European bolt-action sporter stocks always had too much drop; that is, the stock angled down too abruptly behind the action, which had the nasty habit of lowering the butt so far that the comb slapped you in the cheek in recoil. And that comb was almost razor sharp in many cases. The Germans were probably the worst offenders and stubbornly would refuse to change even on a custom order.

Military bolt-action rifle stocks were not suited for sporting because they were made fat and stiff to stand the rigors of rugged field use; the additional wood also made them heavier than a sporter should be. You can, with quite a bit of work if you have the skill, work a military stock down so that it becomes a marginally acceptable (though ugly) sporter stock. This is loosely called "sporterizing." It's far from an ideal solution and the result will depend on the skill of the workman. Nevertheless many of these reworked rifles are still in use and giving satisfactory service.

Winchester entered the market in 1925 with their Model 54, which wasn't much of a rifle in most respects but it came out with a hot new cartridge, the .270 Winchester, that really captured the imagination of shooters and writers alike and became quite successful. Model 54's chief faults were that its bolt handle and safety rose too high for scope mounting without alteration, many parts were punch pressed, which was then considered inferior manufacture, and the trigger also served as a bolt stop.

Winchester did, however, have the good sense to produce the great Model 70, which was introduced in 1937 and which instantly became recognized as one of the world's great rifles. Meanwhile, Remington stayed with that 1917 action until World War II stopped civilian production; it wasn't until after that war that Remington completely redesigned and produced a series of first-rate bolt-action rifles.

Meanwhile, during the 20s and 30s, the demand for sporting bolt-action rifles in America was developing slowly. Such as it was, it was filled by a few custom makers, and by the rifles already mentioned. There also were some imports, and the phrase "made in Germany" was becoming known all over the world. The Mauser plant at Oberndorf, Germany, produced excellent commercial actions for the world's gunsmiths. These were used by such great English gunmakers as Holland & Holland, Rigby, and Westley Richards, among others. They were also used by a few of the top American custom makers as well as some of the better shops in Germany, Belgium, and elsewhere on the Continent. With Oberndorf actions' reputation to lean on, many lesser German manufacturers, sometimes using battlefield pickups, also began making sporting rifles for export. A vast number of these guns were pure junk. Others were just badly designed and nearly all were stocked horribly.

There are a few innovations in bolt-action rifles that took place in this era. About 1910, a gunmaker named Charles Newton was far ahead of his time. Newton developed a number of high-velocity (for the time) cartridges, several of which were adopted by Savage, most of which were built into Newton rifles. Newton's major problem was that he was an inventor, not a manufacturer, and his company soon failed.

Roy Weatherby began his company by employing commercial Mauser actions made in Belgium, but later developed his own action known as the Weatherby Mark V. This action has many original features but the two most important are a locking system consisting of nine lugs and permitting shorter bolt lift (55° vs 90° in conventional rifles). The Mark V also has an oversize bolt, which results

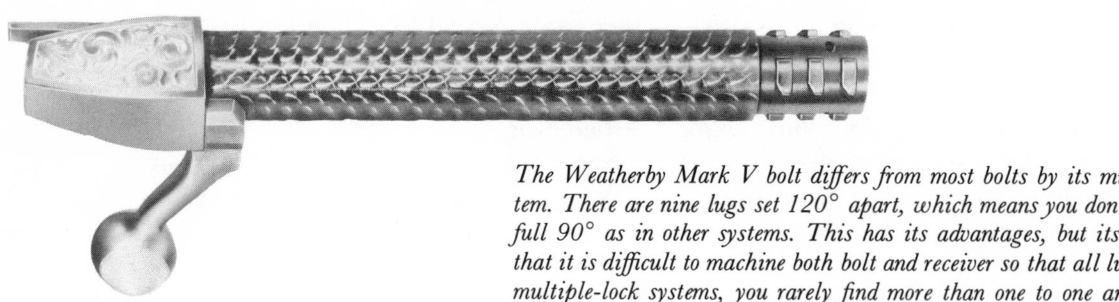

The Weatherby Mark V bolt differs from most bolts by its multiple locking-lug system. There are nine lugs set 120° apart, which means you don't have to lift the bolt a full 90° as in other systems. This has its advantages, but its major disadvantage is that it is difficult to machine both bolt and receiver so that all lugs bear evenly. In most multiple-lock systems, you rarely find more than one to one and a half lugs actually bearing.

in smoother bolt travel. This is accomplished by the larger diameter of the bolt body allowing the outside diameter of the lugs to be smaller than the bolt itself. On conventional bolts, the locking lugs are wider than the bolt body and so require two slots, or raceways, in which to move back and forth. The net result is that there is more to support the Weatherby bolt and working the action is easier. By comparison, one can shake a Mauser or Springfield bolt when it's in the fully open position much as a dog shakes its head.

While I appreciate the smoothness of the Mark V, as I used to like the smoothness of the honorable old Krag, it's not all that big a deal. Wiggling bolts don't bother me, and while there has been recent chatter about making bolts tighter, so they won't rock about like a subway car on a bad track, it's rare that any bolt will bind. At least I've never had one hang up.

Another recent trend has been to tighten the breeching by recessing bolt faces. In the older style rifles — Mauser, Springfield, Remington Model 30, Winchester's Models 54 and early 70s for example — a wee bit of the rear end of the cartridge case used to protrude from the back of the barrel. (You have to grab that rim, or extracting groove, to withdraw the fired case.) As a result, the saying went, the cartridge was the weakest part of the rifle, meaning that if the case blew under the chamber pressure, the gas was dumped into the action where it raced around looking for an exit. That exit often was found by blowing out the floor plate (the bottom of the magazine), blowing the receiver apart, and generally messing up the rifle. Although that happened very, very rarely, nevertheless the potential was there so long as part of the cartridge hung out in the open. Nowadays, led by the design of Remington's post-World War II 700 series, the bolt head is countersunk so it encloses the cartridge base. The bolt's nose slips into a recess in the barrel's breech to minimize the brass exposure. However, it's important (for accuracy) that the bolt not touch the barrel itself, and such manufacturing tolerances were probably not possible in production until recently. Nonetheless, I regard this largely as an improvement that offers advertising copy material rather than significant improvement in action design. I would just as soon have one of the earlier actions.

GAS ESCAPE

While a ruptured cartridge case (with its potential for destroying an action — and possibly parts of the shooter as well) happens so infrequently that it need not concern anyone, a pierced primer is quite another matter.

Its occurrence also is extremely rare, but it can happen, and does on occasion. The usual reason is either a badly shaped firing-pin nose (the result of someone trifling with it — firing-pin noses must be well rounded and very smooth) or a point, a burr for instance, sharp enough to penetrate the metal cup that is the top of a primer. If this happens, gas escapes through that little hole under enormous pressure and into the firing-pin chamber inside the bolt body. From there it is allowed to escape through one or more gas escape holes. Gas leakage can also occur when somebody who doesn't understand handloading gets the wrong powder, too much powder, or something equally senseless and the firing develops more pressure than the gun is designed to handle. In that event, the primer pocket will expand and allow gas to leak out. All modern bolt actions (from the 1898 Mauser on) have provision to protect the shooter's face. But it's still smart to wear glasses.

GUARD SCREWS

The function of the guard screws is to clamp the receiver to the stock. Some actions use two guard screws, some three. Frankly, so long as the rifle is manufactured correctly there's nothing to choose from between them. Both require careful bedding anyway; a receiver can be bent out of shape by turning up the guard screws if the inletting isn't right and this can happen with either system. Thus, other things being the same, the number of guard screws is of no consequence.

.22s

We have been discussing high-power rifles almost exclusively so far, but the .22 action rates some special attention. The pressure generated by a .22 cartridge is far less than that of a high power, so it does not require so strong a lockup. It's also true that no rimfire cartridges can hold center-fire pressures, another reason less lockup is required. The .22 is, moreover, more than a tool of the young — it's a fun gun for everyone. Cheap to shoot, not very loud, it can — depending upon the model — deliver outstanding accuracy. But hardly anybody wants to buy a bolt .22.

Generally speaking, in today's market the .22-caliber bolt-action rifle is a cheaply made, volume-produced product. (The obvious exception is the .22 target rifle, upon which loving care and lavish dollars are bestowed, the only other exception being a single Remington offering, which may or may not last in the line.) This, in my opinion, is a damned shame. I think shooters ought to recognize a decent bolt-action .22 sporting rifle and buy it if one is ever offered again. There was a time, well back in the 1930s, when Winchester made its Model 52 Sporter, a distinguished version of its justly famed Model 52 target rifle. It was one great rifle and it was, as it had to be, priced at a high level. It wasn't bought in sufficient volume to keep it around.

Usually the only lockup required in a bolt-action .22 is the root of the bolt handle (where the handle meets the bolt body); this part of the handle simply turns into a recess in the receiver. Some other specialized target-shooting masterpieces are obvious exceptions.

SAFETIES

Safeties are designed to block the trigger action, the firing pin, or some other part and prevent the gun from an unexpected discharge. In the bolt-action rifle, a safety usually works on the firing pin itself — or should do that if it doesn't. Putting a safety ON will securely lock the firing pin so it can't move forward until the safety is placed in FIRE position. It also moves the firing pin slightly to the rear, to completely disengage the pin from the sear. If it fails to make this disengagement, it is possible to place the rifle on safe, pull the trigger, then push the safety off, in which event the rifle will fire. That's why it is essential that a safety retract the firing pin so the trigger (and sear) is able to move back and forth freely.

Safeties usually have three positions. ON locks both firing pin and bolt, while the middle position locks the firing pin but allows you to operate the bolt to unload the action. There has been a recent trend toward the simpler two-position safety, just ON (firing pin and bolt both locked) and OFF (ready to fire). That's purely an economy move, and perfectly adequate; but at times it's nice to have that middle position. Need I add that the operation of a safety should be quiet? There's nothing like the snap of a loud safety to spook a deer that you've waited hours for.

SHORT AND LONG ACTIONS

The first of the modern bolt actions were developed for cartridges that are usually referred to today as "standard" length, the 7mm and 8mm Mausers and the .30/06. About 1912, the London gunmaking firm of Holland & Holland, Ltd. introduced their famous Magnum cartridges, .300 and .375 H&H; and Savage introduced the .250/3000 and .300 Savage. The two H&H cartridges were quite a bit longer than the standard and would not work through standard actions. The Savage cartridges were shorter than standard and, while they worked in standard-length actions, they did not need an action that long.

Holland & Holland, of course, had developed their Magnum cartridges, which were of the belted variety, primarily for double-barreled rifles. I believe the first major producer of bolt actions of varying lengths to better accommodate short and long cartridges was Mauser. I have, for example, a 1940 Stoeger catalog listing twenty styles of Mauser

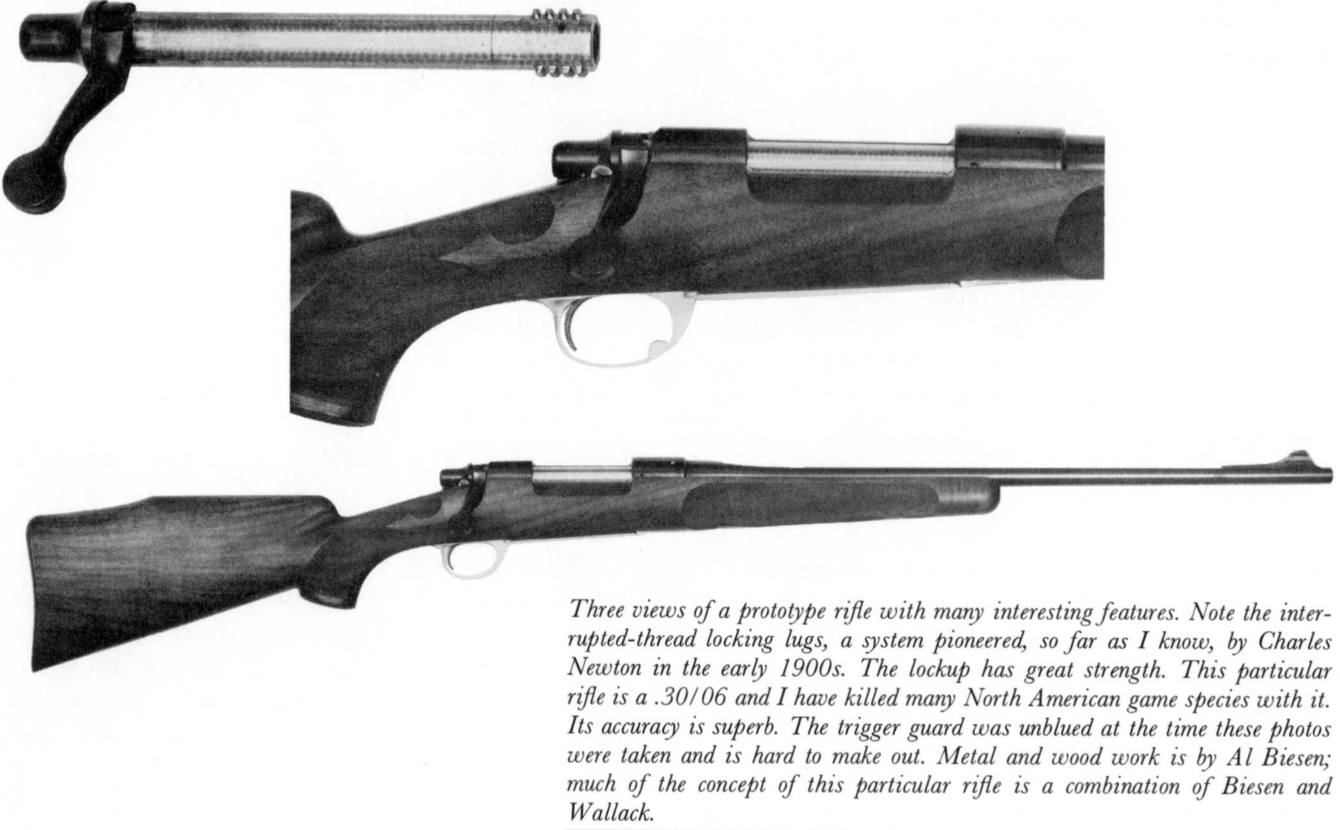

Three views of a prototype rifle with many interesting features. Note the interrupted-thread locking lugs, a system pioneered, so far as I know, by Charles Newton in the early 1900s. The lockup has great strength. This particular rifle is a .30/06 and I have killed many North American game species with it. Its accuracy is superb. The trigger guard was unblued at the time these photos were taken and is hard to make out. Metal and wood work is by Al Biesen; much of the concept of this particular rifle is a combination of Biesen and Wallack.

action, with the "Magnum Mauser" tabbed at $110. That's for an action alone, which the customer had to have barreled and stocked before it became a rifle. (To give a reference point, the Winchester Model 94 lever-action .30/30 carbine listed for $30 in this same book.) Needless to point out, there was not much volume in such costly actions and they are worth a fortune today.

Winchester was the first to offer a standard Magnum-length action in the U.S. when the Model 70 rifle was introduced in 1937. It was chambered for both the .300 and .375 H&H Magnum cartridges. At about the same period, a chap named Ben Comfort won the 1,000 yard Wimbledon match at Camp Perry, Ohio, with a Model 70 rifle chambered for the .300 Magnum and sales were off to a merry beginning.

It has become fairly common for rifle makers to build two basic lengths of actions today, a standard length and a short length — the latter for such cartridges as the .243 and .308. Since the arrival of such hot cartridges of standard length as the 7mm Remington, .300, .338, and .458 Winchester Magnums, there is no real need for such extra-long cartridges as the old H&H Magnums. Roy Weatherby however, who popularized Magnums in the shooting world, still uses longer-than-standard cartridges. His popular .300 Weatherby is still of .300 H&H length, as is his .340, .460, and several others.

Custom gunsmiths have for years altered actions to make them either longer or shorter. The usual procedure for making a standard action handle longer cartridges is to remove enough metal to allow feeding in the big Magnum cartridges. And the usual method for making a shorter action is to cut a small section out of the middle of the action and weld the pieces back together. Such work, of course, requires the services of an extraordinarily competent gunsmith. And there were more actions butchered than skillfully done. The practice has largely ceased today — which is a blessing.

I have always regarded the short actions as nice but not necessary. Nice because they can be made into a neat-looking, somewhat diminutive rifle

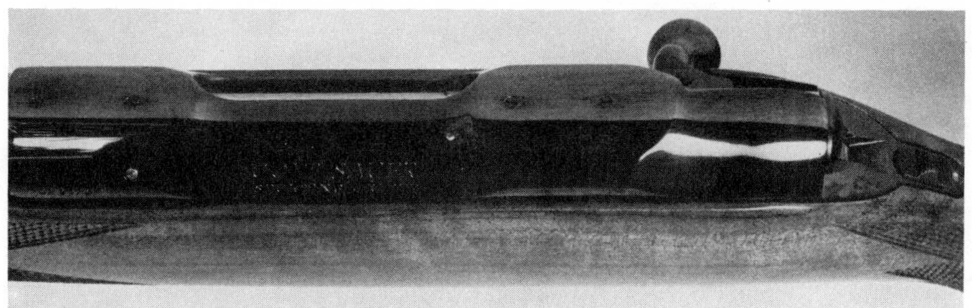

The action of the Colt-Sauer is streamlined to an extraordinary degree. It may appeal to some, but the appearance is far from the classic approach, which calls for square corners where square corners should be and rounded edges where rounded edges should be. The little button appearing at the front of the receiver ring protrudes when there is a cartridge in the chamber. This is a good feature, because you can see or feel when the rifle is loaded.

(provided the makers have the sense to scale everything else down and keep their proportions . . . but they usually don't), a rifle that will be a bit lighter in weight and so a bit faster to handle. This is not really necessary, however, because the longer bolt throw required for standard actions can easily be shortened and so can the magazine. An excellent case in point is the Winchester Model 70 which, in earlier days, was made for a wide variety of cartridges from the tiny .22 Hornet all the way to the monstrous .375 H&H Magnum. All were made on the same basic action and I never heard anyone criticize it. In fact, when Remington first brought out their .222 cartridge (in the Model 722 rifle), "knowing" shooters – by which I mean the solid gun buffs – eagerly bought Model 70 Hornet rifles and had them converted to .222 by custom gunsmiths. It was a tough conversion to make and a pretty expensive one, but these folks considered it worth the trouble and money.

SOME INNOVATIONS

Three actions that bear some individual attention are those of the Colt-Sauer rifle, made in West Germany by the solid old Sauer firm; the Kleinguenther, also made in West Germany by Voere, which they supply on their branded K-14 rifle; and the Champlin, a rifle completely made in the U.S. All three have slightly different locking arrangements and rather distinctive features that bear coverage.

First, the Colt-Sauer: This is one of the most streamlined of actions. You may like it or not, but no effort has been spared to round every corner on the receiver and swoop out large chunks of metal where possible to effect the flowing lines. The bolt body moves straight back and forth; it does not rotate. Locking is accomplished at the rear end of the bolt by three lugs that pop in and out of the bolt body as the handle is turned. A bit unusual, the locking arrangement is both positive and secure. The bolt travel is also smooth and free of the "Mauser Wobble" that's always associated with a Mauser type of bolt. Another distinctive feature of the Colt-Sauer is the removable-clip magazine, in which the cartridges lie in a vertical row, not staggered as in the Mauser system.

Despite the somewhat unusual streamlining, which extends to the stock as well, this rifle fits quite well and is a good shooting firearm. I would have preferred a little less depth through the action – at the expense of less magazine capacity – for a better appearance, but that's a personal opinion.

The Kleinguenther action is a sound, relatively conventional bolt action made in Germany for this Texas firm. One of the leading departures of this action is that it has three locking lugs up front that turn into a Stellite insert. Stellite is one of the strongest of all materials and offers exceedingly durable wear resistance. In use, the Stellite insert is placed into the receiver and the barrel screwed into the receiver hard against this insert. The combination should prove a good one.

A rather startling innovation of the Kleinguenther is the swinging trigger guard. In most actions, the floor plate alone swings down; in this one, the whole guard is pivoted to swing out of the way. This permits access to the removable magazine box

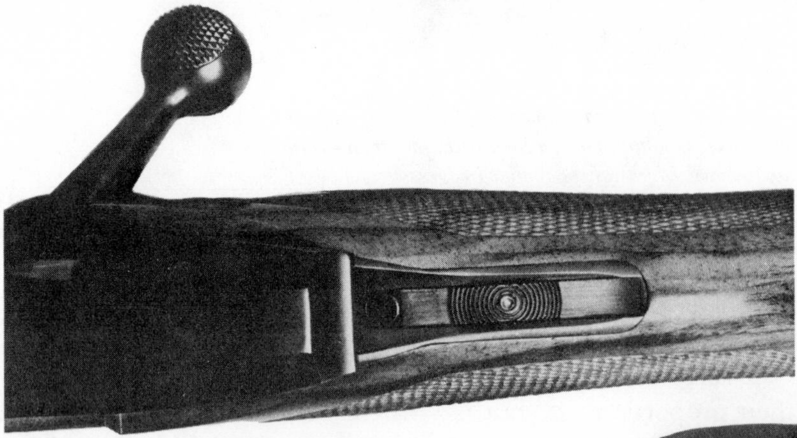

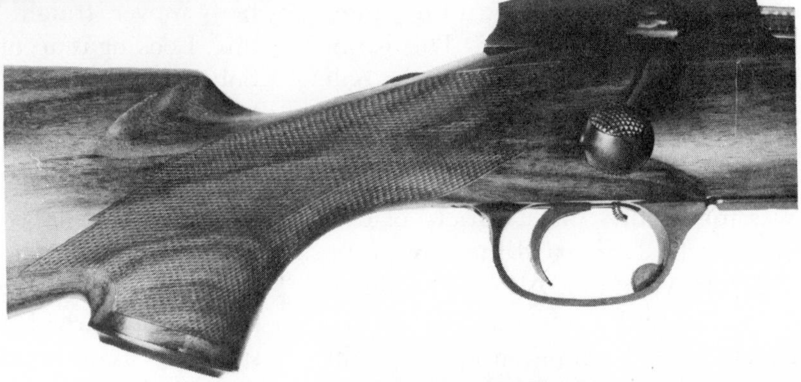

Several views of the fine workmanship practiced by the Champlin Arms Company of Enid, Oklahoma. The bolt action is of their own manufacture and its workmanship is of extraordinary quality. Note the flawless metal-to-wood fit and the generous checkering, which is as perfect as checkering can be made. You will pay a premium price for such a rifle, but your dollars will be well invested.

(you can carry a spare in your pocket), allows making trigger adjustments, and lets you get at the rear guard screw, which is nicely hidden when the guard is closed. I like this feature very much. It offers a neat and finished look and yet everything that needs adjusting is handy. The recoil lug is welded on, a practice that's perfectly acceptable but must make inletting difficult to get a clean job.

The K-14 has one of the shortest firing-pin movements in all the industry — only .158 inch. In metrics, that's only 4mm, which you can compare with the 11mm movement of the Mauser 98. This is an extraordinary ignition system and helps give the rifle good accuracy. As a matter of fact, Kleinguenther guarantees 1½-inch 100-yard accuracy, which is a good guarantee. From all I've heard, the rifles live up to it. This action has a cocking-piece safety which I find a bit awkward and hard to get at, but aside from this it's one of the better actions available and can be highly recommended.

It would be pretty hard not to get excited over the Champlin. The complete rifle is made in Enid, Oklahoma. The workmanship is practically flawless, about as close to the top English guns as you can get, except that the British can't make a bolt action as well as we make them here. This is a better bolt-action rifle than any English bolt gun. Its workmanship is nearly on a par with a Woodward, Boss, or Holland & Holland shotgun.

The Champlin bolt has three stout locking lugs up front with three very long safety lugs behind. It's a neatly designed and made action with excellent lines that complement the fine classic stock lines the company uses. The cost of one of these rifles is about the same as that of five Model 70 Winchester rifles. That means that if you really want the best and are willing and able to put that kind of money into a rifle that's as fine as can be turned out in America, you can get it. Whether one such rifle is worth five others is a question only you can answer. Champlin also is the U.S. distributor for the Merkel shotgun, a fine manufacturer in Suhl, East Germany.

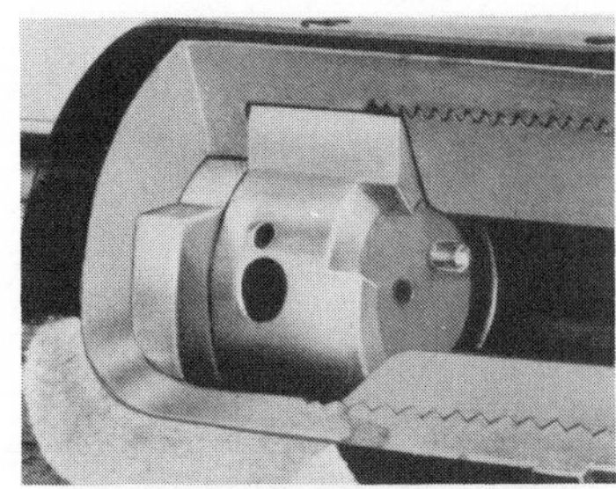

These two views of a Savage Model 110 bolt action show how modern bolt rifles fully support the cartridge. The top photo shows the upper locking lug turned into its locked position. The big hole in the bolt body is a gas-escape hole in the event of a pierced primer, while the small hole is a pin hole to hold the ejector in place (you can see the spring-loaded ejector in the bolt face). The bottom photo shows a cartridge in place in the chamber. Note that the bolt nearly touches the rear barrel face, and note also that the barrel is tightly screwed into the receiver.

THE LEFT-HANDED SHOOTER

There are a lot of left-handed people, and presumably those who designed the bolt-action rifle never even considered them. It wasn't really all that bad in the days when more iron sights than scopes were used, because a lefty could slap his left hand over the action, hook his thumb under the bolt handle, and slam the action back and forth as fast as anyone else. It's a little harder to do that when you have to reach clear up and over a scope. As a result, a number of custom gunsmiths featured the art of rendering conventional actions into a left-handed style. This was usually accomplished by a gear arrangement which, by raising the bolt on the left side, made the bolt body turn the same way it always did. Some 'smiths reversed the whole action. These alterations couldn't be taken lightly. Like shortening an action, it called for really fine craftsmanship. As a result, many were very well done, others were something less so, and some were downright dangerous.

It remained for Savage Arms Corp. to do a little market research and come up with the claim that 10 percent of all shooters were left-handed. Along with this, the company announced a standard version of their then-new Model 110 bolt-action rifle in left-handed style. It was the first genuine, factory-made left-handed rifle. Whether that 10 percent figure was right or wrong, it did serve to call people's attention to the Savage 110 and sales of both versions have been steady ever since. The Savage left-handed innovation also caused other makers to follow suit.

STRAIGHT-PULL BOLTS

Over the years, there have been a few bolt actions on the market of a type known as "straight-pull," meaning that the bolt handle was pulled straight back and pushed straight forward. The up-and-down movement was thus eliminated. This was accomplished by various cams to make the action lock and unlock more or less conventionally.

One of the earliest of these straight-pull rifles was

John M. Browning of Ogden, Utah, was the world's greatest gun inventor. He had a working arrangement with Winchester for many years, designed every autoloading pistol ever made by Colt, and designed machine guns and machine rifles used for years by many of the world's nations. Here are two of the guns he designed for Winchester. Top: Browning's first invention, the Model 1885 single-shot rifle. Bottom: The first model of Winchester's famed Model 94, patented in 1894 and generally known today as "the gun that won the West."

the Canadian Ross, a military rifle of World War I vintage. Chambered for a .280 caliber cartridge, with an oversized cartridge case, this was a very hot rifle. Its big disadvantage was that it was possible to assemble the bolt in a way that the action wouldn't lock but would still fire. This unhappy design feature resulted in the death of a few Canadian soldiers and the rifle soon got a well-deserved bad name. It didn't last long after that. The bad publicity also killed off a cartridge that was years ahead of its time – the .280 Ross. That cartridge was a good number. The most recent straight-pull bolt rifle was the little Browning "T-bolt", so named because of the shape of its bolt handle. This was a .22-caliber rifle, a nice one, but gone now. It just wasn't popular and didn't sell in enough volume to stay in the line.

It's unlikely you'll see any more straight-pull bolts, at least not in the foreseeable future. They remain a curiosity.

THE DOUBLE BARREL

I suspect most people think a double gun is one of the simpler types, possibly rivaling the single shot in this respect. If you are among those who think a double is pure simplicity, accept it as a tribute to the design geniuses who have packed so many intricacies and subtleties into what appears so simple a gun. In truth, more time, thought, and ingenuity have gone into double-gun design than any other. And, significantly, all double-gun inventiveness and evolvement have been directed toward the sporting market. That can be said about no other action system. It's doubtful that any gun evolved more slowly than the double.

The double gun is virtually entirely English in origin, and nearly every improvement made in doubles has come from one or another of the great makers in London, Birmingham, or Edinburgh. Even today, "best" English guns are to the firearms world what Rolls-Royce is to automobiles. There is no competition.

Some years back, in the late 1940s I believe, I had a chance to buy a pair of cased double-barrel rifles made in 1921 by Holland & Holland of London. They were Holland's Royal Grade (which means the finest) and they had never been fired. The story was that they had been ordered by a gentleman from Philadelphia who had passed away before delivery, and now were being offered for sale by his estate. The price tag was $2,100. I was short by $2,095. Today, I wish I'd gone into hock to buy that matched pair; it would have been an excellent investment.

Doubles are made in both shotguns and rifles, very few of the latter and mostly because they are traditional. By this I mean that a double rifle is still preferred by many who tackle the big, dangerous game of Africa. That's part tradition, part sentiment, part good sense, and part plain stubbornness. These heavy double rifles are made for enormous cartridges, the sort that can knock an elephant silly with a head shot, even if the brain is missed. And a double provides the fastest two shots in all gundom, which can be a blessing. Since the English have used doubles in Africa since before they can remember, tradition and sentiment play a large part in this choice. Englishmen just don't consider magazine rifles very sporting, possibly being somewhat conditioned by the general unreliability of the rifles exported to Africa from Germany during the 1920s and 30s. This has all been changed since the advent of the .458 Winchester Magnum in 1956 and, to a large extent, to the popularity given Magnum cartridges in bolt-action rifles by Roy Weatherby.

The .458 Winchester churns up 5,140 foot-pounds of muzzle energy, a stupendous amount of killing power. By comparison, however, Roy Weatherby's .460 Weatherby Magnum develops 8,095 foot-pounds. It has been proven sufficiently that the .458 is enough, but you can see that much more is available if you want that extra margin. Now let's look at the muzzle energy figures for two double rifles: The .475 No. 2 was long one of the more popular heavy bores frequently employed by the white hunter who backed up his "sport." It developed 5,170 foot-pounds. And the whopper of all double rifles, the .600 Nitro Express whumped up 7,610 ft-lbs. So you can see that bolt-action magazine rifles can deliver the goods on the world's toughest game at substantially lower cost and with more reserve firepower. Today, the English firms make a few double rifles each year; there are a few made in Ferlach, Austria; and possibly a few by other makers scattered here and there on the Continent. However, the double rifle is, at this time at least, very close to a thing of the past.

GAINS VS LOSSES

It has been an accepted fact that bolt-action rifles are the most accurate of all. Partly because they are bolt action, partly because they have a one-piece stock. Neither of these points is necessarily true. In fact, I'm not at all sure that one could prove which action system is the most accurate and I'm not sure what it would mean if one could.

It is true that all the benchrest records are held by bolt-action rifles and it's equally true that benchrest shooting has produced the best accuracy that's ever been produced. But there isn't much standard about the present day benchrest rifle. Many shooters use custom-made actions that happen to have a bolt; others use conventional actions but permanently fasten a sleeve outside and all the way around the action to stiffen it. These are really so far from the standard bolt action that any comparison is difficult.

The myth of the one-piece stock is a little easier to shatter. In fact, you can easily make a case for the one-piece stock actually being *less* accurate than a two-piece stock. Unless the piece of wood used is correctly sawn at the mill, properly dried, and then properly wed to the metal, you're going to have a stock that moves with the weather like an old football knee and will consequently bear differently against the barrel and so destroy accuracy rather than help it. In most cases you're probably better off with a two-piece stock although that, too, must be done right or inaccuracy will result.

I have fired many hundreds of bolt-action rifles, a great many of them in out-of-the-box condition. This means that the condition is the same as if you had bought the rifle in your local store, taken it home, pulled it out of the box, and begun to shoot it. Most such rifles have left something to be desired in the way of accuracy; a few of them have proved acceptable; and a very few have proved exceptional. Which means that almost every rifle you buy can be made more accurate assuming you know what to do. These improvements generally include some adjusting of the trigger, checking and probably adjusting the stock bedding, and handloading. But all three of these are things that should only be tackled by someone who knows exactly what he's doing.

In spite of those remarks, the rifle you buy today will shoot better than one you could buy 20 years ago. Just as it comes out of the box.

THE SINGLE-SHOT ACTION

Single-shot rifles — that is single-shot cartridge rifles — are a development of the latter part of the last century. They led directly to the lever action, which we'll come to next. But many shooters and hunters today seek a relationship with the past or prefer to trust to that single aimed shot, so that the single-shot rifle has come back. Whether this is a fad or a more or less permanent movement I can't forecast but I think that these single-shot types will be around a while.

These actions are pretty simple to understand and really don't require much explanation. Their operation is all manual and you can follow the seven steps exactly as they were listed in Chapter One.

Probably the most famous of all the older actions were, not necessarily in this order, Winchester, Ballard, Sharps, and the English Farquharson. There were dozens of others but these are the ones most often talked about today. The Winchester single-shot rifle was the first invention of John M. Browning at the age of 23, and was made by Winchester from 1885 until 1920. Essentially the same rifle is again being manufactured today by Browning. This was an excellent design (as were all Browning designs) and has surely stood the test of time.

The Ballard was another fine action of the black-powder period. It was invented in 1861, had some limited Civil War experience, and was manufactured by several companies until taken over by John Marlin in 1875. A former maker of handguns, Marlin launched his rifle business with the Ballard and made the best of the Ballards until about 1880, when the model was dropped. Although the Ballard was an excellent black-powder action, it could not stand smokeless loads because its construction included a split breechblock and lacked the strength the higher-pressure smokeless loads demanded.

There were many models of Sharps; most common are the older outside-hammer models chambered for the whopping big black-powder cartridges used by buffalo hunters. Later, the Sharps-Borchardt model was perfected, hammerless in style and modern for its time. Unfortunately, the Borchardt never became popular and the Sharps Rifle Company went out of business.

The inner details of a Farquharson single-shot action made by Westley Richards of London. When I got this action years ago it was equipped with a take-down barrel and it had to be threaded, the breechblock bushed, and a new firing pin installed. The Farquharson was made in several styles by a number of English gunmakers.

Meanwhile, English makers catering to their African trade were using the great Farquharson action, which was made in several styles and sizes. Depending on the maker, Farquharson actions vary a little in minor details but generally have a very similar appearance. I have, for example, a Farquharson built originally by Westley Richards which was made for a takedown .303 British barrel (the English service cartridge). Some years ago, I threaded the action, fitted it with a barrel in a wildcat cartridge made by necking the .30/40 Krag cartridge case down to .25 caliber. It's a fine rifle indeed and the Farquharson is a great action.

Another, much older, single shot was the trap-door Springfield. Its name comes from the fact that, after the Civil War, the army had many thousands of muzzleloaders in storage and Springfield Armory altered these by milling away a section of the barrel's breech and inserting a breechblock hinged at the front so that it opened up like a cellar door. This led to further improvements, and in 1873 the .45/70 became the standard military cartridge and was employed in the trap-door action. Today, in a form of sentiment, Harrington & Richardson is manufacturing trap-door .45/70 rifles much the same as the originals. I suspect many of these are being bought by collectors, but surely many of them are being shot too.

Quite likely the most modern and most popular single-shot rifle is the Ruger No. 1. Bill Ruger is both genius and sentimentalist. His genius allows him to design guns that are practical, efficient, priced correctly, and that sell. His sentimental bent usually drives his inventiveness toward classic firearms, often from another age. For example, he foresaw the demand for single-action revolvers and began making modern SA revolvers before any other company could realize what had happened. His bolt-action Model 77 departed from the "California school" that Roy Weatherby established — and others tried to emulate — by having a pure, classic design. His single-shot rifle is a blend of all that's good in some of the long-gone old-timers. However, it is more Farquharson than anything else — which is good — yet it's pure Ruger, which is even better.

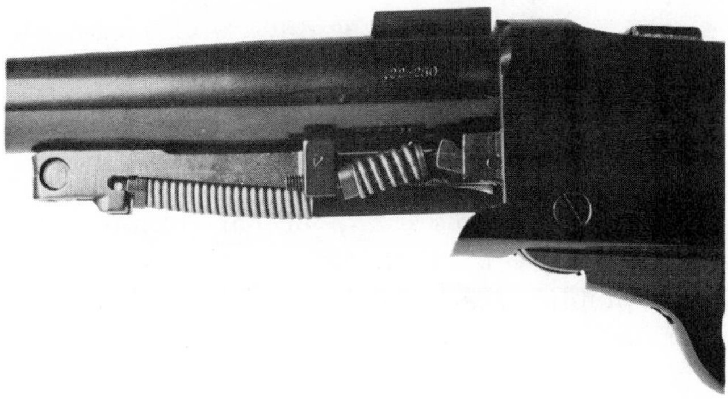

Ruger's Number One single shot is of classic style, but displays Ruger's flair for simple, effective design. Shown under the barrel is the forearm hanger, which allows the forearm to be fastened to the hanger and removes the usual barrel/receiver pressure via the forearm that is often detrimental to single-shot rifle accuracy. The big spring forward is the mainspring, which drives the hammer (underslung in this design) and the smaller spring is the ejector spring.

Single-shot actions are of a type generally called "falling block" which means that the breechblock, usually a massive, nearly square steel block, moves straight up and down. The action is operated by a lever which, on the downstroke, loosens the cartridge, drops the breechlock, cocks the firing mechanism, and extracts and ejects the fired case. One further single-shot action should be mentioned: the old Remington Rolling Block. Made originally in 1867, rolling blocks were continued until 1933 by Remington, and at one time were made in military style for many European countries, including huge orders for Russia. Among the more famous claims of the rolling-block rifle is that three of them were used by the six-man U.S. team that beat the World Champion Irish rifle team in 1874 at Creedmoor on Long Island. The remaining three Americans used Sharps, while the whole Irish team used muzzle-loading rifles. The event was widely publicized at the time and was important in furthering the popularity of breech-loading rifles.

Rolling-block actions are quite simple. The breechblock operates much like an extra hammer in front of the hammer. Closing the block exposes firing pin and the hammer. When the hammer comes down to drive the firing pin forward, it also locks the block closed. I have included it here because rolling-block single-shot rifles are again on the market. However, at least in my opinion, the rolling block, as well as the trap-door Springfield, are inferior actions to the present Ruger and Browning models.

Single shots, of the types we've been discussing, represent the transition between muzzleloaders and the repeating rifle. Moreover, they were made in all sizes from .22 caliber up to, and including, such monsters as were used by the buffalo hunters in the American West and the behemoths employed by British elephant hunters — all this in the days of black powder.

LEVER-ACTION REPEATING RIFLES

Most of the single shots just discussed were, of course, lever actions. The lever-action repeating rifle is quite another matter entirely.

There are today several basic types of high-power lever-action rifles in manufacture, three of them very old designs but still popular. Chronologically, these are the Marlin 336 (originally Model 1893),

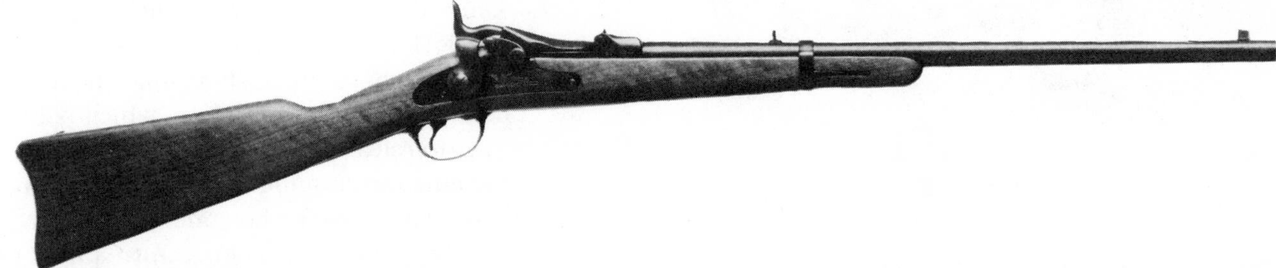

A modern version of the trap-door Springfield, as made today by Harrington & Richardson in .45/70 caliber. The original trapdoor was known as the Allin Conversion, the words relating to the conversion of muzzle-loading rifles to breech loaders shortly after the Civil War following a method perfected by a man named Allin at Springfield Armory. He simply milled out a section of the breech and replaced it with a breechblock hinged at the front. To load, you pull back the hammer and raise the trap door. Lowering the door locks the mechanism ready for firing. This was our standard arm from about then until the bolt-action Krag-Jorgensen was adopted in 1892. Still, many .45/70 trap-door rifles remained in service through the Spanish-American War.

Winchester 94 (originally Model 1894), and Savage 99 (originally Model 1895, improved in 1899). The Winchester and Marlin are what we usually call traditional in style, while the Savage is of modern design, despite its age. At this writing, in 1976, the Winchester 94 has sold around four million, the Marlin more than three million and the Savage something more than one million. No matter how you slice it, that's a lot of rifles. Seven million traditional Winchesters and Marlins, most of them in .30/30 caliber! There are probably as many of these two rifles among shooters and hunters as all other high-power-action types combined.

A newcomer to the lever-action field is Browning's BLR rifle, which employs a turning-bolt locking system (i.e. Mauser) and a breechbolt that is moved back and forth by gearing. The Browning also employs a removable-clip magazine, the Savage a rotary spool, while the Winchester and Marlin use tubular magazines.

Lever-action rifles are called that because their operation is performed by a finger lever, which is moved down and up to accomplish the seven steps of operation. Each brand does things slightly differently, but the two most popular models are similar both in looks and function. Here's how the Winchester Model 94 and Marlin Model 336 work:

1. Firing: Pulling the trigger releases the outside hammer, which flies forward under spring tension to strike the firing pin, which, in turn, crushes the primer to accomplish ignition.

One of the oldest actions of all time is the Marlin 336, shown here in cutaway with parts in fired position. As the lever is moved down, it will unlock and retract the bolt, thus extracting the empty cartridge from the chamber. At the same time, the fresh cartridge will be moved onto the carrier. As the lever is moved back, these operations all reverse. The hammer is cocked, the new cartridge driven into the chamber, the bolt relocked, and the rifle is ready to fire again.

2. Unlocking: Downward movement of the lever pulls a locking block down from its engagement with the rear end of the breechbolt. Neither of these actions possess any mechanical advantage in primary extraction, consequently they are not adaptable to any modern, high-intensity cartridge because they do not exert enough extraction power.

3. Extraction: Grasped by the extractor, at the top of the Winchester and side of the Marlin bolt, the cartridge is drawn out of the chamber as the bolt is moved back by the lever.

4. Ejection: In the Winchester, the cartridge is ejected to the top as soon as the empty clears the barrel, since the ejector is under spring tension. In the Marlin, ejection is accomplished when the stationary ejector in the receiver (left) side is contacted by the empty cartridge, spinning about the extractor hook. The empty is cast out the ejection port on the right side of the action.

5. Cocking: As the bolt moves back, it pushes the hammer down into cocked position compressing the hammer spring.

6. Feeding: The very end of the Winchester's forward lever motion raises the carrier, which lifts a cartridge from the magazine into feeding position. The Marlin accomplishes the same thing as the very first part of the backward stroke of the lever. In both rifles, a new cartridge is allowed to move out of the magazine under spring pressure onto the carrier (often called the lifter). As the bolt is thrust forward by the lever, the bottom edge of the bolt face pushes the new cartridge into the chamber.

7. Locking: The final portion of the lever stroke forces the locking block back up into its recess at the rear of the breechbolt. This final movement also pushes a small pin into place, which permits the trigger to release the hammer. This safety device prevents firing unless the action is fully locked. Both have a further safety feature with two-piece firing pins. The lock must place the rear part of the firing pin into alignment with the front of the pin or it cannot be driven into the primer.

Both rifles are close in design. The Marlin has a round bolt, which is a superior feature in terms of

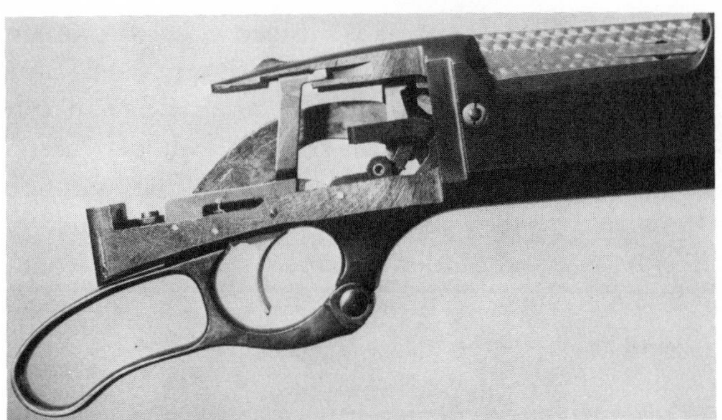

The Model 99 Savage action with stock removed. That curved part you see running up through the middle of the action is part of the lever and its front end moves the bolt back and forth. The first of these rifles appeared in 1895 as Model 1895; the action was slightly altered in 1899 and has remained virtually unchanged since.

strength, and its side ejection allows low and centered scoping. Some of these points are somewhat moot since the lack of primary extraction, while not necessary for the low-pressure cartridges used, prevents either action from being used for a hot, modern cartridge like the .243 or .308. But that means little anyway. The actions are too short for these cartridges. That both these rifles have been around so many years, and that today they are selling in larger volume than ever, is adequate testimony to their excellence.

The Savage 99, even though it's nearly as old as the Winchester and Marlin designs, is a much more modern rifle. Arthur Savage, a streetcar superintendent in Utica, N.Y., when he got the idea, designed well. Perhaps his big advantage was that he had no old models nor habits to get in his way. In any event, he designed a unique action that was able to handle hot cartridges when they came along as far back as 1910–12. Those were the .250/3000 and .300 Savage. And in the mid-50s, when such as the .308 and .243 came along, the Model 99 Savage was able to handle these hot cartridges, too.

Model 99 is a hammerless action. The word hammerless can be misleading; it means that there is no exposed — or no visible — hammer. Many hammerless systems have hammers inside where you can't see them. Others use a spring-loaded firing pin, like the bolt-action rifle. The Savage 99 is of that type, using a firing pin that is tucked inside and out of sight.

One of the Model 99's most distinguishing features is that it uses a spool magazine that has a number of interesting features. As far as I know, the

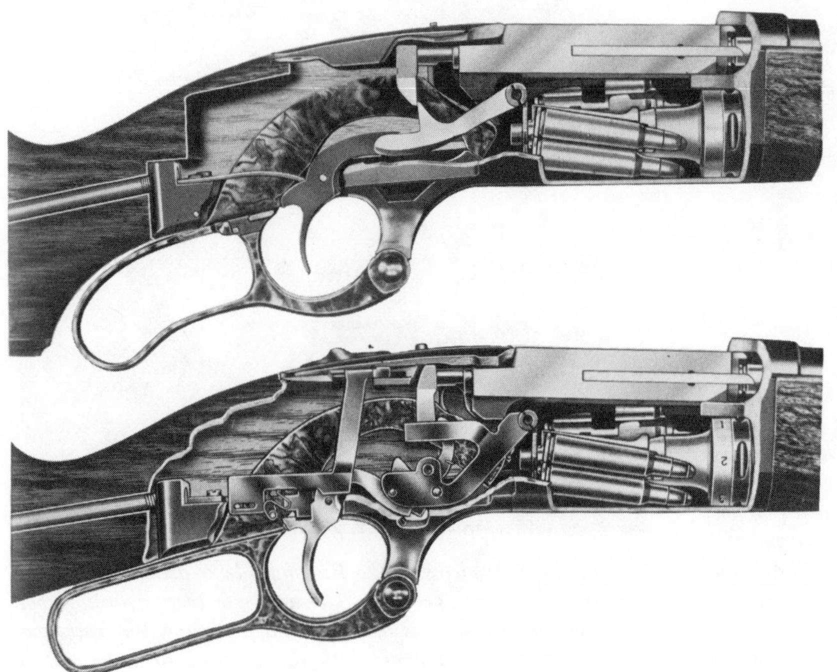

In the older Model Savage 99 (above), the lever action's slide safety is located at the rear of the trigger. This was a positive safety but an abomination to get on and off. It has been vastly improved (below) with a top tang safety. Note in the upper photo that the trigger has a long front extension connected to the sear (which pivots just behind the magazine). Pulling the trigger moves the sear down, releasing the firing pin. This action is a truly hammerless design; it employs a spring-loaded firing pin much like a bolt action. Note, too, the rotary spool magazine in the lower photo, numbered so you can see, through a window in the receiver, how many cartridges remain in the magazine.

spool magazine was first used in the Mannlicher-Schoenauer rifle, an old and excellent well-made bolt-action rifle from Austria. The spool carries its cartridges in what might resemble a revolver cylinder with the outside walls cut away. To load the magazine, you place a cartridge in the exposed recess and press it in place. That exposes another recess, and so on until the spool is filled. In the Savage, the spool is also numbered, so you can peek in a small hole in the left receiver wall and read how many cartridges are left in the magazine. Aside from its uniqueness, the spool magazine does a fine job of protecting the remaining cartridges in the magazine. There's no possibility of their getting battered.

Eliminating the hammer, as Arthur Savage did, has both advantages and disadvantages. In comparison with the Winchester and Marlin designs (as well as the new Browning), with their older-style exposed hammers, each has its advantages. The Savage hammerless action protects the shooter better by providing a solid wall of steel between face and rifle. You can tell at either a glance or a feel if the Savage action is cocked because it has a little pin that sticks up when it's cocked. On the other hand, the Savage must be carried either cocked and loaded and on safe, or without a cartridge in the chamber. With the hammer guns you can carry them on half-cock, in which position they cannot be fired, yet they are easily cocked in a smooth motion as you shoulder the rifle.

Some claim that it's dangerous to put a loaded hammer rifle on half-cock because you have to hold the hammer and let it down gradually while you pull the trigger if you want to close the action without firing it. I'll admit that when you explain it to the uninformed it can sound a little hairy, but I've never directly heard of an accident. And with more than seven million high-power hammer guns, to say nothing of added millions of .22s and shotguns employing hammers still in circulation, it's got to be one of the safest systems ever made.

Savage's 99 does have primary extraction, otherwise it couldn't handle the hot cartridges. It is a

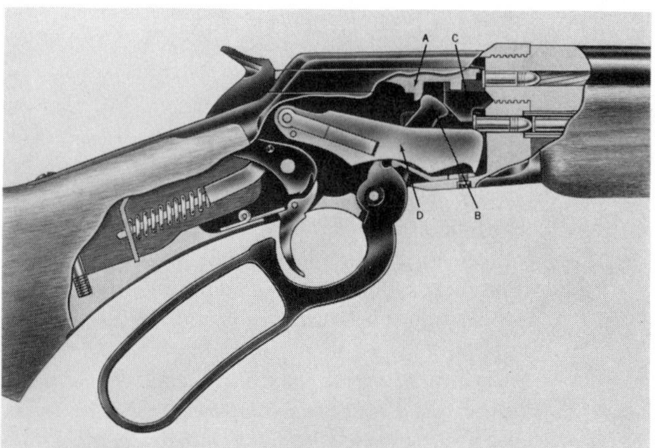

The world's second oldest gun, the Marlin Model 39 .22-caliber lever-action repeater, shows no signs of slowing down as the years go by. (The oldest gun is the Colt single-action Model P.) This Marlin has a simple design that has been virtually unchanged since its introduction in 1891. The cutaway shows the action not quite fully closed. The front of the lever (B) is blocking firing pin (A) so the gun can not fire until action is fully closed. At that time the lever (B) will securely lock the breechblock (C) forward by resting against it. D indicates the carrier that lifts a fresh cartridge into feeding position. The action is rugged and consists of remarkably few parts.

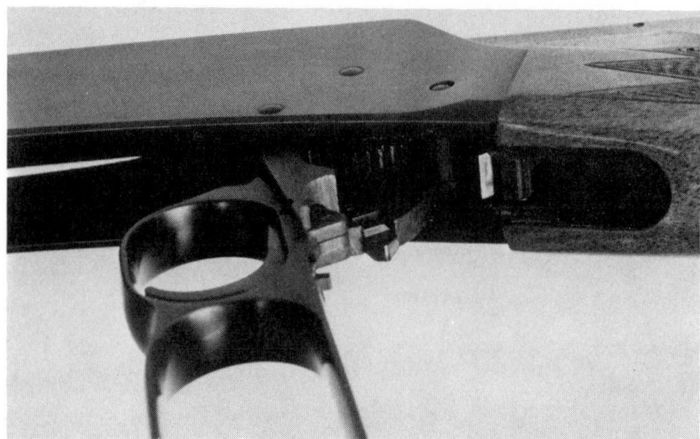

Bottom and side views of the Browning lever-action high-power rifle show its gear operation. The action features a turning bolt head, but the bolt body is moved back and forth by this rack-and-pinion gear system. The old Bullard lever rifle from the mid-to-late 1800s operated similarly.

thoroughly fine action and one that has delivered well for many years. The only fault I can point out is that the older models had a lousy safety. Lousy to operate that is. It was effective, just hard to use. But that's been improved in present production with a top-tang safety.

Browning has been on the market for a fairly short period with a high-power lever rifle that contains a few departures and bears some attention. To begin, the rifle is made in Japan, as are so many these days. It is a rifle with a visible hammer, following the tradition of Winchester and Marlin; its chamberings are .243 and .308. The most distinguishing characteristic of the BLR is that it uses a gear arrangement to move the bolt via the lever. This is totally different from either Winchester, Marlin, or Savage, all of which work directly against the bolt with the lever. The object of the gear is to move the bolt farther than the lever does, similar to the lever principle itself, except that gearing can deliver more force. If you think the application of gears to a lever action is new, be informed that there was a Bullard (from Bridgeport, Conn., and not to be confused with the Ballard single shot) rifle made about a hundred years ago that employed a lever and gear. The principle has also been employed recently with some short-throw lever guns now off the market by both Marlin and Mossberg.

The BLR rifle appears to be a fine product, its action works nicely, and the bolt is of the turn-bolt lockup type with seven lugs engaging recesses at about 120° (as against the conventional bolt action with 180°, or opposite, lugs). A removable box magazine is used in the BLR, but why this was ever designed to hang down more than a half inch from the rifle's bottom line is beyond me. Not only does this occur right at the balance of the gun — that's where you carry it one-handed — making the carry awkward if not impossible, but it also looks like hell. Browning would be well advised to reduce the capacity of this magazine and make it flush with the bottom of the stock. Aside from that objection, this is a fine rifle and quite interesting.

.22 RIMFIRE LEVER ACTIONS

A funny thing happened during the history of .22-caliber lever-action repeaters. Winchester made the first one, the Model 1873, which was chambered for .22 Short or .22 Long, but not interchangeably, before the .22 Long Rifle cartridge was in existence. But Winchester dropped the .22 chambering in this rifle for some reason or another. John Marlin introduced his Model 1891, chambered for .22 Short, Long, or Long Rifle, interchangeably. The 91 was altered slightly and reemerged as Model 1892, then again in 1897, as the famous Model 97. During the 1930s, the 97 was again updated, and redesignated Model 39. Despite the changes made over the years, the basic action is still the same and Marlin's Model 39 rifle is the oldest shoulder-arm design still being manufactured.

The strange part of all this is that Marlin had no competition whatsoever in lever .22s until the 1950s, when Marlin itself brought out a less costly line. They didn't stay in the line too long however, but maybe they did give the idea to others, because pretty soon Mossberg, Browning, Winchester, and Ithaca were in the field. Winchester's 9422 is made in the image of its famous Model 94 .30/30, and the Browning BL-22 is very much along the same lines as is the Ithaca. None of these guns is cheap. They all go for roughly double the price of a .22 bolt-action repeater, but all are also of much higher quality than run-of-the-mill bolt .22s.

Winchester alone offers a .22 Magnum version of this lever rifle (.22 Winchester Magnum Rimfire, known as .22 WMR); it is a longer and slightly larger-in-diameter cartridge. It is more powerful and is not interchangeable with regular .22 rimfires, nor can rifles chambered for regular .22s be rechambered for the WMR.

Another strange, although admittedly not very important, fact about the lever-action rifle is that Remington introduced a .22 lever-action rifle during the 1960s that was aborted almost immediately. This was the only lever-action rifle ever introduced by Remington, the country's oldest gunmaker (in business since 1816).

Let's examine the functioning of the granddaddy of them all, the Marlin 39. An examination of the present Model 39 and the original Model 1891 plainly shows that there have been no vital changes. The company still employs five forgings in the manufacture of this little rifle (two of them for the two-piece receiver, since this particular model is a take-down rifle).

The function of this rifle is much the same as the Marlin 336 and Winchester 94. The essential differences are in the locking and unlocking steps. In the

Marlin, the front end of the operating lever comes to rest under and against a lug on the forward end of the breechbolt in such a fashion that the rifle is locked securely. This calls for close fitting in manufacture but this rifle has been around so long, and so many of them have been fired so many hundreds of thousands of times, that the system is proved beyond question.

Take-down of the 39 is also an interesting feature. You simply loosen a big, coin-slotted nut on the right-hand side of the receiver and break the action into two units from side to side. Buttstock and part of the action stay in one unit, the remainder of the action and barrel are in the other. That permits easy cleaning, simple removal of the breechbolt for cleaning from the breech end, and it shows the rugged simplicity of this fine old action. New 39s come apart a little hard the first few times, since this is a very close fit.

As a matter of fact, the Marlin 39 is one of the few remaining take-down rifles. There used to be a lot of them, the purpose being to allow you to break the gun into two pieces for easier packing and carrying. During the latter part of the 1900s, there were a number of take-down lever-action rifles made and at one time there were a few bolt-action rifles made in take-down style. Take-downs were given up in lever style because the demand for the feature was more imagined than real, and in bolt actions because the cost was high. It was one thing to figure out how to take-down a two-piece-stock lever-action rifle. It was quite another thing to do the same stunt with a bolt. A few British makers made an occasional take-down bolt rifle and a few American custom gunmakers did too. But no one ever made very many.

Take-downs have the unhappy habit of loosening up in their joint, with resultant loss of accuracy. It was pretty difficult to design a system that let you screw a high-power rifle barrel in or out and still retain its tightness. But once the word got out that such rifles wouldn't shoot very straight after being taken down a few times, the market no longer appreciated the feature.

The lever-action system can be properly called our oldest modern repeating system, older even than the bolt. That it has retained its popularity so well over the years is due to a number of factors. First, it's fast, fast, fast. You can work a lever and fire aimed shots with it at a surprising rate after you've become accustomed to your rifle. It's also traditional. This may well be one of the outstanding reasons for its longevity. Maybe that point should be meaningless, but it's a fact that guys buy guns because they are a symbol. And there's no gun going that says masculine like the old "thutty-thutty" that won the West. Speaking of the .30/30, it's still perfectly adequate for a good 90 percent of today's hunting. That statement may be argued but I'll stand by it. There are also some souls just buying rifles for the first time who, having heard .30/30 somewhere along the road, probably on TV, think it's the hottest rifle going. Many are doubtless bought in pure bliss.

It has been claimed that the traditional lever actions are weak, that they can't stand anything hotter than the low-pressure .30/30 or equal. This is partly true and partly false. Winchester's 94 won't stand much more than the .30/30 but Marlin, since it changed to its round bolt design in 1947, will stand a great deal of pressure. I've been told it could easily handle the .308 and .243 except for its length and absence of primary extraction. The Savage 99, of course, is modern in every respect and does handle these cartridges.

It has also been said that lever-action rifles are not very accurate because: (1) they lock at the rear of the breechblock, which allows the block to "give," in other words to provide a sort of spongy support during firing; and (2) because they have a two-piece stock. We'll come to the stock discussion in Chapter Ten. As mentioned before, there is no truth to the one-piece stock myth. Insofar as the spongy breech support is concerned, let me say that the Savage, Marlin, and Browning systems are stout and well supported (actually, Browning's BLR locks up front anyway); the Winchester 94 is more subject to springing.

Technicalities aside, I have fired a great many lever-action rifles in accuracy tests and can report that they are just as accurate in "out of the box" condition as bolt actions. The lever-action high-power rifle, so long as you can find it chambered for a cartridge you want, is ideally suited for fast action in the woods. It's the perfect bush rifle where shots are close and where fast repeat shots may be necessary. And don't sell it short when it comes to accuracy. Such guns as the Savage 99 and Browning BLR, chambered for modern, hot cartridges, can run right along with any bolt gun.

Top: Remington has long made a pump-action high-power rifle, the most modern version of which is this Model 760. It has a rotating-bolt locking system so it handles powerful cartridges such as the .30/06. Earlier Remington pump rifles were chambered for a line of rimless cartridges, the most popular of which was the .35 Remington. Bottom: Pump action .22 rifles were once extremely popular. This is the Rossi, an import by Garcia, which copies the famous Winchester Model 62 which, in turn, was an updated Model 1890. These rifles were popular at shooting galleries across the country some years ago.

THE PUMP ACTION

This is sometimes called slide action or trombone action, but no matter the name they're all the same. So far as I am aware, the first popular, successful pump-action firearm was John Browning's Model 1890 Winchester .22. The first successful high-power rifle pump action was Remington's Model 14, introduced in 1912 and based on C. R. Pedersen patents.

Pump-action .22s were once both popular and common. Today there are very few. I suspect the reason is that it's less expensive to produce autoloading .22s and the market calls for cheap, fast-firing rifles. So in respect to the pump .22 rifle, remember it's slipping away fast. Winchester's original Model 90 was changed a bit in 1906 and again in 1932 and reissued as Model 62. A copy of the Model 62 is being made abroad today and imported by Garcia. It's a slick little rifle. I've owned one since about 1940 and wouldn't part with it. I understand that more than two million of these little rifles were produced before they finally went out of the Winchester line in 1960.

In general, the following illustrates the way in which all pump guns operate according to the seven steps of operation:

1. Firing: First, remember that in every pump gun there is a way of locking the pump handle forward when the gun is cocked. If this wasn't provided for, there would be a tendency to pull the handle back slightly, which would unlock and partially open the action. Therefore, the pump handle is locked forward when the gun is cocked. The handle is connected to the action mechanism by one or two action bars, which extend from the handle to the breechblock. A small part called the action slide lock is used to lock the handle forward. In case you want to unload the gun without firing, pump-action firearms all have some sort of lever or button located out of the way that unlocks the action.

Pulling the trigger causes the hammer to fall and fire the gun; it also releases the action slide lock so the pump handle may be moved. (Sometimes, especially if the gun isn't actually fired, you must push forward just a bit on the pump until you hear a small click. That means the action slide lock is disengaged and you can stroke the action. In actual firing that isn't noticeable, because the recoil of the gun takes care of that forward movement.)

2. Unlocking: The initial movement of the pump handle, transmitted through the action bar or bars, unlocks the breechbolt.

3. Extraction and 4. Ejection: Further backward movement of the pump handle pulls the cartridge out of the chamber and then ejects it from the gun.

5. Cocking: Also accomplished during the rearward stroke, usually by pushing the hammer down, as in a lever action (whether of exposed hammer or hammerless design).

6. Feeding: As the handle starts its forward stroke, the carrier is lifted and positions a fresh cartridge from the magazine into feeding position, and it is then pushed into the chamber by the bolt.

7. Locking: Final closure of the breechbolt, by pushing the pump handle as far forward as possible, relocks the action and locks the pump in its forward position.

It is important to understand that a pump action is meant to be man-handled. You've got to slam it. Failure to do so can easily result in a jam through failure to feed properly. So slam all pumps as if you were mad at them.

For a great many years — actually from 1912 until 1950 — Remington made a very popular high-power pump-action rifle. It was issued originally as Model 14, then updated in 1936 and renamed Model 141. Chambered in a number of exclusive Remington cartridges, the rifle was quite popular in caliber .35 Remington. It was a hell of a deer rifle and widely used for woods hunting. Remington meant this model to compete with the Winchester and Marlin lever guns (as a matter of fact the various Remington cartridges for which this rifle was chambered were rimless variations of several popular Winchester cartridges). In 1952, however, Remington replaced these older models with the Model 760 pump-action repeater, a truly high-power pump rifle with a rotary bolt lockup (Mauser again!) that handles the .30/06, .270 and other hot, modern cartridges that the older design could not handle. The action was also changed to employ a clip rather than a tubular magazine.

In the discussion of lever-action rifles, it was pointed out that only blunt-nosed bullet cartridges could be used in a tubular magazine because of the danger of firing a cartridge in the magazine during recoil should a sharp-pointed bullet rest against the primer of a cartridge lying ahead of it. Remington's models 14 and 141 handled pointed bullet cartridges with a tubular magazine by means of a spiral magazine tube that forced the cartridges to lie in such a way that they could not possibly have to bullet-to-primer relationship. It was an interesting solution to a thorny problem.

Pump actions are fast. In fact, it has been proven many times that an experienced shooter with a slick-operating pump can fire it faster than an autoloader. One reason why pumps are so fast is that one does not have to move the shooting hand as with a bolt or lever. Actually, one doesn't move the action hand either; just pull it back and forward again without changing grip. That makes the pump fast to operate in any repeat-shot situation. And it's equally fast for a left-handed as a right-handed shooter.

Quite a bit of advertising copy has been devoted in recent years to the fact that some pump guns have double action bars. That is, that there is a bar on each side of the pump handle connected to the breechbolt mechanism. The claim is that this is sure to prevent binding, thus assuring smooth operation. On the face of it this does sound logical. But when you consider that the most famous pump shotgun ever made, the Winchester Model 12, has a single action bar, and that many other guns are so equipped, that point becomes silly. A single action bar is just as good as two, assuming a properly designed and manufactured gun. True, Remington employs two action bars on their 760 rifles, but these are elements of an entirely different design and you need not necessarily assume that double action bars are necessary for smooth operation. It just isn't so.

CHAPTER THREE

SEMI-AUTOMATIC BREECH ACTIONS

All you have to do to shoot a semiautomatic gun is pull the trigger each time you want the gun to fire. That means the gun does all the rest of the work; put another way, the energy developed by firing the gun performs six of the seven steps of operation (all except firing).

In an automatic action (machine gun or submachine gun), all seven steps are performed automatically. There are a number of words used interchangeably in regard to semiautomatics, and one term used improperly. A semiautomatic is often referred to as an autoloader or autoloading or self-loading. All these terms are used, they all mean the same thing, and all are correct. The word automatic is often incorrectly used for the semiautomatic gun and this is a mistake. It is in such common use, however, that some acceptance of the term is obvious. The important thing to remember is that it's an error, and that only a machine gun, which has a fully automatic mechanism, is properly called automatic.

Two basic methods of utilizing the firing energy to work the action are employed in automatic and semiautomatic firearms. These are recoil, meaning the kick of the gun, and gas, meaning that the same gas that drives the bullet is used to work the action. There are numerous variations, but these are the two basic forces employed.

While there are many ways to use the gas supply, all modern gas guns operate by bleeding off a little gas to drive a piston, which, in turn, works the action. Recoil operation, on the other hand, breaks down into two basic types – short recoil and long recoil. There's still another semiautomatic system that is similar to recoil, in most respects, but it's a bit different and is called blowback.

RECOIL OPERATION

Each time you fire a rifle, it kicks. That is, it develops recoil, which you feel against your shoulder. This is the force that is used in a recoil-operated gun. To understand this with a simple explanation, visualize a lever-action rifle, such as the Model 94 Winchester .30/30. Now visualize this rifle mounted so that the end of its lever is secured to something solid — as if you clamped the lever in a vise. Now fire the rifle. You know it will kick — that is recoil — backwards; in so doing, it will accomplish the steps of unlocking, extraction, cocking, and ejection.

Take your imagination one step farther. Place a heavy spring against the buttstock and fire the rifle again. This time, after the gun has fully recoiled, it has also stored energy in the heavy spring that will now drive the rifle back forward. As it does, it will complete the steps of feeding and locking and it's ready to shoot again. (If we add something to trip the trigger after the rifle is relocked, it will be a fully automatic machine gun.)

In very basic terms, this is the force that operates a recoil-actuated semiautomatic or fully automatic firearm. Naturally you can't fasten a lever in the vise each time you want to shoot a semiautomatic gun, so gun designers figured out how to make the mechanism recoil within the outside framework of the firearm. Now we have arrived at the real explanation of a recoil-operated gun — the barrel moves.

Sir Hiram Maxim is generally credited with inventing the first recoil-operated gun with his Maxim machine gun. If Maxim came upon it first, John Browning put it on the map. Maxim's invention was perfected in 1884; during the next twenty years, Browning discovered and perfected gas and blowback operation and designed dozens of recoil-operated mechanisms, many of which are still being used.

Recoil operations break down into short recoil and long recoil. In short recoil, the barrel moves a very short distance, from about ⅛ to ½ inch, depending on the type of gun and the power of the cartridge. In long recoil, the barrel moves all the way to the rear.

Recoil operation was popular in rifles for quite a number of years. One example of a popular recoil-operated rifle is the Remington Model 8 (and, later, Model 81), which was in the Remington line from 1906 till 1950. Today, however, there are no recoil-operated sporting rifles being manufactured to my knowledge. The primary reason would seem to be that a movable barrel can't deliver the same accuracy you can get from a fixed barrel. You can certainly get acceptable accuracy, but that's not good enough today.

BLOWBACK OPERATION

John Browning invented blowback operation about 1895; it has since been used by gunmakers all over the world. Guns operated by blowback operation do not have a mechanical locking arrangement, such as the Mauser-type bolt. Locking is accomplished by inertia (defined as the tendency of a body at rest to remain at rest, and a body in motion to remain in motion). Generally speaking, blowback operation is restricted to cartridges developing relatively low chamber pressure. Most handgun cartridges fall into this category as do the .22s.

To visualize why blowback works, you must imagine that you're seated at a long table on which has been placed a row of books. Move just one book far enough to place both your hands, with palms out, between it and the rest of the row. Now, applying equal force to both the hands, spread your hands apart rapidly. You don't have to do it to know the single book will fly off the table while the rest of them will tend to remain where they are but will eventually move. Now let's apply this example to firearms.

Instead of a single book, you have a bullet weighing only 40 grains (in .22 caliber). Instead of a long row of books, you have a heavy breechblock weighing many times the weight of the bullet. When you fire the gun, the gas pressure works equally in all directions but the bullet moves first, because it's so light. The gas, however, is also pushing against the breechbolt through the cartridge case and, just as the bullet leaves the muzzle, the inertia of the heavy bolt has been overcome and there is enough remaining pressure to shove it all the way back. Engineers call this remaining gas the residual pressure. It's not enough to be harmful, but it is enough to work the action. Blowback calls for reasonably

A rather unique design is seen in this Charter Arms "Explorer" model of .22 blowback-operated autoloader. In this little gun, everything is stored in the buttstock and can easily be assembled in something less than a minute. A handy item for the camper.

delicate timing, to be sure the bullet is clear and chamber pressures have subsided enough before the breechbolt opens up. Otherwise, blowback action is no different from recoil. (Many engineers include blowback in the recoil category. This is perfectly valid, but since the barrel doesn't move I prefer to keep it separate, and most gun people do maintain this distinction.) Aside from the steps of locking and unlocking, blowback and recoil operations are virtually the same.

In 1907 and 1910, Winchester introduced two blowback rifles chambered for fairly large cartridges – the .351 and .401, both of which are now long gone. These two rifles were used quite a bit for law-enforcement purposes and were preferred by some hunters. The rifles were, however, quite muzzle heavy, somewhat ungainly, and poorly balanced. As a result they never really achieved much popularity and were eventually dropped. The reason they were unbalanced was because they were blowback. Because the cartridges were fairly powerful, a heavy breechblock was necessary to keep it closed until the bullet got away. Since there wasn't room for a heavy breechblock, Winchester's engineers solved that by an extension rod from the breechbolt up into the forearm, where it was fastened to a heavy weight. That's what unbalanced this rifle, but without that added weight the bolt would have opened too soon with disastrous results.

Blowbacks are balanced by carefully weighting the moving parts, by careful attention to spring tension, all in relation to the cartridge to be used. This will explain why a .22 autoloading rifle chambered for the .22 Long Rifle *high velocity* won't work with standard-velocity .22 Long Rifle cartridges. The action needs that slight extra push to operate consistently.

LONG-RECOIL OPERATION

Long-recoil operation differs from short recoil primarily in the distance the barrel moves. As explained earlier, the barrel of a short-recoil gun moves from about ⅛ inch to a maximum of about

½ inch. In a long-recoil system, barrel and breechbolt, locked together tightly, move all the way to the rear as a unit.

Without question the best-known long-recoil-operated gun is the Browning Auto-5 shotgun, the invention Browning himself called his greatest achievement. The gun was patented in 1900 and there is no way of determining how many autoloading guns have been made under this patent, except that there are "many millions."

Another popular Browning long-recoil firearm was the Remington Model 8, introduced in 1906, which was later remodeled and called the Model 81. Chambered for a line of Remington rimless cartridges in .25, .30, .32 and .35, it was a popular rifle in the woods of the eastern United States for deer hunting, especially in .35 Remington caliber. The other cartridges were meant to be competitive with Winchester rimmed versions chambered for the Model 1894 rifle. The only survivors today are the .35 Remington and, of course, the .30/30 Winchester.

Remington's Model 8 (and 81) operated somewhat like the Auto-5 except that its barrel was entirely enclosed in a long metal jacket. Only about half an inch of the actual barrel protruded at the muzzle. The recoil spring system also included a buffer spring and was enclosed within the jacket.

Both the Model 8 and 81 Remington rifles have operating handles which, when drawn to the rear, unlock the bolt from the barrel extension so the bolt may be drawn back without moving the barrel. It is only when the gun is fired (or when you push back on the barrel) that both parts move rearward locked together.

I doubt there will be many more applications of the recoil principle, except perhaps for autoloading pistols. One of the leading reasons is that most designers today are working with gas operation.

GAS OPERATION

The story goes that once when John Browning was watching the muzzle gases blowing leaves and grass on the firing range, it occurred to him that this force could be applied and harnessed to work the mechanism of an automatic system. Whether the story is true or not, Browning did harness the propellant gases and make them work to operate a gun action. He first adapted an old Winchester .44-caliber rifle by placing a small cap over the muzzle with a hole for the bullet to pass through. The cap was connected to a rod that operated a lever just like a lever-action rifle. Next he drilled a small hole near the muzzle underneath the barrel and filed for patent in 1890. The world's first gas-operated gun was an adapted .44/40 Winchester lever action that could fire sixteen shots a second (that was the full magazine). Next he refined the design and made a .45/70 machine gun which was demonstrated to the hierarchy at Colt as well as to military officials. It fired 1,800 rounds in a little more than three minutes without a hitch.

The gas spurts out of this hole in the Ruger Mini-14 and sharply drives the operating parts rearward. Once the piston, visible at the right below the wooden handguard, moves clear of the port, the gas is exhausted.

Browning's first practical gas design was an automatic pistol, invented in 1895. Browning drilled a small hole near the muzzle and on top of a .38-caliber pistol. In firing, after the bullet passed the hole, some gas was vented upwards where it pushed a lever connected to the breechblock. This lever rotated upward and back in an arc, which served to move the breechblock back causing extraction, ejection, and cocking. On the return, or forward, stroke, it fed a new cartridge into the chamber and the gun was ready to fire again. Locking was accomplished by the straight line arrangement of operating lever, connecting rod, and breechblock.

In 1895, Browning also adapted the gas theory to a machine gun. Called the Colt Model 1895, this operational system was similar to that of the pistol just described except that the gas port and operating lever were on the bottom and were, of course, much larger. The Colt Model 1895 was the first machine gun ever ordered by U.S. forces and saw service in the Boxer Rebellion and the Spanish American War. It was a highly successful design

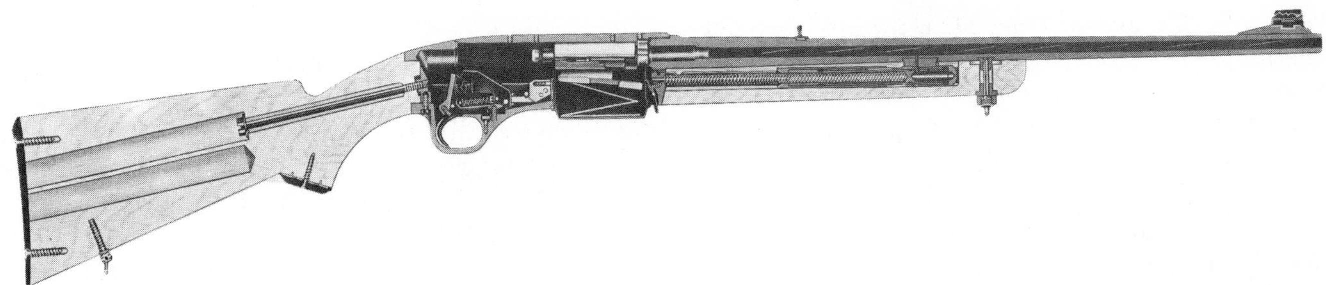

An interesting Winchester rifle that was on the market for a brief period was based on a gas system similar to that known as the "White system," perfected in the 1920s. It didn't stand up to wartime use and so was dropped by the services, but it was satisfactory for sporters. This was the Winchester Model 100. Its gas system was "metered," meaning that once enough gas was in the cylinder to move the piston, the flow was shut off. That was accomplished by having holes in the piston and cylinder line up. Once the cylinder moved, the holes were no longer in line and that shut off the gas supply.

and was eventually succeeded by the 1917 Browning recoil-operated machine gun.

A more successful, or at least more widely used, gun was the famed BAR (Browning Automatic Rifle) model of 1918, which was used in both World Wars and which is quite similar to Hotchkiss designs used in Europe and to the Japanese Nambu models of World War II. The BAR tapped gas from a small hole about six inches behind the muzzle, diverting it down into a cylinder driving a piston backwards to work the action. The BAR fired from the open-bolt position and was a completely reliable machine rifle that fired either fully or semiautomatically by switching a "change lever." John Garand, the Springfield Armory employee who designed the M1 rifle, the U.S. rifle of World War II, employed a similar system for tapping the gas supply, although his bolt arrangement was entirely different.

Some shooters think a gas gun causes lower velocity because it robs the bullet of some of its propellant force. This is not true. The amount of gas bled from the barrel is insignificant and causes no velocity loss whatever. Some also believe the unlocking occurs before the bullet has left the muzzle. This also is not true as we will shortly see.

THE M1 GARAND

This was a great rifle as countless GIs in World War II will testify. Its gas was bled from the barrel very near the muzzle, diverted into a cylinder where it pushed an operating rod to the rear. This operating rod engaged a knob on the bolt (the bolt actually turned, like a Mauser, and so the action is indeed partly Mauser). There was about ⅜ inch of rear movement of the operating rod before it engaged the bolt's knob, which gave ample time for the bullet to clear the muzzle before the bolt opened. Once open, the operating rod drove all the way to the rear carrying the bolt with it to accomplish unlocking, extraction, ejection, and cocking. On the forward stroke, a new cartridge was fed into the chamber and the bolt was relocked. The action of the M1 was excellent and the rifle proved itself in the tropics of the South Pacific, the sands of Africa, and elsewhere around the globe.

The Garand was built around the great .30/06 cartridge. Since that time we have gone to the 7.62mm Nato cartridge, the commercial .308 Winchester; and most recently to the 5.56mm, commercially called the .223 Remington. Each of these has been a step down from the .30/06 in my opinion. The .308 is close and quite adequate. But if this nation ever has to fight a war with the .223 Remington (powered somewhere between the .222 and .222 Remington Magnum) I fear we may well be outgunned. Those who think the infantryman is no longer needed, that wars will be won or lost by nuclear holocaust, simply don't understand history. We need a bigger military rifle than the .223, which I regard as an ideal, intermediate-range woodchuck rifle.

For a short period we had the M14 rifle, chambered for the .308 cartridge. This was a sort of Nato compromise cartridge which made a lot of sense because it permitted interchangeable ammo supplies for Nato forces. Most Nato countries adopted the rifle developed by FN (Fabrique Nationale in Liège, Belgium, an old gunmaking firm that has long manufactured many of Browning's products) while the U.S. adopted the M14. Most of the engineering for the M14 was provided by Harrington & Richardson with an assist from Winchester.

H&R later adapted the M14 operation to their autoloading high-power rifle in .243 and .308 calibers; Winchester produced its Model 100, an adaptation of the same system. These rifles employed a slightly different gas system in that it controlled the supply of gas entering the cylinder. There also was a hole in the piston itself that lined up with the bleed hole in the barrel. As the piston, connected to the operating parts, began to move, the piston's hole moved out of alignment and shut off the gas supply. This is often referred to as a system of metering the proper amount of gas.

THE RUGER "MINI-14"

We now have the new Ruger Mini-14 rifle, a dead ringer for the M1 Garand (well, almost) but built around the diminutive .223 Remington cartridge. It's called the Mini-14 because it appears to be a shrunken M14, the rifle used in Korea which, in turn, borrowed heavily from the M1.

Make no mistake about this little arm — it's a military rifle pure and simple. I would assume that Bill Ruger is after some military, or law-enforcement, market or another. But even if it's of little or no use to the sportsman, to almost anyone who served in World War II or Korea the little rifle will prove of some sentimental attachment and I suspect a lot of people will want to own one.

The Mini-14 is far from a copy of either the M1 or the M14, and it shouldn't be construed as such. Bill Ruger has put his company's considerable design talents to work on this gun — and it shows. If you tried to manufacture an M1 rifle today I haven't any idea what it might cost. But I do recall that a figure of around $85 was mentioned just before World War II. Those costs probably went down a bit as massive war production got underway in this country. Nevertheless, the M1 rifle was difficult to manufacture, even by the standards of those days. To duplicate that rifle today would be almost impossible. What Ruger has wrought is a fine little gun, greatly resembling the earlier military rifles, but made with today's methods, costs, and machines.

THE U.S. CARBINE

David Williams' design for the .30-caliber U.S. carbine during World War II was different. He is the man who invented the "floating chamber," which has been applied to pistol (Colt .22 conversion unit for .45 Auto), shotgun, and machine guns. He also applied a similar principle to gas operation. Instead of bleeding gas from near the muzzle, he bled it from close to the breech. But he also developed a short piston with a total movement of only 3/16 inch. Called an "impinging" gas system, this piston moves very fast and gives the operating parts a sharp, hard whack that sends them flying to the rear. It also is a closed piston, so there is no gas leakage after the bullet passes.

Something fairly similar happens with the Remington autoloading high-power Model 742—gas is bled near the middle of the barrel where it enters a cylinder and drives a piston back to operate the action. This has been a thoroughly satisfactory performer which was issued originally as Model 740 in 1955 to replace the now-obsolete recoil-operated Model 81. First chambered for the .30/06, the 742 is now offered in a wide variety of chamberings. I well remember the first one of these rifles I saw, because I was gunsmithing at the time. To say I wasn't impressed would be to put it mildly. Not only did it seem silly to produce such a rifle in so powerful a cartridge as the .30/06, but it was obvious to me that its accuracy would be terrible. The guy who dragged it into my shop wanted a scope mounted, so he left it and I went about mounting the scope and sighting it in. I don't remember the group size now but I do remember that it shot extremely well and that I was very surprised. I have since fired many of these rifles and, while semiautomatics are not my preference, these Remingtons do shoot with exceptional accuracy.

Aside from the nice H&R Model 360 Ultra, the high-power rifle autoloading field has been pretty much Remington country. It was, that is, until Browning came along with its present high power which they call, naturally enough, the BAR.

BROWNING AUTOMATIC RIFLE

The Browning BAR isn't going to make that much of a dent in the market—it's too high-priced. It is a quality rifle in all respects and I like it very much (my sample is a .338 Winchester Magnum, which has since been dropped) but at nearly $500 (in 1976) I doubt they'll sell too many. This is a more-or-less conventional gas-operated rifle that's available in four standard calibers from .243 Winchester

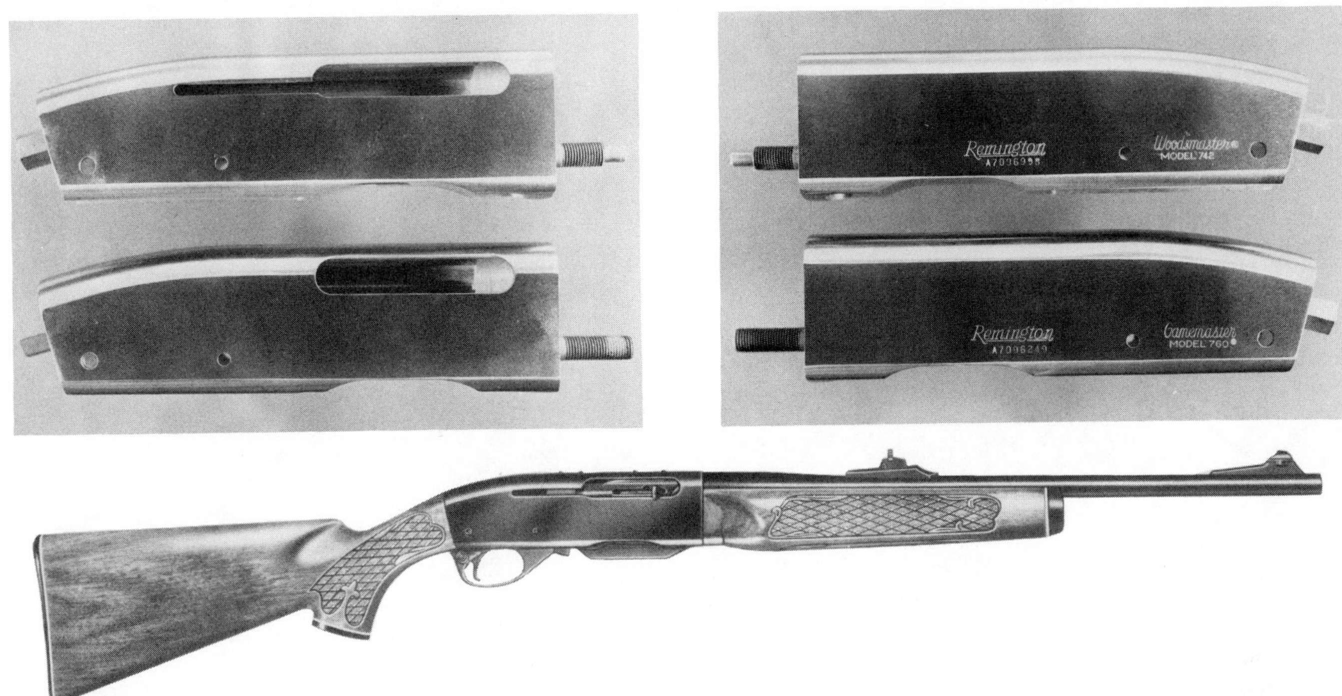

Modern manufacture demands economies and simplicity of design. At top left are two Remington receivers that are identical except that the upper one has an elongated slot for an operating rod. It will be the Model 742 autoloader. The lower receiver will be the Model 760 pump-action rifle. The photograph at top right shows the opposite side of these two receivers after finishing operations and at bottom is the completed Model 742 gas-operated Remington auto.

through .30/06 and two magnums from 7mm Remington through .300 Winchester Magnum. Its action is positive and it can deliver its magazine-full damned fast, as you'd expect. The only real complaint I have is that you have to remove the buttstock to remove the trigger group and the bolt. That's not all that big a deal except that on the .338 model they have a recoil pad and the screws can't be reached without marring the pad.

I believe any rifle should have the capability to be dismounted by its owner for occasional cleaning in a way that doesn't require any act of near magic. The BAR is exceptionally good in its method of getting at the gas system, and I acknowledge that this part may need more cleaning than the bolt and trigger-guard group of parts. But it's inevitable that dirt, water, snow, and other foreign matter is going to get into the rear of this receiver and a better means of getting at the parts ought to have been provided.

CHAPTER FOUR

BREECH ACTION LOCKING SYSTEMS

It is clear that the breech end of the rifle barrel must be securely locked at the time of firing so that the propellant gas is confined and made to perform its assigned task: to move the bullet out of the barrel. It is also clear that we cannot open this lock until the gas pressure has subsided to a safe level and that different pressures require different types of locks. A locking arrangement perfectly adequate for a .22 rimfire cartridge is not nearly strong enough to retain the pressures needed to drive a Weatherby Magnum bullet at high velocity.

The locking system, in short, must be strong enough to hold the cartridge, or family of cartridges, for which the firearm is or will be adapted. The highest-pressure cartridges are those with large, fat, and often long bodies, combined with small bore. Typical examples would be the .264 Winchester and 7mm Remington Magnum. Much lower pressures are generated by cartridges with very large bores. The reason is that the larger the bore, the quicker the gas pressure can get out (other things being constant). Many of the older cartridges must be loaded to lower pressures than a modern rifle will stand because there are old rifles still around. An example is the .45/70. This cartridge was first used in 1873 in the old U.S. Springfield, which never had a particularly strong breech action.

When introduced, the .45/70 was a black-powder load, and black powder doesn't develop as high pressures as smokeless powder does. Even though old-time shooting is experiencing a rebirth today, the ammunition can't be loaded to higher pressures than it was in 1873 because somebody might try to shoot it in an old Springfield rifle. (Such modern rifles as the Ruger single shot, with its massive wedge lock, or the Marlin 1895, with its round bolt, will hold much higher pressures.)

Locking systems are many and varied. Some are particularly suited to a certain type of action. Inevitably some are better than others and there have been some that just do not live up to the claims made for them. We'll discuss the more common types, starting with Mauser's system.

TURNING BOLTS AND ADAPTATIONS

Every turning-bolt type of lockup is usually referred to as being of Mauser type or Mauser induced. That's ample tribute to the man who invented the first practical turning-bolt system.

Early bolts often used a single locking lug, the military U.S. Krag rifle, used in the 1890s, being one of these. (Many of today's .22 rimfire rifles also employ a single locking lug.) The Krag was chambered for the .30/40 Krag cartridge, a fairly good cartridge but one of only moderate power. The bolt with a single locking lug is not as strong as one with lugs on each side of the bolt body and cannot be expected to hold as powerful a cartridge. It also supports the cartridge unevenly, and this unequal effect is detrimental in two ways: It tends to put a shearing motion on the locking lug, and its uneven support is not conducive to good accuracy.

Most of the earlier single-lug bolts also used the root of the bolt handle (defined as that part of the handle where it is attached to the bolt body) as a "safety" lug, because it turned down into a notch in the receiver. The safety lug is one that does not engage in normal operation. That means that there is a small gap behind the safety lug when the bolt is closed. A safety lug is employed in nearly all bolt actions and is intended only to function in the event of failure of the locking lugs. If the safety lug does engage the receiver, it will tend to push the bolt forward and move the locking lug or lugs forward and out of engagement.

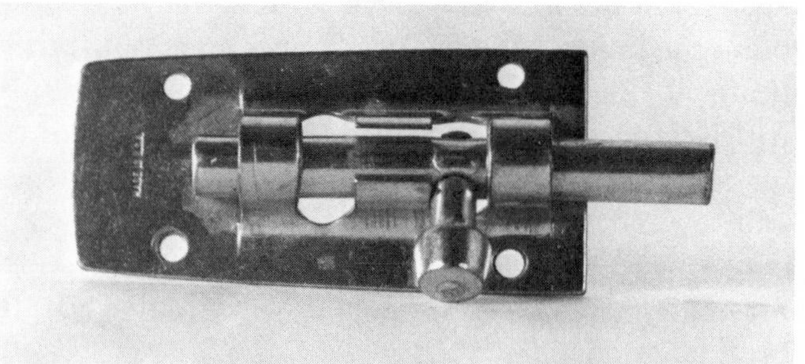

The common turn-bolt action is hardly different from the simple door lock; the only exception being that with the rifle, the thrust is in line with the bolt, while in a doorlock it's at a 90° angle. With both of them, you lift the handle and retract to unlock, and reverse the motion to lock.

Modern .22 bolt-action rifles use the root of the bolt handle as a locking lug. This single lug is perfectly safe and adequate as long as the rifle is used as it was intended.

One of the improvements Mauser made in 1898 over his 1893 design was the addition of a safety lug on the underside of the bolt that turns into a recess in the bottom of the receiver. Mauser's two stout lugs have been used in several millions of rifles, which ought to say enough about their merit. (Moreover, such excellent American sporting rifles as the Winchester Model 70 and Remington 700 have not seen fit to alter that basic concept of locking.) The left-hand Mauser lug is split, to allow the ejector to slide through the notch and toss out the empty case. Winchester and Remington and Weatherby and other current manufacturers employ a different ejector system that makes the left lug a solid unit. This strengthens the action, but whether this added strength was really necessary can be argued.

Among other variations on the Mauser theme are several systems of multiple lugs, instead of the two stout Mauser lugs.

One of the earliest departures was the Newton system of an interrupted thread. Charles Newton was a bright, years-ahead-of-his-time inventor in the early 1900s. He developed very hot, very exciting cartridges that were much more powerful than anything else in existence. And he developed a rifle in which they could be used. Unfortunately, Newton was as poor a businessman as he was good as an inventor and his firm failed, although many of his ideas have lasted. He developed some of the early cartridges that in the years around 1912 made Savage famous, such as the .250/3000, .300, and .22 Hi-Power; his whopping .30 Newton was just about as hot as the .300 Weatherby Magnum — before Roy Weatherby was born. There are still a few of those early Newton rifles around, but ammunition is so scarce it's hardly worth firing them because of

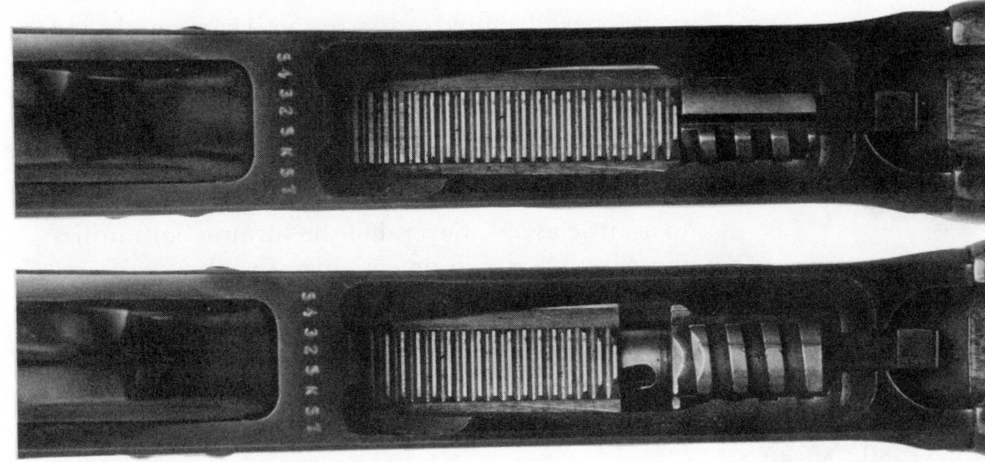

Partially locked (top) and unlocked (bottom) views of the underside of Browning's lever-action high-power rifle. The bolt is driven back and forth by a gear arrangement and front-end locking is provided by the lugs you see. Such a bolt is called a rotating-head bolt.

the collector's value of the cartridges. The interrupted thread Newton used in place of the Mauser lugs is still around however. Similar lugs are used on a number of rotating-bolt rifles, such as the Remington autoloading 742 and slide-action 760. Some Browning designs use them and a variety of other rotating-bolt systems in other than bolt-action rifles have used and are using the threads.

The interrupted thread system has advantages. It's claimed to be stronger than the two, stout Mauser-type lugs. This is an argument I'm not going to get into, primarily because I consider it moot. If the Mauser is strong enough — and it is — why go stronger? The other chief advantage is that it is difficult, some say impossible, to make all the surfaces of a multiple-lug system actually work. All lug surfaces ought to bear evenly and fully, yet it is said that you simply cannot hold tolerances close enough to make all the surfaces engage. The usual rule of thumb is that, no matter the number of lugs that are used, only one to one and a half of these lugs actually touch! But the same is not true with interrupted threads, because the manner of generating (cutting) a thread is continuous.

I have often checked multiple-lug systems and found many of them lacking. Whether or not locking lugs bear and do their job is checked by coating one of the surfaces (the rear of the lugs for example) with Prussian blue, lampblack or some similar material that will make a mark on the mating surface. Then close the action, open it again, and examine both the marked or coated surface and the surface it was meant to engage. Those surfaces that touch will be evident at once. If they do not, the extra lugs are not working.

In his early work on gun design, England's W.W. Greener was extremely critical of multiple-lug locks for double guns. As he pointed out, very few of them actually engaged on all surfaces. The same

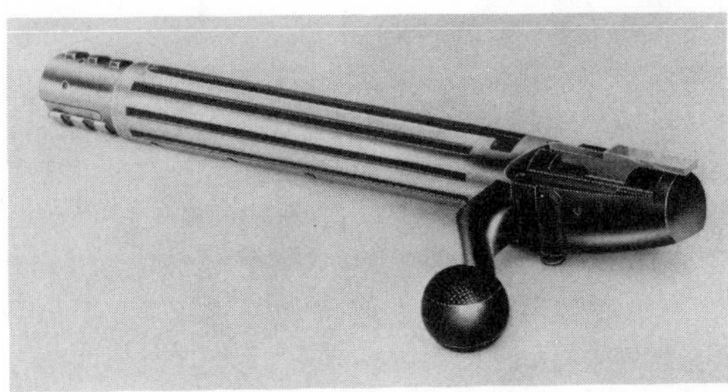

The Weatherby Mark V action has nine locking lugs, an unusual feature of this action being that the outside diameter of the lugs is no greater than the bolt body. This means that the reciever does not require the usual bolt-lug raceways and results in smoother bolt travel.

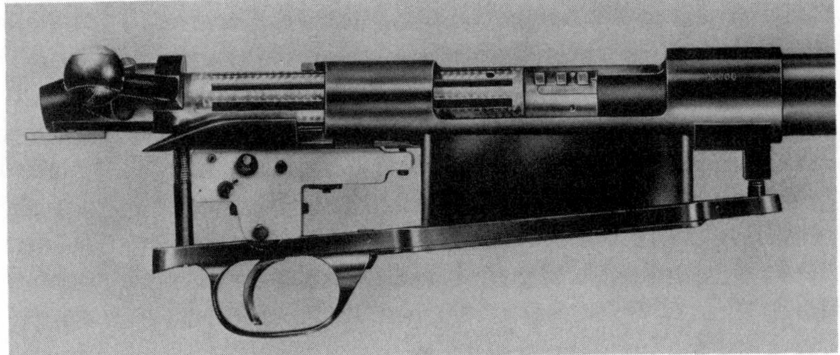

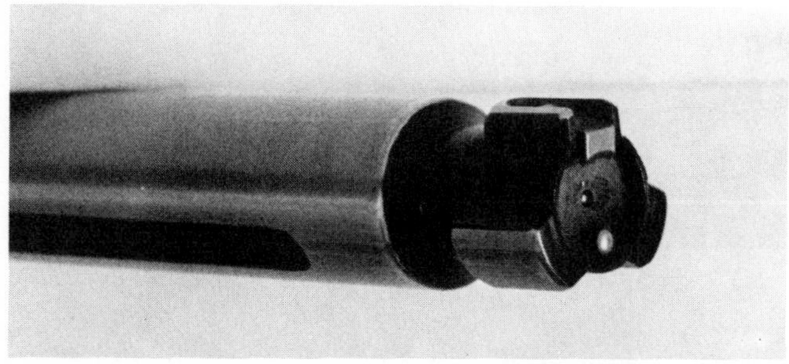

The photographs show side (above) and front-end (below) views, with barrel removed, of the Kleinguenther action made by Voere in Germany. This is a three-lugged bolt that locks into a Stellite insert. Note in the frontal view that the bolt's locking lugs are moving forward into the spaces between the lug recesses. You can see the upper lug recess against which the top lug will bear.

thing is true with any other system — multiple locks are fine and secure, but only when they all work. (It should be mentioned that Greener had an axe to grind. He was one of the better gunmakers of England and had developed the competing cross-bolting system that still bears his name. It was widely copied by lesser gunmakers on the Continent, though most of the copies did not possess the degree of workmanship that Greener guns showed.)

The turning-bolt lock, as applied to bolt-action rifles, was considerably strengthened when Remington introduced its Models 721 and 722 (which were alike except for length) in 1948. This was accomplished by utilizing a spring-loaded ejector (like the Garand) which did away with a conventional ejector operating through a slot in the left-hand locking lug. The result was that two solid lugs could now be used and the action strengthened quite a bit.

Turning bolts are locked and unlocked by turning them in or out of engagement. This was, and still is in many cases, a full quarter turn or 90°. Many recent bolt actions have reduced the bolt lift to as little as 55°. Several of the turning bolts utilizing a pump stroke or gas operation have also reduced the necessary rotation to less than 90°. Again, the Garand is an example. The exact amount of rotation isn't important so long as the lugs are stout enough and/or there are enough of them to get the job done. Reducing the lift on a bolt-action rifle does permit a slightly faster operation, but also brings another problem — stiffer cocking, because the shorter arc must now accomplish just as much cocking force as the 90° turn.

One of the more interesting examples of a rear-lockup bolt action is Remington's Model 788, a plain, inexpensive bolt-action high-power rifle with excellent accuracy.

It had long been thought that the only way to make a good, solid bolt action was to lock the bolt with rugged lugs located up front, as close to the base of the cartridge as you could get. The reasoning was that otherwise you'd permit "springing" in the bolt, and that the cartridge wouldn't be so well supported. The argument appears logical, but apparent logic isn't always all that accurate. Remington blasted the argument with their Model 788, which locked in the rear section of the bolt body. That wasn't the first such lockup, but it was the first modern bolt rifle with rear locking produced in volume by a major American gunmaker. What this rear locking does is permit a nice close fit for the front end of the bolt body, because you don't have to allow space for the lugs to slide fore and aft. (Weatherby solved this with his oversize bolt body, which does have front-end locking lugs.) The superior support given this bolt helps guarantee solid breeching. It also helps eliminate the springing that might otherwise happen.

Another interesting type of turning-bolt lockup is evidenced by the Colt-Sauer rifle. When the bolt is open, that is in the unlocked position, it's perfectly smooth and cylindrical. When turned into the locked position however, three small lugs are forced out of the body and into their recesses. The Colt-Sauer lugs also are toward the rear of the bolt. Front as opposed to rear locking is more complex than it sounds because the receiver must be designed differently for each, so there is a lot more to it than physical location. I do know that both the Remington 788 and Colt-Sauer, as well as a few imports, deliver extremely good accuracy. To state with conviction that the system is as good, or as accurate, as the original system that has been around since 1898 is going to take more time to decide. Besides, I suspect the point might be so close as to be of little or no consequence.

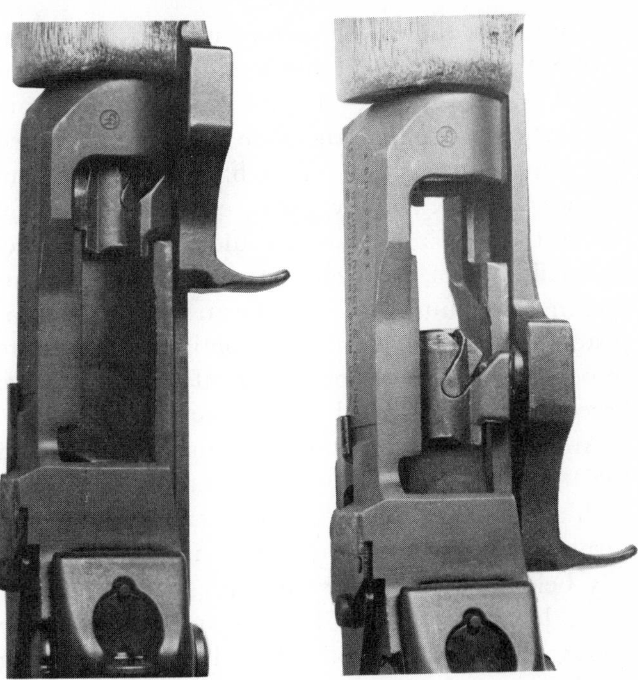

Ruger's Mini-14, close to a scaled-down version of the M1 rifle of World War II, is chambered for the .223 Remington cartridge. At left, the bolt is locked, with the operating rod fully forward; the rifle is in firing position. At right, the bolt is halfway open. The operating rod then moves back a short distance, cams the bolt open by rotating it to the left as in the M1, and the gas-driven operating rod moves the bolt all the way to the rear.

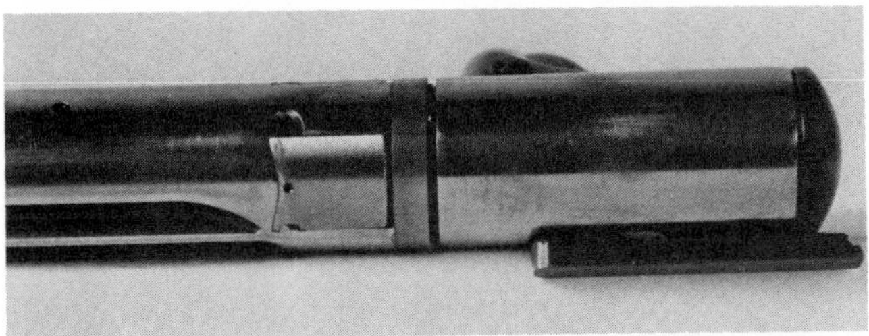

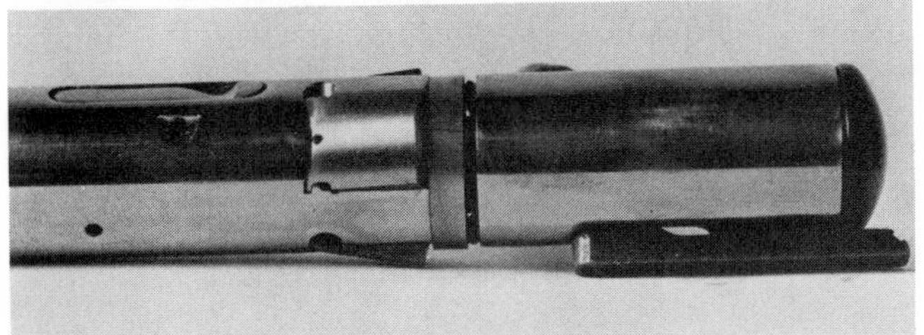

The lockup of the Colt-Sauer rifle is most unusual. The top picture shows the lugs in unlocked position, the lower one shows them locked. Rotating the bolt handle cams the lugs out and into their recesses in the receiver. The system is ingenious and provides a smooth bolt operation; it's a rear lockup, as you can see.

Guns operating with a turning-bolt lock (and this includes such firearms as the autoloader and levers by Browning as well as the pump and autoloaders by Remington) are among the strongest locking systems yet devised.

A couple of interesting departures from the basic Mauser, but nonetheless still turning-bolt lockups, are seen by examining the Winchester Model 100. A gas-operated high-power rifle now dropped from the line, it utilized three locking lugs that were quite large and stout. The degree of rotation was less than the usual 90°, but of more interest is the enclosure of the lug unit within the bolt body. Only the lug unit rotates while the bolt body itself does not turn. A system of gas cylinder, piston, and operating rod activates a cam that rotates the lugs out of engagement, whereupon the bolt body is free to move back and forth.

Somewhat similarly, both Remington's Model 740 autoloader and Model 760 slide-action rifles operate with a bolt carrier that contains the locking lug units. In these Remingtons the lugs are interrupted thread type and thus are multiple lugs operated by action bars and cams. Both actions work similarly, except that the slide action is activated by manual thrust of the pump handle while the autoloader is operated by gas in conventional form. To vastly oversimplify, you could make a slide-action rifle out of the Remington autoloader by attaching a manual slide handle instead of the gas piston. And vice versa. Both actions work quite smoothly, are very strong, and offer very positive breeching and remarkably good accuracy.

Another variation on the turning bolt is seen in the Ithaca Model 51 gas-operated shotgun. This is such a departure that it's hard to categorize it as a turning bolt, yet the bolt does turn and so it properly belongs here. Three small lugs appear on the lower left edge of the 51's bolt and engage three corresponding lugs in the barrel extension along the left side of the receiver. These are plainly visible when the bolt is open. To unlock, the bolt rotates slightly to the left (counterclockwise), only about 10–12° and just enough to disengage, whereupon the bolt can move backwards freely. In locking, the reverse action takes place. The unlocking is accomplished by the initial movement of the operating rod. Ithaca's 51, as well as that company's Mag-10, was designed by Jim Tollinger, a talented engineer and an exceedingly excellent gunsmith in his own right.

SLIDING-WEDGE LOCKS

Perhaps the simplest lock of all is the vertical sliding wedge, as employed in most single-shot rifles. Riding up and down as the lever is actuated, the massive lock rides in notches cut in the sides of the receiver and effectively secures the cartridge in place. Actually, most of these wedges really slide on a slight angle, so that in moving down to unlock, they move slightly to the rear to avoid dragging across the base of the cartridge case. This also allows the extractor to begin its work to break the seal (primary extraction) and slowly move the empty very slightly to the rear. If the wedge dropped perfectly straight down, this primary extraction couldn't occur until the lock had completely cleared the cartridge.

Sliding wedges in the various single shots are usually classed as among the strongest actions ever made. This statement is basically true, but it has its exceptions. In some of the older rifles the steels used were not good enough to stand some of the modern, hot cartridges. Most of the older actions, made for black-powder cartridges, employed large firing pins that require precise gunsmithing to convert to any modern cartridge. (This alteration consists of drilling out the face of the breechblock and inserting a plug made of "drill rod" which can be hardened. This plug is then drilled for the new firing pin, because a smaller diameter pin is necessary with modern cartridges. The usual type of pin installed was called the Mann-Niedner, after Dr. Franklin Mann, the great ballistician, and gunsmith A. O. Niedner. Such a pin could not move backward in the event of a pierced primer.)

Adaptations of the sliding-wedge principle are seen in some other rifles as well. An example is the Model 94 Winchester, which employs two sliding wedges, one on each side of the action near the rear of the breechblock. These are moved down by the first part of the lever stroke to allow the bolt to move back and forth, then are brought up again into locked position by the final closing of the finger lever. A similar, though more rugged, system was used in the Winchester 1886, an obsolete model once chambered for some very large, popular cartridges.

Marlin's 336 utilizes the same principle but its lock is placed across the action, more like that of the single-shot rifle. The upper end of the lock engages the round bolt and provides very secure locking. As a matter of fact, the 336 lock is somewhat similar in operation to the system used on Browning .30 and .50 caliber machine guns. A laterally positioned locking block moves up and down to lock breechblock to barrel. Such a lock, and this applies to all the sliding-wedge types, must be adequately secured in the locked position. Generally speaking, safety of the system is assured in two ways: First, the lock is secured by its linkage with the operating lever or other parts; second, the guns will not fire unless the locks are in position, which is accomplished in a wide variety of ways.

DIRECT-LEVER LOCKS

Marlin's Model 39 .22 rifle is an example of this early, adequate locking system. The basic 39 traces its ancestry to Model 1891; this system has been

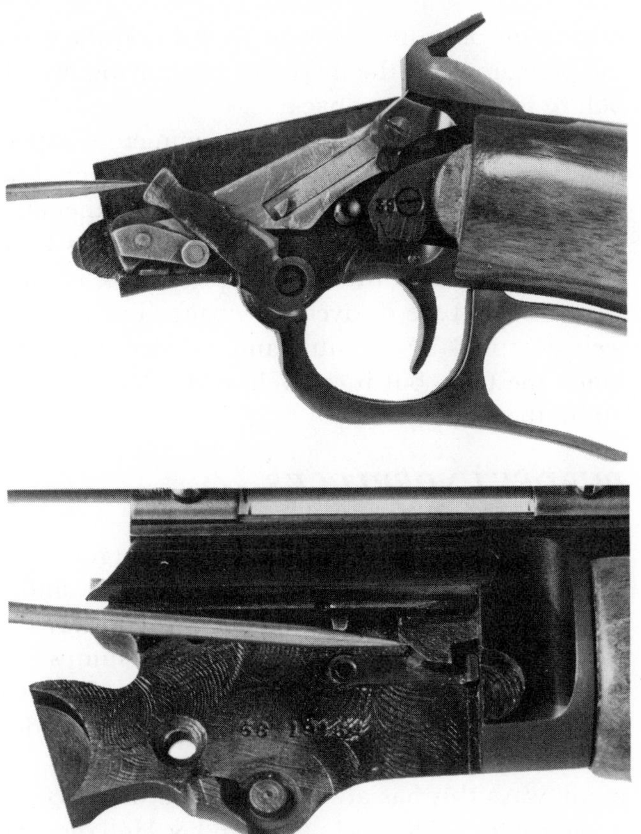

Here is the old, but simple, lockup — the Marlin Model 39 .22 rifle. It was originally the Model 1891, and is the oldest shoulder gun still in production anywhere in the world. The top photograph shows the right-hand side of the action (a take-down action) and the pointer shows the front of the lever that not only moves the bolt back and forth, but also serves to lock the action by coming to rest (below) on the bolt. When these two parts are securely seated, the action is closed tightly.

used virtually unchanged since at least that far back. The system is amply strong for a .22 but, so far as I know, has not been used on any high-power chamberings.

In this action the front end of the finger lever is used to move the breechbolt back and forth in conventional lever style. However, at the end of the forward movement, the tip of the lever moves out of the operating slot in the bolt and against a mating shoulder at the front of the bolt. The result is that it's the lever itself that holds the bolt tightly in the locked position. It's a good system providing very tight breeching for the .22 cartridge and, since it's a straight-line arrangement, there is no tendency for the bolt to move until it's unlocked. The unlocking movement simply takes the lever nose away from the locking shoulder and into the bolt slot to operate the action. Very simple, very neat, and its longevity (more than a million rifles by 1975) suggests its excellence.

HUMP LOCKS

This is the locking system in which the rear edge of the breechbolt top has a hump that is moved up into a recess or against a shoulder to lock the action. Common examples are the Savage Model 99 and H&R Ultra 360 autoloader.

One of the more simple, direct methods of locking, the hump lock certainly serves the purpose and has worked well for many years. This system, by the way, ought to debunk to a large degree that old fallacy about "springing," which some claim is inherent in rear-locking bolts. Certainly the Savage Model 99 has delivered excellent accuracy over the years, and its locking system's strength is attested to by its ability to handle such hot cartridges as the .243 and .308 without alterations.

In this system the lockup is accomplished simply by shoving the rear end of the bolt up into its notch on the closing motion of the operating lever, pump, or whatever system is employed. Unlocking is just the opposite; the bolt's hump is pulled down out of engagement as the first step in opening. A sort of reverse-hump lock is found on the Model 62 and

Here is the rather unusual locking lugs employed by the older Winchester pump action .22s designed by John Browning in the 1890s. This is a Model 62 Winchester, with the bolt open but not retracted. When the action is closed, the lugs drop into the recesses on either side of the receiver. Very simple, very neat.

1890 Winchesters and the current Rossi copy of the Winchester 62. These rifles were favorites of the old shooting galleries. They're all pump-action .22s, and the front end of the breechbolt moved up and out of its locking arrangement, forward and down into it. There were two lugs in this system, one on either side of the bolt, and they just popped down into slots in the receiver to lock the action. Again, simple and neat, but not strong enough for much more than the .22. And because the bolt pops up and moves back and forth pretty high in the air, it's no gun for a scope, which puts it at a disadvantage these days.

INERTIA-LOCKING SYSTEMS

In inertia-locking systems, as described in the blowback section of the previous chapter, locking is accomplished because the breechbolt is much heavier than the bullet, so the bullet moves first. By the time the bullet clears the muzzle, the inertia of the heavy bolt has been overcome and there is enough residual pressure remaining to drive the bolt back and accomplish operation.

Inertia locking can only be used for relatively low-powered cartridges. A .30/06, to cite an example, would require a breechblock weighing about 27 pounds to operate under the inertia principle.

TOGGLE LOCKS

Toggle-system locking is more vividly demonstrated by the Luger or Parabellum pistol. Toggle locking can be either straight-line or slightly over center; either way the lockup is strong and unlocking is usually performed by the short-recoil operational system which raises the toggle joint after maximum pressure has been passed and the residual pressure helps the inertia of the moving breechbolt to move the parts back.

Over the years there have been numerous experimental rifles with actions of the toggle type. One example is a Pedersen design that came rather close to adoption by the U.S. Army between wars I and II. I say this was of the toggle type because the lock was a toggle type delayed blowback. The rifle was well accepted by infantry and cavalry units that made the tests, but it, as well as many others, lost out to the Garand.

PURDEY UNDERLOCKS

Most side-by-side double-barreled shotguns and rifles are locked underneath the barrels by a sliding bar that moves back, to unlock, and forward to slide into engagement with the barrel lumps and hold the barrels down onto the action bar. Invented by the famous London gunmaker James Purdey, the system is still referred to as "Purdey Locks." In many ways this has always disturbed me since the reference to Purdey locks (Holland & Holland sidelocks, Anson & Deeley system, etc.) seems a direct attempt to ride on the coattails of these famous names in London gunmaking. Often, the quality of guns which claim to have "Purdey locks" or "Holland & Holland sidelocks" needs every bit of help it can get. And I think it's a cheap way to exploit a famous name rather than to offer an accurate description of the type of locking employed (which wouldn't mean much to the prospective buyer anyway).

Be that as it may, the locking system worked out by James Purdey is simple, foolproof and has lasted for years. Purdey, by the way, is still in business in London and still making fine double guns.

CHAPTER FIVE

FEEDING SYSTEMS

Feeding is the act of moving a fresh, unfired cartridge from the magazine into firing position in the barrel's chamber. In the single-shot firearm, feeding is simply the removal of a new cartridge from your pocket or cartridge box and sticking it into the chamber. But in any repeating mechanism, integral storage must be provided for ammunition, as well as a simple, reliable method of moving these stored cartridges into firing position.

There are a number of basic magazine types, all invented and in wide use before 1900 and most still in use to some degree. These types are tubular (including forward under the barrel and to the rear, in the buttstock), box (removable and fixed), rotary, gravity hoppers, belts, and drums.

Some cartridges pose difficult feeding problems, so we should begin by outlining some of the problems faced by gun designers when it comes to making a given gun feed with reliability. Any good feeding system must work whether the gun is held sideways, up, down, upside down or in any phase of any of those positions. One of the simplest types of cartridges to feed is represented by the .45 Automatic Colt Pistol cartridge (.45 ACP). It is straight sided, and its round-nosed, jacketed bullet is easy to steer into the chamber. Cartridges with pronounced tapers are more difficult, because, when laid on top of each other they tend to form into a circle, since their front ends are smaller than their bases.

Cartridges with flat-ended bullets, such as wad cutters, which can be as flat as a barn door, are extremely difficult to make feed because they require

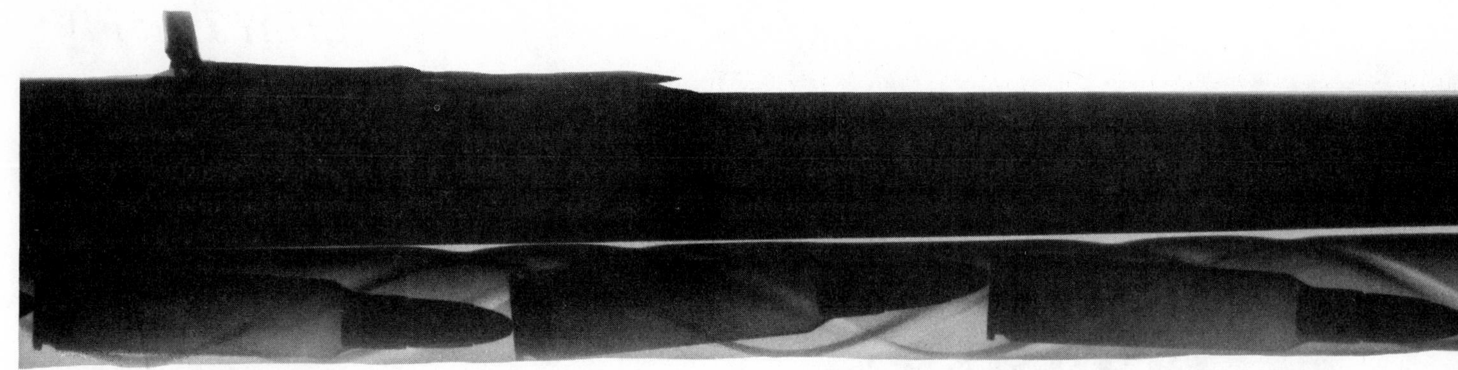

Tubular magazines were used only with cartridges with flat- or blunt-nosed bullets (to prevent one bullet from hitting the primer of a cartridge ahead of it in recoil) until Remington developed the spiral-groove tubular magazine, which forced cartridges to lie to one side or the other. This unusual X ray of such a magazine tube shows how the cartridges — .250/3000 Savage — are forced to lie so that it's impossible for one bullet to contact the primer of another cartridge.

perfect alignment; any deviation and they just won't go into the chamber. Also, rimmed cartridges are harder to feed than rimless, because the rims are a larger diameter, which adds to the taper. Additionally, rimmed cartridges are hard to use in a box magazine because sometimes the rim of one cartridge can get hung up behind the rim of a cartridge immediately below it.

The problems of feeding are also much more important in military automatic weaponry than in sporting firearms. No sportsman wants his gun to jam or fail to feed, and no sporting-firearm manufacturer wants it to happen either. While it is rarely a life-or-death matter for a sporter, in a military weapon, it often is.

Work the action of your gun slowly (in a safe place of course) and watch how carefully the cartridge is guided into the chamber. You can begin to see all the thought that has gone into designing its feeding system. Depending on the cartridge used, it will be fed at a steep or shallow angle or — in the case of a .44 Magnum for example — it will have to be raised for chambering in a level attitude. In any event, it must be guided gently, so the bullet doesn't become damaged and the cartridge case is neither dented nor scratched.

TUBULAR MAGAZINES

These are in wide use in lever-action rifles, .22s, and nearly all repeating shotguns. Generally speaking, only cartridges with flat-nosed, or very blunt round-nosed, bullets may be used in a tubular magazine. Otherwise the tip of a bullet may rest against the primer of the cartridge lying ahead of it in the magazine involving danger that the front cartridge might be ignited by a jar, such as in recoil. That is why .30/30 cartridges have a round or flat-nosed bullet, and also why the .35 Remington has a blunt, round-nosed bullet. There is no problem with .22 rimfire cartridges.

Some years ago, Remington manufactured their slide-action high-power rifle with a tubular magazine, chambered for cartridges with sharp-pointed bullets. In this case they formed a spiral in the magazine tube (see the X ray), which caused each cartridge to lie at an angle in such a way that it was impossible for any primer contact.

At one time, a number of rifles used tubular magazines placed behind the action, up through the center of the buttstock. Only a few rifles are being made today with this sort of tube, examples being the Browning autoloading .22 and Remington's Nylon 66, also chambered for the .22.

Guns employing tubular magazines have a long spring inside the tube that is tipped with a movable plug called the follower. This spring keeps pressure on the cartridges to push them into feeding position when the action is operated. Since, with all tubes located under the barrel, the cartridge must be raised in feeding, there is a part commonly called the lifter or carrier, onto which a cartridge is pushed by the magazine spring, and which is then raised as the action begins its closing movement to position the cartridge for moving into the chamber.

Only one cartridge can be permitted to come out of the magazine at a time, so the gun must have a magazine cut-off latch that is activated at the pre-

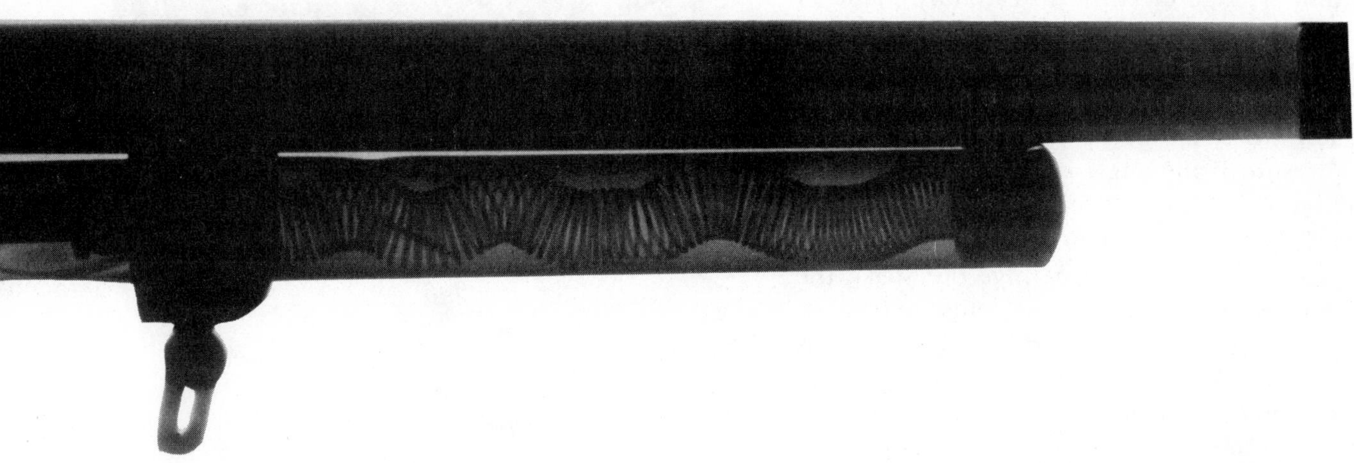

cise time that allows one and only one cartridge to move onto the lifter. As the action is worked, this cut-off latch releases the cartridge and then shuts off the rest of the magazine.

Tubular magazines are found on more guns made in America today than any other type of magazine. They certainly have ample capacity for any sporting purpose, that capacity being limited by the barrel length and/or common-sense restrictions. By that I mean that no shotgun really ought to hold more than three cartridges (two in the magazine and one in the chamber) because (1) Federal law demands it for migratory-waterfowl shooting and (2) if you miss three times, forget it. The six- or seven-shot capacity of .30/30 and .35 Remington lever-action rifles is certainly sufficient, and the usual 24-inch-barreled .22 rifle will hold 19 Long Rifles, 21 Longs or 26 Shorts . . . quite a few indeed!

Tubular magazines, especially for .22-caliber rifles, are probably less prone to problems than removable-clip magazines. Just about the only major disadvantage of the tubular .22 magazine is that you might lose the inner tube containing the spring, without which the whole rifle is useless. Some shooters like to have an extra on hand just to be safe.

ROTARY

The rotary magazine is shaped like a spool. It holds its cartridges in shaped grooves or notches and can be most easily compared to a revolver cylinder that has been cut down to smaller diameter. In the mid-1890s, the rotary-spool magazine was first employed by the Austrian Mannlicher-Schoenauer bolt-action and the Savage lever-action systems. Both these rifles were superb developments; those early Mannlicher spools are a joy to behold, especially as you don't see machining like that these days. The newest gun to use a spool is the Ruger .22 autoloader, which uses a 10-shot rotary magazine.

Rotary magazines are excellent. They provide a special niche for each cartridge, serve to protect the cartridge against battering in recoil (which happens with some other systems), and feed reliably. As each cartridge is loaded, the magazine turns slightly and winds its spring. When the bolt is operated, the spool is permitted to rotate far enough to bring the next cartridge into alignment for chambering. If the rotary spool has any disadvantage it lies only with some of the fat, belted magnum cartridges. A spool to hold the belted magnums for example would require a rifle that was very fat through the action.

BOX MAGAZINES

Box magazines come in two basic styles, those that align their cartridges one directly above the other (most .22 clip magazines are in this category), and those that stagger the cartridges from side to side, as is done in most high-power rifles. Both these basic styles are also available in removable and non-removable types.

The most common clip magazines are those employed in .22 clip-loading rifles and in semi-automatic pistols. It is important to note that these magazines (the correct word is magazine despite the common usage of clip) are carefully made of tempered steel for the very excellent reason that they must present the top cartridge at a precise angle for proper feeding. If that angle is too low, the bullet will strike below the feed ramp and a jam will result. If the angle is too high, one of two other things can happen: (1) the bullet might strike the top of the barrel and jam or (2) the bolt might not engage the rim of the cartridge but strike the cartridge-case body on its side and refuse to feed.

Magazine lips are easily damaged. Usually this damage results from dropping or from trying to use too much force in loading the magazine. In fact, whenever any clip-magazine-fed gun fails to feed, the first place to look for trouble is the magazine lips. Since damaged lips are hard to correct, it's always best to get a new magazine. In fact, I think it's only common sense to order an extra magazine along with the gun, in case of loss, damage, or just for an occasional comparison of the one in use with a new sample.

Clip magazines for any rimmed cartridge, which includes all the .22s, must be slanted to force each cartridge's rim in front of the rim immediately below it. The magazines found on .22 rifles are usually of five- or seven-shot capacity, but sometimes of other odd figures. (In some instances, you can also order a ten-shot magazine as an extra.) Most of today's .22s seem to have magazines that hang down below the stock, right at the balance point (where you'd carry the rifle in one hand). I'd much prefer to see that line flat with the magazine, flush so you could carry the rifle at the balance comfortably. But this "flaw" is even true with Remington's 541-S, the most expensive American-made .22 bolt-action sporter on the market today.

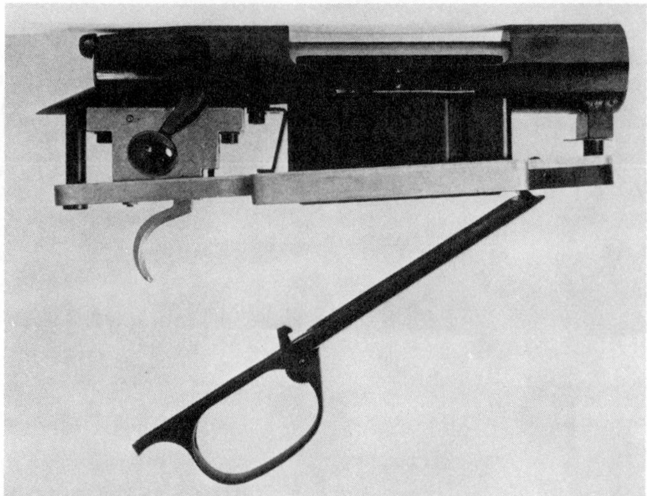

A novel approach to the bolt-action magazine is seen in this Kleinguenther bolt action. The entire trigger-guard unit drops and a separate magazine box may now be removed from the rifle, so you can carry an extra loaded magazine for fast reloading. The opened floorplate and guard also exposes the rear guard screw as well as the trigger-adjustment screw.

Here is shown the hinged floorplate of a Champlin custom rifle. This is a typical Mauser feeding system in which the cartridges lie on either side; virtually every bolt-action rifle, as well as many box-magazine high-power rifles, employ the Mauser staggered-box system.

Most high-power bolt-action rifles use what is commonly called the staggered box, which was originated by Mauser. In this system, the follower is so shaped that it forces the first cartridge to the right. The next cartridge is forced to the left, since the first cartridge now acts as a follower. This procedure continues with each cartridge lying alternately right and left until the magazine is filled. The usual capacity with a cartridge of approximate .30/06 dimensions is five; with the larger Magnums, four is the usual limit.

The original staggered-box magazines, as used in Mausers, Springfields, Enfields, and most commercial sporting rifles, were fixed magazines, meaning that they were not removable. However they did have a removable floorplate to which was attached the magazine spring and cartridge follower. In some of the fancier imported sporters, these followers were hinged at the front with a clasp at the rear end, so they could be unclasped and hinged down to unload the magazine. These were quite attractive and much sought after, although they were generally useless. There has been a recent move, led by Remington, toward making the staggered box magazine in a "blind" configuration. Many high-power bolt rifles do not have a floorplate today, the bottom of the action being solid wood.

To trace the development of these magazines, it's necessary to start with the Mauser. Its system consisted of a solid piece of steel from which was machined the trigger-guard unit. That unit consisted of the trigger guard and magazine box and formed the bottom of the rifle. Once the stock was inserted, between barrel and receiver, the whole rifle fastened together with two screws – one in front of the magazine box and one behind the trigger guard. Then the floorplate, with its magazine spring and follower, could be inserted.

That same basic unit was also used in the U.S. Springfield; the Enfield, on the other hand, departed by having a separate magazine box that simply fitted into the receiver bottom and was held in place by the trigger guard. The Enfield guard also held both screws and provided a floorplate like the Mauser. The famous Model 70 Winchester also followed the separate-magazine-box route and it, and the earlier Remington 30, used spacers in the box to accommodate the different lengths of cartridges for which the rifles were made. But these rifles still retained the floorplate; in fact, the Model 70 incorporated a hinged plate, although far less fancy than some of the German floorplate-release systems.

The next step was to eliminate the floorplate entirely, as has now been done in many American-made rifles. But they still retain the separate magazine box, which is simply stuck in the stock along with the magazine spring and follower. It may not be quite as neat, but it works just as well and I, for one, don't mind it on a rifle that is used for hunting. It saves a little production money, and that's important today. Besides, I'd rather not have a floorplate than have one made of plastic, which might have been an alternative. Put another way, I'd rather have a high-quality floorplate made of steel; but if I can't have that, then I'd prefer the blind bottom.

There are a few high-power rifles with removable magazines; among bolt guns, the Savage can be ordered this way as can the Remington 788 and Remington's slide and autoloading high powers plus Browning's autoloading and lever rifles. This trend is likely to continue, for a lot of hunters like to have a removable magazine of this type. Moreover it's a handy feature that allows easy loading and unloading as you get ready to hunt and come back into camp. The opportunity to carry extra loaded magazines is far easier than carrying loose cartridges, too. I'd say this was a clever move and one that ought to be expanded.

One of the early military features of this basic Mauser box-magazine system was its clip-loading feature (now, the correct use of the word clip). Cartridges were packaged in five-shot clips that were held in a row by their extracting grooves, while the ends were closed with a tiny brass lip. The receiver of the rifle had clip slots into which was placed a clip of fresh cartridges. Pushing down with the right thumb, you bent that tiny brass lip back and shoved the five cartridges from the clip into the magazine; then slammed the bolt home and you were reloaded. The same system was used in the U.S. Springfield and Enfields and in some commercial rifles used for target shooting with the .30/06 cartridge, such as the Model 70 Winchester National Match rifle.

A variation on the clip idea was employed in the M1 rifle, which used a factory-loaded clip containing eight cartridges. When the M1 fired its last shot, the old clip was ejected and the bolt stayed open. You then placed a new clip in the action, pushed it down, and got your hand out of the way fast for the bolt to close. In this rifle the clip remained inside the rifle until the last cartridge was

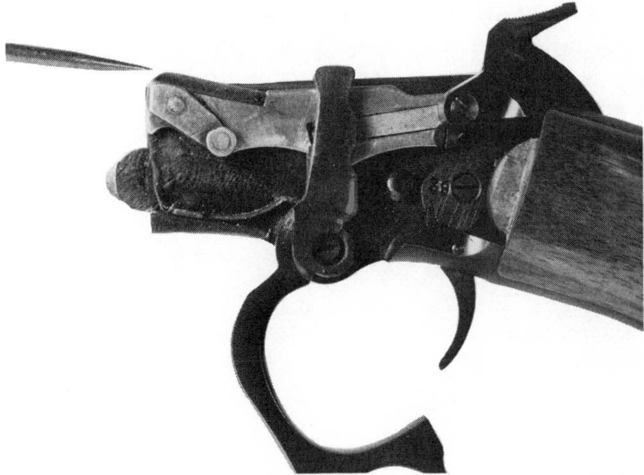

The carrier (somtimes called the lifter) on a Marlin Model 39 .22 rifle in the raised position. The pointer shows where a new cartridge is raised to position to be fed into the chamber. When lowered, a cartridge from the magazine is permitted to move back onto the carrier.

fired and ejected. M1 clips were made of tough spring steel and were hard to reload by hand. The rifle would not function without a clip, which was criticized by some, but even so the M1 is acknowledged to have been the best rifle of World War II.

Feeding cartridges out of box magazines by the breechbolt is relatively simple and foolproof. In general, the procedure is for the advancing bolt to engage the top of the cartridge positioned at the top of the magazine. As the cartridge is moved forward, its nose (bullet) is guided up a feed ramp that angles the cartridge upwards and starts it into the chamber. Meantime the base end of the cartridge is permitted to rise gradually. In older-style bolt faces, like the original Mauser, the cartridge head simply slides up the bolt face and under the extractor hook (which engages the extracting groove of the cartridge). Newer rifle bolts are made with a recessed bolt face, which prevents the cartridge from slipping up the bolt face. What happens with the newer extractors is that the cartridge is driven up and out of the magazine box and, at a certain point, becomes entirely free of magazine and bolt. By this time, however, it's in the chamber and cannot fall out. Final closing of the bolt causes the extractor to slip over the rim.

It has been my experience that a correctly engineered feeding system is much more complicated than it appears. Years ago, as a working gunsmith, I learned, after some trial and error, that feeding systems were an excellent thing to leave alone. Alteration of an existing rifle action to make it feed an altogether different type of cartridge was a thing to be avoided like the plague if you didn't want to go broke. It was an easy matter to rebarrel a .30/06 for a cartridge such as the .270 or .25/06 because they were basically the same cartridge case. But to alter an existing bolt-action made for the .30/06 for something for which it was not designed (a belted Magnum or .45/70, to give a couple of examples) was a tricky proposition not worth the effort.

GRAVITY FEED

Probably the earliest type of feeding system for a multifiring gun was the gravity hopper, such as was used on the Gatling gun. So long as you put the cartridges in the hopper with the bullet end forward, and kept the gun fairly level, there was no problem. But gravity feeding was obviously not any final solution to a feeding system for modern firearms.

LOADING

Loading any magazine is pretty much a straightforward proposition and really needs little or no elaboration. You simply follow the manufacturer's directions. In the event they are not available, common sense ought to dictate.

If you can avoid jacking every cartridge through the action each time you unload, so much the better. That's why a detachable magazine is so handy, or a floorplate or magazine tube that you can remove. Use any means to avoid jacking them all through the action because there is always a danger that a round may fire, and there is also a certainty that these cartridges will become scratched.

You can carry your extra ammunition on a hunting trip in any one of a number of ways. I prefer to have a few spares in a handy and otherwise empty pocket. They won't rattle if you're careful. Then I long ago developed the habit of carrying a small backpack in which I habitually carry such things as foul-weather gear, compass, matches, emergency Space blanket, camera, lunch and a box of spare cartridges. You can carry whatever you wish and it'll be out of the way and fairly handy.

CHAPTER SIX

EXTRACTION AND EJECTION SYSTEMS

Extraction and ejection are often confused. Extraction is the act of withdrawing the cartridge from the gun barrel. Ejection is the flipping out, or removal, of that cartridge from the gun itself.

Extraction is a good deal more complicated than it appears, and much variation in extraction systems occurs. There are four basic requirements for satisfactory extraction: (1) a smooth chamber in the gun barrel; (2) a cartridge case of correct dimensions and proper hardness so the rim won't tear out; (3) an extractor hook, or claw, sufficiently large that it won't tear out part of the rim; (4) satisfactory primary extraction to break the grip a cartridge has gotten on the chamber walls.

It will be obvious at once that a good deal more extracting power is necessary for the .30/06 than for the .22 rimfire. What is less apparent is that the hotter the gun gets from sustained rapid fire the more difficult extraction becomes. That's of little importance to any sportsman, but it is a serious military requirement, and forms one good reason why a proven military system can hardly fail to work under sporting pressures.

PRIMARY EXTRACTION

This is the area where an extractor is subjected to its greatest challenge. There is a small angle that appears on a high-power rifle bolt, where the handle joins the bolt body (a little to the left of the top when the bolt is open), called the extracting cam.

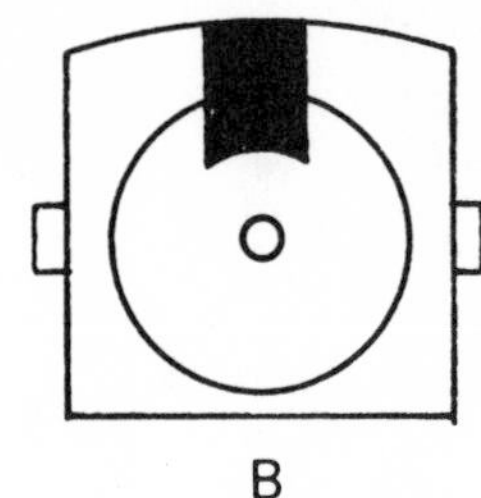

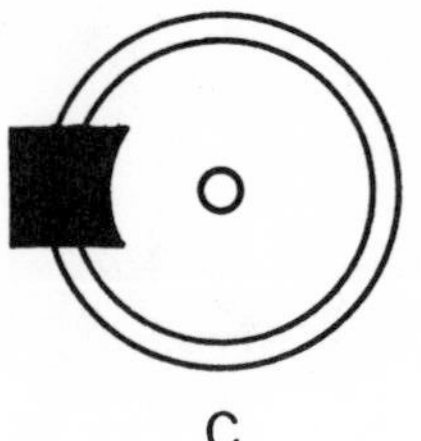

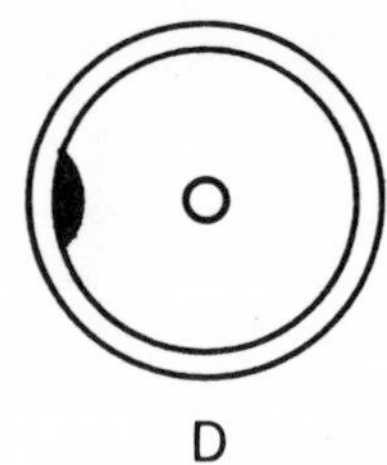

Some common cartridge extraction systems. Figure A, double extractors, as found in many .22 rifles. Figure B, top extraction, as found in the Winchester Model 94. Figure C, Mauser extractor with wide claw, also seen in most older bolt-action rifles and the present Ruger Model 77. Figure D, the Remington bolt extractor, a simple spring-steel ring inserted into the bolt head with extractor indented.

There is also a mating cam on the receiver and, as the bolt is opened slowly, these cams meet to gradually move the bolt backwards as the handle is lifted. This mechanical advantage provides the primary extraction.

One of the reasons a bolt action is so popular for high-pressure cartridges is that it has about an 8- or 10-to-1 ratio (meaning that if you apply 1 pound of effort to the bolt handle it translates to 8 or 10 pounds of extracting power). By contrast, due to the relationship of lever to bolt, a traditional lever-action rifle has only a 2-to-1 ratio. (These figures are approximate, for all bolts are not alike nor are the traditional lever guns exactly alike either.)

If a cartridge case sticks in a bolt action (it's usually due to faulty handloaded ammunition) it can be most difficult to remove, even with the great mechanical advantage of the bolt. You can even stomp on the bolt handle with your heel if the case is real stubborn. While this practice isn't recommended it has been used many times. And often the net result many times also is that the extractor hook is torn through the cartridge rim. That places the rifle effectively out of service until the stuck case can be satisfactorily removed. (Such removal should be done by a gunsmith — many chambers have been ruined by shooters trying to pry out a stuck case.)

You won't see an extracting cam on every bolt action; one exception is a to-be-introduced rifle with interrupted-screw locking lugs. Since the lugs are cut at an angle (the pitch of the threads), opening the bolt has the effect of making the lugs act as extracting cams and they are able to provide positive primary extraction.

EXTRACTION TIMING

Extraction may take place when there is no pressure remaining in the firearm (as is the case with every manually operated gun), when there is still some pressure remaining, or when there is enough residual pressure remaining to retract — or help retract — the breechbolt.

Propellant gas develops very high chamber pressure, up to approximately 55,000 copper units of pressure (cup) in some modern rifle calibers and this pressure builds progressively. (Pressure used to be designated as pounds-per-square-inch — psi. The term was a misnomer; the measurement was never made in pounds, but the figures were useful for comparative purposes. Now the industry uses cup — lup for lead units of pressure — and the figures may be interchanged with the old psi. To measure, a special gun is used incorporating a hole in the chamber wall and a copper disc [lead for low pressure] which is compressed upon firing. A measurement of the compression gives the cup.) You don't go from zero pressure to 55,000 cup instantly; nor does pressure drop instantly when the bullet leaves the barrel. Take the .30/06. At peak pressure, it attains approximately 50,000 cup of chamber pressure. But by the time the bullet has reached the muzzle, that pressure has already dropped to about 12,000 cup. And when the bullet is only a few feet from the muzzle, the pressure is down to about 5,000 cup. It's perfectly safe to unlock the bolt by now and this remaining residual pressure will aid in extraction. While of no importance at all in a manually operated gun, this matter of timing is important in semiautomatics.

RECESSED BOLTS

The shooting world was pretty accustomed to the Mauser system of a big extractor lying alongside the bolt with a big hook that securely grasped the extracting groove of a cartridge. The system had been employed in bolt-action rifles practically since their inception. Even the M1 was no exception, for it employed a similar extractor. Consequently shooters were startled when Remington introduced the recessed-bolt-head system in their Models 721 and 722, both issued in 1948.

There were a number of innovations in this model (721 and 722 were the same except for action length, depending on the cartridge for which they were chambered), one of them being a new extraction system that replaced the Mauser clawed hook. It was accomplished by recessing the bolt face so the cartridge head would fit inside to a depth of nearly ⅛ inch. The recess was undercut and into this undercut was snapped a small spring-steel ring with an indentation on one side that became the extractor hook. Where the original Mauser extractor operated by letting the feeding cartridge slide up under the hook, the new Remington system was designed to ride over the extracting rim as the bolt handle was closed.

The recessed bolt also eliminated the large extractor slot cut in the rear of the barrel, permitting an extraction system that was responsible for a new breeching technique that is also substantially stronger. Not incidentally, it's also less costly to manufacture. Most of today's bolt actions, or turning-bolt actions for that matter, are equipped with a recessed bolt head. Some are partially enclosed, like the Ruger 77 which retains the Mauser type extractor but provides the recessed feature for more than half the bolt head's perimeter.

While the recessed bolt extractor doesn't seem to provide much area to grasp the cartridge, the system certainly works, for it's been in wide use for many years now including Remington's use of it in their Model 740 autoloading .30/06, which would have to rate as the gun most likely to rip out a rim if anything would. It hasn't, and similar systems have been now adopted by just about everybody making high-power rifles.

EXTRACTOR POSITIONING

The position of the extractor, that is at what part of the circle it should grasp the cartridge, is of primary importance in the direction ejection must take. For the next role of the extractor is to help provide the force for ejection.

Positioning is determined by the action itself more than anything else. In the Winchester 94 for example, the extractor is placed on top of the bolt. So the 94 ejects its cartridges straight up in the air. Most guns eject spent cartridges either directly to the side or up and right. There are advantages and disadvantages to all these systems, but few are of major importance unless they interfere with something. For example, the Winchester 94's top ejection prevents mounting a scope directly over the action. Depending on whether or not you think a scope is essential, this may or may not be important. There also are several bottom-ejecting guns including Browning's autoloading .22 rifle.

DOUBLE EXTRACTORS

Many .22 rifles have double extractors, one on each side of the bolt. Actually, only the right-hand one is a real extractor, the left-hand one is merely a guide that holds the cartridge against the right-hand extractor. The right-hand extractor is sharp, with a well-defined undercut on its rear surface. The left-hand extractor is more of a small spring with a little bump, and its sole function is to help hold the case in place.

EJECTION

Ejection is relatively simple compared to extraction, except that most guns require full rearward movement of the breechbolt to provide it. If the fired cartridge is not flipped out of the mechanism cleanly and on time, a jam will result. Ejectors can be categorized easily into three kinds: fixed, movable, and plunger. Even though plungers can accurately be called movable, they are sufficiently different to be classed by themselves. The simplest type is the fixed ejector.

Fixed ejectors are found chiefly on autoloading pistols; they are simply a small post, sometimes just a cut in the frame. In either event they require a slot running the full length of the slide. The ejector functions when the slide moves back carrying the fired case on its face held by the extractor. When the slide is nearly all the way back, the base of the

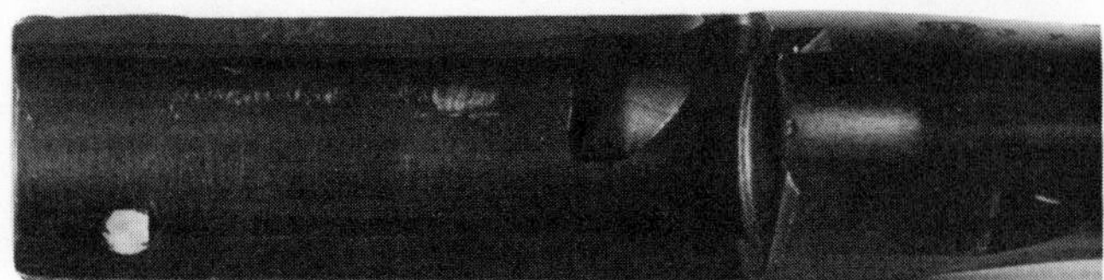

A Remington gas-operated autoloading gun's barrel extension contains the ejector, which is visible at lower left as a shiny spot. It's nothing more than a small plug inserted into the extension; when the extracted cartridge gets that far back on the bolt face, its edge contacts the ejector and it is flipped from the gun.

left-hand side of the cartridge strikes the ejector. By shoving forward on the left side, the cartridge is forced to rotate around the extractor hook and is thrown clear of the action. Some .22 rifles also have fixed ejectors; they are quite simple in their function and completely reliable.

A movable ejector is one that works exactly like a fixed ejector except that it pivots back and forth and no slot is required running the full length of a breechbolt. The ejector simply swings, or is forced, into position at the last moment. Movable ejectors are found on nearly all bolt-action rifles made up until about the end of World War II. The Mauser, for example, has a spring-loaded ejector which rides along the bolt body until the bolt nearly reaches the extreme rear part of its movement, at which point a slot running through the left-hand locking lug allows the ejector spring to push the ejector itself into the slot and thus to strike the left side of the cartridge.

The U.S. Springfield 1903 rifle works similarly, except that the ejector is forced into position by the rear surface of the left locking lug, rather than employing a spring to perform the act of moving the ejector into position. Both systems work equally well, and have since the 1890s. There are also many variations on the movable-ejector system but they are essentially as described in their function.

PLUNGER EJECTORS

There's nothing new about this type of ejector. So far as I know it was first used by John Browning and can be found on the Winchester Model 94. It consists of a spring-loaded piece inserted into the bolt face, which simply pushes against the cartridge head. When the action is closed, this ejector spring is compressed. As the action opens, the ejector pushes against the cartridge and, as soon as the front edge of the empty cartridge clears the action, it is flipped out.

One of the first .30/06 rifles to use a plunger ejector system was the M1 of World War II, actually introduced in 1936, but John Garand had been working on this particular design since about 1925. (Garand had been working on designing auto-loading rifles since about 1919. An earlier rifle was unlocked by primer actuation, meaning that a large-diameter firing pin was employed and that when firing took place, the primer itself was allowed to set back, pushing back the firing pin which unlocked the rifle. However, the Ordnance Department in 1925 adopted a new cartridge for the service rifle which was known as the M1 cartridge. It used a 172-grain bullet, instead of the former 150 grain, and the powder was changed to a new duPont powder called Improved Military Rifle, or IMR. This change produced problems with the original Garand design so he began the design of what eventually became the M1 rifle in 1925.)

Consisting of a round, flat-nosed pin, about ⅛ inch in diameter, and backed by a strong, small spring, ejector and spring are assembled into the bolt face so that the ejector protrudes about 1/16th of an inch. In the M1, a hook-type extractor was used, and today's rifles use either the hook type, considerably modified, the Mauser — as employed by Ruger — or the spring-clip type, as used by Remington. Often the force generated by these ejectors is so strong that they bend the case mouths before the latter are tossed out of the rifle. (That's a problem for the reloader, who usually gets around it by simply removing the ejector from his target rifles and picking the empty cartridges off the bolt face by hand.)

It should also be noted that nearly all turning bolts rotate across the face of a fired cartridge as the bolt is opened. There is a certain amount of friction involved, which means the bolt face must be clean and smooth, as must the nose of the plunger-type ejector. A few rear-locking bolts, chiefly in .22 rifles, have a non-rotating bolt head (the front part) and thus obviously do not rotate.

There are other types of ejectors too numerous to detail and too infrequently encountered to be important. One that should be mentioned, however, is that used on older Winchester pump-action .22s, such as the 1890 and Model 62 (a faithful copy of which is available today as the Rossi, a Garcia im-

In a long-recoil-operated gun, be it rifle or shotgun, bolt and barrel travel all the way to the rear locked together. Then the bolt stays back while the barrel moves ahead and strips itself off the fired cartridge. Here you see the Browning Auto-5 with the bolt locked back, the barrel moving ahead. This is the extraction step, although the barrel is the part that is moving. Once the barrel clears the cartridge, the latter will eject — that is be flipped out of the gun, a new cartridge will then feed out of the magazine and release the bolt to complete the steps of operation.

port). This system was unique in that the lifter moving a fresh cartridge up from the tubular magazine was used to shove the empty up and off the bolt as the bolt moved back.

The angle of ejection is of no small importance to target shooters. That is, the angle of ejection is of importance to the other shooters on the line, for there's nothing to break up your concentration like a hot empty landing on your neck. This is often taken care of in range construction, but the annoyance can still happen.

Empties are usually tossed out at an angle of about 45° up and right, although there is no universal rule about it. And they often come out of the gun with considerable force. Autoloaders often pitch all but the last empty in a forward direction, because the bolt is moving forward again before the empty clears. The last empty will fly directly to the side or perhaps a bit to the rear if the gun is one in which the bolt stays open after the last shot is fired.

One of the most useful (and fascinating) tools employed by today's gun designers is the Fastax camera, which takes slow-motion pictures. The slam-bang of operating parts can be carefully studied, with the result that engineers can perfect extraction and ejection as desired. I have studied a number of these photos taken by the H. P. White Laboratory and they are truly fascinating.

CHAPTER SEVEN

TRIGGERS

Different types of firearms have different types of triggers, a mechanism that is somewhat more complicated than it might seem. Perhaps the simplest is the most direct, such as that used on a lever-action rifle, in which the top of the trigger directly engages the hammer. Pull the trigger and the nose moves out of engagement with the hammer and lets the hammer drive forward to fire the gun. But trigger pulls are hard or light, smooth or rough, good or bad. Even the direct trigger can be one or more of those things. A trigger pull should be: (1) consistent; (2) crisp; (3) with as little movement as possible; (4) smooth; (5) heavy enough to be safe; (6) light enough to permit an easy letoff. The direct trigger can be regulated by the distance from finger curve to the pin on which it pivots, and by the distance from that pin to the nose where it engages the hammer. This trigger is a simple lever, so the better the mechanical advantage, the easier will be the pull.

The part of the trigger that engages the hammer is the "sear," a generic word for that part of any firearm that holds back the firing mechanism. Its mating notch in the hammer (or firing pin) is the sear notch. The fit of the sear in the sear notch, which includes the angle of both surfaces, their depth, their hardness and their smoothness, will dictate the decency of the trigger pull. Some people stone sears and sear notches with a fine, hard Arkansas stone to make the surfaces smooth. The procedure is all right provided the angle is not changed (which is easier said than done). The simplest way to "improve" the trigger pull of such a hammer gun is rough and cruel — but it does have good results. You just cock the gun (with the chamber empty), stick a wide-bladed screwdriver under the hammer thumbpiece and twist, as though you are trying to make the hammer fall. While exerting this pressure, pull the trigger. A few treatments like this will smooth out some of the roughness and improve the pull. I'm not necessarily recommending this procedure, although I have used it. The screwdriver won't help the finish of the tang under the hammer spur a bit but that can be protected by a piece of cardboard.

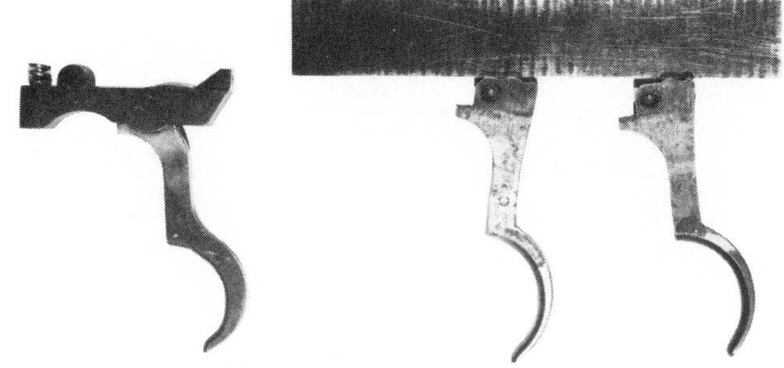

The military two-stage trigger. On the left, a Springfield 1903 trigger and sear complete with sear spring. On the right, two Mauser triggers that work the same way. The left Mauser trigger is in rest position, while the right one has had the slack taken up. Note the two small lumps, or fulcrums, at the top edge of the trigger at different distances from the pin. Taking up the slack, because of the mechanical advantage, is a light pull and you can see how far it moves the trigger. Then a short movement of the trigger will release the firing pin. Most of the rear surface of the Springfield trigger's sear is engaged when the rifle is cocked. After taking up the slack, this engagement will be reduced to a scant fraction of an inch.

DOUBLE MILITARY PULL

Most military rifles have what is generally called a double trigger pull, which is often called more unflattering things by those unused to it. But to those who have become used to the old Springfield, Mauser, and other such excellent rifles, there was never anything whatever wrong with their triggers.

The reason for the double pull is to provide more area of contact for the sear, thus more safety. (If you slam the bolt hard in combat, you damned well want the rifle to stay cocked and not fire from the jar of closing the action.) More area of sear engagement means a longer trigger pull, far too long to be practical. So a sort of double fulcrum was used at the top of the trigger, making the initial pull light and distinct. Called slack, the trigger moves about ⅛ inch when you take up the slack. At this point the pull noticeably stops and you begin your squeeze. Once you learn to take up the slack, it becomes second nature and presents no problem whatever. In fact, you can stone and hone a Springfield or Mauser trigger to give an exquisite letoff — crisp and sharp and light — once the slack is taken up. And, once you're used to it, the military double pull is just as fast when a whitetail buck jumps out from a blowdown right in front of you as any other trigger. It's all in getting used to it.

If you must stone a sear, the best way to do it is to place the part in a machinist's vise with the angle to be stoned level with the vise jaws. Then use a hard Arkansas stone with a bit of oil. Failure to follow this procedure will probably result in destroying the correct angle as well as the pull.

Most shooters, however, don't like it. And there's no question that modern triggers are better and are just as safe. However, there is one comment that should be made about altering the military trigger. It was a fairly common practice — and may still be — simply to shorten the military pull by removal of the slack. This can be done with a little screw-on device that you buy, or it can be done by drilling a hole and sticking a pin through the guard to hold the trigger back just that far. It can be done in a number of other ways. The objection to removal of the slack is that it lessens the sear engagement to a degree that can be dangerous and can cause the rifle to fire by jarring off when the bolt is slammed shut.

The only reliable way to adjust the original military pull, if you can't live with it, is to replace the whole trigger with one of the excellent replacement triggers available. The business of remodeling military rifles isn't nearly as big as it was in the years immediately following World War II but there is still enough activity in old war rifles that you might want to be aware of this.

MODERN BOLT-ACTION TRIGGERS

The first modern bolt-action-rifle trigger appeared on the Winchester Model 70 when it was introduced in 1936. There is no question that this rifle, perhaps second only to the original Springfield sporter built by Louis Wundhammer in 1910, has been the most important sporting bolt-action rifle ever designed. While it had many outstanding features, its trigger must rank among the most notable of them. It was the first of the modern slackless or over-riding triggers, offering a fine pull with crisp letoff, and it provided adjustment.

Trigger pull on a rifle ought to be between 3 and 5 pounds, measured by a small scale (or by actual weights) at the center of the finger curve when pulled straight back. There is no excuse for a heavier pull; it indicates something lacking in manufacture. On guns used for hunting purposes there isn't much need for a pull weighing less than 3 pounds, although some prefer them lighter. A 3-pound pull is light enough, so long as there is no creep.

In 1936 Winchester introduced the Model 70 rifle with the first improved bolt-action trigger. It remains essentially the same today. Trigger and sear are pinned to the receiver separately, unlike the old military style, where the sear was pinned to the receiver and the trigger pinned to the sear. The Model 70's engagement is that fraction of an inch between the forward part of the trigger and the sear nose hanging down. When pulled, the trigger releases the sear, which is then pushed down out of the way by the firing pin. This trigger can be adjusted but only if you know what you're doing. In my opinion this trigger is still the equal of anything designed since the only criticism of it is that it is more difficult to adjust than some newer designs. Once properly set, however, the 70 trigger will stay that way forever.

Creep in a trigger is defined as a scratchy movement that hesitates, jumps a bit, and stops again before the gun fires. It is sometimes compared to a rusty barn gate. There should be no lost motion in a decent trigger pull and no hesitation. In fact, you shouldn't feel anything as you squeeze a trigger — when it goes off, it should be like breaking a glass rod. And there should be no follow-through, no rearward movement after the trigger releases the sear. Alas, not all triggers are that neat and nice. Many of them can't be, particularly with autoloaders. But there is no excuse for not having such a good trigger on a bolt-action rifle. And the Winchester Model 70 first achieved such refinement.

Winchester accomplished this by a unique design that completely changed the usual trigger/sear relationship. The Mauser system pinned the trigger directly to the sear; pulling the trigger forced the sear down (in a very slight, though insignificant, arc, since the sear was pinned to the receiver at its front end). Winchester pinned both sear and trigger to the receiver so they were independent of one another. And they arranged the trigger to hold the sear in place by putting the sear and sear notch engagement up front. When cocked, the sear acts like a platform underneath the firing pin's cocking piece to effectively hold the pin back. It only requires small pressure on the trigger to disengage trigger and sear, whereupon the sear is allowed to be forced down by the firing pin spring. If you will, the firing pin simply overrides the sear, shoving it out of the way when sear and trigger are disengaged. It works cleanly because the leverage employed is so advantageous.

Unfortunately, those who assemble Winchester Model 70 rifles do not always seem to know how to adjust this fine trigger. It is capable of much finer adjustment than is usually provided for a gun you pick out of the box. When properly fixed, it's as good a trigger as any to be found today — more than forty years after its introduction. Not only is it simpler than most of those that followed, it also requires less wood removal from inside the stock, which is of no small importance.

All the excellent trigger assemblies now in use are built along this basic idea. That is, all of them allow the sear to provide the platform that holds the firing pin cocked. Then the trigger disengagement allows the sear to be shoved down (sometimes in an arc, sometimes straight down) which, in turn, permits the rifle to fire. Except for the Winchester, nearly all the other triggers are inside a housing that is simply fastened to the receiver bottom. All are adjustable (and all are easier to adjust than the Model 70) and many of them may be partially adjusted through the trigger guard without disassembling the rifle.

These adjustments consist of: (1) weight of pull; (2) follow-through — after the trigger is pulled; (3) forward movement — before the trigger is pulled. When any of these triggers is properly adjusted, you should feel no trigger movement at all, and the weight of pull should be what you want it to be. I would caution against the tendency to try to make it too light in any hunting rifle. You won't need it lighter than three pounds in the first place, and if set too light there is always the chance the adjustment may malfunction and you won't have the necessary tools to readjust it in camp. Thus, you'll have a useless rifle.

RELATIONSHIP BETWEEN TRIGGER AND SAFETY

Safeties come in vastly different shapes, styles, and methods of operation. Some, like most bolt-action-rifle safeties, lock the firing pin directly. Others, like the common cross-bolt safety used in many pumps and autoloaders, simply lock the trigger so it can't be moved.

A safety that locks the firing pin must move that pin back far enough to disengage the sear and firing pin. The reason for this is pretty plain: If it did not, it would be possible to put the safety ON, pull the trigger, and push the safety OFF, in which case the rifle would fire. That would happen because the pin hadn't been retracted and there was just enough engagement to cause the friction to break the sear/firing pin engagement when the trigger was pulled. At this point the only thing holding the firing pin back is the safety; so when it's released, it goes off. You can see this happen in a bolt-action rifle: When you put the safety ON, watch the cocking piece where it appears at the end of the bolt and it will move back a perceptible amount.

But the design is different with any safety that simply blocks the trigger, a system commonly used on pumps, autoloaders, double guns, and some others. These are perfectly "safe" safeties as safeties go. It's obvious that if you can't pull the trigger you can't fire the gun. But it's equally obvious that if the firing pin, hammer, or whatever the system employs is not held firmly back, it can be jarred hard enough to fire. This is one reason why it is a lot harder to get the same letoff you can get on a good bolt-action trigger — there has to be more movement in any trigger that is used in direct conjunction with the safety.

The foregoing might help explain why so many experienced shooters will tell you never to trust the safety. A safety is all well and good, and it ought to be used. But the commandment that says *thou shall not ever point any firearm at any object at which one does not intend to shoot* had safeties in mind in addition to common sense and politeness. Indeed, most of my big-game hunting has always been done with a loaded magazine, but with the firing pin down on an empty chamber. There's no need to have the rifle fully loaded and ready to fire until you see game, unless you move into an area where you have a reason to expect to see game momentarily.

Bird hunting is another matter; here it's best to be ready with the safety on. This is where common sense must prevail. You soon learn where you might reasonably expect to shoot, and there is no reason to be ready to do so until there's a good chance you'll have to. A loaded gun is one that has a cocked firing pin or hammer under heavy spring tension. All that's keeping the firing mechanism from flying forward is a scant fraction of an inch of engagement between two pieces of steel. It just makes sense to keep that in mind and be safe.

SHAPE

You rarely hear much about the shape of the trigger bow, which is the part of the trigger that you see and that you press. But the shape of a trigger, as with most parts of a firearm, is important both to looks and to function. The trigger is traditionally curved because your finger is curved, and you want to be able to get a good grip on the trigger. You want to distribute the pressure over as much of your finger as you can, because that will make the actual pull seem lighter.

And since we all spend a great deal more time looking at our guns than shooting them, it helps if those guns look good. Other things being equal, there is no reason why a firearm can't be shaped so it looks good instead of ugly. A pleasing curve on a trigger is attractive and should complement the remaining lines of the rifle. Contrarywise, a handsome, well-shaped rifle with a trigger dangling like a well-used nail would look like hell.

The trigger should also lie in the rear part of the trigger guard, with ample room to ensure there is no chance of its contacting the guard either at the bow of the guard or where the trigger comes through the guard out of the action. And, up above and out of sight, there must be sufficient clearance from the wood stock so that no swelling or warping can interfere with the trigger's movement.

DISCONNECTORS

When you press the trigger on an autoloader, it fires and goes through all the remaining steps of operation automatically, but it doesn't fire again. It won't do that until you relax the trigger and pull it again. That's because the trigger is disconnected during the operation and isn't connected again until you relax it. This happens in a variety of ways, all of them quite simple and foolproof.

Were it not for this disconnector, some guns would fire again and keep firing until out of ammunition — or until you got your finger off the trigger. Others would not fire at all, because the failure to cock would only result in letting the hammer or firing pin ride forward slowly behind the bolt without sufficient force to achieve ignition. The function of the disconnector is to disconnect the trigger and sear after firing, so that the sear is again free to engage the hammer or firing pin so the gun will recock and cannot be fired again until the trigger is relaxed. That relaxing of the trigger permits trigger and sear to reengage so another pull of the trigger will fire the gun.

Ruger's Mini-14 trigger employs the same basic disconnecting system first used by Browning on his autoloading shotgun in 1900. It was also employed on the M1 rifle of World War II, among many others. Here trigger and hammer are in position to fire; pulling back on the trigger will disengage the front top of the trigger and the hammer will fall. The rifle will operate and recock before the shooter can release his finger, so the hammer will be caught by the rear hook. When the trigger is relaxed it will permit the rear hook to disengage and the front to engage as shown here.

That little button right in front of the firing pin hole in this .45 Auto is the disconnector. Located in the frame, it is moved up by spring pressure, down by the slide. The disconnector must be up for the gun to fire; when the slide is fully closed and the gun locked, the disconnector is permitted to move up into a small recess in the slide and the gun can be fired. When the slide opens, it pushes the disconnector down, breaking the engagement between sear and trigger and the gun cannot be fired again until the trigger is relaxed.

Another disconnector that has remained basically the same since 1900 is once again Browning's. This is simple indeed; the hammer has two small notches on the front and back sides of a horn that might be a hammer thumbpiece if the gun were of an outside-hammer design, whereas the trigger's top is shaped like a U, with notches both forward and back. Upon firing, the trigger is depressed and held back. As the action recoils within the gun, the hammer is pushed down, at which point the rear horn notch engages a corresponding notch in the back end of the top of the trigger. After the reloading cycle has been completed, the trigger is relaxed. That permits the hammer to disengage from its

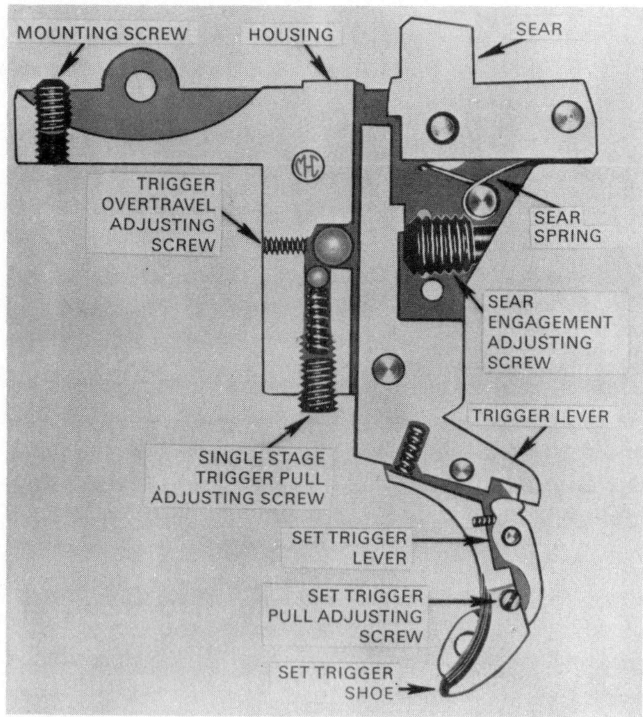

M.H. Canjar has beem making great triggers for many years and his are perhaps the best known of the type called two-lever design. The sketch shows a single set trigger (it can be brought with or without the set attachment) which is set, or cocked, by moving the trigger shoe forward until it clicks. To fire, you simply touch the little piece that sticks out in front of the shoe as shown. When that happens the shoe flies up with enough force to move the trigger lever and fire the rifle. When the rifle is cocked, the firing pin will press against the sear, which will be held up by the top of the trigger.

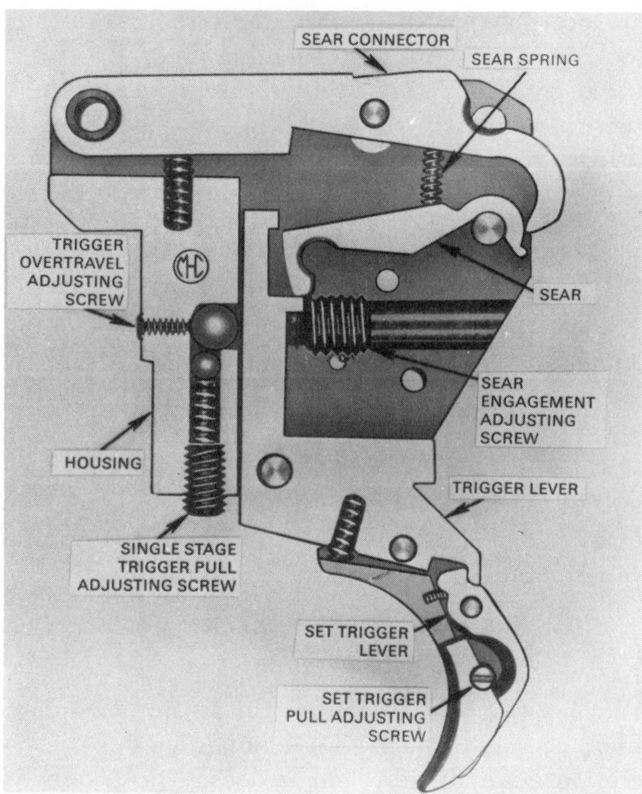

This is a Canjar three-lever trigger, which is made for such target rifles as the Winchester Model 52, for which a fine trigger pull is required. The simple addition of another lever further reduces the pressure needed to fire by increasing the mechanical advantage. In this case, the front of the sear will be forced up by the sear connector when the rifle is cocked. Slight pressure on the trigger will release the sear which, in turn, will release the sear connector and permit the rifle to fire. Quite complicated, but a very excellent pull results.

rear hook, move forward and up slightly, whereupon it's caught by the front hook —the sear. Now, when pulled again the gun will fire.

SET TRIGGERS

A set trigger is sometimes called a "hair trigger" — generally by writers who say bullet when they mean cartridge, dum-dum because it sounds ominous, or cordite because they read it some place. In general, they don't know what any of these terms mean. Set triggers are capable of being set so that a very light touch will fire the gun. Some of them can be adjusted so fine that you can actually blow against the trigger and the gun will fire. The set trigger has a place, but it's only on a target rifle or pistol and preferably only on target rifles and pistols used in International Match shooting (under rules of the International Shooting Union, or ISU). Even there, the use of a set trigger is debatable; some like them, others don't.

The set trigger is available in two styles: double-set triggers, in which case there are two triggers employed, and single set. The latter only has a single trigger. A double-set trigger is set by pulling the rear trigger until it clicks, or "sets." Then a light touch on the front trigger will fire the gun. (There are variations of the double-set trigger, but this is the most common type.) Single-set triggers are set by pushing them forward until they click, or set. Another type of single-set trigger is that offered by Canjar. A push forward of the trigger causes a small projection to move out in front of the lower part of the trigger and a tiny touch on this projection will fire the rifle.

The purpose of any set trigger is to provide a fine, light trigger pull under the theory that the shooter can better control his shot, especially when he's shooting in the offhand (standing) position. Some shooters even go to the extreme of sandpapering their trigger fingers so their feel will be extra delicate. For those who like them, a set trigger can have a distinct advantage in this type of shooting, but that's about the only advantage any set trigger really has.

Double-set triggers and sears are not connected. They work this way: When you set the rear trigger you're pulling a rather long arm, that is part of the rear trigger's front end, down into a tiny notch in the front trigger. You're also compressing a spring so the rear trigger is under spring tension. When you touch the front trigger, it disengages the rear trigger whose long front arm is now allowed to fly up under spring tension and kick the sear out of engagement. That trigger arm kicks a small part fitted to the sear called the kicker. You can also fire a double-set trigger by pulling directly on the front trigger without employing the set principle; this trigger has a long arm that is far enough back to reach the kicker, but its mechanical advantage is poor and the pull this way is awful. Double-set triggers provide a tiny adjusting screw and, depending on the quality of manufacture, some of them can be set very light. What I've described is the common Mauser double-set trigger; others are much more complicated with multiple levers and capable of far finer adjustments.

The large light-colored metal housing under the receiver is the trigger unit employed by Kleinguenther in his "Insta-fire" rifle. Look at the small, square opening located in the top center of this unit and you'll see the sear resting on the trigger with ever so fine engagement. In firing, the top of the trigger is moved ahead just enough to break this engagement, whereupon the sear will be shoved down by the firing pin and the gun will fire.

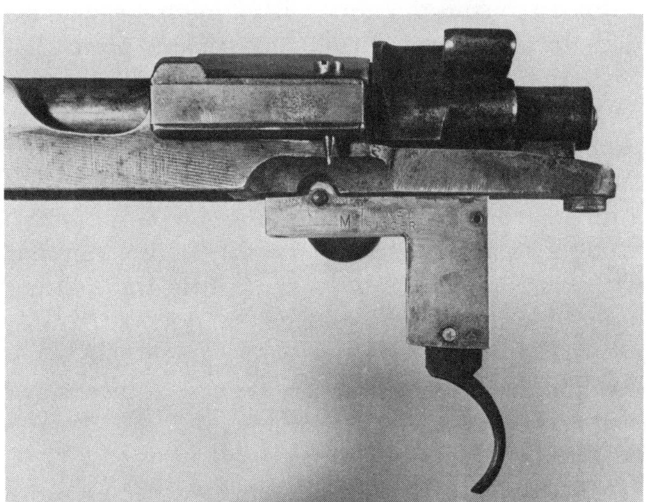

One of the things I have always liked about the Timney trigger is that it takes up very little room in the stock. One reason is that its sear moves straight down rather than in an arc. This excellent trigger is shown on a military Mauser action.

The double-set trigger isn't all that advantageous, even if it does provide a good letoff. It also sets some parts in motion before ignition which causes movement, no matter how slight. It also takes time, no matter how slight. So the set trigger isn't necessarily an advantage. In fact, some consider it a disadvantage.

At one time, during the years between the wars when a lot of German plants were exporting guns, the double-set trigger, "butter-knife" bolt handle and razor-sharp comb were pretty standard trademarks. None of them were worth a damn on any hunting rifle and the American public finally realized it. I repeat, a double-set trigger has no place on a hunting rifle.

Single-set triggers work somewhat similarly, except that the regular pull is, or can be, excellent. This is especially true of the Canjar, and if you want to experiment with a set trigger, this would be the one to try. If you don't want to use it, you just use the trigger conventionally and can forget it's even there. But when you need it, you can push the trigger forward and touch the little button.

Canjar's single set also has a wide trigger, which is a reminder that wide triggers are available for most rifles. Called "trigger shoes," they are fastened to the standard trigger by two very small screws and their advantage is that they distribute the pull over a wider part of the finger. The net result is that a pull will seem lighter, since you have more flesh bearing on the surface. These shoes have been around for years. Recently Pacific (the reloading-tool people) introduced a wide line of shoes for most popular guns. One thing to remember: When you take the metal out of the stock, be sure to remove the shoe first. It's wider than the slot in the trigger guard!

Some triggers resemble a mousetrap when exposed to scrutiny. This one is a Colt-Sauer trigger with tang safety (the long bar running back and forth). When such a safety is incorporated into an action, trigger design becomes more complicated, and requires the removal of a lot more wood. Removal of too much wood from the action area can be serious because stiffness and support are needed there.

SOME VARIATIONS AND EXCEPTIONS

Once upon a time, Winchester made a .22 rifle with a thumb trigger. As the definition indicates, the trigger was operated by the thumb positioned on top of the tang where a shotgun safety is usually found. The bottom of the rifle was clean and neat. This never became popular and was abandoned long ago.

Target shooters are precise folks, and demand exceptionally fine triggers. Many target rifles employ extremely complex multiple-lever trigger units that allow for extremely fine adjustment and an extremely fine, delicate trigger pull and letoff. Some of these devices are quite complicated and expensive. I have a pre-War Walther .22 rifle on which I've done considerable gunsmithing to make it into a sporter. It started life as a Walther Olympic model and is listed in the 1940 Stoeger catalog at $250 (the same book shows the Winchester Model 94 carbine at $30). But I have not fiddled with the complicated Walther trigger – it's a real gem and housed in a big unit that I prefer to leave just the way the Walther people made it.

It might sound like it would be easy to be hopelessly confused if you own several guns all of which happen to have different triggers, including perhaps, variations in weight of pull as well as two triggers vs single, set triggers, and so on. It has been my own experience that, assuming you do a lot of shooting and are familiar with your guns, this will not happen. I can get off two shots as fast with a two-trigger double as I can with a single trigger or autoloader. And the same with a pump or lever action. In fact, I can get off repeat shots pretty fast with a bolt action, too. Nor does the military pull with its two-stage taking up the slack present any problems on a hunting trip when I have to shoot fast. This is true even if I have two rifles with me and switch them off. It must be emphasized, though, that you have to be thoroughly familiar with your guns because you must do these things without thought. If you have to stop and think, you're finished. So practice, and you will find when the moment of truth comes that you have acted fast, unconsciously, and correctly.

CHAPTER EIGHT

FIRING SYSTEMS

The purpose of any rifle's firing system is to ignite the powder charge which, in turn, burns to develop propellant gas to drive the bullet out of the barrel. The earliest firing systems usually consisted of a piece of smoldering punk that was stuck in the touchhole directly against the powder. A little later the matchlock was developed, but differed only in that it offered a mechanical means of moving the smoldering fire to the touchhole. Next came the wheel lock consisting of a device wound up like a watch mainspring which, when the trigger was pulled, was allowed to spin against a flint to throw a shower of sparks into a "pan" containing some loose powder. This was followed by the flintlock, in which the flint itself was fastened in the hammer and, when the trigger was pulled, struck a piece of steel to throw sparks into the pan.

Along about 1840, percussion ignition was developed and has not changed significantly today except that today's ammunition is compact and self-contained. Percussion ignition requires a blow to fire a primer which, in turn, ignites the propellant powder. The percussion cap was used with muzzle loaders and in a variety of ways during the transitional period from muzzle loading to breech loading. Today's primer is essentially the same as an 1840 percussion cap.

Modern ammunition employs two different types of primer: that used in rimfire cartridges, where the priming compound is spun around the inside of the rim, and that used in center-fire cartridges, where a separate, self-contained primer is seated in a pocket in the cartridge case. The priming compound is used in minute amounts, because it is extremely violent and explosive. There is, in fact, enough power in the primer alone to drive a bullet deep into a gun barrel even if loaded without a powder charge.

The firing mechanism of a rimfire rifle is constructed to cause the firing pin to crush the rim (any part of the rim) of the cartridge against the breech end of the barrel. In a center-fire firing system, the pin must strike the primer itself, located in the middle of the cartridge. A rather substantial blow is needed for ignition, and that blow must be delivered consistently. There are numerous variations in the ignition chain, including manufacturing tolerances for the cartridge case, for barrels, and for the several parts of a center-fire cartridge primer. Put all these together and a considerable variation can exist.

For rimfire ignition, the barrel must be positioned correctly in the receiver and the cartridge must position itself against the breech end of the barrel with the bolt face snugly behind the cartridge. An accumulation of dirt or grease between cartridge rim and barrel will soften the firing pin's blow and cause variations in ignition.

In a center-fire cartridge, the primer must be seated at the bottom of its pocket in the cartridge case, otherwise part of the firing pin blow will be wasted because it must first drive the primer all the way into its pocket. Similarly, some primer cups (that's the part you see) are softer – or harder – than others and these variations will have an effect on ignition. Finally, there is a difference in primers between those for handgun cartridges and those for rifles. Since the firing-pin blow of a handgun is softer than that of a high-power rifle, primers used for handgun ammunition are more sensitive. (This sensitivity is achieved by using a softer primer cup so the lighter blow will crush it easier and more positively.) If you use a rifle primer in a handgun cartridge, it will sometimes fail to fire. If you use a pistol primer in a high-power rifle cartridge, it will fire but it might rupture and spill gas into the firing-pin hole. This is of concern to the handloader, because rifle and pistol primers are made to the same size and can't be identified once removed from their packages. If you're not a reloader, it helps to know about it because it's one more of the complexities of gundom that are too often oversimplified.

SIMPLE FIRING-PIN SYSTEMS

Simple isn't really the right word, but by using it I mean those that are simple to understand; they are pins that are directly connected to a hammer. Most of these pins are an integral part of the hammer and the most common applications are seen in revolvers. There is a hole in the frame to accept the firing pin and when you look through this little hole you'll see the primer of a center-fire cartridge – or the rim of a rimfire cartridge. When you pull the trigger and the hammer flies forward, it will hit this primer and ignite the priming charge.

There isn't much mystery connected with such a blow; it's just like the cap pistol you had when you were a kid. Both types fire from a percussion blow; the difference is that the cap pistol simply makes a noise, whereas the firearm's primer sets off a chain reaction that ignites a powder charge that develops propellant gas that drives a bullet.

Firing pins used for center-fire and rimfire cartridges must be positioned differently, since one must strike in the middle, while the other must strike off center. They must also have different profiles. Rimfire firing pins are flat on the end but may be round, square, or rectangular in shape. They come in all sizes and shapes. Their function, again, is to smack the cartridge's rim hard enough to crush the soft metal and deliver a good, sharp whack to the priming compound located inside. It will be obvious that the larger in diameter the face of such a pin is, the harder must be the blow.

The center-fire pin, on the other hand, must hit the primer as nearly dead center as possible and it, too, must deliver a good whack. It must indent the primer cup with enough force to crush the priming compound, which is located directly under the cup. The pin however must *not* pierce the cup nor allow it to rupture. So the center-fire firing pin must have a spherical nose and it must be nicely polished and smooth.

The next simplest firing pin is the combination of firing pin and hammer. It's one of the oldest systems and one of the most reliable. Typical examples are the Winchester Model 94 and Marlin Model 336. In both these rifles you can see both the hammer and the rear end of the firing pin, so an understanding of their function is easy. The same system is used in most of the so-called hammerless guns (which actually have a hammer inside the receiver where you can't see it). These range from the Browning Auto-5 in use since 1900, to the M1 Garand to the modern gas gun. One of the reasons this type of firing system is so widely used is that it's simple . . . and positive. There's nothing like a big hammer to give you the necessary whacking blow to fire a primer.

The third common system is that used in most bolt-action rifles — the Mauser-type spring-loaded firing pin. It is an excellent system, positive and reliable.

TYPES OF FIRING PINS

The three major types of firing pins are inertia, supported, and fixed. An example of an inertia pin is in the Colt .45 autoloading pistol. The pin is not long enough to reach from the hammer to the primer and relies on getting a good enough whack from the hammer to be driven far enough to fire the primer. A limp firing-pin spring holds the pin back in position for the hammer to connect. The advantage to this pin is that it's quite safe to carry this gun with the hammer down on a live cartridge. There's no way the gun can fire until it's cocked. This kind of pin cannot be used on a high-power rifle, however.

The supported firing pin is found in the Winchester Model 94. When the hammer goes down it stays down and supports the pin.

The fixed firing pin, once used on a couple of sporting .22s, is now found only on machine guns. It's designed to be used on a gun firing from the open-bolt position and works by firing the cartridge as the bolt fully closes. This is not worth much for any sporting purpose, because firing from an open bolt is not conducive to decent accuracy. (You can't expect the gun to stay still while the bolt is flying forward.)

There are also a very few examples of rebounding hammers still seen. These are hammers that act like the supported Model 94 but then the hammer is allowed to "rebound," or move back — in some instances about ⅛ inch. These are apt to be associated with older black-powder rifles and I know of no modern guns that use the system. Keep in mind that, with certain action systems (single-shot rifles for example), it is necessary to retract the firing pin slightly before the action can be opened. Failure to do so will make the firing-pin nose drag through the primer with resultant difficulty in opening and the possibility of damaging the nose.

THE BLOW AND INDENTATION

We can establish certain requirements for the firing system (including the primer):

(1) The primer must fire consistently with a blow of a certain energy or weight.

(2) The primer must not fire when struck with a blow less than the minimum (that is, primers must not be too sensitive).

(3) The primer, or the rim of a rimfire cartridge case, must not rupture or be pierced.

While those limits are required for ignition, there is a far narrower range of specifications within which more perfect ignition will result. And more perfect ignition will produce more perfect accuracy. This will explain why firearms intended for target use are refined to the point where their ignition systems provide the quickest, surest and (most important) most uniform ignition possible.

Quickness is known in the trade as lock time. It's important to the target shooter, because he has learned to study wind, mirage, and any number of range conditions to the point where when he shoots, he wants that gun to fire instantly. The slightest slowness in lock time can easily make a 9 out of a perfect 10-hold. It's easy to make an action with fast lock time; but quickness is generally associated with light weight and that combination doesn't always result in consistency. So the problem of lock time in a target rifle is more complicated than it sounds at first.

For example, the 1898 Mauser and the 1903 Springfield actions have a firing-pin travel of about ⅝ inch. That's quite a long way. Most of today's modern bolt-actions have firing pins that travel about 3/16 inch, or roughly only one third that distance. Since both systems provide sure ignition, the modern rifle can be shot with a little more accuracy (other things being the same) because its lock time is faster.

The 1903 Springfield was a Mauser copy and one of the changes made by U.S. Ordnance was the addition of a two-piece firing pin. This change has been generally and pretty universally condemned as subject to breakage and having a tendency to cushion the blow, thus providing weaker ignition. In theory, both points are of some validity but I can't agree that they are really all that bad. It's true that Springfield firing pins have broken on occasion and it's probably true that a sloppy fit between the main firing-pin rod and the striker could result in a spongy ignition blow. Despite all this, the famed 1903 rifle set many marks for accuracy until better rifles came along. And that took a long time. The Springfield action has never been popular for benchrest shooting (the true test of accuracy) for reasons that aren't clear. As a practicing gunsmith specializing in benchrest rifles, I was in at the start of the sport and would guess that only a very few Springfields ever showed up on the line. I'd suspect major reasons might be that there were many military Mauser actions available and that it wasn't too long before the Remington 722 made its debut and pretty well took over benchrest for a few years before being replaced by the custom actions of today.

The so-called speed locks, some of which are available as kits for such older rifles as the Mauser, Springfield, and Enfield, and with which most modern bolt actions are equipped, achieve their speed by using very strong springs. Quickness is achieved both by lightweight parts and by heavy, powerful springs. As there is a limit to how light you can go in weight, the difference must be made up in spring pressure. Today's firing systems are a good blend of the two.

Lock time can, of course, be measured. It is defined as the elapsed time between the moment the sear releases the firing pin or hammer and the moment the primer is crushed and explodes. In the 1903 Springfield, the interval has been timed at approximately .0057 second; lock time of .002 second is considered exceptional.

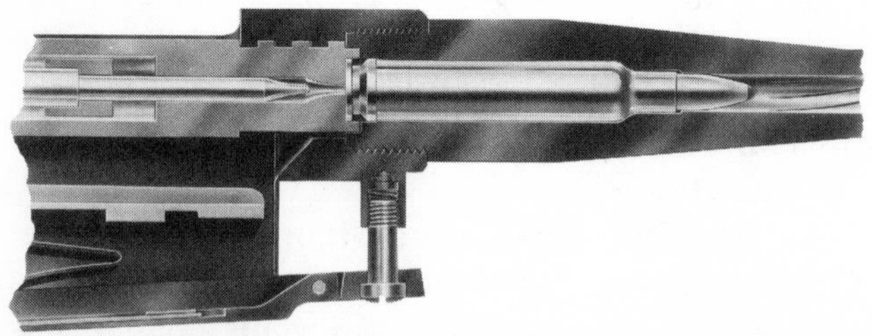

The Weatherby firing system, with its spring-driven firing pin, is typical of modern bolt actions. Note that the shape of the firing pin recess inside the bolt corresponds to the firing pin itself; this stops the forward movement of the pin.

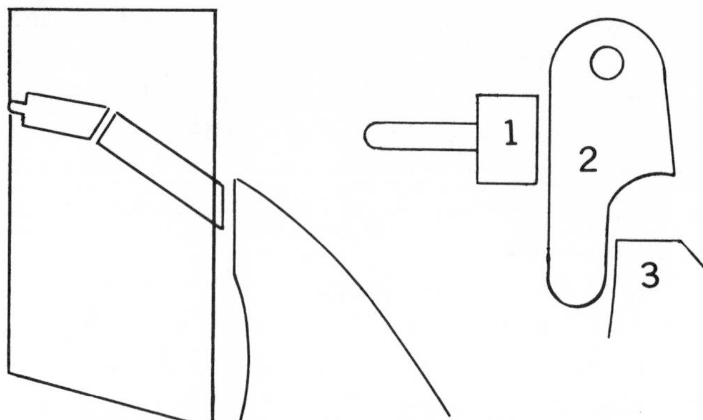

Left: In one Farquharson in my collection, the firing pin is in two pieces to make the difficult angle from hammer to primer. It's an unusual way to accomplish the blow and one that is less than satisfactory, because the blow is cushioned despite the massive hammer. Some of the force is wasted in driving one pin against the other at this angle.

Right: Ruger's Number 1 single-shot action obtains a straight firing pin blow by using a transfer bar (2) that rests against the firing pin (1) and is struck by the hammer (3). The result is a straight-line ignition without wasting force. The Ruger hammer is underslung and pivoted at the bottom of the action.

Another factor of importance in firing-pin blow is the angle of the pin — and often the number of parts between hammer and primer. Some guns are constructed in a way that some rather unusual contortions are required to get the firing blow delivered to the primer. Already mentioned is the 1903 Springfield, with its two-piece firing pin. A somewhat similar system is employed by Marlin on its 336 lever-action rifle. This is a safety feature pure and simple in the Marlin. The short rear end of its firing pin is urged downward at its front by a small spring. This serves to disconnect the two parts of the pin when the action is unlocked. But when the lever closes, the lock rises and pushes this rear end of the firing pin into line with the front of the pin. Thus, the rifle won't fire unless it's closed and locked.

I have a fine English Farquharson action manufactured by Westley Richards which I converted to a sporting rifle many years ago. It required considerable action work to accommodate the rather hot cartridge for which I chambered the barrel. The firing pin is a two-piece affair which is angled as shown in the diagram. As you can imagine, the blow required must be more than necessary with a straight pin in order to drive one pin against the other with sufficient energy to fire the primer consistently. I would not call this an efficient design, even though the Farquharson action is justly admired. It must be noted, however, that this is a rare model of the Farquharson; most of these actions do not have this kind of a firing-pin setup. In fact, most Farquharsons have an excellent firing pin.

This problem of severely angled firing-pin travel has been solved ingeniously in the Ruger single-shot action. Ruger's hammer is positioned low, so that when cocked, it lies "flat on its back" and parallel to the bore, pinned by the same pin as the finger lever. The rear end of the firing pin is nearly on the bore's center line and the hammer cannot be made to strike the pin itself since a solid wall of steel prevents it. Moreover there isn't room enough for the hammer to swing through such a wide arc.

What Ruger has done is to place what he calls a "transfer block" in the breechblock. This part is pinned at the top, contacts the rear of the firing pin, and extends down far enough for the hammer to whack it. The effect is that the hammer flies through its arc and transfers its impact through the transfer bar to the firing pin. This ingenious solution to a thorny problem eliminates the extreme angled firing pin as well as the two-piece pin, and it permits a hammerless action leaving a thick, protective wall of steel between the action and the shooter's face.

FIRING PIN PROTRUSION

An important detail in firearms' manufacture is the control of firing-pin protrusion. This is usually controlled by the shape of the shoulder behind the striking point. It is most important in center-fire high-power rifle cartridges, which develop enormous chamber pressures. Too much protrusion could easily cause a pierced primer, with the result that gas under pressure would rush back into the bolt body via the firing-pin hole. The normal protrusion in such a rifle is between .055 and .065 inch, or roughly 1/16 inch (.0625). Less protrusion will not give consistent ignition, more will introduce the element of danger from a pierced primer.

A rimfire rifle also must have a limited protrusion, otherwise snapping the firing pin without a cartridge in the chamber would cause the pin's nose to hit the barrel each time. This would soon ruin the pin and mar the barrel where it must support the rim for consistent ignition.

Firing pin protrusion in many rifles is restricted, as shown. A shoulder on the pin abuts the shoulder in the bolt; otherwise the pin would impact the breech end of the barrel if snapped without a cartridge in the gun.

LUBRICATION

Many of today's lubricants are designed for extremely cold weather and if that's what you use you're not going to experience what some hunters had to go through. One day, many years ago — when I had a gunsmith shop in New York's Adirondacks — it was bitterly cold. A friend who had been hunting dropped in quite annoyed that his pet Model 70 Winchester had failed to fire when he had a good buck in his sights an hour or so earlier. Bill sat the rifle down and began complaining, so I picked it up and looked it over. It appeared to be in order, but then I took the firing-pin assembly out of the bolt body and pointed out the trouble. A coating of fairly heavy grease covered the mainspring. It had congealed in the extreme cold and only allowed the firing pin to ooze forward, far too slowly to ignite a cartridge. We cleaned out the grease and dried out the firing-pin recess and Bill went back to his hunting. The moral is that, unless you're using one of the modern light oils specifically made to flow at low temperatures, you're far better off to keep your firing mechanism clean and dry. If you must lubricate use powdered graphite.

TYPES OF SPRINGS

There are three types of springs in general use for firing mechanisms: coil, leaf, and V. There is nothing whatever wrong with any of the three types, so long as each is correctly made, hardened, and tempered. The leaf is probably the least used of the three today although you still find it on many older guns. It is quite dependable. However, if not made correctly it has a tendency to break more readily than a coil spring. The V spring, used on most of the top grades of double shotguns, also must be made correctly to give good service.

Today, however, almost everybody is using coil springs. They are cheaper, easier to assemble, easier to make, and totally reliable. Given low-cost manufacture, there is no question they are more dependable than any other type of spring.

THE CASELESS EXPERIMENT

A few years ago, Daisy (the air-rifle people) introduced a revolutionary concept they called V/L, a "shooting system with caseless ammunition." It was revolutionary, it was different, and it didn't last very long. But it's still of interest. What Daisy did was to take a .22-caliber lead bullet and attach a "short rod of propellant on its base." There was no conventional brass cartridge case and no primer. The ammunition consisted simply of a bullet with propellant stuck to its base. Ignition in the Daisy V/L system was accomplished by heat from a jet of heated air created by a spring-driven piston behind the firing chamber. The system was ingenious and can be compared to the way a diesel engine operates, in that the heat generated by compression is sufficient to ignite the propellant. In the case of a diesel it's the fuel mixture; in the Daisy it was their propellant.

No reasons have ever been given for the V/L's failure that I am aware of. I can guess that shooters weren't sufficiently interested in such a departure. I can also guess that the movement of the big spring and piston was enough to move the gun during their travel motion. Put another way, lock time in this system had to be very, very slow. I can also imagine that the ammunition storage problem must have been monumental. You couldn't carry the caseless ammo loosely in your pocket and propellant deterioration may have been a factor.

Just the same, the Daisy V/L was an experiment in a different method of firing. It worked sufficiently well to get on the market, but obviously not well enough to reach the sales goals projected for it and the project is now dead.

CHAPTER NINE

THE RIFLE BARREL

The earliest guns were not shoulder-fired —they more nearly resembled small artillery. Early barrels were made of wood. A bit too much gunpowder and the barrels burst, and so they were often wrapped with wire. The wire wrapping added strength, and as a matter of fact, wire-wrapped artillery barrels were used until comparatively recently. Then wooden barrels gave way to metal, and then to improved metals, as the science of metallurgy developed.

The methods by which barrels have been made over the years have closely followed modern machine-tool development. In fact, the American Industrial Revolution, when America began to turn from an agricultural society to an industrial giant, was formed around two industries: firearms and textile machinery. Of the two, firearms is the older, since its ancestry can be traced to the earliest settlers; the textile industry was started in 1790 by Samuel Slater along the banks of the Blackstone River in Pawtucket, Rhode Island.

It would be useless to review some of the older methods of making gun barrels, but it might be of interest to review, in an oversimplified way, the methods used during the early and mid-1800s. Barrels were not bored out of solid steel as they are today; rather they were made by wrapping metal around a steel bar, welding the joints, and then withdrawing the bar.

Such barrels are variously called Damascus, twist, stub, or laminated (and sometimes a combination of those names). There are variations in each one of them but these are mostly of interest to the technological historian. Early barrels were iron, later ones usually a combination of iron and steel. Some of the twist barrels (to use that term generically) were excellent, being a good combination of steel — with its properties of strength and elasticity — and soft iron. Others were pretty nearly pure iron and wouldn't stand as much pressure.

Barrel quality also depended on the skill of the various workmen who forged and welded them. It was important (and very difficult) to keep scale out of the welds and equally important to keep the metal at the right temperature (in a charcoal fire) and hammer it correctly to achieve perfect welds. The hammering had another important effect in that it strengthened the metal by inducing a molecular rearrangement; we know this as forging, and a forged product usually has greater strength than most other types of manufacture.

After these barrels were rough-formed on a steel bar called a mandrel, they were rough-ground on the outside and rough-bored inside. A visual inspection would now disclose serious imperfections (if there were any, the barrel was scrapped at this point). Assuming no visual defects, the barrels were then proofed by loading them with a prescribed load and firing them in the confines of a "proof house." Some barrels burst open from poor welds or other defects. Those that did not were finished and then proofed again. In England and most other European countries where gun proofing is a government function, this initial proving is called "provisional proof." The final proof is "definitive proof."

As steels improved, the gun industry moved to barrels bored from a solid steel bar. Initially called "weldless" barrels, they had many advantages over the older methods. As is usual among gun people, however, there were countless arguments over the relative merits of both ways and there's no denying the beauty of a fine twist barrel. I suspect the development of smokeless powder had as much to do with the demise of twist barrels as anything else. Smokeless, which became popular during the 1890s, developed considerably higher pressures than black powder and so demanded stronger barrels. It also burned hotter, so it demanded tougher steel than black powder did. That's why, if you have a fine old rifle made during the days of black powder, you should not shoot smokeless loads in it unless the barrel is stamped "for smokeless powder."

Steel is made tough by the addition of certain alloys; made harder by the addition of other alloys. The most common gun-barrel steel today is known as SAE (for Society of Automotive Engineers) 4140. It's an alloy consisting of chromium and molybdenum, popularly called chrome-moly. This steel is abrasion resistant, high in tensile strength, and readily machinable. It satisfies the requirements for nearly all gun barrels in use today.

Some of the very hot cartridges, including the .264 Winchester, 7mm Remington, some Weatherby Magnums, and the .220 Swift, are hard on barrels. This means they create such heat that a barrel will be rapidly eroded. The solution has been to switch to stainless steel. Stainless has all the desired attributes of 4140, but is much more difficult to machine. It does, however, add great abrasion resistance and thus longer barrel life for these hot calibers.

Most .22 rimfire rifles do not develop especially hot pressures and do not require a steel as tough as 4140. So most .22 barrels are a softer, milder steel, actually an alloy of carbon and manganese. This combination is much easier to machine and just as suitable for the purpose. There are many high-power rifles made that are used solely for hunting — which means they won't be fired very often —whose barrels also are made of this softer carbon-manganese steel. Again, it's perfectly suitable for a .30/30 deer rifle whose owner might fire two or three boxes of cartridges in a lifetime. But it is not suitable for a shooter who *uses* his rifle.

THE RIFLE BARREL

Nobody knows who invented rifling, the spiral grooves in a gun barrel that give the rifle its name and that give a rotational spin to the projectile to keep it flying point on. Rifling was used in Europe in the 16th Century, so it has been around a long time.

In the manufacture of a rifle barrel, the bore is first drilled and then reamed up to what is called "bore diameter." Let's use the common .30 caliber as our example, in which case the barrel is reamed to an exact diameter of .300 inch. Now we have a perfectly smooth, precise hole through the barrel that appears absolutely smooth but which really has circular tool marks, no matter how slight, in its surface. At this point barrels are sometimes honed, or polished, to make this surface even smoother.

Barrel drilling is generally considered the most critical operation in barrel manufacture. The stationary barrel drill is shaped like a v at its drilling end and has a long groove running the full length of the drill, as well as a small hole all the way through. The hole is to force cutting oil to the cutting edge and to carry the chips back out along the v groove. The barrel itself is rotated at high speed and the drill fed into the barrel blank. It usually takes approximately 45 minutes to drill a barrel.

Assuming no flaws in the steel and a properly sharpened bit, the bore should be drilled dead straight. It seldom happens that way, however. Most barrels are drilled reasonably straight, but nothing is perfect in this world. Barrels are straightened after drilling and reaming – sometimes several times, depending on the manufacturer. Now, it must be understood that a slightly crooked barrel can shoot with accuracy, can deliver shot after shot into the same point of impact so long as other things remain the same. But there are a number of other factors that can prevent a barrel with a crooked hole from delivering consistent accuracy. The primary reason is that the bore is not concentric with the outside form of the barrel. This means that as it heats up during shooting, the barrel will warp slightly, since one side will heat quicker than the other. The result will be that the shots will begin to "walk" across (or up or down) the target. On the other hand, a barrel that has been straightened has been forcibly bent and may tend to return to its original shape when heated. To avoid this possibility, barrels are usually "normalized" after straightening. This process consists of bringing the barrels up to a certain temperature in an oven and letting them soak in the heat for a certain amount of time, after which they are allowed to cool gradually.

After straightening, the usual procedure is to turn the outside diameter of the barrel, with the result that the tube will now be consistent in wall thickness – or concentric.

I spent many years as a custom gunsmith and during my career I fitted some 1,500 new barrels to customer's actions. Barrels are threaded and screwed into the receiver, but I employed a method a little different than most gunsmiths. Using an excellent South Bend toolroom lathe that had a large spindle hole, I was able to suspend the barrel through the entire lathe headstock. I had mounted a chuck on each end of this spindle and, using a dial indicator, both ends of the barrel were trued. The procedure then allowed me total access to the breech end of the barrel and it assured the action would be in perfect alignment with the bore. It permitted another interesting experiment: Before working on any barrel blank, I could turn the lathe on and look through the hole while the barrel was spinning. Any deviation from dead straight showed up instantly! I suspect I only saw one or two among all those barrels that I would have called "dead straight." I don't know that they shot any better than other barrels, however. Other things being the same I'd rather have as straight a tube as possible, and one that's concentric.

I can't recall the number of times I've had people come in the shop with the request to "cut a few inches off her so she'll swing easier." Lo and behold, I'd cut her off to find that where she was cut, the bore was off center by as much as 1/32 inch. That's not right, and that kind of a barrel isn't going to shoot with much accuracy.

Rifling, as mentioned, is the system of grooves running down the barrel that give a bullet its spin. Only with the spin will a bullet have stability. It can be compared with throwing a football. Get a good spin, make the ball fly point on, and you can sneak it between two defenders closer together than a pair of chorus girls. Let the football tumble end over end, however, and you lose speed, accuracy, and ultimately the ball.

We've been using the .30-caliber rifle as our example and a .30-caliber bullet measures .308 inch. That's 8/1,000th of an inch larger than the bore diameter of .300 inch. Therefore, the rifling grooves are cut to a depth of .004 inch, making a groove diameter of .308 inch, or the same as the bullet. The reason is that the bullet must be driven into the rifling and the latter must bite into the bullet to make it accept the spin. The spaces between the grooves are called the lands.

Once again, there are tolerances. Rifle bores usually measure very close to .300 inch. Groove depth can run a little deeper than .308 and often goes to .3085 or even .309. There is excellent reason for this. The rifle barrel must perform with ammunition of any and all brands, just as ammunition must fit rifles of all makes. All of this is controlled by an organization known as the Sporting Arms and Ammunition Manufacturer's Institute (SAAMI, always referred to as Sammy) which establishes the standards so that Federal ammunition will fit a Winchester rifle and a Winchester cartridge will fit a Marlin rifle and so on.

When bullets are manufactured, they are made to tolerances. For example, a set of bullet-forming dies will be used to make several million bullets before the die is retired. That means the die is going to wear, so that the first bullet made from this die will be smaller than the last. A bullet die, for a huge-volume run, will be made a little undersized – say .307 inch – so that after several million bullets have been formed, the die is now producing bullets measuring close to .309 inch. Maybe that doesn't sound like much, but a difference of .001 inch can raise merry hell with the chamber pressure if it's the bullet that's bigger than the hole. Generally speaking, today's ammunition is far closer to dimension than was true even as little as fifteen years ago.

Nearly all rifling twist is to the right, although the British usually twist to the left, as does the Colt revolver. Almost everybody else twists right hand. According to the best information I have, the British believe that on this side of the equator, rifling works better with a left-hand twist. I've heard it said that Colt uses a left-hand twist because the torque of the bullet going through the barrel will tend to tighten the barrel in its threads. Who knows? It really doesn't matter.

What does matter is the amount of twist, which is always expressed as one complete turn in so many inches. In a .30-caliber rifle, for example, the usual rate of twist is 1 turn in 10 inches, expressed as 1–10. The longer and heavier the bullet, the faster the twist must be to keep it stabilized. To be more specific, the .30/06 handles bullets from 110 to 220 grains in most standard loads. A relatively slow twist of 1–14 will handle the 110-grain load, 1–12 will stabilize most 180-grain bullets but 1–10 is needed for the 220 grain as well as a few of the exceptionally long 180s. Some claim a bullet shouldn't be overstabilized. In other words, you use a rate of twist that's just enough to stabilize the bullet in question. I've never seen this proven and have therefore never felt overstabilization was a sin. If in fact it is really possible.

Whatever else is said about rifling twist – don't believe it. Some incredibly wild things got printed about the ballistics of the 5.56mm military cartridge (.223 Remington), for example, in stories out of Vietnam. They claimed the bullet was purposely understabilized so it would chop a more ghastly wound; that it tumbled end-over-end and ripped through flesh like a saw. These stories were, to put it politely, ballistically impossible. And the worst part of it was that some who should have known better picked them up as gospel. I repeat, no bullet that isn't stable in flight can possibly fly true. Nor can it fly far.

A somewhat odd form of twist that has been used from time to time is called "gain twist." The name is descriptive since the rate of twist accelerates toward the muzzle. It might start, for example, with a twist as slow as 1–20 at the breech where the bullet starts down the barrel and be gradually increased to 1–10 by the time it reaches the muzzle. Gain twisting is very old. I have no idea how old, but it was extensively tested by the late Dr. F. W. Mann, who was one of the world's leading ballisticians around the turn of the century. It also has been tried in modern benchrest shooting with no superior results that I know about. Gain twist has some theoretical advantages but they don't appear to work in practice.

The number of grooves in a rifle barrel has long been a subject of discussion, rumor, argument, and chatter. It has some bearing on performance, but not as much as is sometimes claimed. One of the problems in such a discussion is that you often run up against a boneheaded individual who has had a bad (or good) experience with one type or another. Therefore it's good or bad depending upon that one experience. To illustrate: During World War II, in an economy move, Remington, which had a contract to make vast numbers of 1903 model Springfield bolt-action rifles for the Army, produced hundreds of thousands of barrels with only two grooves. (The norm was four in a Springfield.) Some of these barrels shot very well, others didn't. That's to be expected. They were rifles made during wartime under conditions of extremely high pressure to "get the iron out." Under those conditions they'd have produced some lousy 4, 6, 8, or 100-groove barrels. As well as some good ones.

RIFLING SYSTEMS

Rifling systems vary in the shape of lands and grooves as well as in their number. All the systems work, have worked, and in some cases are still working. Some of the major ones include:

SCHALK-POPE

This is generally simply referred to as the Pope system, after the legendary barrelmaker, Harry M. Pope. The system was found best for lead bullets and, while originally used so far as I know by George Schalk, it was popularized by Pope.

Harry Pope was a crotchety genius, a graduate engineer (M.I.T.), who worked most of his long career in a dingy Jersey City, New Jersey, loft atop one of the huge industrial plants in the area. Pope is generally acknowledged to have made the best — that is, the most accurate — barrels for lead-bullet shooting. Making his own barrels with painstaking care, he fitted them to such single-shot actions as Winchester, Ballard, Stevens, and others.

As the sketch shows, this rifling system was extremely shallow. Its grooves were wide and so shallow that their center was actually bore diameter and the net effect was considerably more bearing, or grip, on the bullet. In a way, you could almost say that the system provided an extra land in the middle of each groove.

Other barrelmakers of the period made barrels that were probably just as fine as Pope's. Many claim, for example, that George Schoyen of Denver made a better barrel. Still, it's the system we're talking about because it is distinctive, and it bears Harry Pope's name. It must also be added that a good deal of the Pope legend was launched by the late Lucian Cary, who wrote a couple of stories many years ago about a noted barrelmaker whom he called "H. M. Pyne" which were printed in the old *Saturday Evening Post*. Every man and boy in America who knew a lick about guns in those days knew that H. M. Pyne was Harry M. Pope, a good friend of Cary's.

When Pope, or one of his contemporaries, made a rifle, he also made a bullet mold to fit that particular barrel. Further, the Pope system generally included a false muzzle that was rifled right along with the barrel. Its purpose was to allow the shooter to load the bullet from the muzzle, perfectly guided by the false muzzle. Then he loaded a primed cartridge charged with powder, with a wad over the powder to avoid spilling, from the breech. Most of the famous riflemen of the period around 1890 until World War I used this type of rifle and they used

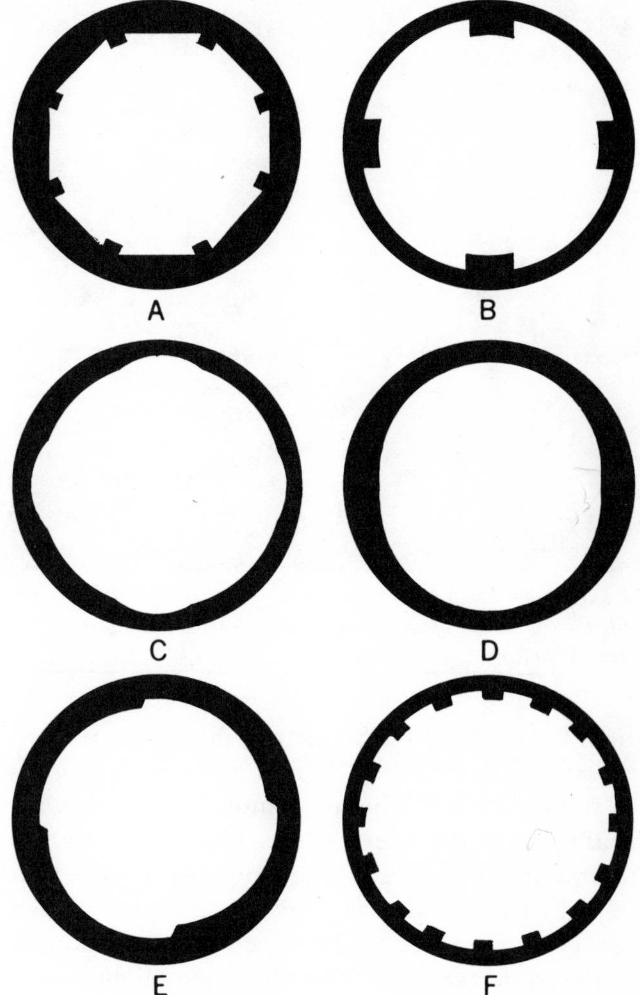

These are the more common, and some of the more interesting, forms of rifling used over the years. A *is the type used by Harry Pope and referred to as Schalk-Pope. It is basically a system of very wide, very shallow grooves, so wide and so shallow that the middle of the grooves remain at bore diameter, giving, in effect, an extra land at that point.* B *is the Enfield system, the most commonly used of all. It consists of square lands and square cornered grooves; the number of lands and grooves is often determined by the caliber.* C *is the Metford form which was popular in England during black-powder days for sporting rifle use. It consisted of rounded grooves making cleaning very easy.* D *is the Lancaster oval bore which hardly appears rifled at all. At one time this system enjoyed popularity. It works despite its unique appearance.* E *is the Newton parabolic system. Realizing that only the driving edge of the lands did any work, Newton eliminated the other edge. The system worked and worked well but no better than other types.* F *is a multi-groove system consisting of many lands and grooves and most commonly known as the Marlin Micro-Groove system. The exact number of lands and grooves depends on the caliber; it is claimed that this system grips a bullet more gently but more fully.*

Hundreds and hundreds of rifle barrels or bolts, depending on the kind of steel. This is the way steel is received at a modern gun plant; it will later be cut to proper length and go through countless machining operations to become a precise rifle part. The photo is from the new Marlin plant.

them for rest and for Schuetzen shooting. (Schuetzen shooting came over from mid-Europe; primarily it consisted of shooting standing — "from your hind legs," as Pope used to say. The Schuetzen rifle also boasted palm rests, long tanged buttplates that helped in steadying the rifle. As an added attraction great schooners of beer were often consumed by the contestants. But they did some mighty great shooting from the standing position.)

ENFIELD

The Enfield rifling system deserves to be called standard because it is in the widest use. Cut with square corners, the number of lands and grooves can be 4, 6, 8, or just about whatever the designer wishes to make it. The precise number usually depends on the caliber, with more lands and grooves in the larger calibers. The system is also the easiest type to cut, and this is as good a place as any to explain how the longitudinal grooves are cut in a rifle barrel.

Until the 1950s, most rifle barrels were rifled by cutting — using a long rod with a tiny cutter at the end that was drawn through the barrel and rotated as it was moved. The degree of rotation corresponded to the twist rate desired. Each pass removed a very tiny bit of metal — there was very little space for a large chip. And after each pass of the tool, the rod had to be turned slightly to cut the next groove. A bit at a time, the grooves were cut to final depth . . . slowly and laboriously and calling for extremely fine craftsmanship. There was nothing mystic about rifling a barrel — it simply took a damned good man a damned long time.

In the early days, twist was achieved by a long, large wooden rod in which grooves of the correct pitch were cut and in which an end of the rifling rod rode. As the rod moved back and forth it was forced to follow the twist in these grooves. The system worked well except that a different twist rod was needed for each twist cut. But early gunsmiths cut few different twists.

In later days, tools were manufactured by Pratt & Whitney purely for rifling. They resembled a long lathe bed and had a slanted bar mounted over the approximate center of the machine. This was called a sine bar; it could be set to any desired angle and caused the rifling rod to rotate as it was moved back and forth to the pitch set on the sine bar. But in the 1950s or thereabouts, some enterprising engineers learned how to rifle a barrel by pulling a carbide "button" through the reamed bore. This button literally swaged, or pushed, the grooves into place. The process took a few seconds and produced barrels with extraordinarily fine finishes, with remarkable consistency from barrel to barrel and — the final plus — better average accuracy than with older methods of cutting.

This carbide button is about an inch long and has reverse rifling, a mirror image of the rifling if you prefer, so that when it's forced through the barrel it leaves the system of lands and grooves just as wanted. The system of button rifling is in nearly universal use today.

METFORD

An older system formerly used by the English who preferred it for black-powder rifles because it was simpler and easier to clean than the Enfield system. Metford rifling had no sharp corners, but gripped the bullet just as well and performed equally well. It was experimented with in many rifles using jacketed bullets and, while it still performs perhaps as well as any other system, it has not been popular since black-powder days in England.

LANCASTER OVAL BORE

This is one of the more interesting rifling variations and is extremely old — dating at least back to 1835. It simply consists of two grooves, but very wide and on a shallow radius so that when you peer through the bore it almost appears totally smooth. Nevertheless it is rifled, to standard depths, and it does spin the bullet. Moreover, tests have proved it as good as any other system. Originally developed during black-powder days, it fouled less and was easier to clean than other systems. Oval boring has been used recently in American commercial arms. How long it will last, I can't guess. But such experiments go on continually.

NEWTON

Among the many innovations of the inventive Charles Newton in the early 1900s were several rifling systems. One of these was the Lancaster oval bore; another was a variation of the oval bore that became known as the Newton segmental system. It was really a modified Metford system and that's all Newton ever claimed it was.

NEWTON PARABOLIC

Around 1918, Charles Newton modified his segmental rifling system to give a short radius on the driving edge of the lands; this became known as the parabolic system. (Only one edge of the land actually does any of the work; this is the driving edge. The other edge simply has to be there.) There is little evidence Newton's parabolic rifling was any better, or any worse, than the popular Enfield system. To the best of my knowledge it hasn't been used since the early Newton experiments, at least not in any quantity.

MARLIN MICRO-GROOVE

In 1953, the Marlin company secured a patent on a system of rifling that they call Micro-Groove and that consists of many more grooves and lands than standard. The basis of the patent lies in the angle of the driving edge. Not only does the Marlin system have a multi-groove system, but these grooves are much shallower than in the conventional Enfield system. For example, to take a standard .30-caliber rifle which has, as we have noted earlier, a bore diameter of .300 inch and a groove diameter of .308 inch. In the Marlin system, however, while the groove diameter must remain at .308 inch (because that's the size of the bullet), the bore diameter must be larger than .300 inch . . . say about .302 inch. The reason is that there are more lands. Despite the apparent discrepancy, there really isn't one at all because the same amount of space is displaced.

Marlin claims better accuracy for its system because it grips the bullet more tightly, yet its shallow lands don't dig into the jacket as far. Given a perfectly concentric bullet, this won't matter. But given an off-center bullet, the Marlin system should produce superior accuracy, since the lighter bullet grip in the barrel will distort it less.

COLD FORMING.

This is a rather revolutionary method of manufacturing a rifle barrel that I first learned about in the 1950s. I was introduced to Dr. Gerhardt Appel, from Germany, who had perfected a method of manufacturing hypodermic needles by a cold-forming process before the War. The method was highly successful and, when Germany began World War II, Dr. Appel was enlisted by Germany to produce machine-gun barrels for the MG 42 gun. Apparently, many hundreds of thousands of these barrels were made by the Appel process.

I remember going to Detroit to visit the doctor, who had his big — a little larger than a big station wagon — machine set up a small shop in that machine-tool city. I had the opportunity of discussing the process with Appel and watching the machine make a few barrels; then I obtained some sample barrels and made quite a few tests on them.

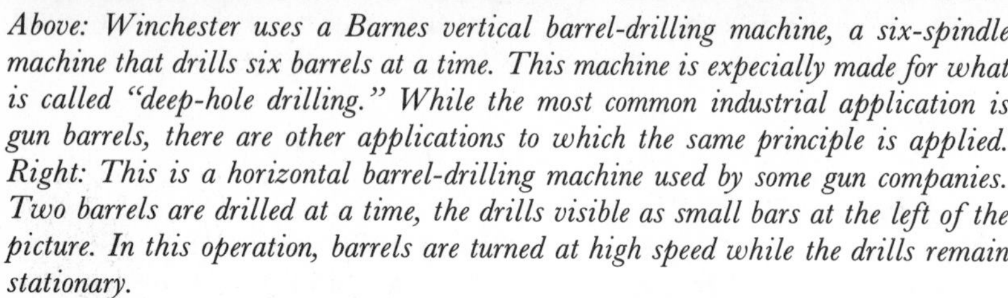

Above: Winchester uses a Barnes vertical barrel-drilling machine, a six-spindle machine that drills six barrels at a time. This machine is expecially made for what is called "deep-hole drilling." While the most common industrial application is gun barrels, there are other applications to which the same principle is applied. Right: This is a horizontal barrel-drilling machine used by some gun companies. Two barrels are drilled at a time, the drills visible as small bars at the left of the picture. In this operation, barrels are turned at high speed while the drills remain stationary.

The process is complicated. You must first have a drilled and reamed steel bar. Let's say, just for the sake of example, that it is about 16 inches long and 1⅜ inch in diameter. Its bore is larger than .30 caliber. Located inside the machine is a mandrel not unlike the rifling button just described. It contains the rifling in mirror image and to exact dimension. The barrel-to-be is placed in the machine, positioned over the mandrel, and the machine turned on. At this point, rapidly revolving shafts begin to whir and rotate and cams force "hammers" to push against the steel bar so rapidly and so forcefully that they actually reduce the steel to a plastic form as it passes over the mandrel. The bar is fed through the machine and, as it passes over the mandrel where the hammers strike it, the inside assumes the reverse shape of the mandrel. The other accomplishment of the machine is to elongate the barrel to about 24 inches. What comes out of the machine then is a barrel, longer and slimmer than when it went in, completely rifled inside, and with a smooth finish. Moreover, each and every barrel is theoretically identical as to inside dimension.

The Appel process has a number of advantages: the hammering is cold forging and possesses all the advantages of that process, namely greater strength through rearranged molecules. The smoothness of the internal surface and its surface hardness provide significant advantages and its speed of producing a barrel has significant production plusses. But the process, as operated by Dr. Appel, was flawed. Appel had to buy his barrel blanks already drilled — that is, he had no control over the drilling operation. In addition, his barrels were not reamed, which means that the drilled hole had a rough surface. In the process, despite the heavy hammer forging, these drill marks were not always erased. The second big disadvantage was that the blanks were not straightened prior to forging, and thus came out just as crooked as they went in. There's no question in my mind that if Dr. Appel had had better blanks to work with, he would have produced a superior product indeed.

In fact, the process led me to some pretty exciting thoughts. For instance, insert a thin-walled piece of stainless-steel tubing into a piece of tough

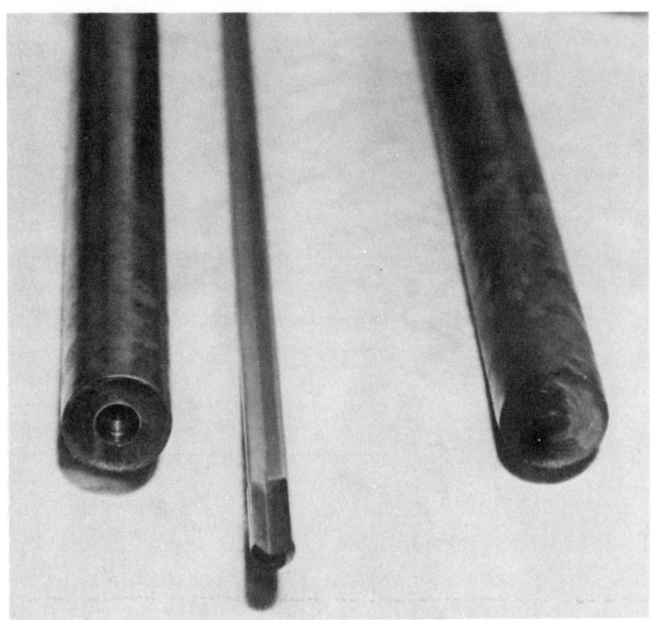

Left: The undrilled barrel (left) and (right) after drilling, with a deep-hole drill (center). Note that the drill is V-shaped and that the V runs its full length. In use, the barrel is spun at high speed, the drill advanced slowly. Oil surges through a small hole and forces the chips out along the V-groove. It usually takes about 45 minutes to drill a barrel. Right: Before (left) and after reaming, with a reamer in the center. These reamers are pulled through the barrel and are known as "pull reamers."

aluminum alloy tubing and forge the whole thing as a unit. If that worked, you could produce a light barrel with a tough surface that ought to give long barrel life, withstand high pressures, and yet produce an extremely light barrel. One of its advantages would be that you could use a tougher stainless alloy than now can be used for barrel steel, because the tough alloys are so hard to machine. Forging can produce any rifling configuration desired, and it can even produce the chamber so that the only remaining operations necessary would be to thread the shank to screw it into the action and turn down the outside.

I still have an Appel barrel on one of my rifles. It's a .30-caliber barrel and a nice, clean one inside. I reduced its outer dimensions to light sporting weight and chambered it for a wildcat cartridge that was the .275 H&H Magnum necked up to .30 caliber. The .275 was a fine English 7mm Magnum cartridge, and what I wound up with was something like the present .300 Winchester Magnum, although not quite so powerful.

Some companies are cold forming today, one of them being Winchester, which, of course, controls its internal surfaces and straightness better than Appel could. The forged barrel as produced by Winchester is an excellent barrel. The people at Winchester have shed a little more light on the Ap-

Left: After drilling, which leaves a rough, undersize hole, the bore is reamed up to size. Here is a Pratt & Whitney two-spindle reaming machine that is ready to pull the reamers through the bore. Note the cutting oil and chips under each reamer; oil, under pressure from the other end, forces the chips out the bore. Several reamers are used to bring the bore to exact size and to provide as smooth a surface as possible.

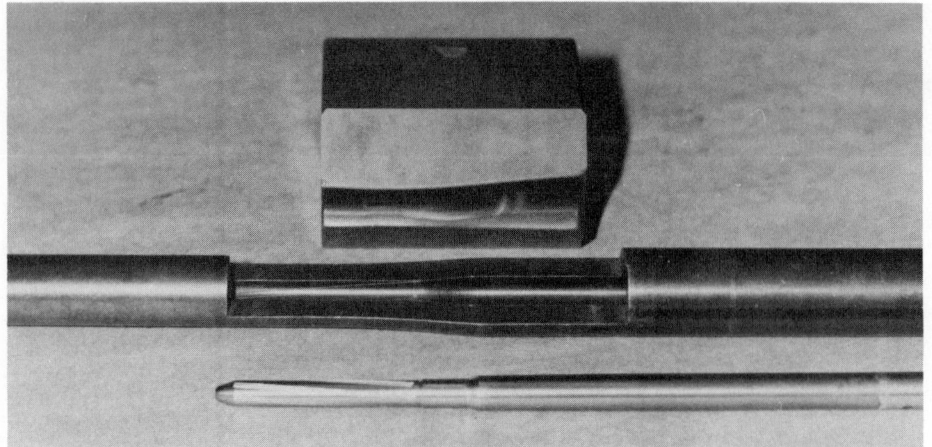

The Appel process of cold forming barrels is used by Winchester. The photo shows (top to bottom) a carbide die, a sectioned barrel partially formed, and a carbide mandrel. In use, the barrel blank is of larger diameter and shorter length at the start than at the finish. Inserted into the machine, the set of dies move rapidly back and forth, so rapidly that they literally "plasticize" the steel and cause it to accept the shape of the mandrel. The result is a barrel of smaller diameter than when it entered the machine, perfectly rifled and chambered.

pel process of cold forming barrels. Their machinery is made by three different companies and Winchester claims to be probably the only major sporting-arms manufacturer which is cold forming a chamber in a rifle barrel. Winchester further claims these advantages for cold-formed barrels:

1. Bore and rifling surface finish are superior.
2. Bore and rifling dimensions are more consistent.
3. The barrel is straighter.
4. There is a 20 to 40 percent saving in material.

I would agree with all these points except to comment that the third doesn't necessarily follow. Winchester's procedure *may* produce straighter barrels than the company's competitors but, if true, it's not the result of cold forming alone. Winchester further advises that cold forming has the disadvantages of a huge initial investment and high maintenance costs. But they claim it is more economical than the button process. By which they mean on an overall basis, and they would know this better than I. I cannot accept the thought that, if it was really that much better, other companies would not employ the same system, since the same machinery is available to anyone.

I remember long ago doing business with a maker of barrel blanks. He shipped me a blank that he declared was the finest he had ever produced. He never did say just how he came to this reasoning, but I had seen him at work and knew that he could tell by the feel of the very first cleaning patch after he was finished rifling. In any event, I chambered this barrel and it didn't perform all that well. It shot well, but no more than average. This so infuriated the barrelmaker, who claimed I'd ruined his barrel, that he never spoke to me again. The point is that nobody, not even the skilled craftsman who makes it, can tell precisely how any barrel will shoot until it gets shot. To support that argument, I once barreled an action for a skilled shooter in Massachusetts with a run-of-the-mill barrel from a barrelmaker not especially known for superaccurate barrels. This rifle shot like a house afire and, in fact, the owner won a world record with it at benchrest shooting.

There are some who believe it takes a certain magical (even mystical) length to produce good rifle accuracy, as, for example, a barrel should be 23.45 inches long. Not 23 inches nor 24, but 23.45. This is nonsense. Within reason, the exact barrel length doesn't mean a thing.

I used to have a customer in central New York State who was one of the finest woodchuck shooters I've ever known. A dentist, he would go out after lunch and park his car where he could watch the far side of a huge meadow where the shots ranged from 300 to 600 yards. He'd listen to the Yankee ballgame and shoot chucks. Then, a couple of hours later, when the sun had moved, he'd drive around to the other side of the meadow and do the same thing. Doc never shot at any chuck less than 300 yards away, and moving around gave him shooting at the chucks that had been near him. In any event I'd built Doc a good-shooting, heavy-barreled .243 Winchester with which he did some remarkable woodchuck execution at a full 600 yards. Then one day he brought the big gun back and asked me to cut the barrel to 19 inches and turn it as light as possible. He wanted to make a deer rifle

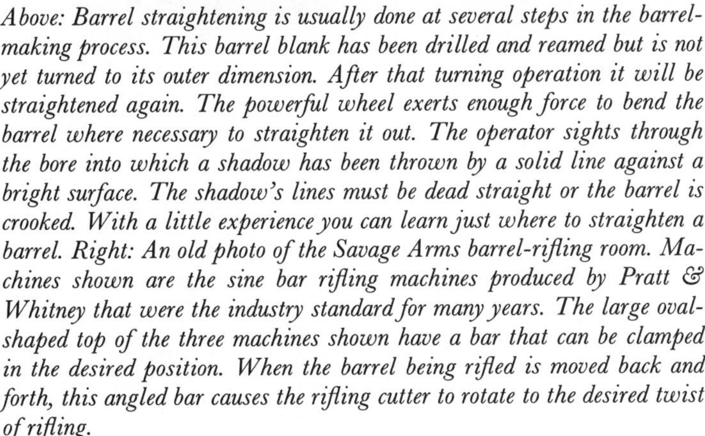

Above: Barrel straightening is usually done at several steps in the barrel-making process. This barrel blank has been drilled and reamed but is not yet turned to its outer dimension. After that turning operation it will be straightened again. The powerful wheel exerts enough force to bend the barrel where necessary to straighten it out. The operator sights through the bore into which a shadow has been thrown by a solid line against a bright surface. The shadow's lines must be dead straight or the barrel is crooked. With a little experience you can learn just where to straighten a barrel. Right: An old photo of the Savage Arms barrel-rifling room. Machines shown are the sine bar rifling machines produced by Pratt & Whitney that were the industry standard for many years. The large oval-shaped top of the three machines shown have a bar that can be clamped in the desired position. When the barrel being rifled is moved back and forth, this angled bar causes the rifling cutter to rotate to the desired twist of rifling.

out of it. I did so, he put the same scope back on it to see how it shot, and the most remarkable thing happened: He did not have to change the scope adjustment and the rifle shot just as accurately as it had before. That's unusual and I cite it only to show that such things do happen, although they are by no means the rule. It is my belief that, so long as other things remain the same, a given barrel will deliver the same accuracy no matter what its length, shape, or weight. Within reasonable limits of course.

The weight and shape of barrels depend on a number of factors. First of all, a barrel must be large enough in diameter to hold what goes on inside. This simply means that a rifle chambered for the .300 Winchester Magnum must have a bigger barrel than one chambered for the .30/06. That is, it must be larger in diameter at the breech end because the chamber is larger and the pressure is higher. It need not be any larger at the muzzle. (Pressure is always highest at the breech and diminishes toward the muzzle.)

A barrel's shape and weight depend on its use, too. A target barrel is heavier than one for hunting because it can be held more steadily, will not heat up so fast, and therefore is more apt to retain its zero over a string of shots. A target barrel is not necessarily any more accurate for the first shot out of a cold barrel (the most important shot out of a sporter) nor for a three-shot string either, for that matter. You can accept the fact that a light, short, sporter barrel can be just as accurate for three shots as nearly any target rifle, assuming a good barrel and proper load. Weight and length purely of themselves have no bearing on that sort of shootability.

Nobody much cares what a target rifle barrel looks like. How it shoots is the only criteria. But the barrel on a sporter is quite another matter entirely, for it is a part of the total rifle and contributes to its looks. You must, for instance, completely although subtly, shape a stock differently for a 24-inch barrel as opposed to one of 20 inches. Moreover, the shape used in turning the barrel is a matter of the rifle's cosmetics and considerable subjectivity is encountered. I used to admire greatly the shape Winchester used on its featherweight Model 70 back in the 1950s. In fact, I turned out a large number of custom barrels using the same configuration, because I liked it so much. Others didn't like the shape at all, so it's all a matter of personal preference. (It must be admitted that the most popular sporting rifle barrel shape consists of a short cylindrical section just ahead of the receiver about 1¼ to 1½ inches long, then tapering sharply for about 3 inches, from which point it tapers gradually to the muzzle.)

Some years ago it was felt that a barrel had to be long to be worth anything. There was a bit of truth to that with black powder, and there's some very slight truth to it now. But the point is really pretty moot. To examine it more closely, if it's a target rifle using iron sights (instead of a scope) there is an advantage to a longer barrel because it provides a longer sighting radius and thus lessens holding error due purely to sighting. And a longer, heavier barrel can also be held more steadily. It is true, too, that you can obtain slightly higher velocities from a longer barrel than from a very short one. A 26-inch tube will shoot faster than one of 19 inches, for instance. But, while the difference is measurable, it's also not noticeable in the field. It may be concluded that, even though a short barrel does cause a slight loss in velocity, a short barrel is no handicap in the field because the difference in length is too small to be practical. Furthermore, a short barrel is so much handier that it is often more useful than a longer tube.

These considerations do not apply to single-shot rifles, however, because there is no length of action to contend with. You can have a single-shot rifle with a 26-inch barrel that's no longer than a 20-inch barreled autoloader. That gives you all the advantage of a little more velocity with the handiness of a short rifle. These are determinations you must make yourself. But, for the record, be advised that the velocity loss from a short, handy barrel need not concern you particularly.

Many years ago the octagon barrel was popular. It had a recent blush of popularity again with the big boom in commemoratives during the 1960s, but octagons now appear to have gone back into obscurity again. They have a built-in nostalgia and some buffs very likely find them of interest because of that. Other things being the same, an octagonal barrel will shoot the same as a round one but it will cost more, because it's more complicated to make. There is also a steady, though small, demand for semioctagon barrels, however. These are produced by several European firms and distributed by a few specialists in this country. These barrels do have a certain appeal but their selection is strictly a matter of looks and you make your choice based on that aspect alone.

DOUBLE RIFLES

Barrels for double rifles are joined just as those of a double shotgun. These rifles are almost always made for whopping English express cartridges for dangerous game, the few exceptions being a few small-bores made for wealthy Englishmen or Americans with nothing more useful to spend their money on. I can cite as examples a James Woodward .303 British double rifle (the .303 being the British service cartridge, hardly an elephant stopper) and a Westley Richards chambered for the .22/3000 R2 Lovell (an American wildcat cartridge of years gone past).

Nearly all British doubles (only a few were or are made on the Continent) are side by side doubles. (There is a story about a Tim Murphy, one of Morgan's Riflemen, who mortally wounded British General Simon Fraser off his horse with a spectacular 200-yard shot at Saratoga during the Revolution. The shot probably happened, and was quite a feat — but it's also supposed to have occurred with an over/under rifle!)

The alignment of the barrels on a double rifle is a lot more difficult than that of a shotgun, simply because only a single projectile is involved. The process is called "regulating," and it's accomplished by firing. Both barrels of a double rifle must deliver their shots to the same spot. Since a right barrel will shoot to the right of the mark, and a left to the left — because the barrels are off the center line — it follows that they must be made to converge. And since rifles shoot differently when held at the shoulder than when clamped in a vise, the only satisfactory method of regulating is by actual shooting. *With the load that will be used.* It also follows that two loads won't shoot to the same point of impact, except in rare instances.

In regulating, the barrels are positioned in several places by spacers. A couple of shots are fired, the spacers are refitted, and the guns are fired again. This is repeated until both barrels are precisely right. Infinite care, and long experience, plus the skill to remove metal no thicker than a layer of smoke, is required for this regulating, which should help explain why a double costs so much money. There was also a time when workers in other countries were satisfied with far less pay than American workers. Indeed, that was even true in different parts of America. But the days when you could pay a skilled Japanese craftsman a bag of rice a week are long gone.

BARREL LIFE

The subject of barrel life — how long a rifle barrel will last before it's shot out — is one about which much mystery exists. First, the rifleman's term "shot out" is applied when a target barrel loses its gilt-edge accuracy. When a barrel that's been shooting half-inch groups consistently suddenly starts to shoot larger groups, it's shot out. That won't mean a thing to the average deer hunter who shoots his rifle five or six times a year or maybe less, but it's a decided factor to any shooter who uses his guns to any degree. Barrel steel has a direct bearing on barrel life, but there are several other factors that bear as well. Chamber a soft, mild steel-carbon-manganese barrel for the .220 Swift, .264 Winchester, 7mm Remington, or one of the other hotshots and your barrel will be shot out in less than a thousand shots, possibly far less. That's why stainless steel is used for these fiery cartridges.

We're talking about barrels being shot out due to *erosion*, which, in turn, is defined as washing away, just as a bank of earth is eroded by rain water cascading down and floating out the soil. Steel barrels erode the same way inasmuch as the intense heat of firing produces a much higher temperature than the melting point of steel. So the surface of the bore melts very slightly. But only very slightly. Then, it is rapidly cooled by the mass of steel underneath. The extremely rapid flash melting and cooling causes miniscule flaking, which is then pushed out by the next shot fired. We are talking about incredibly small amounts of metal, but when you project them over many shots, it builds up to a significant amount. That amount is accelerated with hotter cartridges and it's accelerated even more by rapid shooting. So, especially if you have a red-hot cartridge, shoot it slowly and avoid getting the barrel excessively hot. On the other hand, there are .22 rifles that have fired hundreds of thousands of shots with no sign of wear. The late Colonel Larson, an exhibition shooter who shot for Marlin using a Model 39M that he bought himself over the counter, put more than a million shots through that one rifle. (He used .22 Shorts with "gallery" bullets that break up on impact.)

Improper cleaning probably ruins more barrels than shooting. Whereas shooting out barrels happens at the chamber end, because that's where the greatest heat occurs, cleaning ruins them at the muzzle. Always clean a rifle from the breech end if that's possible. There are many rifles where it can't be done, however, and you must clean from the muzzle. This presents two difficulties: It is hard to properly clean the chamber since you're working from the other end, and it's hard to get at. The major problem is that your cleaning rod is going to rub the rifling at the muzzle. Since this is the last point at which the rifling can guide the bullet, it's the most vital point. There are cleaning devices designed to center a cleaning rod and you'd be well advised to use one.

LINERS

When a barrel becomes shot out or otherwise worn, or if it is desired to change the cartridge to a smaller bore, or if you want a new barrel but prefer not to disturb the looks of the original for some sentimental reason, there is a way. This is called relining, and it consists of drilling out and reaming the original barrel to a precise measurement and then soldering a barrel liner in place. The liner will be a thin-walled tube nicely rifled and often already chambered. The English firm of Parker-Hale did a big business in barrel liners at one time, mostly in .22 caliber.

Often, when a barrel becomes shot out, the owner has it rebored and rifled to a larger caliber. Say, if you have a .220 Swift that's quit shooting well, it can be rebored to .30 caliber for example (actually it can be rebored to any large caliber so long as the reaming will clean out the old rifling). This can then be used for a .30/06 or .308 or whatever you wish that is compatible with the action used.

The gunsmith doing the job should re-mark the barrel with the new chambering. I remember quite a few years ago I got a letter from someone who had bought, second-hand, a rifle that bore my stamp on the barrel. He was mad as hell. He claimed the gun shot very poorly and I had produced a rotten job. So I asked him to give me the number on the bottom of the barrel, which he did by return mail. What I learned astounded me. The job upon leaving my shop was a .22 caliber; what this man had was a 6mm rifle. That meant that someone else had rebored the job and rechambered it but had left my name on! As you can see, there are many ways in which you can get burned.

INTERCHANGEABLE BARRELS

These are rarely found on rifles, but on occasion one will be seen, especially on some of the finer English guns. It's relatively easy to build a double rifle with two sets of barrels in different calibers; it's quite another to build a bolt-action rifle with interchangeable barrels that can be depended upon to maintain accuracy. Some rifle barrels are made with inserted chambers; this is a more common occurrence with machine-gun barrels and is seldom necessary in the sporting field. Machine-gun barrels often use inserted chambers made of Stellite, or some other hard metal (carbide is another), because they offer longer barrel life.

PROOFING

The twist barrels used in early barrel-making days were proofed before finishing to disclose any imperfections. The same procedure is used today, although there is much less reason for it now. In most of the world proofing is done either by the government or, for example, by the "Gunmakers' Company" (London) and the "Guardians of the Birmingham Proof House" (Birmingham). In America, proofing is handled by each manufacturer. Not only is the American system more democratic — it's also less costly, and you can assume, correctly, that any gun made here and bearing the name of a reliable producer is safe and dependable.

In England the gunmaker must run to the proof house with his rough-bored barrels to obtain "provisional proof" just as he did in the days of twist barrels. Then, after the gun is finished, he must return to obtain the "definite proof." Nearly all guns imported into Britain must also pass British proof; notable exceptions are those of most major American manufacturers.

Today's proofing consists of placing the gun in a steel box after loading it with a "proof load," generally about one third more powerful than a standard load, and firing it remotely. If no imperfections are evident, the barrel is stamped with the maker's "proof mark."

HOW BARRELS ARE FASTENED

Most barrels are fastened into the receivers by

An older system of fastening barrel to receiver is seen in this Savage Model 23AA which happened to be my first gun (at the age of 12). The barrel and receiver were made of one piece of steel in this series which also consisted of a .22 Hornet, .25/20, and .32/20. Mine was a .22 Long Rifle. While an excellent rifle, which has long been off the market, it did not have an ideal breeching system and, I suspect, was costly to manufacture.

threading. These threads usually are, and should be, closely fitted and the barrels are turned up tightly by holding them in a rugged barrel vise and using a large and heavy action wrench capable of giving the operator vast leverage to get a tight closure. Other barrels are screwed just as tightly into a barrel extension, which, in turn, is fastened to the receiver; in such cases the breechbolt locks into the barrel extension.

Most cheap .22s are pinned in place, the shank of the barrel and the hole in the receiver providing a fairly close fit. This is a perfectly acceptable method and one used on a surprising number of higher priced rifles. I'm just old-fashioned enough, however, to think that the barrel on a good .22 rifle ought to be threaded though.

This subject quite naturally leads into those accessories that are fastened onto barrels, such as sights, forearms, gas cylinders, operating rods, and, often, all manner of things that have little to do with the basic operation of a barrel. There are a couple of old wives' tales that ought to be put to rest once and for all. One of them is that you must never cut a slot in a rifle barrel, because, it's said, the barrel will never shoot as good since the slot will upset the vibrations. This is pure nonsense. I have to admit that I used to believe it myself but have learned the truth. Another says a one-piece stock shoots more accurately than a two-piece stock. That's just as wrong and, again, I had to learn this one the hard way. (One sage once said it was more important to learn what has been tried and failed to work than much of anything else. He had a point.)

Slots simply don't make a good barrel shoot poorly. Moreover, a one-piece stock is no more conducive to accuracy than a two-piece. But a great deal depends on what kind of a lash-up is employed to hold various attachments onto the barrel. Ruger and Browning, in their single-shot rifles, have provided a "hanger," attached to the receiver to which the stock is fastened so it won't touch the barrel. This is one solution, and it's an accepted one. Under this situation barrel and stock should not touch. Anything on a barrel that touches the wood is going to affect accuracy, just as accuracy is affected when you rest the barrel against a fence post or a tree. All these things affect accuracy because they restrict vibration. If they do so the very same precise way for each shot, the accuracy will be the same. But if there are variations (and variations occur when barrels heat up) then accuracy will suffer.

It is extremely difficult to categorize in this area. Gas guns require a gas cylinder, piston, and some method of transmitting the force through an operating rod back to the action. You can't avoid this. How to accomplish it is what counts and there are far too many systems to enumerate here. It should be said however that the requirements of a hunting rifle are vastly different from those for a target rifle. By this I mean that a hunting rifle has to be deadly, absolutely sure, for the first shot. And it will help if it's also accurate for the first three shots. Beyond that, it really doesn't matter. If you haven't bagged your buck by the time you're fired the third shot you may as well forget it.

So your hunting rifle should be tested differently than your target rifle. Fire one shot from a clean, cold, and very slightly oiled bore. Clean the rifle, lightly oil the bore, and set it aside again for maybe a half hour to cool off. Then fire another shot. It should come very close to the first impact. Move your sights to where you want the point of impact and repeat. When you have determined that your hunting rifle is capable of putting that first shot from a cold, clean, lightly oiled bore where you want it then, and only then, see what it will do for a three-shot group. More than three shots for this sort of rifle are not necessary. Another benefit you'll realize from this sort of shooting is that your barrel will last longer.

RIFLE CHAMBERS

The word "chamber," with regard to barrels, refers to that portion of the breech end of the bore that is reamed out to accommodate the cartridge. The chamber must be precise, smooth, and dimensionally correct. Chambers are usually cut with a succession of reamers to the correct depth and then polished. It may be easiest to follow the procedures used by a custom gunsmith, because they are not buried in production jargon on automatic machinery, although the result is essentially the same.

With the barrel turning slowly in the lathe, a drill bit (an ordinary drill bit), smaller in diameter than the roughing reamer, is used to remove some of the excess metal. Then the roughing reamer is fed slowly into the barrel, removed often to clean chips out, and lubricated with liberal applications of cutting oil. The roughing reamer will cut most of the chamber within a few thousandths of an inch, leaving the remainder for the finishing reamer. Both roughing and finishing reamers have a pilot that exactly fits the bore to keep the reamer in alignment and, of course, the reamer is fed into the barrel in a perfectly straight line with the bore.

Next the roughed chamber is carefully cleaned and the finishing reamer used for the final cutting. This reamer also – usually – cuts the "throat," which is the tapering of the breech ends of the lands so the bullet has a seat. This was sometimes called the leade (or leed). Using the GO and NO GO headspace gauges, the chamber is cut to a depth that will accept the GO gauge but will not accept the NO GO gauge. After final reaming, the chamber is carefully wiped clean of chips and oil and then polished, with the lathe running at high speed. With a good finish reamer, the amount of polishing needed is minimal.

HEADSPACE

Headspace is a mysterious word that has a simple yet most vital meaning; it refers to the fore-and-aft distance provided for the cartridge. If this distance is too short, the cartridge isn't going to go in far enough to allow the action to close. If it's too long, the cartridge will go in too far and, when fired, the propellant gas will create a dangerous situation that can manifest itself in a number of ways. A more precise definition is: the distance between the bolt face (in closed and locked position) and that part of the chamber that prevents further forward movement of the cartridge. This differs for various cartridges. Some definitions, and typical cartridges, include. *Rimless*; From the bolt face to a point on the shoulder, the shoulder being defined as the sharp taper down to the neck that holds the bullet (.30/06). *Rimmed*; From the bolt face to the front of the rim (.30/30). *Belted*; From the bolt face to the front of the belt (.300 Winchester Magnum). *Straight*; From the bolt face to the cartridge-case mouth (.45 ACP).

Obviously, excessive headspace can be a function of either rifle or cartridge. If rifle, the chamber has been cut too deeply – meaning that the barrel will have to be set back (which can usually be done). If cartridge, it's another matter entirely, often a function of faulty reloading. Some reloaders have learned, to their dismay, that they can create excess headspace easily and innocently by shoving the shoulder of a rimless cartridge back too far or by trimming the case mouth of a straight case back too far. Those are obvious. The result is that the cartridge goes in too far and the primer usually pops out a little after firing. What also can happen, and is less easily understood, lies in the case of a reduced load in rimless cartridges. A reduced load is one usually used with lead bullets that use less powder than normal. They are used for target shooting where a lower noise level is sometimes desired and where the shooting may be over shorter ranges. They are also easier on barrel life. Reduced loads are also frequently used for edible small game to destroy very little meat. When a reduced load is fired, the blow of the firing pin is often sufficient to drive the cartridge forward a little bit, but the resultant pressure is not enough to fully expand the case. If the same case is reloaded enough times with reduced loads, the firing pin shortening it a little each time, eventually there will be excessive headspace with accompanying nasty results such as blowing out primers, separating cases in the middle, and even spilling gas into the action.

RIBS

The rib on a rifle barrel usually takes the form of a short rib on which are mounted rear, open sights. Sometimes a short rib is also employed as part of a scope mount. Ribs, however, are really one of those little niceties that one finds on expensive custom rifles. They're nice but not really necessary. Still a nice rib sure does dress up a rifle barrel. These attachments had their origin, I believe, in the British way of doing things, where a neat, folding rear sight was installed for each range. Sometimes these were up to 500 yards, which meant that there were five little sight leafs, each one folding down neatly into the rib when not used. Some refer to them as a "British dress parade" of sights, but such people have no regard for exquisite workmanship. Regardless of whether they are functional or not (you don't often make a hit with a .465 No. 2 Nitro Express double rifle at 500 yards), they are slick as hell and time-consuming to make. I've made ribs, and I've made them with those little sights, but it's a job I'd prefer not to tackle again. That may explain why you see so few of them. The rib for use as a scope

Gun blueing is a messy process. Here, a rack of rifle barrels is being lifted out of the blueing bath at a major arms plant. The barrels are rinsd in hot water and then oiled.

mount base, or for part of a mount base, is another matter entirely. It's easier to make and looks just as neat. There are some rifles that require it, or something similar, for scope mounting. One of these is Ruger's Number 1 single-shot rifle. You can't mount a scope on the receiver as on a bolt action, because it's too short. So Ruger supplies what is known as a "quarter rib." This means short, and it serves as a base on which to anchor the scope mount. It also looks elegant.

RECOIL COMPENSATORS

From time to time the use of a device known as a recoil compensator comes to life. Briefly, these are devices designed to direct some of the propellant gases upwards (and sometimes slightly back and up) and thus reduce recoil and muzzle jump. Every time that life is breathed back into these gadgets, there is ample laboratory evidence offered to prove they work. Maybe so. But nobody is ever convinced for very long and the things die down again for another generation. I guess I've straddled a couple of generations for I've seen them come and go twice already.

There are two basic methods of accomplishing this feat. One is to attach something to the muzzle by threading it on (which means threads must be cut in the barrel), with a hole large enough for the bullet to go through. It has a vent on top and a cavity against which the gas is supposed to push. It does this to some degree, and tends to pull the gun forward and push the muzzle down. But it has another side effect: If you're not wearing ear protectors, it will knock your hearing silly for a week. Another way of performing the same feat is to drill (or otherwise cut) a hole or several holes into the upper side of the barrel itself out near the muzzle. They make the same claims.

I admit that I subscribe to the old Harry Pope opinion on this subject. Pope said, "The only holes that should be drilled in a rifle barrel ought to be as close to the muzzle as possible, and just in front of it."

BARREL LENGTH

Barrel length is measured by poking a rod down the barrel of a gun and measuring the distance from the closed bolt face to the muzzle of the barrel. By Federal law, a shotgun or high-power rifle must be a minimum of 16 inches long, a .22 rifle at least 14 inches. These Feds operate in strange ways. What the law means is that you cannot take a rifle and manufacture a handgun out of it with a barrel shorter than the above, or you have a sawed-off rifle and you are illegal as hell. If the gun was originally manufactured to be a rifle it must always retain the above minimum barrel lengths.

There are some small rifle actions that would

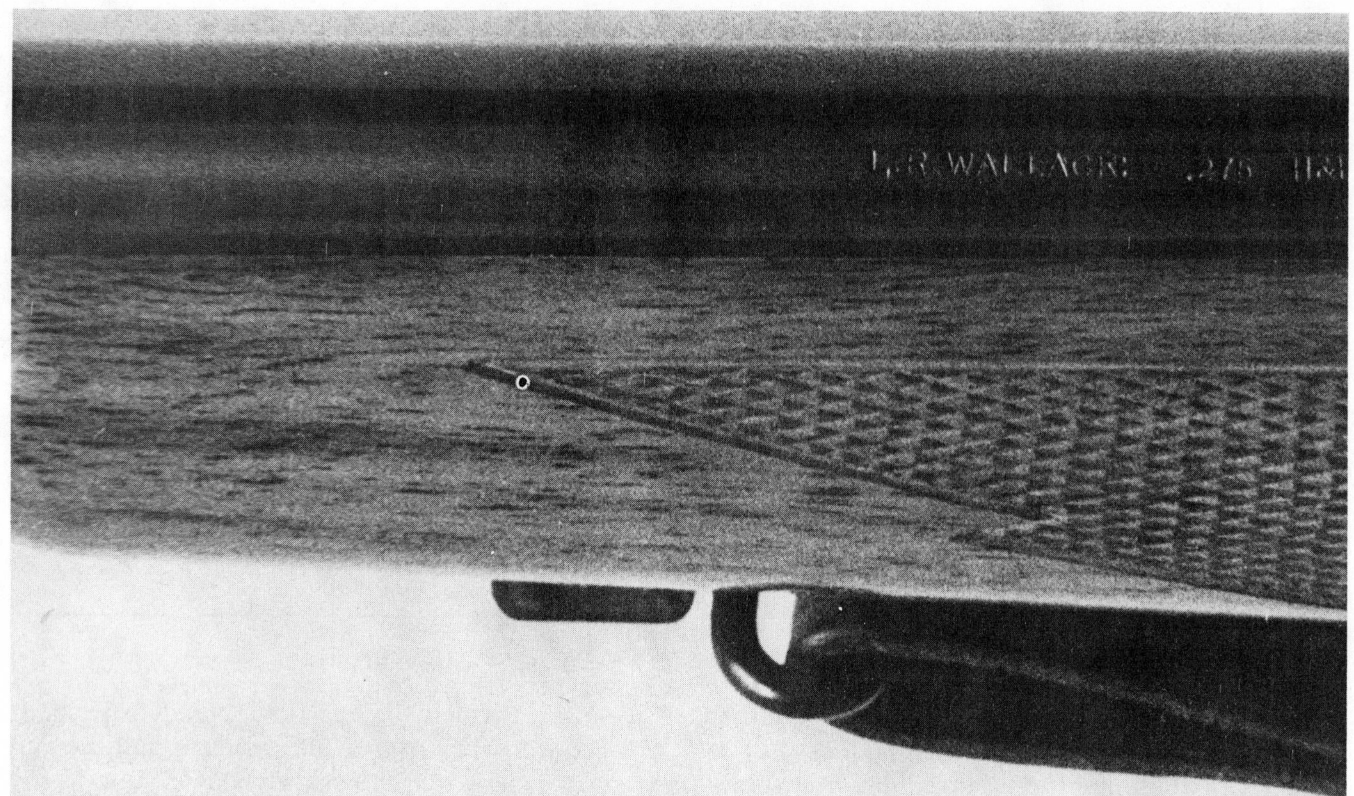

The custom maker should stamp his work the same way as any factory. This is a standard way of doing the job—stamp the barrel where the name can be seen clearly along with the caliber. I always found it good practice to repeat my name underneath the barrel out of sight and assign a coded number. Then this number along, with all pertinent details of the job, were entered into a log.

make a great pistol; a case in point is the Remington short-bolt action that has been withdrawn from the market but appeared for several years as Model 600 and 660 in calibers .65 and .350, both short Magnums of considerable power. (Remington's "Mohawk 600," a promotional rifle, uses the same action.) At about the same time Remington made its .221 Fireball pistol using the same action. The Fireball is indeed a fireball, since it packs close to the wallop of the .222 cartridge. It is a legitimate handgun because that's the way it is manufactured. But if you attempted to take one of these actions and make a handgun out of it, you would be breaking the law.

CHAPTER TEN

THE GUN STOCK

Nowhere in all gundom will you hear more varying opinions, more references to ancestries, and more downright prejudices than when discussing stocks. Even at that, most of what you hear is wrong! This is not to set myself up as the only authority who's right all the time – far from it. Subjective opinion is strong regarding the gunstock, although a vast amount of the discussion can be categorized.

Subjectivity comes more into its own with regard to the shape of a gunstock than any other single factor. For example, there is what is popularly called the "California school" of stock design. That refers to the style popularized by Roy Weatherby. The opposite is called "classical." Admittedly the terms are about as accurate as calling a politician a liberal or a conservative. Just the same, there are extremes in stock design and what pleases you is right for you. Another excellent analogy would be women: Some like blondes, some like brunettes. Some are leg men, others focus their attention on the bust. These things are purely subjective. There is no reason, except personal preference, to choose one over the other.

So be it with the gunstock. Let me say at the outset that I am strongly in the classic stock corner in every respect. By the same token, I have great respect for what Roy Weatherby has done in the world of guns and, for those who prefer that general look, Weatherby presents an excellent product. Before getting further into the subject, let's review some terms.

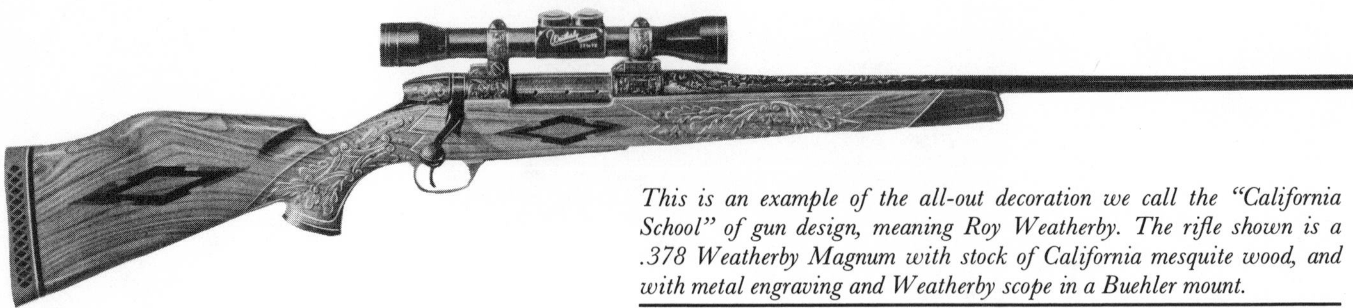

This is an example of the all-out decoration we call the "California School" of gun design, meaning Roy Weatherby. The rifle shown is a .378 Weatherby Magnum with stock of California mesquite wood, and with metal engraving and Weatherby scope in a Buehler mount.

Butt: The rear end of the stock, generally from the action back and often referred to as the buttstock (especially on any gun with a two-piece stock).

Butt plate: A protective pad covering the rear surface of the butt, often of steel, plastic, or rubber. If soft and cushioned, the buttplate is sometimes called a recoil pad.

Heel: The top of the butt with gun in normal position.

Toe: The bottom of the butt with gun in normal position.

Comb: The top line of the buttstock, the front end of which is called the nose; the rear is the heel as already defined.

Cheekpiece: A raised portion along the side of the stock extending from the comb down in varying shapes which is designed to be an aid in aiming with a scope sight.

Monte Carlo: A top line (comb) with a dip down to the heel that lowers the buttplate while keeping the shooter's eye level relatively high.

Pistol grip: Which really needs no definition.

Drop: A distance, measured at comb and heel (two measurements), from a continuation of the centerline of the gun bore.

Pitch: The angle formed by the buttplate and the continuation of the bore's centerline.

Length of pull: The distance from the center of the trigger to the center of the buttplate.

Cast-off: The amount the buttstock is out of line (to the right) with the bore's centerline.

Cast-on: The same as cast-off, but to the left. Normally a right-handed person requires a small amount of cast-off, a leftie a small amount of cast-on.

Forearm: The part of the stock lying forward of the action, sometimes called a fore end.

Inletting: The fitting of metal into wood.

Bedding: The fitting of a barrel (usually a rifle barrel) in its channel in the stock.

MATERIALS

Stocks are made of a variety of hardwoods. Sometimes the nature of the gun to be built dictates the type of wood demanded. By this I mean that a hard-recoiling monster like the .458 Winchester Magnum requires a much tougher piece of wood than a .22 Long Rifle – to use extreme examples.

The wood used must be capable of holding the action in place during recoil, sometimes for many thousands of shots. A wood that splits easily, or that warps freely and does not have stability, is of no use in a gunstock. Gunmakers learned long ago that the most desirable wood for a gunstock was walnut, because it has a combination of strength, weight, and stability that is equaled by few other woods and exceeded by none. There are, however, two distinct types of walnut. These are English walnut (*Juglans regia*), which is native to all of Central and Southern Europe and the Near East; and American or black walnut (*Juglans nigra*). English walnut is the very best material available anywhere at any price. It alone possesses the most desirable hardness, closeness of grain, and beauty of figure that make it the first choice of anyone who knows anything about guns. Black walnut is the next best choice.

English walnut is often called "French walnut," largely because that country has produced most of this wood for many years. The same wood has been called a wide variety of other names such as Circassian walnut and others. English walnut is the proper name and the name of the edible walnuts with which we are all familiar. Early colonists brought seedlings to America with them. Today,

This is just about as fine an English walnut stock blank as you'll ever see. Such wood is rare today and, if you can find it, you will pay close to a king's ransom. It would be tragic to buy such a blank and not have it worked on by one of our top stockmakers.

many of these trees are grown in California under irrigation and yield lots of nuts and some reasonably good wood for gunstocks. I say "reasonably" good because this wood does not compare with that from a tree grown slowly, in the harshness of high altitude, and in soil with little richness where it must struggle for its very survival. The force-fed, irrigated American variety will have coarser grain and will not have the figure and color of its European cousin.

The most magical of all names in gunstock wood is Circassian walnut, a term highly promoted by gunmakers a few generations back. True Circassian walnut is the same species of tree that grows in France (or California); the only difference is that it comes from an area in the USSR north of Turkey. No gunstock wood has come from this part of the world for many years; in fact, most stock wood sold as Circassian came from France anyway. Circassian always was more myth than reality. Which is neither here nor there for the wood is equally good.

European walnut picks up its color – some of which runs from nearly white, through the reds and oranges, to brown and black streaks – from the minerals in the soil. (This is why two identical seedlings, one planted in an irrigated walnut grove in California and the other near a mountain top in France, will produce vastly different wood. The latter will be far superior, especially in terms of its grain characteristics and coloration.) Grain, the direction in which the fibers lie, gives the stock its strength and stability. Color lines do not always follow the grain line, although they usually run close to that followed by the grain.

The finest grain, and often the finest colorations, come from wood cut near the butt of a tree. An ancient walnut tree that's three or four feet or more thick at the butt will, when properly dug out of the ground and correctly sawed, produce dozens of exquisitely figured gunstock blanks. The areas around burls and branches often yield interesting grain patterns. By now you should have a mental picture of some wood buyer standing next to an ancient walnut tree on the slopes of a mountain far from civilization somewhere in France or northern Italy. He buys the tree, directs its felling (which must be done just right or the tree may split), then directs digging out the butt at a depth of several feet. This then is pulled, pushed, and dragged to the sawmill where it must be carefully studied before any cutting. Alas, however, the chances are that the buyer is buying for a furniture company rather than a gunmaker. In this event, hundreds and thousands of potential top-grade gunstock blanks wind up as furniture veneer.

As this is being written, in 1976, there is little European walnut available in the higher grades, and what is available is extremely expensive. In terms of 1976 dollars, the highest-grade English walnut gunstock blank (that means the roughly sawn stock wood with no labor expended) is valued at from several hundred to nearly a thousand dollars, depending on the exact grade of the wood itself.

The American black walnut tree is second in preference for gunstocks, and produces a good stock that is used by most American gunmakers. Some American walnut has fine figure and some has good coloration too. No matter how good American walnut is, or how pretty, it is coarser than European which means it isn't as strong. You can usually cut American walnut checkering to not more than about 18 lines per inch while some makers cut up to 28 lines in good English walnut.

There are some guns that ought to be stocked with American walnut despite the superiority of English. An American classic like the Winchester

94 just wouldn't look right with an English walnut stock.

Despite the ravages of gunmakers over 200 years and furniture makers and occasional other uses, there is still a surprisingly sufficient supply of black walnut available. Most of it today comes from the Ozark Mountains. Even though gunmakers are gobbling up prodigious quantities of trees annually, the supply continues to hold up. Yet, you can read in old accounts that during the early 1800s the supplies of walnut were being exhausted and some substitutes were being used.

Substitutes are still being used today. There is an item in the trade called a "promotional" brand, meaning that it is the same basic model as, say, the Ajax Model 100 except that instead of being stamped Ajax, it may be stamped Centurion Model 10. But it will be exactly the same as the famous and popular Ajax 100 except it will have a "walnut-finished hardwood" stock. This means birch or elm or sycamore. It also means a lower price and the manufacturer doesn't care what the retailer charges for this promotional branded gun while he prefers that the Ajax 100 continue to retail at its "suggested price." You will often get a good buy, however, with one of these promotional guns.

The same thing is often true with private branded guns, guns that are also virtually identical to some famous models but appear at Sears under the Ted Williams brand, or Western Auto's "Revelation" or whatever. Depending on the specifications made by the private-brand buyer, this gun may or may not have a walnut stock.

There are a lot of other woods that have been used for gunstocks over the years, some of them acceptable, some of them excellent but so rare as to be improbable, and many of them unacceptable. (There is little point in expending a lot of costly labor on the wrong kind of wood.) Stocks have been made of maple (hard, rock, or sugar maple), apple, pear, myrtlewood, cherry, beech, and many other woods. A large number of Kentucky rifles were made with maple and some with cherry stocks. Neither wood is as good as walnut although there are some who will argue that point.

The gun you buy will probably have an American walnut stock if it's one of the better grades of American gun. If it's a very high-quality import the stock will be English walnut and the same if it's a quality American custom gun. If it's a lesser brand, you will probably have a birch or elm stock. Those are generalities and subject to changes. Some of the wood being used on today's "finer" imported guns is a shame. I have seen, on today's market, gunstock wood that is English walnut all right but that is so plain and of so poor a color that the manufacturer really ought to hide his head in shame rather than market the product at the prices he's asking. I acknowledge that good wood is hard to get, but there is no excuse for offering at suggested prices of more than a thousand dollars guns that have stocks that are about as handsome as a pine plank.

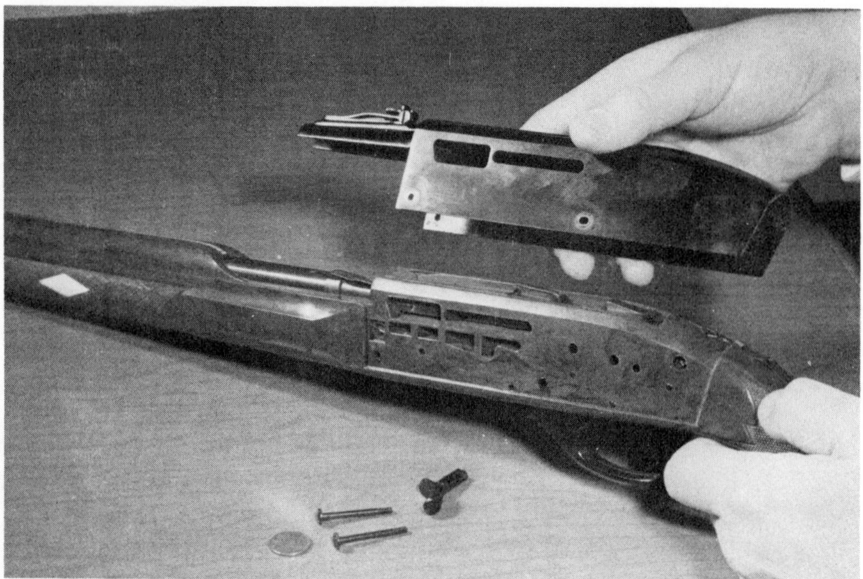

The Remington Nylon 66 with receiver plate removed. In this outstanding breakthrough, the entire stock and receiver are a single piece of nylon and the steel breech bolt rides back and forth in nylon.

TECHNOLOGICAL BREAKTHROUGH

Some years ago Remington provided the shooting world with an unheard of development — the nylon stock. This was introduced on the Model Nylon 66, a .22 Long Rifle autoloading rifle that quickly became one of the industry's best sellers. Remington and its parent company, DuPont, worked together on this project with the result that a structural nylon (called Zytel 101) could be used as both a stock and receiver. That became a double-departure for not only was the stock made of nylon; so was the receiver, all formed in a single piece. A thin steel cover over the action makes it look like it has a steel receiver. In developing this rifle, Remington engineers discovered that nylon needs no lubrication — another strong point. The little rifle actually has only a barrel and breechbolt, among its major parts, that are steel. The steel breechbolt rides back and forth in nylon and, after firing hundreds of thousands of shots the engineers could measure the wear on the steel bolt, but not on the nylon!

The other leading features of the Nylon 66 are that it has strength and stability far beyond that of wood. At the time of its introduction, Remington showed a heavy automobile running over the rifle, which presumably came up shooting as well as ever after that test. Remington colored the nylon brown or black so you had a choice of color. There was no great pretense to make the nylon look like wood — for which Remington should be praised, because the gun stands on its own feet.

The big surprise to me is that Remington has not carried this concept beyond the .22 stage. At least to my knowledge they haven't; but I should think the military potentials might be enormous. They did launch two abortive nylon models on the heels of the 66 but both were quickly abandoned. These were a lever-action .22 (the first lever-action rifle Remington had ever marketed) and a bolt .22. Both flopped because they did not sell.

There have been many other plastic stocks over the years (I assume you can call nylon a plastic), one of the old favorites being something called tenite. Some of these warped when left out in the sun and they were generally terrible. Today's plastics are much improved and I suspect you can look forward to seeing more plastics in guns rather than less. I view this as both good and bad. Quite frankly I think the Remington development with their Nylon 66 is good. Not that the rifle interests me from any personal viewpoint except for the breakthrough that it represents. I certainly have no desire to own one. But that's strictly a personal reaction (and I saw a Nylon 66 long before it was ever introduced to the public). I do respect and applaud the research and development that went into this little rifle.

LAMINATIONS

During World War II, German gunmakers had difficulty getting adequate supplies of gunstock wood so they came up with laminated stocks, consisting of strips about 1/16 inch thick and glued together. These made adequate military stocks and solved what had to have been a critical problem.

Following the war — and where the idea came up first, I have no idea — a number of American experimentalists used laminated stocks for totally different reasons. In the late 1940s, a friend of mine named John Franks experimented with laminations and was among the first, although by no means the first, to do so. The main purpose of laminating was, unlike the German reason, to help prevent warping of the rifle stock which would change the zero. The solution, if that's really the right word, was to place two pieces of wood opposite each other with opposing grain so that one would offset the other.

Laminating was held back for many years because most glues were water soluble and who wanted a gun whose stock would come unglued in the rain? Once the modern epoxies came along, this wonderful world was wide open for the laminated school of stock construction. Some of these experiments led to alternating light and dark colors; one that I can recall even had a strip of purple wood running down its center.

This is a strictly personal opinion but I have always believed that a laminated stock, no matter what woods were employed, looked awful. You can also dispute part of the warping theory since wood absorbs moisture and, despite opposing grain structures which can and will offset each other, it's also true that both pieces will swell when the air gets humid and that this swelling will present different pressures against the barrel and so affect accuracy.

These things get quite complicated; the laminators thought they had all problems licked but found out it wasn't so. The cure-all hasn't yet been found. When it comes to sound gunstock design there really hasn't been much new in years and years.

DESIGNING A GUNSTOCK

There are few people capable of designing a gunstock that has the right proportions and I don't care whether he's in the research-and-development section of one of our leading companies or runs a one-man custom shop. Actually, most of the better ones are in the latter category. I'm told by some factories that their machinery can't reproduce certain curves and shapes, which is something I can't accept. Some of the worst stocks are turned out by people who call themselves custom gunsmiths. It seems that one definition of "custom" means anything not produced by a large factory. That's ridiculous, but it's accepted by too many people who ought to know better.

There are a lot of custom stockmakers. There are a few very good ones and a very few whose work is excellent. These men are true artists. Constructing a gunstock properly is sculpting of the highest order. I have shown the work of several of these men whose work I consider to be in the front line of American gunstock artistry. There are a few others capable of work as fine and there are also a few small companies turning out truly fine work entirely of their own manufacture. Moreover, the custom departments of America's largest companies are also capable of turning out excellent custom work. In many cases, however, the work of these larger companies, especially in terms of stock design, is not up to the standards of our finest custom craftsmen.

THE RIFLE STOCK

The rifle stock differs considerably from the shotgun stock in that the latter arm is *pointed* rather than aimed. Except in rare instances, rifles are intended to be aimed precisely in order to deliver a single bullet, as opposed to the shotgun's charge of several hundred pellets. Perhaps the only significant instance where a rifle is fired by pointing, like a shotgun, is that of a quick shot at short range such as is sometimes necessary when pursuing a wounded dangerous beast in heavy cover. All of this means that the *fit* of a shotgun stock is much more important, because when the gun is shouldered it must be automatically pointed where you're looking. In the case of a rifle you can accommodate your body to the stock rather than the other way around.

Rifle stocks come in two basic types: the one-piece stock common to nearly all bolt-action rifles, and those whose buttstocks are separated from the forearms because there's an action in between. Two-piece stocks are common on lever, pump, and many autoloading rifles. It is said that the one-piece stock is more accurate. This is untrue. Rifle accuracy depends upon a vast number of factors, among which are bedding of both action and barrel in the stock. These factors are important, but whether the stock is a single piece of wood has no bearing on the subject — other things being the same. Let's put that tale to rest right now. It's not true.

As a matter of fact, I believe it to be true that the usual rifle with two-piece stock in out-of-the-box condition will deliver as good accuracy — if not better — than a rifle with a one-piece stock under the same situation. The reason is that there's less wood to act adversely against the accuracy potential of the metal parts. It's easier for example, to make the front end of a buttstock fit the rear end of an all-metal receiver evenly and to secure it tightly with a through-bolt than it is to bed the whole length of an action as in a bolt rifle. When the forearm is properly attached, and most makers have learned how to do this, such a rifle will deliver decent accuracy. One-piece stock bolt actions can be tuned up (usually) to shoot better than when you took them out of the box, but the average guy hasn't the slightest idea how to perform that operation and he shouldn't try.

INLETTING

The act of cutting out the wood to let in the metal parts is called inletting. Let's take a bolt-action rifle: For a custom stock, where the stockmaker works with a stock blank, he first trues up the top and one side. These must be perfectly straight and square, because he will make all his layout lines from these surfaces. Some wood may be removed with power tools, but most will be cut away with chisels, gouges, and scrapers, all honed to razor sharpness. The custom gunsmith will completely

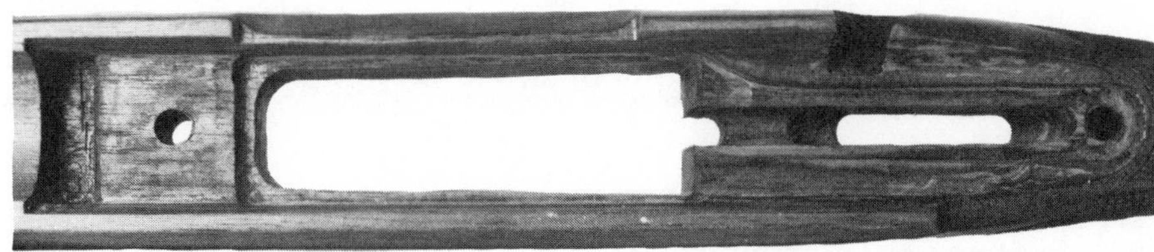

This is reasonably good inletting for a Model 70 Winchester action in English walnut. I did the work, so am free to criticize it. A couple of chisel marks at the bottom of the recoil-lug channel mar its looks; most of the other marks you see are from lampblack, the agent used for spotting.

inlet the barreled action (with all parts removed); then, one at a time, will add trigger and other parts and make the necessary cuts for them. When he has achieved the inletting to his satisfaction, he will inlet and apply the buttplate, grip cap, forearm tip, and whatever other attachments have been ordered. All this before any shaping is done. Under these circumstances, and while there are a few tricks to the trade, inletting is a purely mechanical function. The wood should appear as an exact mirror image of the metal with the proper clearances in certain places to allow movement of such parts as the trigger so they won't bind. The fit of metal to wood, inside as well as outside, must be such that you couldn't fit a human hair anywhere between steel and walnut. There is simply no excuse for anything else and if you've ordered a custom stock and it has any gaps, you have been taken.

The stockmaker has allowed for the proper measurements, such as drops, pitch, length of pull, and so on, before he ever touched an inletting tool. It takes time to make such a stock and it will cost you a lot of money, but if you can appreciate good workmanship, you'll get more value for your money here than just about anyplace else I can think of.

The custom maker now shapes his stock, rough cutting away some of the excess wood by band saw, even chipping carefully with a sharp hatchet in some cases. Final shaping, however, gets down to such tools as chisels, gouges, spokeshaves, and files. Each stock must not only conform to the dimensions specified by the buyer, but it must also match the metal parts, because the completed product must look as though everything belonged. By this I mean that slightly different shape concessions would be made for a Model 70 Winchester stock than for a Mauser or than for a Springfield and so on. These things are accomplished by eye and by touch and feel. You can't train anyone to do them because no two artists work precisely the same. (You can duplicate a stock exactly, but that's not what I'm talking about.)

What a stockmaker does to make a fine handmade stock is easier to understand than how a large manufacturer produces his. The latter has to perform the same basic steps to transform a blank into a finished stock, but he attacks the problem from a different direction entirely. First of all he sticks a "center" in each end of the blank. One of these will be the driving center, which means it will rotate as the machine tells it to. Then the stock, along with up to 23 others depending on the equipment, is placed in the turning lathe — a machine similar to those used in the furniture industry. With a pilot made out of cast iron, the machine is turned on and as many cutters as there are stock blanks go to work. The machine is guided by the pilot and the net result is that all of the stocks are turned to the shape of the pilot.

Inletting is accomplished in the same basic manner, after outside shaping — a reversal of custom procedure. Final inletting is done by hand in most cases, but not all. The quality of most American inletting is reasonably good, given the price charged for the particular model. The quality of inletting of the two-piece stocks, however, is generally better than that for the bolt action.

Final finishing of the outside is accomplished by hand. Here again this depends on the process each company uses. Some manufacturers will sand down their stocks with the metal parts in place, which is the best way to get a nicely matched surface. Stocks are then numbered with the action's serial number so that, after the metal is blued and the stock is finished, the same two will come back together in final assembly. This procedure is not followed by all makers nor for all models. The worker simply holds the stock against sanding belts to finish a stock after which the finish is applied. The modern stock finish is a high-gloss acrylic of some sort on most production guns, which gives you that shiny surface many admire, but I hate. I must admit the surface is tough as nails and resists bull briars and shirt buttons pretty well. I still don't like it and I don't mind seeing the scratches of honest use on a gunstock.

On the other hand, the custom stockmaker fin-

Top, bottom, and side views of a very special rifle concocted by Al Biesen and me. We collaborated on the design of wood and metal around a basic new action that may some day be produced, and Biesen did the actual work. The reason you can't see much of the trigger guard is that it is aluminum and had not been blued when the photos were taken. The rifle, a .30/06, is in my possession today, shoots like a house afire, and has taken several nice heads of North American game.

ishes his stock by getting it down to perfection by hand sanding with very fine paper. He then fills the pores either by the old method of applying varnish (high-grade bar varnish) and sanding each coat down to the bare wood until all pores are filled. Or he uses an epoxy, which he spreads over the whole stock, then sands down to bare wood, filling the pores with a single operation. Finishing then is applied with a couple coats of his favorite blend — often GB Linseed oil.

Two-piece stocks are handled differently by the custom stockmaker. Inletting the action is just as important if the rifle is to shoot with accuracy, with particular attention necessary to the fit of the very front end of the buttstock against the rear wall of the receiver. Not only must these surfaces meet evenly and fully, they must also be secured in that position. Securing them is difficult when the buttstock is fastened by a screw through from top tang to bottom tang; it's a much better arrangement to use a stock-through bolt that runs from the rear into the receiver and serves to hold these surfaces together tightly. Most modern rifles with two-piece stocks are constructed with this through-bolt arrangement, but many older style models are not. Some custom stockmakers alter such old actions in order to use a through-bolt and the result does help accuracy. If the older method is used, the screw must fit tightly against the wood, and the top and bottom tangs must also be carefully bedded to help hold the stock in place.

Most custom stockmaking for two-piece rifles involves single-shot rifles; very seldom does anyone spend custom-stock dollars on such as the 94 Winchester, 336 Marlin, or Remington pump or autoloaders. One of the inherent problems with stocking a single-shot rifle lies with the forearm. If the forearm is fastened to the barrel and also bears against the front wall of the receiver, an accuracy problem can result. Nevertheless, that's the way it was done for many years and only recently has it been determined that the ideal way to support such a forearm was to install a "hanger" to the action's front wall and fasten the forearm to the hanger, not the barrel. This hanger is simply a piece of metal that extends forward far enough to allow forearm fastening.

Like all such solutions, however, this is not always the most desirable and there will be occasional rifles that will shoot better with another kind of lash-up. One such option is simply to fasten the forearm to the barrel and allow a gap between the forearm and action body. This can be a little bit unsightly to some eyes, but it does eliminate one problem. The gap, by the way, must be sufficient to allow for stock movement during recoil. That isn't much movement at the juncture of forearm and action face, but it doesn't take much movement to cause inaccuracy and you must remember that a barrel vibrates violently when it's fired.

Some years ago, just on a hunch that a two-piece stock could be accurate and, at the same time, that a rear-locking lever action could also be accurate, I had Marlin make up a special heavy-barreled rifle

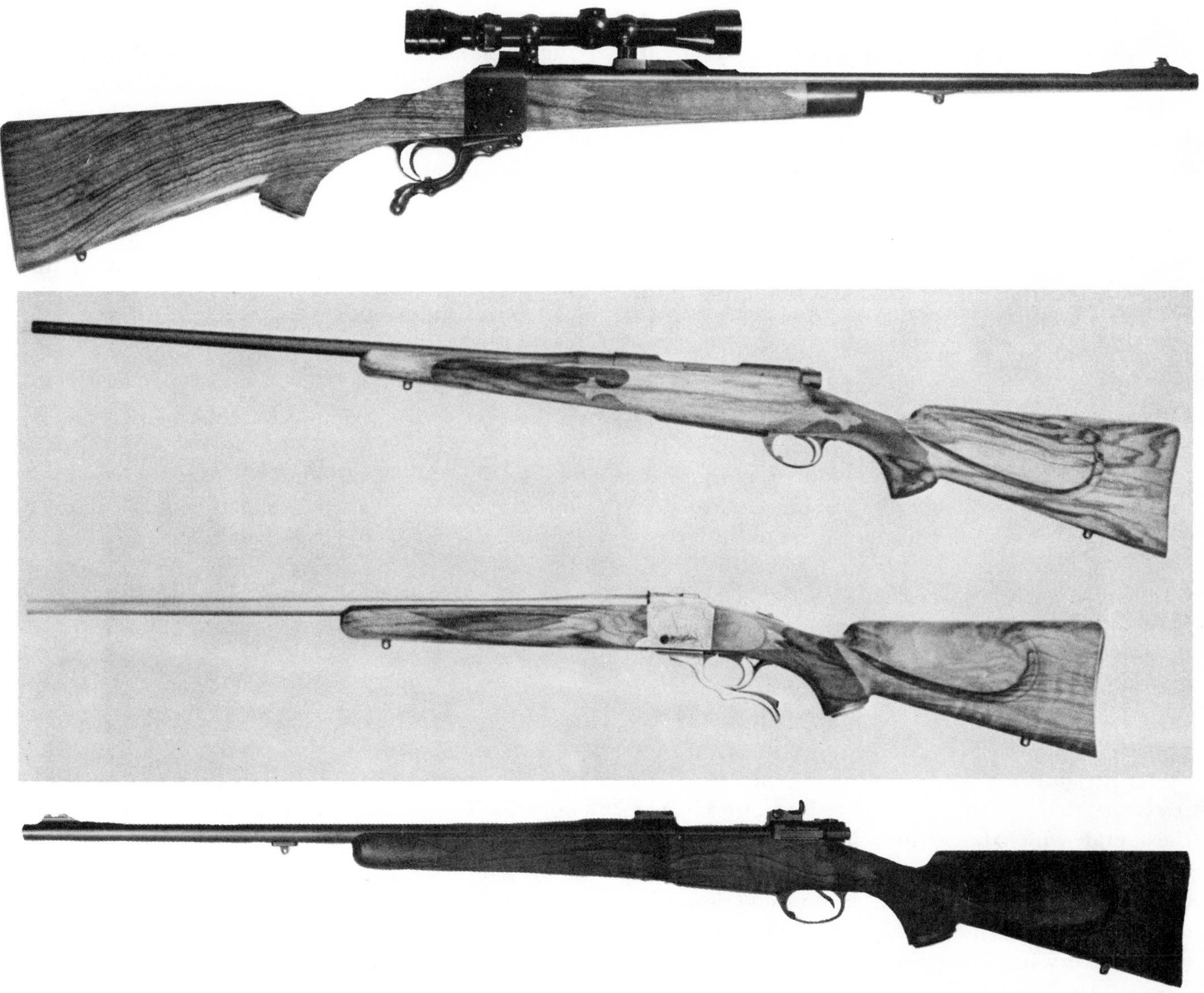

Top: view of a Westley Richards Farquharson action on which I did all the gunsmithing and stocking. The scope is a Redfield 2x7X in modified Redfield mounts which I formed into a short rib. The grain of this wood is perfect, in that it flows down toward the butt, although it is a rather plain-grained piece of English walnut. Center: Joe Balickie of Raleigh, North Carolina, stocked these handsome guns. Top is a Model 70 Winchester caliber .270 in English walnut and using a Blackburn trigger guard assembly with Biesen grip cap and butt plate. Below is a Ruger No. 1 in 7mm Remington Magnum stocked in English walnut. Bottom: A .375 H&H Magnum on the 1917 Enfield action with metal work by Tom Burgess and classic stock by Earl Milliron. This is just about as handsome as a rifle stock can be made. Note that the stock is virtually straight, meaning that the comb is just low enough to clear the opened bolt and that the drop at heel is no lower than the comb. This makes a heavy-recoiling rifle more pleasant to shoot since it keeps the recoil in as straight a line as possible.

using their 336 action and a very heavy barrel with their patented Micro-Groove system. The buttstock was conventional, but the forearm was about 2 inches square and secured directly to the barrel with a single screw. There was a substantial gap between forearm and action. In benchrest tests, using handloaded ammunition, this rifle delivered remarkable accuracy, delivering groups of around a half inch at 100 yards. I was using Sierra 180-grain match bullets, the rifle was a .30/30 caliber, and I used a Lyman 20X Supertargetspot scope. A little later the same rifle was fired by the late Frank Jury, an expert rifleman who worked for Lyman at the time, and he obtained similar results. It all goes to prove that a lot of what you hear isn't true at all. Two-piece stocks certainly can shoot, and so can lever actions.

In production rifles of the lever, pump, and autoloading types, all of which employ two-piece stocks, the forearm fastening is vastly different from that on a single shot. That's because you generally have a magazine tube, a gas cylinder, or some other device latched onto the barrel and receiver. Sometimes these are held by bands surrounding both barrel and wood; in other instances they are held by screws, and most pump forearms are simply fastened to the front end of the operating rod or rods. Others, like the Browning Auto Rifle, are held in place by setting the forearm's rear into a notched recess in the action face, then holding the front end in place by a screw that doubles as a swivel base.

So there are many ways of accomplishing this fastening, but the designer is always faced with the problem of accuracy, for the relationship between barrel and separate forearm and action is critical for good accuracy.

Production bedding of the buttstock often takes some surprising twists. Marlin rough inlets its buttstocks, then places the receiver in place and exerts pressure fore and aft, so as to force the two parts together. Then they apply electricity to heat the metal, which burns its way into bedded position. Some wag labeled this "bedding by electrocution." The method may work in production, but it must be done judiciously since charred wood won't be very stable very long.

THE FLOATING BARREL

A floating barrel is one that doesn't touch the stock. It is strictly supported by the threads that hold it in the receiver. There are those who think a barrel will shoot more accurately if there is no stock contact. And then there is the opposite school of thought.

First, we should examine just what floating means. I say this because I have seen countless riflemen slip a dollar bill between barrel and forearm and, if it slides back and forth, call it a floating barrel. That's not true, because the mere act of resting the rifle on its forearm can bend the wood enough to make contact. Moreover, the act of firing causes the barrel to vibrate, and, unless the stock clearance is ample, the barrel will whip against the wood. To illustrate how a barrel vibrates during firing, visualize a length of pipe held tightly in a vise at one end. Smack the pipe violently with a big hammer. That's pretty much the same thing that happens when a rifle is fired. The severity of the vibration depends on the caliber.

I realize those who back the floating barrel have a lot of merit on their side and, for a purely target rifle, there is no objection to its appearance. In a hunting rifle the story is totally different. Any wide barrel channel leaves room to gather rain, snow, pine needles, twigs, lint, and any number of other foreign objects that have no place there and that you probably can't remove readily in the field. Besides, it looks like hell. And on top of all that, it won't shoot any better than a properly bedded barrel. A properly bedded barrel (one-piece stock) is one that is snug and tight all along the channel sides so you can't see any space at all. Then the wood is relieved underneath so it does not touch the barrel except for about two inches at the front of the stock. (If a forearm tip is present, the bedded area will be behind the tip.) This area must exert upward pressure. There is universal disagreement on how much pressure this ought to be. Some say a certain number of pounds; but they neglect to say how that's measured. My own rule of thumb has always been that you judge this by tightening the front guard screw. Once the bearing area touches the barrel, further tightening of the screw will cause the stock to bend and exert pressure on the barrel. From the point of contact you should get about one additional full turn of the screw before you have the action down solidly. That will approximate 1/32nd inch, but the exact amount will depend on how many threads per inch are in the screw and these vary among the manufacturers. Anyway, that's only a rule of thumb.

You can easily check my theory since most bolt-action rifles when received from the maker do not have enough pressure at this point. Simply loosen the guard screws a little, then slip one or two thicknesses of cardboard – such as a business card, matchbook cover, etc. – under the barrel at the front of the forearm. Retighten the screws and see if she doesn't shoot a lot better. A little experimenting might be in order to know how much paper you'll need, but I've found this trick will make about 90 percent of factory rifles shoot a great deal better. When you've got the right amount of shims in

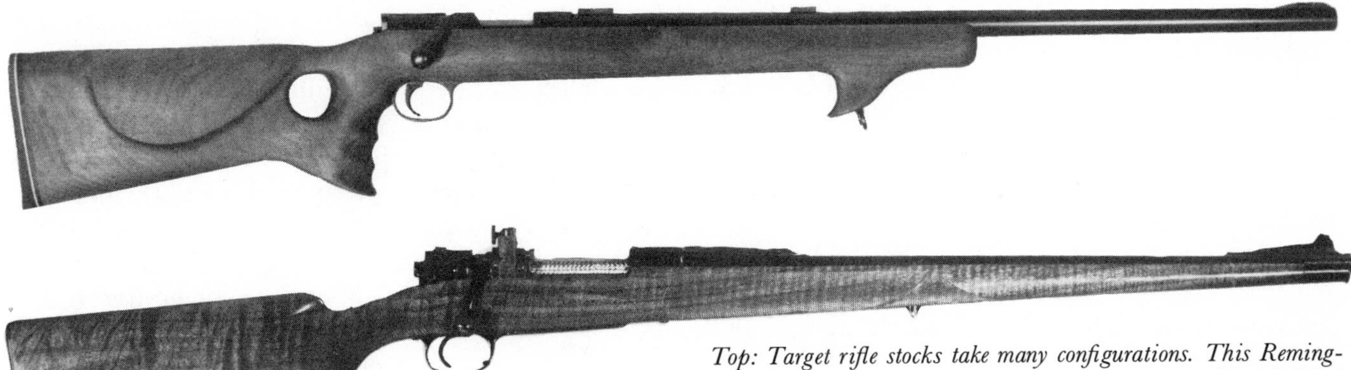

Top: Target rifle stocks take many configurations. This Remington Model 37 .22 Long Rifle has a Biesen custom "thumb hole" stock; note forearm stop for left hand. This rifle was made strictly for prone shooting. Bottom: The Mannlicher style stock is a full-length affair that originated with the Mannlicher-Schoenauer rifle many years ago. This one is a Biesen job on a Mauser action. The original Mannlicher-Schoenauer rifle was difficult to stock: it was held together by rotating the floorplate 90° and that called for some very capable stock work.

place, it's a simple matter to run a razor blade along the stock and trim off what shows. Then it's a simple matter to use a pipe cleaner and a little brown shoe polish to color the paper edges and only the flinty-eyed will know what you've done. Jury rig or not, this is a good solution to most factory high-power bolt guns' accuracy.

There is another school of thought that also believes the barrel should bear just forward of the receiver for a short distance. I doubt this hurts anything, but I also doubt it does much good so long as the receiver is bedded right. The bedding of a bolt-action high-power receiver is critical; whether flat on the bottom or round, it should bear evenly for its whole length. That's a lot easier to say than to do and the neophyte who sets about to build his own stock will lack the necessary knowledge to bring this down in an even manner. It's all too easy to bend a receiver with the guard screws without knowing it's happening. Believe it or not, I've seen some actions bedded in such a bent fashion that you actually couldn't get the bolt in. And that's some accomplishment when you consider how sloppy a fit some of the older military bolts are. Probably the worst offender in this regard is the Mauser military, because it has a thumb slot in the left receiver wall that can encourage such bedding if you're not careful. This is why the experienced stockmaker works from the blank and drops his receiver straight down, since the whole bottom flat on a Mauser is on one plane. It should be the same distance from the top of the blank at front, rear, and middle.

Every high-power bolt-action rifle has a recoil lug located at the lower front of the receiver. The purpose of this lug is to take up the recoil and thus hold the metal parts in place without "shucking" (a term of the trade used when a receiver moves in its bedding). Ideally, this lug should bear evenly against the wood. Realistically, only a few of them even touch it, let alone bear fully and evenly. That's because it's not all that easy to accomplish since the cuts must be made very precisely and, while American industry has learned how to machine metal to precise tolerances, it has a long way to go with wood.

To be practical and perfectly honest, it isn't really all that vital that a recoil lug bear! Heresy? Maybe so, but it's true, especially with any action that has a large flat or round bottom surface so long as the bottom is well bedded. Take a Model 70 Winchester for example, and I used to see a lot of them where the recoil lug didn't offend the wood at all by battering against it. This was especially true with many of the vaunted pre-64 models by the way. But so long as that big bottom flat was down on the wood, the action stayed put and the rifle shot well. And the same is true with most other actions, whether flat or round. The main requirement is that the more surface available the better the bedding, and some designs remove more wood than necessary for magazine, triggers, and other appendages. By the same token there is no disputing the fact that a rifle that has been perfectly bedded in a good piece of walnut will shoot better than one that isn't so precisely done — other things being the same.

Over the past twenty or twenty-five years there has been something called glass bedding, using a fiberglass or resin material to fill in gaps that shouldn't have existed in the first place. To use this concoction, you first applied a chemical agent to the metal parts so the gunk wouldn't stick to the metal. Then you applied the goo, stuck in the metal parts, wound up the screws, and let it harden. When finished you had a glass-bedded action that was a mirror image of the metal. Sound good? Sure. And it's a decent way to repair a stock that's been ruined by removal of too much wood. Some of those who promote glass bedding tell you that all you have to do is dig out enough wood (the way they tell it, it sounds like you could do the job with a hatchet) so the metal goes in the stock, then fill it up with goo, fasten the barreled action, and you've got the bedding job of all time. If you're satisfied with that sort of work, that's your business. But I think it a shoddy way to build a gun. In fact, I regard glass bedding as a poor substitute for workmanship in the first place. Its only legitimate use is to repair a stock that wasn't made right initially.

When Sturm, Ruger introduced their Model 77, they adopted an innovative recoil-lug setup by installing the front guard screw at a rear and downward direction, at about a 45° angle. The purpose is to pull the receiver rearward in addition to down. The idea is pretty slick and it helps pull the recoil lug against its shoulder in the wood. I haven't examined enough Ruger 77s to know that they all do what they're supposed to but, given careful inletting, this should certainly help. Given sloppy woodwork, it isn't going to help at all.

One of the best stocking ideas, although I think it looks bad on a sporting rifle, is the German military idea of placing a steel recoil shoulder within the stock. Its appearance on a sporting rifle leaves much to be desired since it requires some sort of nuts on either end to hold it in place. But it does serve to hold the action where it belongs and it permits the use of inferior wood, which is an advantage in wartime.

To illustrate some of what I've been talking about in terms of bedding let me use a rifle of my own as an example. This is a Model 70 Winchester .338 Magnum that was sent to me before the rifle was introduced, in 1958 I believe. It's a "toolroom" model, a prototype made in the toolroom and the caliber designation is handstamped because the .338 was not yet in production. The original bedding in this stock is pretty bad. Despite this lack, the rifle shoots superbly in the original stock (with cardboard shims under the barrel at forearm tip). In fact, it consistently shoots 3-shot groups at 100 yards of about a half inch with handloaded ammunition. It shoots so well that I have now restocked the rifle in a good piece of English walnut, figuring that such a good shooting rifle deserves a better stock. In the original factory stock, the recoil lug had a little bearing along its outer edges. There was some bearing along the big flat behind the recoil lug, but a chunk of wood was ripped out that made the bearing less than 50 percent; the bedding was a little better farther back along the flat and really good in the middle of the action. I didn't expect it to shoot any better with the new stock — it doesn't — but at least it looks a lot better and I'm happier.

It's all very well to criticize the products of our large factories and there are dozens of things I could point to and ask why it was done this way when that way would have been so much better. But gun factories like any other industry must make a profit to survive. Their employees get a paycheck every week, their salesmen are paid, and those who handle their products at wholesale and retail levels must also make a living. A small change in a model, which might seem insignificant, might cost a dollar at the factory level. That will raise the cost of the finished product to $2 (plus the 11 percent excise tax) and that $2 could put the model higher than its competition and ensure that it didn't sell. Manufacturers are required to watch these things carefully and still produce thousands of guns a year to keep meeting payrolls.

This isn't the same with small gunmakers and custom stockers. So you can't expect the same quality from Winchester or Remington that you'll get from Champlin Arms, Al Biesen, Joe Balicke, Earl Milliron, or a few other artists. On the other hand, these men could not produce guns on a production basis. And even if they could who would buy them? There just aren't that many people willing to pay that kind of money for a top product, just as there are very few with the means to buy a Rolls-Royce automobile.

Figure 1

Figure 2

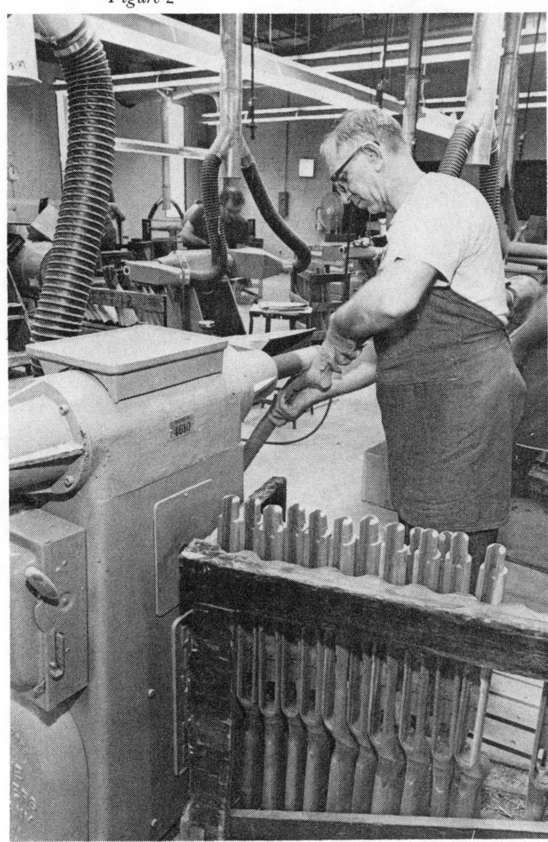

Machines can do a lot in modern gun making but Figure 2 shows that it still takes skilled hands to finish sand a stock. In Figure 1 a tape-controlled automatic machine controls stock manufacture.

STOCK SHAPE

The basic measurements of a rifle stock are generally fairly standard, except in custom work. Too many people won't realize, or even comprehend, that stock shape is what makes a rifle look handsome or like a crooked 2x4 that has been filed a bit here and there. It costs no more to make a factory stock attractive than to make it ugly. The same number of cuts must be made. The same amount of wood is removed. There are an incredible number of badly shaped stocks on the market and there seems to be little or no interest on the part of manufacturers to improve this phase of their product. Much of this is because they don't know any better. The rest is a basic stubbornness in that they can't recognize good stock design.

There are a couple of reasons for this unseemly condition. One of them is what I call the military mind. A lot of the influence on American gun design has come from the military and the military career man really doesn't know much about sporting rifles. There are and have been a few exceptions, but by and large most military types are out of their element when it comes to a sporting rifle. The late Col. Townsend Whelen was a friend of mine. I knew him fairly well toward the latter part of his long and distinguished career, and I recall him with reverence. But the Colonel made a lot of mistakes in the later days in his writings, chiefly because he was so militarily indoctrinated. But people believed what he said because of his reputation.

Another reason for poorly shaped stocks is a basic unwillingness to change. It took a long time for the bolt-action rifle to evolve into a sporter; just as it took a long time for the Kentucky rifle to evolve into the Plains rifle. I have to say that some stocks aren't shaped any better than those of the 1920s.

A third reason is that most designs are created by engineers who work around machining capabilities and who are neither shooters (in most cases) nor artists. That's why a custom stockmaker (and I'm speaking of only a handful of the top men) can shape a stock so it looks right. He is both a shooter and an artist.

It must be said here that the best-shaped stock of any commercial high-power bolt-action rifle on today's market is that produced by Ruger as the Model 77. Bill Ruger is an intelligent person and an uncommonly brilliant gun fancier. This is combined with a clairvoyance that seems to produce the right product for the market at the right time. With that as background, when Ruger decided to make a bolt-action high-power rifle, he brought into his New Hampshire plant a skilled stockmaker named Len Brownell from Montana. Len designed the stock — with Ruger peering over his shoulder, I'm sure — and directed the production. That's the logical way to operate and I wish more companies would follow the example. It must also be mentioned here that it is *my opinion* that the Ruger bolt-action stock has the best commercial shape being produced. That doesn't mean it's everyone's choice. Ruger's has the "classic" shape, which means that it has no inlaid pieces, no Monte Carlo, no cheekpiece. Just a simple, straightforward, excellent gunstock design. Let's examine a couple of these things that Ruger has left out.

Monte Carlo: The little step at the heel of the butt that allows the comb's top line to slope down forward. The theory of a Monte Carlo is that it's necessary when you're using a scope because it helps get your face up to the higher line of sight. The forward sloping comb line, it is claimed, pulls the stock away from your face in recoil and is supposed to be more comfortable.

Let's see what really happens. First, the nose (front) of the comb is restricted in elevation, because it must be low enough to allow the bolt to clear in the open position. So we have the first constraint: The comb nose must just clear the opened bolt. The next constraint results from recoil being in a straight line, which is a continuation of the axis of the bore. That means the lower the buttplate is placed, the farther from the bore axis it will be and the more the gun will tend to rise in recoil (and the more the shooter will feel that recoil). This is why the classic stock design places the heel of the butt ½ to ⅝ inch lower than the comb. This produces recoil in a straighter line and the result is more comfort and less muzzle climbing.

Closely allied with this discussion is the *cheekpiece*, which appears in many forms, some of which are pleasing to the eye, some of which more closely resemble a limp pancake draped over the stock, as a colleague of mine once described them. A well-shaped cheekpiece can be an attractive addition to a stock whether classic or California. It's also supposed to help raise the face to scope height and, in combination with the Monte Carlo and forward-sloping comb, help reduce the "felt" recoil (real or imagined) of the rifle.

It has been my experience that the more severe the Monte Carlo and the greater the forward slope, the worse the gun will hit you in recoil. This happens because, when the rifle recoils, it moves away from your face; then it pivots around the fulcrum (center of the buttplate) and rises at the muzzle. The net result is that the stock whacks you sharply on your cheekbone. The classic stock is far less apt to do this, since it's less apt to part company with your cheek in recoil and there can be no reconnection because there has been no separation.

The claim about a cheekpiece being necessary to raise your face to scope height is also not true because the same thing can be accomplished by widening the comb at this point. This is what Ruger has done. He has simply supplied a slightly thicker comb at the front end and the result is exactly the same with far fewer production problems. What this all adds up to is that you need neither a Monte Carlo nor a cheekpiece. If you prefer to have one or both, that's your choice but don't be misled by those who say they are necessary. It has gotten to the point that most manufacturers add them because their competitors do. Then those who write advertising and catalog copy have to justify the existence of those items. First thing you know most shooters have accepted the concept and it becomes gospel. Things like this have never stood in the way of Bill Ruger and Ruger has gotten away with his ideas because he was right. There have been other free thinkers in the gun world who have followed the same philosophy but haven't made it. In some cases, they were wrong; in others they didn't have the marketing know-how to get their products in distribution or off the shelves once they got in the stores.

On the other end of this discussion is Roy Weatherby. Most gun fanciers like myself do not subscribe to the school that Roy established for reasons that are easier to understand than they are to explain. It must be said in all fairness, however, that the Weatherby concept has been successful and that he has had a greater impact on all shooting since World War II than anybody else including Bill Ruger.

Weatherby's influence has led to the proliferation of Magnum cartridges. He also introduced and promoted the California school of stock design. For lovers of the classic, the California stock is flamboyant, ornate, even — as expressed by the late Lucian Cary — lurid. Nonetheless, the Weatherby stock has been widely copied by almost

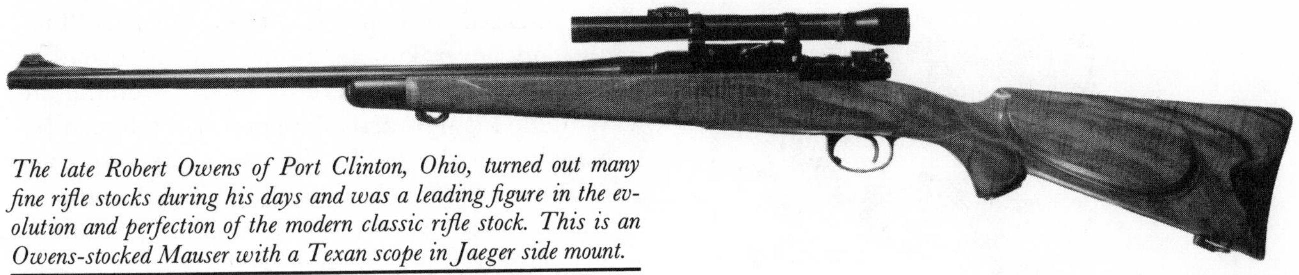

The late Robert Owens of Port Clinton, Ohio, turned out many fine rifle stocks during his days and was a leading figure in the evolution and perfection of the modern classic rifle stock. This is an Owens-stocked Mauser with a Texan scope in Jaeger side mount.

every major firearms producer in America and abroad. Nearly everybody produces stocks with Monte Carlos, cheekpieces, slanted forearm tips, white line spacers, a few inlays here and there —features nobody dared use before World War II.

Whether these additions are good, bad, indifferent, or whatever is beside the point. The point is that they were established and promoted by Roy Weatherby, and have had an enormous impact on the styling of American firearms ever since. Another phase of the Weatherby impact has been stock finish. Before Weatherby, it was normal procedure to finish stocks with a dull oil finish that was really quite desirable. Its attributes were that it didn't glisten like a signal mirror when the sun hit it in the field and, if it got scratched, you could simply dip your finger in a little stock-finishing oil and rub the spot and it would virtually disappear. Then they started varnishing the stocks of cheaper guns, which invariably led to a bit of chipping off here and there and pretty soon the stock looked like a dog with the mange. The only remedy was to completely remove the varnish and refinish the stock with that desirable oil finish.

When Weatherby came along, he started using a high-gloss finish along with some of the exotic stock woods (Oregon myrtle, maple, and other light-colored woods) that shone in the sun like a bright and shiny pearl button. It started a trend. Today you can hardly buy any gun that doesn't have a glossy finish, most of which are tough plastic finishes that you can't remove short of blasting. They will turn the toughest brush and are very protective. I frankly don't like them; maybe people buy them because that's just about all that's available.

SHAPE

There's a lot more to stock shape than Monte Carlos and cheekpieces. A good rifle stock is a work of art. Genuinely and legitimately. It's of the same substance as sculpture because that's precisely what it is.

I have always maintained that the beauty of a stock rested in two principal areas: the shape and the wood, especially its figure and color, in that order. I would much prefer a properly shaped stock made out of a plain stick of English walnut than a poorly shaped stock made from the handsomest wood. Proper shape is an extremely hard thing to describe and it's such an area of personal preference that what pleases me best may not please you, and what pleases another person might not please either of us. I have no use for a stock that is badly shaped, made of poor wood, or adorned with flamboyant inlays or the like. I do admire precise workmanship and I have illustrated this text with a few examples of stocks that I consider excellent. They are the products of a few custom stockmakers or small factories that produce the complete product.

It is impossible to discuss stock shape without including the shape of the metal parts as well. Probably the most important single part made of metal that can influence the looks of a bolt-action rifle is the shape of the bolt handle which must be correctly shaped to complement a well-shaped stock. There are no — repeat no — correctly shaped bolt handles on the commercial market today. This is why most custom stockmakers will reshape your bolt handle or replace it with one of their own manufacture. There are some other metal parts that are of nearly equal importance in the final looks of the job, the other major parts being trigger guard and floorplate, cocking piece, and receiver. Unless these parts are of the correct shape and contour, the stock won't look right no matter how well it's done.

It may seem insignificant and trivial, but if a part is changed, say a pistol-grip cap that's a little smaller is substituted when the stock is nearly fin-

This is my own checkering on a Mauser-action rifle chambered for the .240 Weatherby Magnum with bolt altered by Al Biesen. The shape of the bolt handle is of vital importance to the finished design and appearance of a fine rifle. Biesen does one of the finest jobs in the business.

ished, it will require that the whole butt end of the stock be reshaped to match. The ordinary eye may not see this, but the artist who makes the stock can — and that's what you're paying for.

By no means does this mean that each and every bolt handle, each and every stock should be shaped exactly the same. There are many variations of correctness, just as there are many artisans plying the trade. This matter of shape is all-important, but is extremely hard to discuss because there is so much personal whim and subjectivity involved.

The effect of recoil is also largely a matter of stock shape. Take a relatively mild-recoiling cartridge coupled with a poorly shaped stock and you have a combination that can produce a "felt recoil" that is painful. On the other hand, take a hard-recoiling rifle, like the .338 Winchester Magnum, as an example and stock it correctly and the recoil will not be as painful as you might expect. By this I do not mean that when you have a hard-recoiling big rifle it's not going to come back at you. It will, simply because there will be a lot going on inside that barrel. But when badly stocked, a .30/06 can slap you silly. When correctly stocked, a .338 can seem like a pussycat.

It follows that correct stocking is essential for any of the hot magnums; otherwise the owner is going to be so scared to shoot them that he would flinch badly and never kill his game. An old friend of mine, who used to be an outfitter in Wyoming, always made his new arrivals shoot at the bench before taking to the field. "Just to make sure their guns were still sighted," was what he said. Actually he was closely observing the shooter's reaction. When he saw a guy with a .300 Weatherby who was scared to death of it, this outfitter would suggest trying a .243. And if the hunter shot the .243 with no trouble, as was the usual case, that was what he hunted with. Far better to shoot a lighter gun that you're not afraid of than a bruiser you're not going to hit with.

CHECKERING

The function of checkering is to provide a non-slip surface that helps you hold the gun in place. Since it is functional, it may as well look nice and add to the appearance of the stock. Checkering's appearance depends on several factors: the pattern selected, the quality of the execution, and the wood used for the stock. There are a few rifles that actually look better without checkering, two significant examples being the Winchester Model 94 and Marlin 336 T with straight grip. They really don't need checkering because it doesn't help the grip that much.

There was a trend a few years ago to use impressed checkering. This was accomplished by squeezing the stock between a pair of steel dies that contained the checkering. Applying a combination of heat and pressure, these dies pushed their way into the wood and the result *looked* like checkering. Almost any pattern could be used. Impressed checkering only appeared on production rifles and all the major companies tooled up for the system because it was quick and thus cost less. But impressed checkering had its problems, too. First, the stock had to be precisely finished as to its dimensions. A little too much wood, or not quite enough, and the dies didn't meet the wood perfectly, resulting in uneven patterns. The gun manufacturers found that wood was much more difficult to hold tolerances on than metal, chiefly because the final sanding is done by men, and the human element is less consistent than modern machinery. These uneven patterns looked like hell and were difficult, often impossible, to correct.

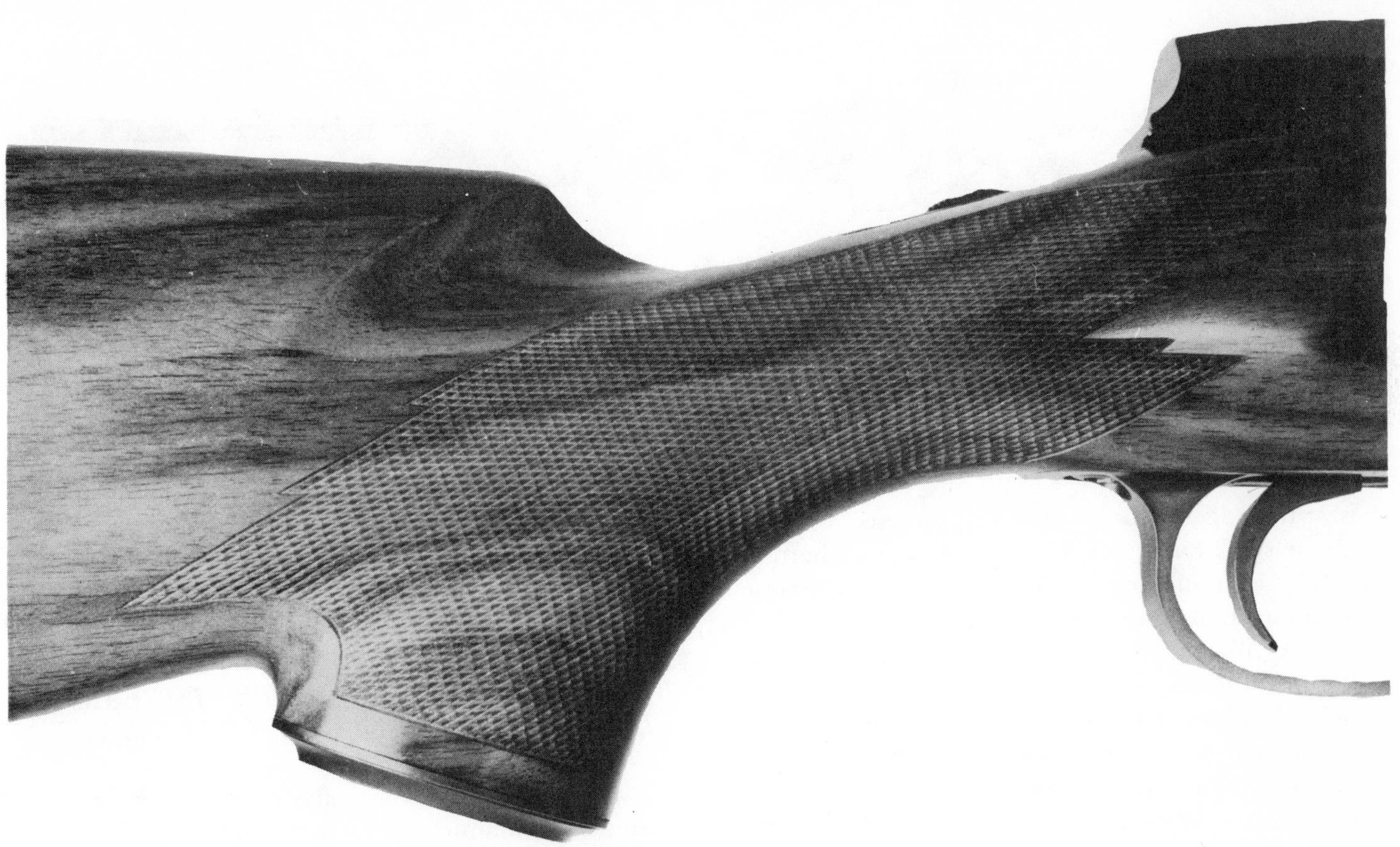

You won't find much better checkering anywhere than on this Champlin custom rifle. Its execution is flawless.

The gun-writing fraternity was quick to complain about impressed checkering, primarily because it was not functional. By shoving the diamonds into the wood, the impressed treatment was really checkering in reverse. Instead of having the diamond points to help you hold the gun, you had the ridges that were normally the bottom of a real checkering pattern. The surface was actually quite slippery — more slippery than plain wood in many cases. These considerations have led to a general retreat away from that kind of "progress" and most of today's guns have returned to cut checkering that gives you some grip.

There are as many checkering patterns as there are people checkering and one sees some pretty weird patterns. A pattern should be tasteful and ought to complement the stock to fulfill its double duty of providing grip and adding to the gun's appearance. Since cut checkering takes time, it will be obvious that the less checkering a manufacturer gives you, the less will be his cost to produce a gun. That's why patterns are often skimpy on less costly models. These often have a couple of square inches on each side of the grip, the same on either side of the forearm, with occasionally a panel of the forearm's bottom surface thrown in. Better grades usually have a good amount of checkering on both sides of the grip and are fully checkered around the forearm. Sometimes the custom stocker cuts his checkering entirely by hand, sometimes he uses a small electric cutter. Either way, it's hand-cut checkering and the result is the same.

The usual rule of checkering is that the diamonds should be three to three and a half times as long as they are wide — a 3½–1 ratio. Sometimes this is changed to provide a more elongated diamond, especially on some guns made on the Continent. Diamonds are usually brought up to a point but you will occasionally see a fine English stock on which the diamonds are left flat on top. While I don't like this nearly as well, and submit that it doesn't offer as good a grip either, it is exceedingly hard to accomplish. This means the checkerer must get each individual groove to the same precise depth or his truncated diamonds won't be even.

The most common sin in checkering is to run

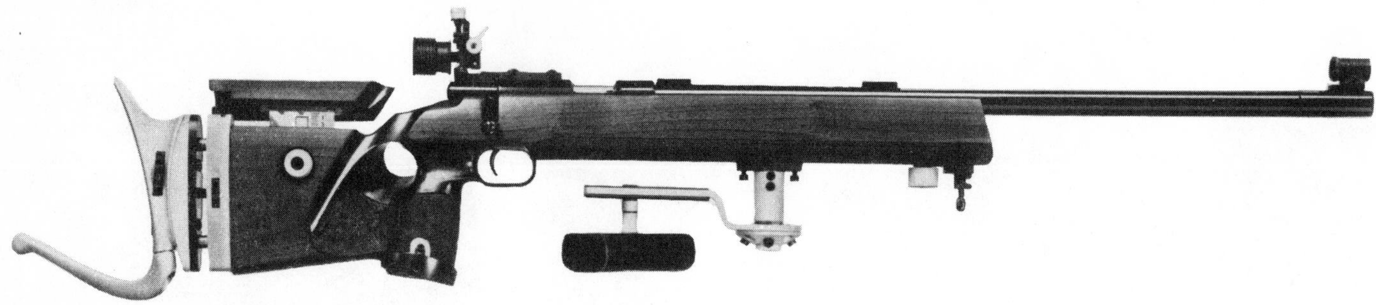

No, not Rube Goldberg, but a serious target shooter's delight made by Anschutz and imported by Savage Arms. Made in .22 Long Rifle for International target shooting, the butt and comb are both adjustable, as is the forearm rest.

past the edge of the pattern and produce a groove in the stock outside it. It's easy to do, and hard to correct once its there. Borders are often cut around a pattern to help reduce the incidence of such overrun. As a result the best checkering is that with no border and no overruns. And when you pay top dollar you have every right to expect that.

When a top stockmaker errs in his pattern — say he chips the top off a diamond in the pattern — he must resort to surgery. This means he must cut a hole, fill it with a plug of the same wood (and match the grain), then carefully file the plug down to the surface and recut the checkering over the plug. When finished, it will never be detected. It's a nasty job, but it will save a stock on which many hours of work have been lavished and in which a considerable investment already has been run up.

Sometimes carving is substituted for checkering and it can be just as functional. I believe carving is not as popular as it once was, but it is still occasionally seen, especially on some older European guns. Perhaps the most commonly seen carved stocks were those on German and Swiss Schuetzen rifles, built exclusively for offhand (standing) position shooting competition. Today's counterpart is Olympic and ISU (International Shooting Union) match shooting.

Specialized stocks are required for such specialized forms of shooting as ISU, benchrest, prone, and varmint shooting. The ISU stock is meant to be used in the standing position and is generally useless for anything else. A benchrest stock is massive and designed to lay on the rest atop a shooting bench in a manner that provides no movement and also offers consistency from shot to shot. Similarly, a stock meant for exclusive prone shooting (flat on your belly) is tailored for that sort of shooting and a varmint rifle stock also has certain refinements chiefly because a varmint rifle generally has a slightly heavier than standard barrel.

BUTT PLATES, GRIP CAPS, FOREARM TIPS, SWIVELS, MONOGRAM PLATES

The gun stock is not completed unless it has a butt plate; the remaining items listed above are in the "nice but not necessary" class yet most of them belong on any decent rifle.

A butt plate is meant to protect the butt of the stock from abuse and chipping. It should be made of fairly thick steel and be reasonably hard. Drop a rifle a short distance, in a way that it will land on the toe of the butt, and a soft butt plate will bend and you'll probably chip out a piece of wood. Plates are also often made of thick plastic and these seem to be serviceable. Rifles of heavy recoil often wear a rubber pad. The best looking such pad, in my opinion, is the smooth one that's about ½ inch thick. The less desirable pads are those known as ventilated pads which pick up dirt, dust, and dozens of small loose objects. I also feel these are too soft and spongy. Rifles seem to bounce away from my shoulder when I fire them and I have a feeling that this may contribute to poor shooting.

Years ago pads were also made of what we used to call hard rubber, a material that is gone today, having been replaced by various plastics. Most best-grade shotgun butts have no pad at all; the wood is finished like a pad and checkering in the wood itself finishes the stock distinctively. You are not supposed to mishandle such a gun.

Occasionally you'll see a fancy butt plate that's

skeletonized in some form or another. These are perfect devils to install, but they add a bit of class. I made and installed one on a rifle of my own many years ago that was made out of a commercial plate and I assure you I'll never do another because it was an awful job to get it in position. The wood is checkered in between.

Buffalo horn was used as butt-plate material at one time by some European gunmakers and is still seen on occasion. Horn is another material that has largely been replaced by plastic. Often a thicker butt plate is used to lengthen a stock in a perfectly legitimate way for a new owner or for whatever reason. This is often accomplished by the substitution of a thick pad, other times it's accomplished by a piece of buffalo horn an inch or so thick.

Occasionally you'll see one of those fancy butt plates with a trap door (grip caps too) which is intended to carry a couple of spare cartridges, a flare, cleaning equipment, or whatever. These are really quite useless in my opinion, being too small for a change of socks although I suppose you could stick a little fishing line and a couple of hooks in there. The modern hunter rarely needs this sort of survival storage place. If he needs survival equipment, he'll need a hell of a lot more than you can stick in a trap under a butt plate.

Grip caps serve the same general purpose as a butt plate, although they're less important for function. They do function though and a well-shaped grip cap is a decided addition to the looks of any rifle. These caps are usually made of steel; those of the best shape are usually the products of custom stockmakers like Al Biesen who makes and sells a line of them. Others are made of buffalo horn and sometimes of a very contrasting wood, like ebony. You can buy small blocks of ebony — and sometimes buffalo horn — from such gunsmith supply houses as Bob Brownell or Frank Mittermeier. These are heavily waxed to prevent splitting and may be used for forearm tips or for grip caps. You often can make a forearm tip, then a grip cap, from the scrap.

A forearm tip is non-functional, yet it does add a lot to the looks of a rifle. Many don't think so and that's their right. In any event, a forearm tip should, I think, be a square fit and not slanted, as so many are today. And it also should not have a white spacer between tip and stock. That's my feeling, but an awful lot of them today are slanted complete with white-line spacer. Tips are usually fastened by drilling a hole in both stock and tip and fitting a dowel, then gluing the tip to the stock. Final shaping is accomplished after the tip is glued in place and care is taken to be sure the barrel doesn't exert pressure against the tip; bedding should be just behind the tip.

Swivels for the gunsling are usually fastened to the stock, although the front swivel is often fitted directly to the barrel itself, or, in some guns, to a band surrounding barrel, stock, and magazine tube. Swivels come in fixed types as well as in various forms of quick-detachables. The QDs are preferred by many because they can be taken off the rifle so fast. I've come full circle on swivels; I used to prefer the QD, now I would rather have the permanent swivel.

A monogram plate, located on the underside of the stock near the butt, always looks neat and classy. It doesn't do a damned thing but it pleases the ego of the man who owns the gun. You can have your initials engraved there. These plates are usually gold or silver, although I made those I've installed out of pre-Lyndon Johnson nickels which are very close to German silver and take a nice polish without tarnishing. These nickels must be filed to an oval shape, then bent to conform to the bottom line of the stock shape. The edges must be beveled and the coin inletted carefully into the wood. Once it is deep enough, you drill a hole and fit a wood screw, rounding its top so it just meets the bottom surface of your monogram plate. Then remove the screw, tin (with solder) the screw top and monogram plate bottom, wind the screw back in, and place the plate in position. Now apply heat with a soldering iron until the solder grabs and your plate is in place. File it down to the wood's surface and finish sand and polish. The result will look nice indeed. Sometimes these plates are made in the shape of a shield or you can get more imaginative if you want.

One of the most difficult tricks in any of this work is to locate things like inlays, swivels, and the like precisely where you want them. You don't have that problem with a butt plate or grip cap because these are located before any shaping is done. They're simply placed at your centerline on the stock blank after the barreled action is in place.

CHAPTER ELEVEN

SIGHTS AND SCOPES

The purpose of sights on a rifle is to aid in aiming. Some sights are simple, others very complex. Rifle sights that come on the gun when you buy it are known as open sights. Peep sights, which have a hole in the rear sights, are often called aperture sights. Both open and peep sights are known as iron sights, which simply separates them from a scope which contains lenses.

A rather wide variety of open sights are supplied with factory rifles; most of them are useless for any practical purpose. Many are so flimsy and poorly made that they are worthless from any direction. Second, open sights are hard to aim with any degree of precision. And they are, most of them, only adjustable by banging them back and forth in their dovetail slot. By all odds however, the worst feature of any open sight applies regardless of its quality. This is that your eye must focus on the rear sight, front sight, and the target. All at once. This is something the eye simply can't do. The eye is incapable of focusing on three objects so far apart and at such varying distances.

Bad as open sights are, some are far worse than others. The worst kind of an open sight is the one known as "buckhorn"; it has high and wide ears that obscure most of the landscape in the vicinity of the target. There are some old-timers who think a buckhorn is just the berries, but not too many of these oldsters know what they're talking about. There also is a semibuckhorn that merely has shorter horns. It's in the same category.

Open rear sights come with square U or V notches. Often there's a white line running verti-

Any sight mounted in a dovetail is driven in from right to left, driven out from left to right. These dovetails are very slightly tapered. The photo shows a brass drift pin in position to drive the sight out. Always use brass, aluminum, or plastic to avoid marring the sight or barrel.

The very wide V with white triangle is reputed to be the fastest type of rifle sight available and has been popularized over the years as best for following up wounded dangerous game. This photo shows the standard sighting equipment on a Winchester Model 70 .458 Magnum.

cally from the notch down. (This is usually silver-filled in a fine British rifle.) Square notches are most often used for target shooting and should be accompanied by a square front-sight blade with a wide, flat top. U notches serve with most any front sight — square or round top V and the V notch is sometimes wide, sometimes small and narrow. V notches too are used with any type of front sight.

Rifle manufacturers stick the cheap open rear sight on their rifles for a couple of valid reasons. They know that a high percentage of gun buyers will buy a scope, so there's no merit in furnishing an elaborate rear sight. Others will buy a peep and discard the open sight. Another factor is that whatever is added to the rifle at the time of purchase (that is, whatever is added at the factory) is subject to 11 percent excise tax. If the factory mounts a scope and ships as a unit, you pay 11 percent tax. If you bought the scope separately you pay no tax on the scope. That 11 percent tax, however, is a good thing because it goes into separate funds that are reimbursed to the States for wildlife use in proportion to the number of hunting licenses sold. The whole thing started in 1934 and is known as the Pittman-Robertson Act. The tax is collected on guns and ammunition. It's a tax the sportsmen asked for, and one they asked to be maintained when other excise taxes were dropped during the Johnson Administration. Hundreds of millions of dollars have been collected over the years and all the money has been redistributed and used for habitat improvement, research, and similar beneficial programs.

If a sight becomes loose in its slot, it may be tightened easily by slightly peening the edges of the dovetail slot, as shown. Just give it a couple of taps and try the sight again, keep it up until it can be driven in snugly.

There was a time when scopes were neither as good nor as rugged as they are today, and it was wise to have open or other iron sights handy in case the scope got whacked, fogged, or otherwise knocked out of commission. That's not true today so there is really no use whatever for an open rear sight; still it's not a bad idea to have one of those folding rear sights on the barrel and that's what most better guns come through with today. If you don't want to use it, just lay it flat along the barrel

Champlin Firearms mounts a rib on this octagon barrel with a wide V sight for dangerous game. The rifle is a .458 Winchester Magnum. Note the fine checkering on this sample.

and it's out of your way. If you have one of the standup variety it's sometimes necessary to remove it so it's out of the way of the scope. The only time, aside from a scope accident, that an open sight is useful is for dangerous game — Africa's "big five" (elephant, buffalo, lion, leopard, rhino), certain Asian game like tiger, and the grizzly and brown bear in North America. The wide v sight is a British favorite for such game and is usually used when following up a wounded beast in heavy cover. It is claimed to be the fastest sight for that purpose.

Correct use of the open iron sight is to place the front sight in the notch so that the top of the front sight is even with the top of the rear sight. Holding the front sight higher than that is used if the shot is longer than the distance for which the rifle is sighted. Some folks prefer to sight in by placing the front sight bead in the bottom of the notch which is known in some parts as "drawing a fine bead." Maybe so, but it's damned hard to see in poor light and, if you plan to use the open sight, I'd recommend using it correctly.

FRONT SIGHTS

Front sights come in various shapes and sizes. Early front sights consisted of a simple blade that stuck up at the muzzle. Later, the dovetail slot was adopted (dovetails are tapered and sights are *always* driven in from right to left, so if you must remove them be sure to drive the other way) and simple front sights were driven into the slots. The recent trend is toward a ramp sight, which not only looks much nicer but also is easier to use in sighting.

The configuration of front sights is usually a square blade, sometimes wide, sometimes thin. A wide blade is better; despite the common impression that you can "sight finer" with a thin blade, it's not true. Such blades are often slightly slanted on top and sometimes have a gold insert, which is really copper, sometimes a red plastic insert, and sometimes an ivory insert, which is also usually plastic. These inserts are most often set in at an angle to pick up light and are usually well protected by the steel blade. I've always considered red one of the best colors for a front sight and my old trick was to use a dab of red nail polish that would transform any blade into a red one. And it could be scraped off if you got tired of it. A gold bead is a good choice too, since it picks up light well and stands out against woods or snow so long as there is adequate light. The white ivory bead is excellent except when there's snow on the ground. Beads also come in a round configuration, usually sitting atop a thin blade; they can be small or large, fine or coarse. The round bead is all right for hunting, but best with a U rear-sight notch.

Certain special iron sights for match shooting (there are rifle matches that specify iron sights) employ special front sights that are usually of the globe variety into which various adapters can be fitted which include blades of varying sizes and rings also of various sizes that can be used to circle the bull's-eye. Unless he's using one of these globe sights, the marksman usually blackens his sights by smoking them, since the soot doesn't give a glare from the sun and much finer aiming can be done.

PEEP SIGHTS

The peep, or aperture, sight was invented by Lyman personnel toward the latter part of the 19th century. It's simply a hole that you look through as opposed to looking at a rear open sight. The eye, being the accommodating organ that it is, automatically centers itself in the aperture so that all you have to do is concentrate on the front sight and

Typical of iron sights used by competitive shooters is this Redfield Olympic Front, which accepts inserts that can be posts of varying widths, circles to surround the bullseye, and so forth.

A Whitworth rifle from England with the typical lineup of sight leafs. Such sights are precise and expensive to produce. This rifle is equipped with sights to 300 yards. On occasion you will see them out to 500 yards, which is ridiculous, because no one has any business shooting at game at that distance with open sights.

the target. For the best use, the peep should be located as close to the eye as possible.

Most peep sights have a disc that can be unscrewed. This disc has a rather small hole and is pretty good for target shooting. If you're a hunter and you've bought a peep sight for a hunting rifle, the best advice I can give you is to unscrew the disc and throw it away. You'll do far better just to sight through the hole the disc screws into. It also will allow you to see more of the area around your target, which means getting on target faster, and getting faster repeat shots. It may surprise you, but you'll shoot just as accurately as with the disc. Peep sights never really caught on the way they should have. When they first came out, only the more astute riflemen realized how good they were. The old foofs, who made up the ranks of most hunters, stuck with their buckhorns.

Probably the best, and the most famous, receiver sight ever made was the old Lyman 48, although other excellent peep sights were made by such firms as Redfield and, later, Williams. Today the good peep receiver sight is close to a thing of the past. Lyman's 48 is gone and Redfield only lists extremely fine (and high priced) target receiver sights. The whole market has gone to scopes. In a way this is a shame, because the peep sight is a far better arrangement than any open sight. But it's nowhere near as good as a scope either. One of the few rifles today that comes equipped with a fairly decent peep is the Ruger Mini-14. This Ruger peep, however, hides too much of the surrounding area to be practical for hunting. But then the Mini-14 is not a hunting rifle.

SCOPES

The biggest reason a scope is the excellent aiming device that it is, is because it has a single aiming device — usually a crosshair or tapered post —which you simply place where you want the bullet to hit on the target. There is nothing else to line up. The single plane makes aiming much easier and eliminates many errors.

There are scopes for rifles, shotguns, and pistols. There are scopes for target shooting, varmint, and big-game hunting. There are scopes that do not magnify at all and there are some that magnify up to 30 power (expressed as 30X). There are light scopes, heavy scopes, and scopes for almost any purpose for which guns are used. There even are scopes that have built-in range finders and other models that compensate for the trajectory of a bullet. There are cheap scopes for .22 rifles that have plastic lenses and there are expensive scopes that have extremely fine lenses ground to extraordinarily close tolerances to eliminate virtually all imperfections. Now there are "scope-type devices" that place a red dot on the target.

Before getting deeper into the subject, here are a few definitions.

Field of view. The width of the area you can see at 100 yards. Normally the higher power a scope has, the smaller the field of view.

Eye relief. The distance from your eye where you can see the complete field of view. Generally this is around 2½–3½ inches and this distance is necessary to protect your head from a hard-recoiling rifle.

Variable power. A scope which can be changed in power by turning an adjustment. A scope designated 3–9X, for example, has a range of power (magnification) from 3 to 9X or anywhere between.

Fixed power. A scope with one power, which cannot be changed.

Lenses. The glass, or plastic, lenses that provide the magnification. Plastic lenses are molded, have some surface irregularity, are easily scratched, and absorb moisture. Glass lenses are ground to precise specifications, are heavier than plastic, and do not absorb water. Glass lenses are usually coated, which increases light transmission (making better visibility at dawn and dusk). Coated lenses transmit 90 percent of available light, uncoated lenses only about 55 percent.
Reticle. The sighting or aiming point in a scope. Most of today's scopes have centered reticles, which means that they always remain in the center of the field of view when corrections are made. Older scopes moved the reticle across the field of view and sometimes wound up way off center. The most common reticle is crosshairs, but there are many variations, from tapered posts to dots.
Parallax. The most difficult word for anyone to understand in scope language. Briefly, and somewhat oversimplified, it means focus. More precisely, it occurs when the reticle is not positioned at the actual optical center of the scope. Some scopes, notably the precise target scopes, can be adjusted for parallax at different ranges by moving the reticle back and forth until it's optically centered. You can tell when parallax is present (it should not be) by placing the scope on a firm rest and, without touching it, move your head back and forth, up and down. The reticle should not move across the target. If it does, parallax is present. You can eliminate parallax at only one distance, excepting adjustable target scopes. Most hunting scopes are parallax-free at 100 yards and this provides minimum parallax at other distances. To check your scope, make the test noted above at a precise 100 yards.
Adjustments. Most scopes are internally adjustable for windage and elevation, but there are a couple of brands on the market that are non-adjustable in which case they require a mount with adjustments built in. The literature accompanying each scope will tell you the value of each increment of adjustment. A scope is just as easy to adjust as any other sight; in fact it's simpler than most iron sights. A quality scope will give very precise adjustments; some lower-cost and low-quality scopes cannot be depended upon for precise adjustments.

A variable scope has adjustment for power, usually with a ring, which should turn with considerable resistance to prevent accidental turning.
Fogging. In the early days it wasn't wise to bring a rifle into a warm room or cabin from the outside cold. To do so was to cause the inside to fog up because the moisture inside the tube condensed. Next morning the reverse happened and many shots were missed because of fogged scopes until hunters learned to leave their guns out in the cold all night. Now fogging is a thing of the past in any quality scope (so long as its owner doesn't remove the seal) because they have been filled with nitrogen (dry gas) in manufacture and permanently sealed. The seal is the secret and a scope is a very smart thing to leave alone when it comes to repair jobs.
Resolution. Crisp detail throughout the field of view, without distortion or curvature anywhere in the viewing area.
Eyepiece. The piece at the rear, or eye, end of the scope that you can screw back and forth. It contains the "ocular lens."
Objective. The front end of a scope containing the "objective lens."
Turret. The sealed housing which contains the windage and elevation adjustment systems.
Erector system. A system of lenses located in the approximate middle of the scope which re-invert the image. It is important to realize that you do not really look through a scope, you look into it. And you see an image — as opposed to looking directly at the object. You know that when you look into the ground glass of many cameras the image is upside down. It's the same in a scope. The erector lenses invert the upside-down image so you see it right side up.

Scopes that maintain the reticle in the center of the field accomplish this feat by moving the entire erector system (containing the reticle) when you make adjustments. The old way only moved the reticle.

.22 SCOPES

Most scopes for .22 rifles, many of which retail for about $8–$14 (1976 prices) are a joke. They have plastic lenses, poor adjustments, and are not fit to put on any decent .22. These same scopes are often

The rifle is a fine pre-war Walther Olympic action .22 Long Rifle that I altered to a sporter and restocked, the scope a Leupold with 1-inch tube. The combination shoots like a dream.

sold as a loss leader in a "package" price (i.e., rifle and scope) by some mass-merchandisers when the price is even lower. Try to adjust one of these scopes and you'll often find that you can wind the dial a couple of revolutions before anything moves. Then it moves all at once. That can be frustrating and — worse — it can dampen the enthusiasm of some youngster for shooting in general and for shooting with a scope in particular. There are, however, some brands that are better than others, and some individual scopes even at those prices that are surprisingly good.

If you have a good .22 rifle, and there are a number of fine .22 sporters that are capable of excellent accuracy, it should wear a decent scope. Fortunately, scope makers have at long last awakened to this market segment and they supply decent .22 scopes at higher prices as well as mounts that can be used to mount a high-class hunting scope on any .22 with dovetail base. This is an excellent plan; one of the fine scopes available is Redfield's 4X with ¾-inch tube at $36.50 (in 1976) featuring glass lenses and an accurate adjusting system. Bushnell also has a pair of fine .22 scopes with ⅞-inch tubes, one a fixed 4X and the other a 3–8X variable selling in the same general price range, and these models come with an integral mount that fits dovetailed receivers. I don't doubt that in the near future other scope makers will offer such scopes or that at least you can mount any quality hunting scope on a fine .22 rifle simply by using a mount that will fit the dovetail.

THE HIGH-POWER RIFLE SCOPE

It is no secret that scopes were used as far back as the Civil War. Some of the famed riflemen of those days used monstrous slug guns that were capable of extraordinary accuracy at great ranges. And they often used a scope. These scopes were of very poor quality by today's standards, and they usually were as long as the barrel. Later, similar scopes were used by buffalo hunters for some of their long-range shooting. But scopes for hunting never really achieved popularity in this country until the bolt-action rifle became popular. You can even pinpoint the date: about 1937.

The story of the slow but steady rise to popularity of bolt-action rifles following World War I is told in Chapter 2. Suffice it to repeat here that the giants of the industry were slow to respond and that many early commercial bolt-action rifles were equipped with bolts or safeties that interfered with a scope. However, in 1937 Winchester introduced the Model 70 rifle equipped with a bolt handle and safety that did not interfere. The company even placed two holes in the top of the receiver ring (the front part) for a scope base, but they neglected to drill a hole in the receiver bridge (the rear part) which meant you couldn't mount a bridge-type mount (like the modern Redfield Jr. and its various copies) unless you drilled and tapped a hole. And that was a tough hole to drill, because Winchester left that steel nearly undrillable!

Meantime, a few scopes were imported from Germany, most notably the Hensoldt and Zeiss, at very high prices but of fine quality. In America, with the use of scopes being promoted by such writers as Captain E. C. Crossman, Paul Curtis, and Townsend Whelen, the first successful side mount was developed by Rudolph Noske of California. It consisted of a bracket mounted to the side of the receiver by three stout screws and two taper pins — a difficult mounting job. This base had a dovetail on top and its mating part was fastened to a pair of rings that held the scope. Held in place by a lever, the scope could be removed or replaced at will. The early Noske side mount was copied by the famous gunsmithing firm of Griffin & Howe, who used a two-lever lock, and by Paul Jaeger of Jenkintown, Pennsylvania, who used a single lever. So far as I know, both mounts are still being made, but most shooters use a top mount today.

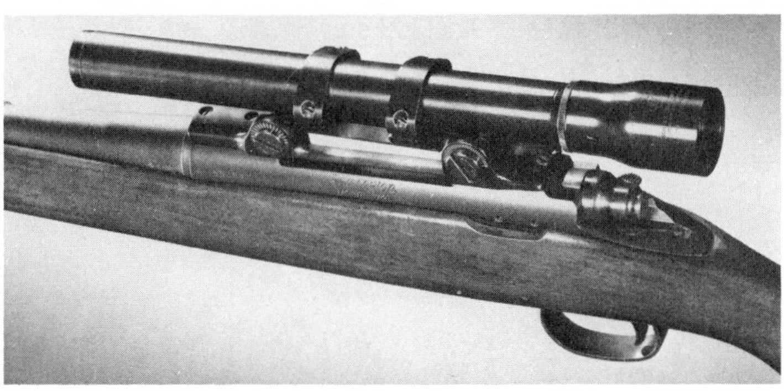

Some scopes, like the Bausch & Lomb shown above and above right, are made without any internal adjustments and require a mount with adjustments that move the entire scope tube. The two views show the rig both on and off the rifle. Movement is made by turning the rear screw, which moves the eccentric cones and raises or lowers the scope tube. The front screw moves the scope tube to one side or the other. These mounts are satisfactory and work well, but they are not nearly so popular as the internally adjustable system. One big advantage to the B&L system you see here: Since the adjustments are in the mount, you can have mounts on as many rifles as you own and simply move the scope from one to another. You'll always be sighted in.

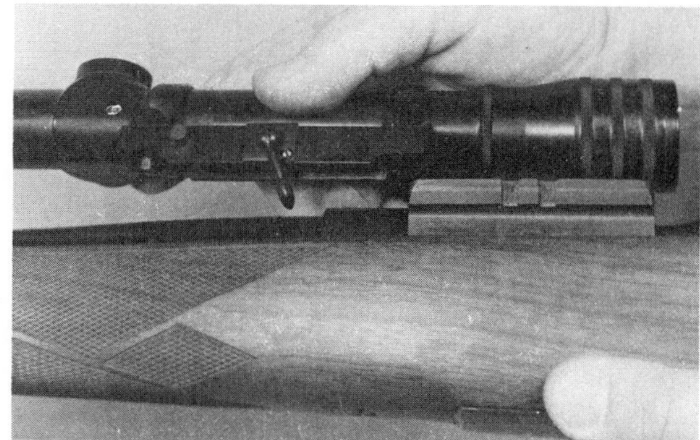

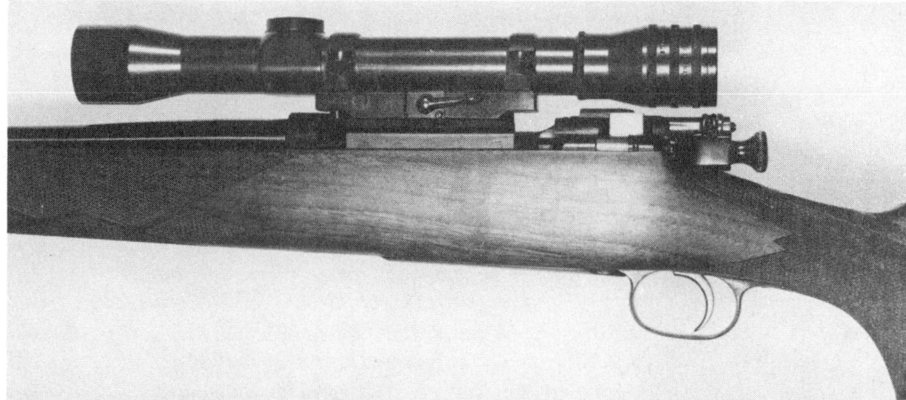

Three views (above, left, and below) of the Jaeger side mount. This is an excellent mount, secured to the receiver side by three screws (which are mounted as blind screws) and two taper pins to assure they'll stay put. The advantage to such a mount is that the scope can be removed quickly and the iron sights used. The iron sight on this rifle is a Lyman 48. The rifle is a Springfield .30/06 which I built some years ago and have since sold; the scope is a Kollmorgen (now Redfield).

Noske also designed a model with longer eye relief so it could be mounted forward of the bolt handle. Otherwise, bolt handles had to be altered and American gunsmiths began doing a pretty good business at this. (They still modify many bolt handles.) This alteration consisted of either cutting off the old handle and welding on a new one (which called for good welding capability) or heating the existing handle and hammering it into a new shape that would provide a sufficiently low contour. This also called for skilled work, since the cocking and extracting cams are both located at the back end of the bolt and must remain hard after the handle alteration. Then the receiver and stock both had to be filed out to accommodate the new shape. Small companies sprang up with new safeties to replace the old military wing types. All of this had to be done to properly mount a scope on a Mauser, Springfield, or Winchester 54 rifle.

The introduction of the Winchester 70 led to much easier scoping and the way was paved for scope popularity. The two pioneering companies were Lyman – with their very fine Alaskan model, a 2½X scope that was a fine instrument indeed – and Bill Weaver. Weaver started his company in El Paso, Texas, with a scope called the Model 330 (it was about 2X and it retailed for around $27.50). At the same time, he also made a low-cost pressed-metal mount so all a gunsmith had to do was drill and tap four holes. Lyman and Weaver had the market, one at the high-price end, one at the low-price end, up through World War II. At the end of that war many other companies got into scopes. Most notable among them were Kollmorgen, a fine old optical company that first made scopes under the Stith name, then under their own name, and finally sold that part of the business to Redfield. Leupold & Stevens, in Portland, Oregon, also got into the business at about the same time and have been making rapid strides in market share in recent years. Meantime a young GI named Dave Bushnell spent some service time in Japan and came home with an idea. He bought some first-class American scopes, went back to Japan, and said "make me scopes like these." They did and the rest is history.

This widespread proliferation of scopes made the American shooter and hunter really scope-happy. Most shooters think pure magnification is the reason for a scope's excellence. But what really counts is that it puts the target and aiming point in the same optical plane – you have no objects in varying optical planes to align or on which to concentrate. Magnification has its use all right. Take the most popular scope power of all, 4X. This means your target appears four times closer to you. A deer at 100 yards appears to be at 25 yards, and so on. That is an advantage.

There are two major kinds of scopes today and

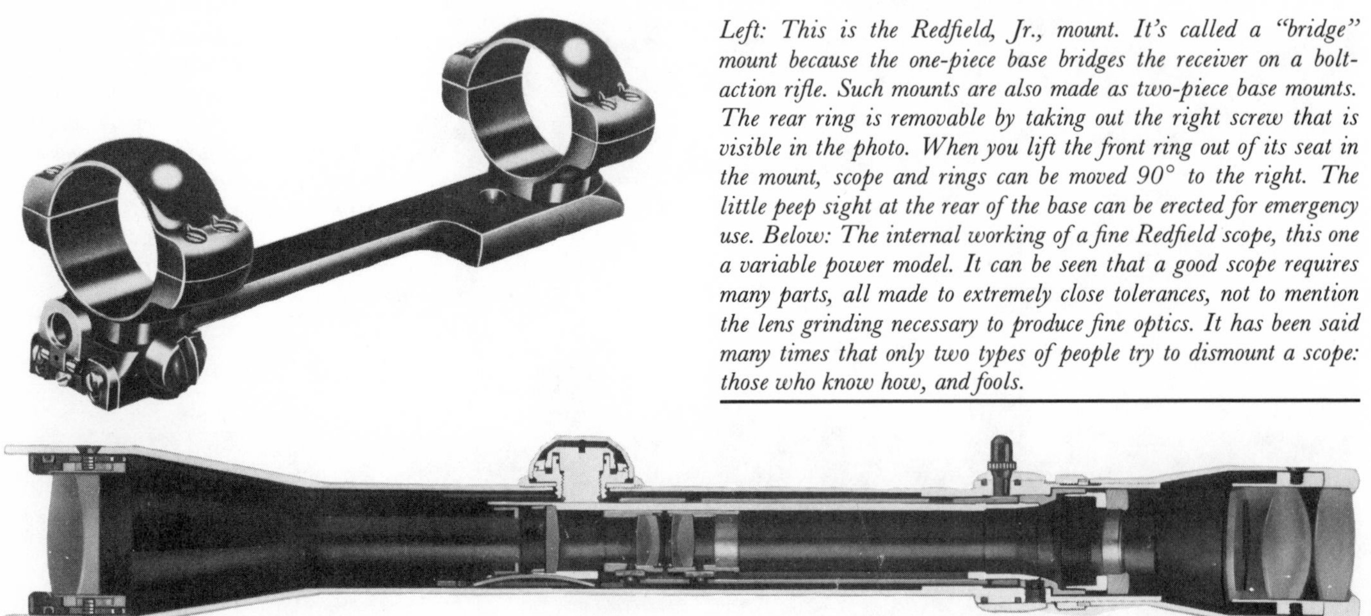

Left: This is the Redfield, Jr., mount. It's called a "bridge" mount because the one-piece base bridges the receiver on a bolt-action rifle. Such mounts are also made as two-piece base mounts. The rear ring is removable by taking out the right screw that is visible in the photo. When you lift the front ring out of its seat in the mount, scope and rings can be moved 90° to the right. The little peep sight at the rear of the base can be erected for emergency use. Below: The internal working of a fine Redfield scope, this one a variable power model. It can be seen that a good scope requires many parts, all made to extremely close tolerances, not to mention the lens grinding necessary to produce fine optics. It has been said many times that only two types of people try to dismount a scope: those who know how, and fools.

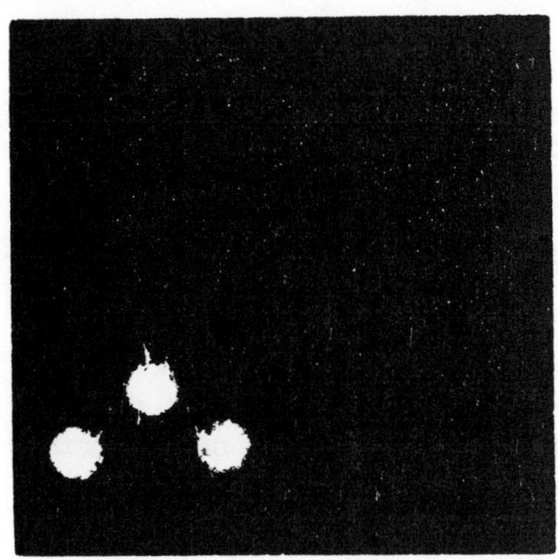

Above: This 3-shot group was fired at 100 yards with a Winchester Model 70 .264 Winchester Magnum with new Leupold 24X scope and 140-grain factory-loaded ammunition. The group measures ⅝ inch. This is extraordinary accuracy, especially with a factory rifle out of the box. The new 24X Leupold scope proved equal to the task of delivering superior accuracy. Right: These three examples of benchrest sighting equipment show how nonstandard this type of shooting is. The top picture shows a fairly conventional setup; the shooter has placed a piece of tape from the muzzle to the front scope mount to help break up mirage waves from the barrel. In the middle picture, the shooter has slipped a long tube over his scope for the same purpose. In the picture below, the shooter has offset-mounted his scope for reasons probably best known to himself.

each can be further broken down by use. The kinds are target and hunting. A typical example of the target-type scope is seen in the Lyman Supertargetspot. This scope has changed little in outward design for many years. It all began years ago when Wray Hageman and John Unertl both worked for J. W. Fecker in Pittsburgh. The Fecker Company made rifle scopes. Unertl went off on his own and formed the John Unertl Optical Company, which is run today by his son and widow. Unertl made excellent target scopes for years, which were popular in benchrest shooting, and for a short time made a line of hunting scopes as well. With his death a few years ago, however, the company has placed less and less stress on the shooting market.

J. W. Fecker made target-type scopes for some years but is now out of the picture. Meantime, the late Wray Hageman went to Lyman and put them in the scope business. When I started benchrest shooting in 1947, I had to buy a Lyman Supertargetspot in 20X (which was the highest power at the time). This was the scope to buy. It still is. The scope has changed a little — I suspect the optics are better than those in my 30-year-old model and I know the mounts are better. These scopes have a fixed reticle and adjustments are made by moving the whole tube. They are mounted on dovetail scope bases usually screwed on the receiver ring and on the barrel. There is a recent benchrest trend, however, to using a long sleeve that is bonded permanently to the receiver and to mount the scope on the sleeve. The theory is that it will provide better accuracy if both bases are mounted on the single surface.

Something of a variation in this design is provided in the Redfield 3200 target scope, which was introduced in 1967. The major change is in the mounting system, which is rigid and has internal adjustments (as are true of hunting scopes). The Lyman, on the other hand, permits its scope tube to slide back and forth and you must pull the scope back after shooting because it tends to stay in place while the rifle moves back under it. The net effect is that the scope "moves forward" each time you fire in order to protect the delicate lenses.

Redfield also has added a receiver-mounted target scope in 16, 20, and 24X powers and Leupold has just announced a similar target scope in 7.5, 10, 12, and 24X. These scopes are designed to be mounted on the receiver in the same manner as a hunting scope and both have internal adjustments. Leupold calls these scopes "AO," which means adjustable objective; the objective end of the scope can be screwed in and out, and then locked in place, to provide focus at ranges from 50 yards to infinity.

At this writing, scopes of the Lyman type are still the most popular with benchrest shooters, who are going to use whatever will give them the best advantage. But what is true today may change tomorrow. It is still the feeling of many benchresters that more improvements can be made in scopes than anything else, and that this applies especially to mounting methods.

VARMINT SCOPES

In the late 1940s, 1950s, and part of the 60s, most varmint shooters used target-type scopes for varmint shooting. In fact, I used two scopes, one of which was the big 20X Lyman Supertargetspot that I also used for benchrest matches. I killed more chucks and crows using that scope than any other single scope I've ever had. I also used a 10X Unertl target-type scope quite a bit. There were a couple of good reasons why these were the kind of scopes used then: We needed a lot of magnification because we never took shots at less than 300 yards on a woodchuck. It simply wasn't sporting to take closer shots with a rifle that could literally hit a mouse every time at 200 yards. And hunting-type scopes were not made in anything much larger than about 6X. There was a fellow named Litschert who made an attachment for the ordinary hunting sight that worked by unscrewing the objective lens of the scope then screwing on the attachment. But this had two disadvantages. First it had a different optical plane, which meant you had to keep it good and tight or it would wobble and the plane of the attachment would revolve around that of the scope. Second, it added considerable weight as well as additional length at the front end of the scope and that unbalanced the scope so it received a wrench each time the rifle recoiled. These gadgets were popular for a while but soon went the way of a lot of gadgets.

Today, scope makers have learned how to make precise hunting-type scopes with objective lenses that are not too large and in magnifications up to 24X. The actual diameter of the scope at the objective end on these models is 2 inches. That's about what it was for a 6X scope twenty years ago. These are extremely fine scopes, many of which have a variable feature with a range of from 3–9, 4–12, 6–18 and so forth. Those with the higher powers give you an adjustment at the objective end so you can focus the scope for the exact range over which you'll be shooting. It might well be said that the varmint shooter never had it so good with so much choice. If I had to pick just one of these, I'm not sure I'd be able to make a selection, unless I flipped a coin.

You must remember that as power (magnification) increases, field of view decreases. A 2¾X scope for instance, can have a field of view at 100 yards of 55 feet. On the other hand, a 24X scope at the same 100 yards has a field of view of some four feet! Keep in mind, however, that other things being the same, the lower the power the greater also will be the light-gathering capability.

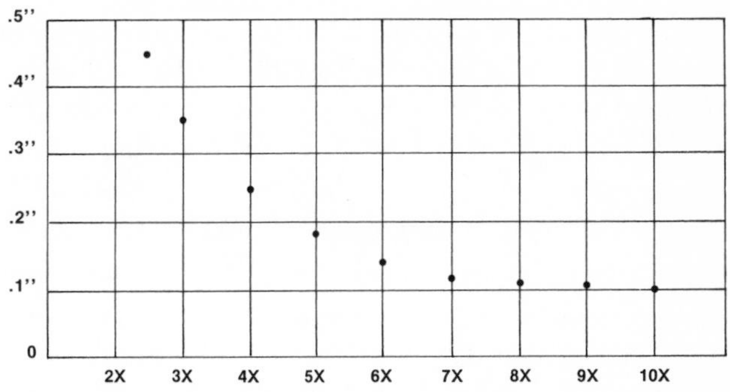

Aiming error of a scope at 200 yards is plotted on this chart. Note that a 2½X scope has an aiming error of approximately .45 inch, while the error is reduced to about .1 inch in a 10X scope. This assumes a quality scope in perfect adjustment. Very little aiming improvement will be noted as power increases beyond 10X and virtually none will be noted beyond 20X. By comparison, open sights of good quality used by a person with good eyesight will have an aiming error at 200 yards of about 2 to 3 inches. A peep sight will fall somewhere in between the open sight and the scope.

HUNTING SCOPES

Most scopes sold are in 4X. It's probably safe to say there are as many 4X scopes sold as all other powers put together. The 4X scope is actually an ideal compromise and I suspect if I could only choose one scope that would be it for a hunting rifle. But that also depends to some degree on what sort of hunting I planned to do as well as on where I planned to do it.

If your hunting is entirely in the close puckerbrush that's found in most parts of America, your shooting will be at short range – say less than 50 yards. No matter what most people tell you, there's more game shot at less than 50 yards than beyond that distance. These shots are seldom in open country which means that to some extent there's some kind of cover. And that means a scope is an advantage. When your shot is at 50 yards or less you don't need magnification but you do need light gathering, because that's what enables you to sight at dawn or dusk or in deep shade anytime during the day. The ideal scope for this sort of hunting is around 2–3X. That gives plenty of magnification, the widest possible field of view, and the most light gathering you can buy. More than once I've fooled a wise old whitetailed buck in the deep woods when he was smart enough to slip behind a blowdown where he was hidden. So long as you see the movement and realize there is a deer there – and provided you know where the rest of your party is – you can look over the cover with your scope and chances are you'll see the animal. Possibly enough of him to shoot. You can't do that with iron sights. Regardless of what you may hear (usually from oldtimers who have never used a scope), the use of a scope on such a deer rifle for close-cover hunting is a decided advantage. Generally speaking, the closer you will be to whatever game you are going after and the darker it is in the woods where you are going to have to shoot that game, then the lower the magnification of your scope should be.

One type of scope that is increasing in popularity is the variable power. Among the more popular ranges are the 2–7X and 2½–8X, either of which would be most useful if a man had to have just one scope. The range of power is adequate for nearly any hunting situation. Another fine variable range is from 1¾–5X. At the low setting, a Redfield offering gives an unbelievable field of nearly 70 feet and is a little shorter, a little lighter in weight, than the 2–7X. Larger variables also come in 3–9X which begin to get a bit large and heavy for the ordinary hunting rifle. Still, they are meant for hunting and if you expect a shot at pretty long range this is a good compromise scope.

It has been my experience that most people who buy variable-power scopes usually leave them at one setting. It's true that when you see game you're quite apt to forget about the variable feature and just take the shot. This will be true no matter what the setting. And I've done just that. On a Quebec caribou hunt one year I was shooting a prototype .30/06 with a Redfield 2–7X variable scope. It was my last day and I still hadn't found a good bull, though I'd seen many good animals. Hunkered down out of the wind and snow I turned and saw five good caribou bulls working their way past me. They were about 150 yards away and their direction would bring them to about 100 yards and then away again. Feeding as they moved, they were covering ground at a surprisingly fast pace. Knowing it was my last day, and this was my last chance, I completely forgot to turn the variable dial up to see which was the best head. Instead, I eyeballed them, made my selection and dropped him. To this day I'm not sure he was the biggest. At the time he ranked about 13th on the Boone & Crockett woodland caribou list; but B&C has since lumped all caribou in Quebec and Labrador into a single classification even though there are both woodland and barren-ground caribou in both places.

If you will do a lot of walking and a lot of climbing, both size and weight are factors to consider. The larger the scope, the more it will weigh and the more it will snag brush. Yet, if you're a sheep or goat hunter, some extra magnification will come in handy once you get in position. It's getting there that hurts. The Redfield scope people have done a great deal of pioneering in the scope field. One of their pioneering efforts in 1970 was the Widefield, which involves a flattening and elongating of both eyepiece and objective ends of the scope. This reduces the vertical field and extends the horizontal field of view. It also allows the scope to be mounted a little lower in many cases. This excellent idea has been copied by other manufacturers.

As a rule, the higher-quality scopes are made with aluminum-alloy tubes finished with what the trade calls a "hard anodize." This was the brainchild of Kollmorgen, originally a Brooklyn-based manufacturer of periscopes for the Navy. Before the hard anodize, which was borrowed from an aircraft-industry practice, aluminum scope tubes were subject to easy scratching. You can lay a file on a hard-anodized aluminum tube and run it across the surface. Then look at the file and see that its edges are turned but there is no mark on the scope tube. This was quite a development and is used throughout the industry today. A few lower-priced scopes have steel tubes but they're not as good as aluminum alloy, being heavier and subject to scratching.

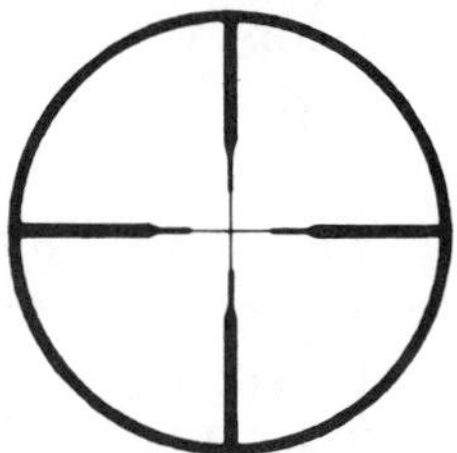

This is an excellent reticle because it offers very fine wires at the center to permit close sighting in at the target; at the same time it has coarse posts that can be readily picked up when hunting in fading light. You can easily center your target no matter what the conditions are.

RETICLES

There are almost as many reticles as there are scopes, but the most common, and still the most popular, is the plain crosshair. The varmint shooter wants pretty fine wires, the target shooter wants extremely fine wires, and the hunter wants them rather coarse. There is some degree of compromise in that reticles are also made with quite heavy wires running almost to the center where fine wires then fill in.

Another popular reticle is the tapered post and crosswire, which means there is a single horizontal crosshair with a tapered post sticking up from the bottom. The wire serves to help you keep the rifle level. And then there are dots, of varying sizes, that sometimes float and that sometimes are at the in-

Weaver is out with this Qwik-Point sight for shotguns, .22 rifles, and high-power rifles used in close shooting. The device is optical. You look into the lower part while the superstructure superimposes a red dot where you want to hit. The device is useful, and works nicely. My objection is that it has so much height that it appears, and is, quite cumbersome.

tersection of the crosshairs. So far as I know, the dot was invented by the late T. K. Lee, one of the old-time exhibition shooters who also was a target shooter. He called his product the "tackhole dot" and Lee himself was known as Tackhole Dot Lee. Lee made his dots by dropping a very tiny amount of some gluelike substance on the intersection of the crosshairs (which in his case were made of spider webbing). For some reason he was able to produce a perfectly round dot while many of his competitors produced "dots" that were more square than they were round. Dots are available in various sizes (they're all round today) from as small as ⅛ inch at 100 yards to one that will cover 4 inches at that distance. The dot is a popular reticle and a good one.

Weaver is now out with a different concept that they call Quik-Point. This is a rather small optical sight that projects a blaze-orange dot over the target. It's meant for relatively short-distance shooting, in good or poor light, and it's intended for shotgun game as well as game animals. It should be a boon to the shooter in heavy cover. In use, you simply look through the eyepiece with one or both eyes open, place the orange dot where you want it, and shoot. Its major disadvantage is that it stands quite high on the gun.

The sort of reticles to beware of are those that hide too much of the landscape. This used to be a failing with many imported scopes. Back in the early days of scopes, the Germans especially liked to put complicated reticles in a scope that hid too much of the field of view. Bushnell offers an interesting reticle called the Command Post. This is a standard scope with standard crosshairs except it has an added reticle with a big, tapered post that flips up or down by magnetic persuasion when you move the selector ring. It's meant to be used when dusk comes along, because the bigger post is more easily seen in poor light.

LENS CAPS

All scopes ought to be protected by lens caps which should always be of the solid type that must be removed before you can shoot. Many plastic see-through caps distort the image, and, if you sight through them, your shot may be off. The caps protect the lens from dust in your gun rack, from dirt and dust when in the field, and really ought to be in place at all times except when you're actually shooting or are about to.

SIGHTING IN

Sighting in with a scope has posed problems for many shooters and I've seen some terrible waste of ammunition trying to get things squared away. That should now be a thing of the past. I have a little Bushnell pocket-size Tru-Scope that sells (in 1976) for about $25 that's the slickest way to sight in I've ever seen. I've always been skeptical about such devices but I'm sold on this one.

To check it out I ran it through its paces with a rackfull of rifles that I know to be sighted in. Damned if it didn't show them all to be sighted in on the button! Sure it varied a hair or so and was dead on in just one or two instances, but a barrel doesn't always shoot where it looks, either. The point is that using this device, you can be within a couple inches at 100 yards with just about any rifle you care to name. You can do another thing with it. Take it on your hunting trips and, once you've got your rifle sighted in at home before you leave, check just where this device puts your crosshairs. Then check again when you are ready to hunt. This saves sighting shots that might spook game in hunting country. You should always check your rifle after it's been shipped on an airplane, or stuffed in a car trunk anyway. This lets you do it fast and easy. You'll save the $25 pretty fast with the cost of today's ammunition.

SCOPE MOUNTS

The methods by which scopes are attached to rifles has led to more inventiveness than most other gun subjects and, by and large, also to more gadgetry that hasn't worked. The two systems that have lasted the longest, and been copied the most, are the Redfield and Weaver systems. The Weaver mount consists of two separate bases that are attached to the rifle, with a set of rings attached to the scope. They are attached by slipping the scope onto the left side of the mounts and hooking it there, then moving it down to its final position and tightening a large, coin-slotted screw.

If the Weaver system is simple and foolproof, so is the Redfield. This started out as a bridge-mount base, meaning that a single piece of steel was used as the base extending from the front receiver ring back to the receiver bridge (on a bolt action), usually being fastened by two screws up front and one at the rear. Today, Redfield offers two-piece bases as well. Redfield's rings differ from Weaver's in that the front ring is designed to be placed into the base at a 90° angle to the right. Then, the rear end of the scope is swung into position and a screw set in place to hold the rear ring in its part of the base. With two opposed screws, the Redfield mount offers windage adjustment in the mount if you need it. As proof of how good the Redfield mount is, it has been copied so faithfully by Leupold that the rings and bases are interchangeable! Keep in mind that as these words are written both these companies have a reputation of manufacturing just about the finest scopes in the world. If Leupold had been able to design a better mount they'd certainly have done so.

One of the worst bugaboos involving scopes has always been a loosening of the mount screws. This happens under recoil especially when the screws were perhaps not tightened quite enough in the first place. Some years back you had to check the tightness of your mount screws regularly and faithfully.

In my gunsmithing days, I always put a drop of shellac on each screw before winding it in good and tight. There were some who advocated putting a drop of iodine on a screw. But all that did was to rust it in place, which was a poor idea. Then, shortly after I got into the advertising business, I met a Professor Krieble, who had been a professor at Trinity College in Hartford, Connecticut, but who had invented a magical goo called Loctite. This remarkable stuff had just been placed on the market and the operation was very small. Loctite was what is called a sealant and it is the kind of stuff that remains liquid as long as it remained unconfined. But, once confined, say as when applied to a screw and wound home, it will tighten into a plastic that fills every single nook and holds the screw like mad. The good professor died a short time later, but his company is going mightily and Loctite is not only used by almost every major manufacturer of anything that has to be screwed together, but also is one of the greatest boons to keeping scope mounts in place that there ever was.

For those who like to have the capability of using open sights in addition to a scope, there are several options. One is to use a swing mount that lets you swing the scope aside and have the open sights available. There also are mounts that have an opening so you can leave the scope as is and sight through the opening and through the open sights. Or you can use one of the side mounts mentioned earlier that lets you zip the scope off quickly. Much as I like the precision of a side mount like the Jaeger or Griffin & Howe I frankly see no need for them today. You don't really need to remove a scope that fast and, if you do, you can get a Redfield or Weaver off quick enough. I also don't like the swinging mounts no matter who makes them. We've had swing mounts for thirty years and none has lasted very long. Neither do I care much for the super-high see-through mounts; you have to get the scope up high to see under it and I prefer a scope where it ought to be – down low.

The height of a scope mount should be just high enough to position the scope so its eyepiece will clear the bolt handle, if a bolt action. And just high enough so the objective end will clear the rear sight or barrel. To this end, you can select the proper height of bases and rings to accomplish that objective. You also should be able to position the scope far enough forward so that the eyepiece is far enough from your eye to be comfortable in your normal shooting position. Sometimes this can't be done with some rifles, some scopes, or some shooters (those with abnormally long necks, for example), so the solution is to use the extension rings which permit more movement ahead or aft, whichever is needed. Often the location of the scope's turret will dictate which you need.

From time to time someone comes up with the idea that it would be a great thing if rifle manufacturers built their guns with built-in scope mounts. Or at least with knobs or holes or something to which one could hang a scope. This has been accomplished most recently by Ruger, who supplies his Model 77 bolt rifle with or without Ruger scope mounts. It seems not everybody wants to be restricted to what the gunmaker says he ought to have. The customer wants his freedom of choice, so Ruger offers the rifle either way: with Ruger top mounts or with holes drilled and tapped like everybody else. Then you can fit your Redfield, Weaver, Lyman, Leupold, or whatever right onto it.

The Sako rifle, imported by Garcia, also is equipped with its own mounts, which fit a tapered dovetail running fore and aft on the receiver. This is a good setup, quite satisfactory, and reliable. Since the Sako rifle comes without any other sights whatever, you are required to use either the Sako or other rings such as Redfield on these integral bases.

PART TWO

AMMUNITION & BALLISTICS

INTRODUCTION

This part of this book concerns itself with the ammunition, with what it contains and how it performs inside the gun and how its projectile performs once it's airborne and when it arrives at the target. This is sometimes referred to as the science of ballistics, internal ballistics for the goings-on within the gun and external ballistics for the rest of it.

As a science, ballistics is deep, mysterious, and highly steeped in some of the highest order of mathematics. We'll avoid that sort of thing. What really counts is the practical business of what happens. Before getting started however, a few definitions are in order. There will be other terms; these will serve as a starter.

Cartridge. A cartridge is a complete unit consisting of the brass, case, primer, propellant powder, and bullet.

Primer. The tiny component that is exploded by the firing pin's blow and, in turn, ignites the powder. Primers are sensitive, powerful, and small.

Powder. The propellant. When ignited, it burns to generate gas which propels the bullet.

Bullet. The solid, single projectile used in a rifle or handgun.

Caliber. A term used to measure the bore of a firearm but having no relation to its power or performance.

Magnum. The word simply means big, as in a "magnum of champagne." As a matter of interest, Smith & Wesson owns the copyright for the term in handgun use, but in riflery and shotgunnery it's in the public domain.

CHAPTER TWELVE

AMMUNITION

Ammunition, in general, consists of center-fire and rimfire types. Today, given the trend back to muzzle loading, we have that to contend with as well. In fact that may be a logical place to start, because it's the least confusing.

Long ago ammunition consisted of powder and ball. The powder was black powder, the only kind available, and the ball was a lead ball that was poured into a mold to take the requisite shape and size to accommodate the bore of the gun being employed. Not always, but usually, both gun and bullet mold were supplied together by the gunsmith to assure some sort of reliable fit. To use the muzzle loader, you poured the required amount of powder down the bore and seated a bullet on top of the powder. Ignition in the earliest days was accomplished by sticking a smoldering wick of some sort through a little hole in the breech that touched and ignited the powder. The next refinement was the wheel lock followed by the flintlock. There is a lot of present-day interest in these old systems; it may be a large step backwards, but vast numbers of people are shooting these guns and apparently having a lot of fun doing so.

One of the greatest inventions in the gun world was the percussion cap. And perhaps the shortest lived. Invented in about 1840, the percussion cap replaced the flint and only lasted until the development of the self-contained cartridge as we know it today. The first successful modern cartridge was used in about 1852 so while the percussion cap didn't last long, its impact was monumental.

In percussion cap ignition, the flint-system pan

was replaced with a little part called the nipple, which stuck up and to the rear and contained a small hole that extended into the barrel where the main charge lay. Instead of the shower of sparks, on which the flintlock depended for ignition, a small cap containing fulminate of mercury was placed over the nipple. The new hammer had a concave face that fitted over the nipple and came down to whack the cap. When it did so the fulminate exploded and drove a hot fire into the powder to ignite it.

Like the flintlock, they're making cap-and-ball (percussion) guns today faster than at any time in history, except for a couple of early wars, and shooters are gobbling them up like mad. It's hard to perceive the attraction for these oldies but it's real.

The first modern cartridge was developed by Frenchman Louis Flobert and exhibited at the Paris Exposition of 1851. It consisted simply of a small pinch of "percussion-cap material" with a small bullet perched on top. Flobert showed the cartridge along with a small rifle he had developed for target shooting. The development caused little stir, but it was observed by two American visitors named Horace Smith and Daniel Wesson. They returned with the idea and added a very small charge of black powder to the combination. Thus was born, in 1854, the .22 cartridge. Today's .22 Short is hardly changed, at least in outward appearance.

The .22 Short was entirely self-contained. It was what the military calls a "fixed" round. Smith & Wesson sold their operation to Winchester and went into the handgun business. Revolvers of that day used a cylinder that was bored out from the front, but the charge holes were not bored through. It was necessary to leave a solid wall of metal at the rear to contain the thrust of the charge and only a nipple for the cap was fitted at the back end. It remained for Rollin White to patent the bored-through cylinder that made self-contained ammunition possible. Smith & Wesson bought this patent and, for the patent's life, defended it vigorously. Until the patent expired in 1870, no other gunmaker could bore his charge holes through the cylinder and thus could not use the self-contained cartridge. This resulted in a literal stranglehold on the market by Smith & Wesson and they made the most of it. The dam broke in 1870, once the patent expired, and a host of competitors joined the fun; but while it lasted, Smith & Wesson achieved a position of dominance.

At that period, Smith & Wesson manufactured ammunition as well as firearms, so it was a simple matter to mate the two products. The original Flobert design used a .22-caliber bullet, as we have noted, and no powder charge. Smith & Wesson slightly lengthened the cartridge and added a small amount of powder. Flobert's original cartridge was continued until about 1950 as the "BB Cap," the initials standing for "bullet breech"; the reference implies a superior method of loading. BB Caps were used for short-range indoor target shooting for years along with CB Caps (Conical Ball), which have also been discontinued.

RIMFIRES AND CENTER-FIRES

The first fixed ammunition was for rimfire and it worked by utilizing a soft copper or brass cartridge case with a rim that had a space between the two layers of metal into which was placed the priming compound. (Priming compound is handled moist; it is a sensitive, violent explosive.) Ignition is caused when the firing pin strikes any part of the rim, which must be supported by the breech end of the barrel. This forms a sort of hammer and anvil situation; the blow fires the primer and it, in turn, ignites the powder.

All early cartridges were rimfires, from the tiny Flobert up to such larger numbers as the .44 Henry, the renowned ancestor of the modern Winchester. Among the more popular rimfire cartridges of all time were, in addition to the .22 Short and Long Rifle (which came along many years later), such as the .25 Stevens, .41 Remington derringer, plus the .32 Short and Long and .38 Short and Long. All were chiefly for handguns. One of the better numbers was the .41 Swiss Vetterli, the military rifle of Switzerland, firing a 300-grain bullet with a charge of 55 grains of black powder.

The .25 Stevens rimfire load deserves a few more words. It was a fine cartridge and I remember it well as a small boy. I never owned one myself, but an older friend did and he used to hunt squirrels with it and sometimes let me go along. Time has a way of obscuring reality, but memory tells me that little Stevens rifle shot to beat the band. It probably didn't, but the cartridge was a good one. It fired a 67-grain bullet (.25 Long; it was also available as a Short) at a muzzle velocity of 1,130 feet-per-second. The .25 Stevens finally departed in the 1930s and its loss has been lamented considerably, although it has been replaced by the .22 WMR (Winchester Magnum Rimfire) which fires a 40-grain bullet at 2,000 fps. The introduction of the .22 WMR has largely stilled the clamor for bringing back the .25.

All rimfires have one severe limitation: The rim of a cartridge must be crushed in order to make it fire, so it follows that the rim must be soft. And it also follows that a soft rim cannot be made very strong. As a result, the rimfire cartridge is limited to relatively low-pressure loads. If the pressure developed were too high it would be easy for the case to rupture, spill gas into the action, and blow the rifle apart.

The pressure generated by the .22 WMR is about as high as you can go, and the rifles built for this cartridge must be carefully constructed, particularly with regard to firing-pin shape. Too sharp a pin could easily weaken the metal enough to rupture, which would result in an unpleasant gas spill under high pressure. Fortunately, when Winchester designed the .22 WMR cartridge, they deliberately made it in such a way that it's impossible to get the cartridge into the chamber of any existing rifle not specifically made for it. Nor can older rifles be chambered for this cartridge.

The rimfire has another disadvantage: It requires a rim. This is purely a physical characteristic, but its very means of ignition requires the rim for ignition. This means it eliminates rimless and belted cartridges, both of which are practically essential to modern, efficient automatic and semiautomatic operational systems.

In the mid-1800s there were a couple of developments that led to the center-fire cartridge as we know it today. One of the earliest was the Maynard system — developed by a Washington, D.C., dentist — which employed a rimmed cartridge case (but without any priming mixture inside) made of brass and enclosing the powder charge and bullet. The rear of the case contained a small pinhole and ignition was accomplished by percussion cap (actually the Maynard used a roll of caps almost identical with those of a toy cap pistol) the flame of which was funneled through the hole and into the powder charge. This, one of a number of roughly similar systems, was an outgrowth of a way of doing things since the American Revolution. A powder charge and bullet were paper wrapped as a unit. These were called "cartridges" and were loaded (from the muzzle) as a unit to facilitate reloading on the battlefield. The paper that wrapped the unit was consumed during firing.

To follow the history of a fully self-contained cartridge very briefly, one of the first was the mid-1800 cartridge developed by von Dreyse for the Prussian needle gun described in Chapter Two. This system used a paper-wrapped unit containing bullet, powder, and primer. Von Dreyse placed the percussion cap near the front of his cartridge, requiring a long firing pin to penetrate through the powder charge to the cap. Hence the name needle gun.

In 1836, a Parisian named LeFaucheux invented a cartridge called the pinfire, which had an ignition pin extending from its head. When loaded in the gun, the pin protruded in a manner that it was struck by the hammer and driven into a cap in the cartridge for ignition. Pinfire cartridges, which were most often seen in shotgun cartridges, lasted a rather long time. The Smith & Wesson Volcanic development, which consisted of a bullet with hollow base into which was packed the firing cap plus a powder charge, was reminiscent of von Dreyse's needle gun.

These developments slowly led toward the development of the center-fire cartridge as we now know it. The center-fire cartridge has its self-contained primer in the center of the base, seated in a pocket. The bottom of the pocket contains a flashhole through which the flame can move into the main body of the cartridge case and ignite the powder. The first such cartridge used in the U.S. was called a "folded-head" cartridge, and was widely used from about the late 1860s until the 1880s. Chiefly used in military firearms, it saw some use in civilian guns as well.

The folded-head cartridge outwardly resembles a rimfire — there is no apparent primer. That is located inside, where you can't see it. You can see two indentations in the outside of the cartridge case, however, about ⅛ inch forward of the rim, which is what holds the primer in place. The blow of the firing pin is sufficient to crush the primer and ignite the powder. The result is that cases for folded-head cartridges were made of soft copper, because they had to be crushed. And that meant low pressures.

One of the early folded-head center-fire cartridges. You can see the crimp marks in the side of the case. Even though this outwardly resembles a rimfire, it has a center-fire primer inside it and requires a blow in the center for ignition.

In the 1860s, two army colonels, one in England and one in the U.S., each perfected a system of center-firing that was vastly superior to anything yet devised. Both systems are still in use virtually the same as they were originally designed. The English officer was named Edward M. Boxer and the American was Hiram Berdan (of Berdan's Sharpshooters of Civil War fame). While both systems are still in use, it's the Boxer primer that is now used in America and the Berdan primer that's used in Europe!

There is very little difference in these two primers in terms of their basic principle or performance, but for reloaders the difference is vast. Any priming system requires an anvil to support the explosive against the blow of the firing pin or hammer. The rear of the barrel in a rimfire serves this purpose. A cap pistol has a solid surface against which the cap lies when the hammer comes down. Similarly, a center-fire primer, such as the Boxer and Berdan, also requires an anvil. In the Boxer, the anvil is built into the primer and there's a single flashhole into the main part of the case. In the Berdan, on the other hand, there is an anvil built into the cartridge case itself with two small flashholes.

If you're a reloader this is important because the Boxer system is the more easily reloaded, since a reloading die's decapping rod can easily locate that single, large flashhole and push it out of the pocket, making it a simple matter to seat a fresh primer. A Berdan primer, on the other hand, must be pried out with a picklike tool making the job much harder.

BASIC CARTRIDGE TYPES

There are several basic types of cartridge. The rimfire, already described, is a sample of the rimmed cartridge by virtue of its definition. Another typical rimmed cartridge, but a center-fire this time, is the common .30/30. A rimless cartridge is one that has a base no larger than the rear of the case body. An example is the .30/06. Rimless cartridges come in straight-sided cases, like the .45 Automatic pistol cartridges, and bottle-necked cartridges, like the .30/06. And they come in sizes that have smaller rims than bodies (an example being the now-obsolete .284 Winchester). The purpose of such a shape is to provide a larger case body, with more powder capacity, and still use a standard bolt face.

There are other, lesser-known, examples such as those known by the fancy name of "rebated rim." In the opposite direction are a number of semirimmed cartridges, like the .220 Swift, where the case body is a little smaller than the rim. The rim itself is standard, again to fit a standard bolt face. All these cartridges have a groove machined into the cartridge for the extractor to grab, which is called the "extracting groove."

Back in about 1912 the great London gunmaker Holland & Holland, Ltd., introduced a line of proprietary cartridges that featured a belted case head. This represented a major development and provided a far stronger cartridge than any other type. The best known of the originals are the .375 and .300 H&H Magnums; today there are a wide variety of belted magnums based on the same idea.

WILDCATS

A wildcat cartridge is one that is created by a custom gunsmith or reloader as opposed to one of the major arms producers, and that must be handloaded. A typical example of a wildcat cartridge for years was the .22/250. Its name means that it was simply the .250/3000 Savage cartridge with its neck squeezed down to .22 caliber by running it into a die of the proper size. It got to be so popular (its capacity was excellent for .22 caliber) that it was finally legitimatized by Remington and the .22/250 is now available in factory-produced rifles and ammunition.

Very few wildcat cartridges have ever achieved such lineage; most are destined to be bastards forever. But the experimental rifleman and his gunsmith have prodded and goaded the giants into producing better and better rifles over the years. A

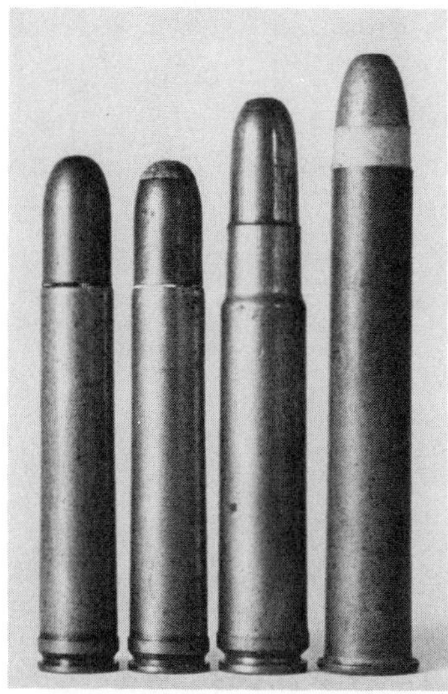

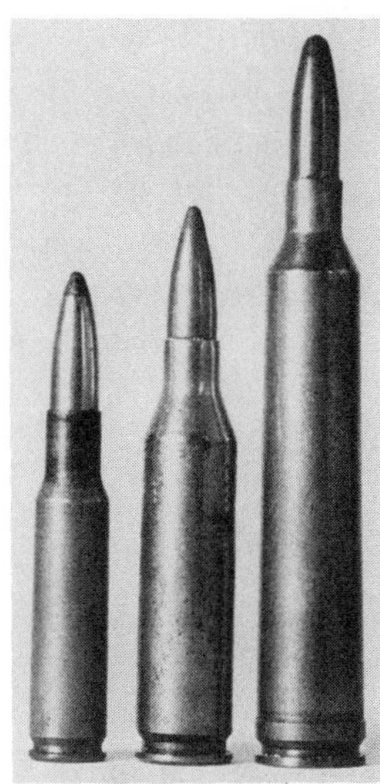

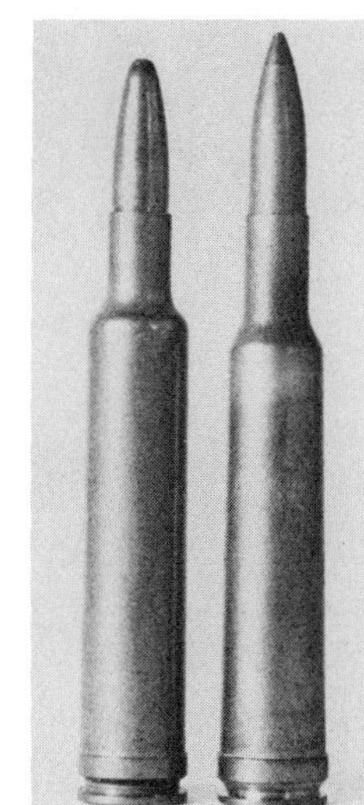

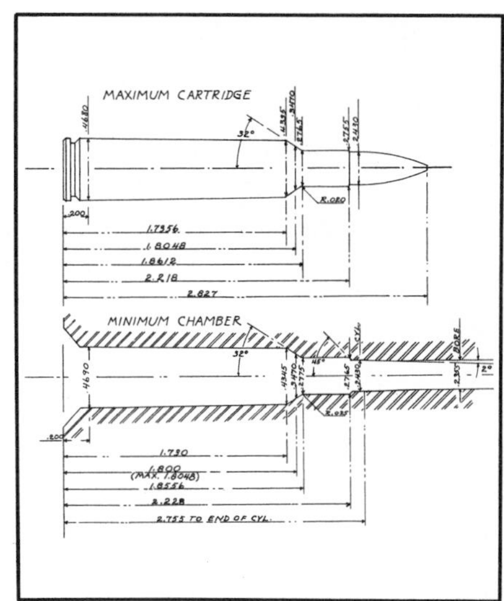

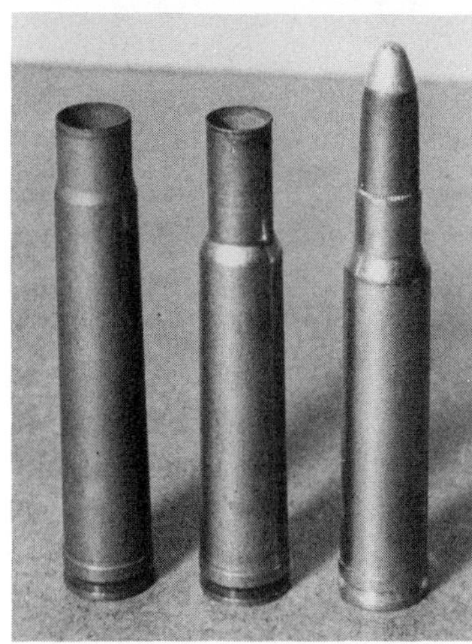

Top Left to Right: Four of the most monstrous cartridges of all time. These are the .458 Winchester Magnum with solid bullet; the same with soft point; the .460 Weatherby Magnum; and the Sharps "Big Fifty," a .50-caliber 3¼-inch cartridge used in Sharps rifles during buffalo-hunting days. The Sharps .50 was just about the largest cartridge used in the West. The extremes in varmint cartridges include the .222 Remington, one of the finest of all short- to medium-range cartridges ever; the .243 Winchester, one of the finest medium- to long-range varmint cartridges; and the .244 H&H Magnum, a British attempt to make a supervelocity rifle that was a bust because the case is far too large for the 6mm bore. On the left is Weatherby's .240 Magnum and on the right the venerable Holland & Holland .240 Apex. Both are 6mms and both work in a standard action. In my opinion, the .240 Weatherby is one of the great cartridges and I think it deserves a lot more popularity than it enjoys. Shown is a typical chamber blueprint giving all the pertinent dimensions. The .243 Rockchucker cartridge was designed by Fred Huntington of RCBS fame and was a forerunner of the present 6mm Remington cartridge. The drawing was made by F.K. "Red" Elliott, the famous maker of chambering reamers for the custom gunsmith trade. Bottom Left: Forming one cartridge case from another is a simple operation. The .375 H&H cartridge (left) is lubricated and run into a .338 Winchester Magnum forming-die. The result is shown in the center. Then the neck is trimmed back and the case loaded, as at right. You now have a .338 cartridge. The same procedure may be followed with many cartridges. Bottom Right: An ancient sub-caliber adaptor is shown here for the .32/40 rifle that will allow you to fire the small .32-caliber revolver cartridge for practice. Today there are many such adaptors, from a .222 Remington insert that will fire .22 Long Rifles to a .300 Winchester Magnum using .30 Carbine cartridges.

classic example of this is Roy Weatherby, who started as a wildcatter, then began producing his own ammunition, which removed him from the wildcat status. Moreover, his impact with his Magnums has had profound results in the products of the industry's giants.

METRICS

They tell us that the United States is going to "go metric" one of these days. Indeed, they now tell us the temperature each day in both Fahrenheit and Celsius. The cost of conversion by American industry will be unbelievable and the whole subject isn't really of much interest to us here except as it relates to calibers and bore sizes.

All European cartridges have always been in millimeters, generally in two figures. For example, the 8mm Mauser cartridge is referred to as the

8x57mm. The second figure is a measurement of the length of the cartridge case. This is necessary because there are many 8mm cartridges available on the Continent. Rimmed versions of European cartridges are followed by the letter R, as 9.3x72R, this being one of the larger bore cartridges fairly popular in some German double rifles.

When the day comes that all cartridges are called by metric numbers I know I'll be long gone and I suspect most of you will be too. I also suspect that your pet 7.63x60mm will also be known as the "7.63x60 Wasp" or some other pet name. And I further suspect that the full name will soon be shortened to just plain Wasp.

CHAPTER THIRTEEN

CALIBERS

The subject of calibers is one that is so often misunderstood that it's pretty amazing. For example, in my home state of Rhode Island there is a law that permits hunting woodchucks with a ".22-caliber rifle." That would seem to be pretty plain language, but you should hear what some of the definitions are! One day, while talking with a State Conservation Officer, we brought up this subject. I asked, "What about the .222?" He replied, as though I'd asked a nasty question, "Don't bring up the .222." In some quarters the .222 is considered *larger* than .22 caliber, just because it has that extra digit in its name. Rhode Island says it's OK to use a .220 Swift, but you could get in trouble with a .222.

This is not only silly and stupid but it demonstrates a remarkable lack of knowledge among those officers who are supposed to know something about guns. For both the .222 Remington and the .220 Swift use bullets of exactly the same diameter (which happens to be .224 inch).

This introduces the fact that names need have nothing whatever to do with the actual sizes and are often chosen for their sound, for their alliteration, and for their promotional aspects; or perhaps to ride the coattails of another, already popular, cartridge.

It may be accepted that any cartridge adopted by the U. S. military will be a success. There have been a couple of exceptions, but not very many. For instance, look at the .45/70 which was adopted in 1873. That was during the period when the West was being opened up and the big, fat cartridge was just the ticket for those pioneers who faced elk, buffalo, and grizzly bears. The .45/70 faded after about the 1920s and began to quietly go the way of all older, no longer really useful, things. But today the .45/70 is bigger than ever! Now look at the .30/06, an all-time runaway success and, in spite of its age (since 1906), still one of the best-selling and finest of the world's sporting cartridges. Other popular cartridges that are or have been popular because they are or were U.S. military standards are the .30/40 Krag, .308 Winchester, and .223 Remington.

The same thing is true across the world. The British .303 has long been one of that country's favorites as a game rifle, as has been the German 8mm Mauser. So has the 7mm Mauser been popular over the world. Keep in mind that the German arms factories (and the Belgian plants) made rifles for many of the world's armies. Most of these were in 8mm or 7mm caliber and that's one of the prime reasons these two cartridges have been so popular so long all over the world. Where the .308 and .223 will eventually wind up on the pecking order is hard to say. The .308 wasn't a military standard very long, and the .223 is too new to evaluate.

THE NAMES

Rifle cartridges are often given names. This may have started seriously with the .22 Hornet back in the late 1920s, and the Hornet remains one of the most unique cartridges in existence. It began life as a wildcat and was the first cartridge for which commercially loaded ammunition was made before a commercial rifle was available. There were a couple of more later, but they never became successful. The little Hornet was pushed hard by a number of custom gunsmiths and writers of those days, to the point where the big companies tooled up and produced ammunition and rifles, in that order. The Hornet was followed by the .218 Bee, .219 Zipper, .220 Swift, and a vast flock of wildcats, most of which are but dim memories in the minds of many of us over the age of fifty.

Let's continue this rundown of the .22 caliber. In the first place, there are .22 rimfires — .22 Short, .22 Long, and .22 Long Rifle, all employing lead bullets and all used for sporting and target purposes in both rifles and handguns. Certainly these are the world's biggest selling guns and ammunition and come in both standard-velocity and high-speed loads. The former (in .22 Long Rifle) are a little below the speed of sound, the latter a little above it. All target ammunition is loaded to standard velocity, below the speed of sound (about 1,100 feet-per-second at sea level).

As already mentioned, the .22 Short cartridge was developed by Smith & Wesson and first marketed in 1854. A little later the .22 Long came along and, in the 1890s, the .22 Long Rifle. Both the Long and Long Rifle use the same length of cartridge case but their bullets are quite different in that the Long uses the 29-grain .22 Short bullet, while the Long Rifle has its own 40-grain (37 grain in hollow point) bullet. The .22 Long was, and remains, a bastard cartridge. It should have been dropped long ago. It has no practical use and I suspect it's handed over the shelf to unsuspecting customers who ask for "Longs" when they really mean "Long Rifles" . . . or perhaps who don't know what they mean. The industry would do all of us a favor if they just buried the .22 Long and forgot it.

On the other hand, the .22 Short is most useful. Its noise level isn't much more than a pellet gun, its accuracy is excellent (with target cartridges that are loaded to rigid specifications) and it is finding considerable use today among competitive pistol shooters. Several models of pistols are made exclusively for this tiny cartridge. Other .22 Short cartridges were made for gallery use (are you old enough to remember the shooting galleries at every carnival?). These generally used a disintegrating bullet made from sintered metal that simply disappeared on impact in a little cloud of dust.

I suspect as much research-and-development time and money have gone into the development of the .22 Long Rifle as any other cartridge. It is available in standard and high velocity, lead and hollow point, and also in superbly accurate match ammunition used by the world's leading target shooters. Moreover, .22 ammunition is loaded by every major maker all over the world.

Back around the 1890s, Winchester introduced a bigger .22 rimfire cartridge, which they called the .22 WRF, for Winchester Rim Fire. (Remington called their version of the same cartridge the .22 Remington Special.) This cartridge was longer and its bullet of larger diameter, so it couldn't be used in any other .22 rifle. Both companies made special rifles to handle it. The .22 WRF (and Remington Special) used a bullet that measured .228 inch; all

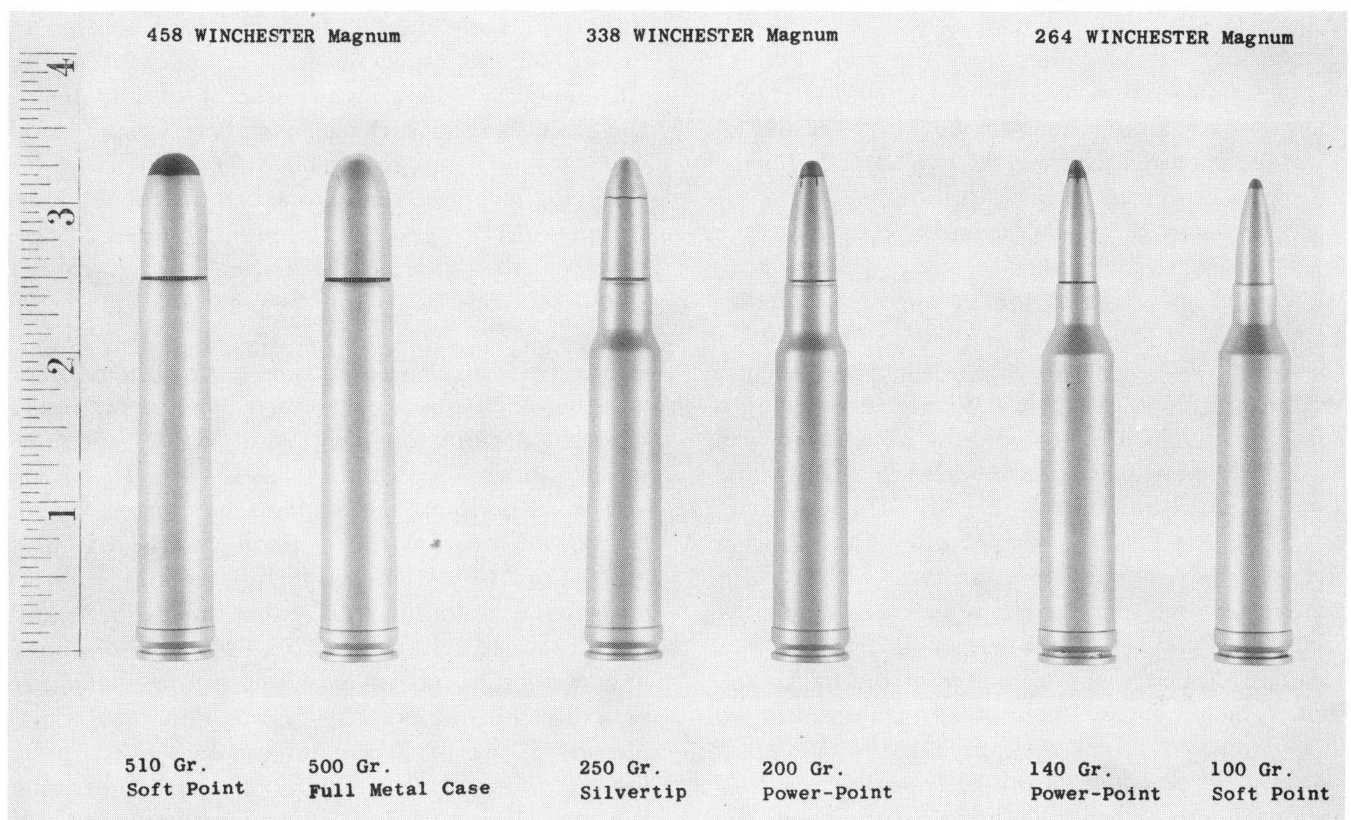

A "family" of cases based on the same belted Magnum basic design. All three cartridges are the same length and work through any standard action and all three are superb for the purposes for which they were designed. The original "parent" for these belted Magnums was the .375 Holland & Holland Magnum first produced in 1912 by the famous London gunmakers of the same name.

other .22 rimfires use a bullet that measures .222 inch. The WRF is gone now, even though a few older rifles are still around and the ammunition is still listed. Then, a few years ago, Winchester produced their .22 WMR (Winchester Magnum Rimfire), a considerably hotter cartridge that uses a jacketed bullet, instead of a pure lead one and is of .224-inch diameter. This means you cannot stick a WMR cartridge in any existing .22 rifle, and you cannot rechamber such a rifle for the WMR. This new cartridge has proved excellent for somewhat longer-range shooting, usually to about 150 yards, and has quite a bit of sock at that distance.

CENTER-FIRES

Despite their names, almost all .22 center-fires use a bullet measuring .224 inch. This means you can take any given barrel blank (an unfitted, unchambered barrel) and fit it to any suitable action and then chamber it for any cartridge from the .218 Bee to the .220 Swift – or .220 Weatherby Rocket for that matter. First though, the exceptions: The .22 Hornet was made with a .223-inch barrel and the earlier .22 Savage Hi-Power (which was many years ahead of its time) was .228 inch. This needn't bother you unless you're a reloader, in which case you use a .223-inch bullet for the Hornet and a .228-inch bullet – if you can find it – for the .22 Savage; but you can't find many of the old Savage rifles so that point becomes academic. As you can see, cartridge numbers and names are meaningless.

In the old days, cartridges were named with a series of numbers, as .30/30, .45/70 and so on. Sometimes these were extended to add another set of numbers as in the .45/70/500. These were black powder designations, where the first number gave the caliber (.45 inch), the second gave the powder charge in grains (avoirdupois, there are 7,000 grains in one pound), and the third represented the bullet weight, also in grains. Thus the .45/70/500 shot a .45-caliber bullet propelled by a charge of 70 grains of black powder and its bullet weighed 500 grains. These numbers have hung on with a few of the famous old cartridges such as the two named plus the .30/40 Krag, .32/20 and .44/40.

Propelled by the late Warren Page, at that time *Field & Stream* magazine's shooting editor, both Winchester and Remington in the mid-1950s introduced a cartridge in 6mm caliber. Winchester made their case by necking down the .308 Winchester, the simple and classic pattern of producing a new cartridge. Remington did the same thing with the .257 Roberts cartridge. Winchester's was called the .243 and Remington's the .244. The cartridges were a little different in shape, although both were of approximately the same size and capacity. But one turned out to be a runaway success and the other was a disaster. What happened?

What happened was a matter of the basic concept. Winchester saw the 6mm as a compromise, so they produced theirs in both 80- and 100-grain loadings. They reasoned the 80-grain bullet would be ideal for long-range varmint shooting and the 100-grain load deadly on deer-size game. Remington's concept was that the 6mm was a varmint rifle. They produced their ammo in 75- and 90-grain bullet weights and their rifle had a twist of rifling that was too slow to stabilize a 100-grain bullet. Moreover, their rifle — as a varmint rifle — was a bit heavy. The result was that Winchester's .243 ran away with the market — fast. The .244 Remington sat on shelves. Remington doesn't make too many mistakes; they realized they had made an error and reintroduced the same cartridge with a new name (6mm Remington), this time with 80- and 100-grain bullets and a new rifle with the correct rifling twist. Rifle and cartridge now sell very well.

I still regard these cartridges as a tossup. There are those who claim the 6mm Remington is a better cartridge, but my own experience has been that the .243 has a slight edge. The point, however, is really too narrow to be valid. Besides, my favorite 6mm cartridge is the .240 Weatherby Magnum anyway.

Another cartridge with a strange name is the .250/3000 Savage. It's an old-timer now, dating to before World War I, and it was named because it fits a .25-caliber rifle and fires an 87-grain bullet at a muzzle velocity of 3,000 fps. That was pretty sensational in those days and the cartridge became an instant success, especially in the Model 99 Savage rifle. The .250 Savage was pushed into oblivion by the 6mms a few years ago and there was a period when nobody was making a rifle for it. Now it's back again, and I think to stay — it's a fine cartridge and it deserves to. It might be pointed out, however, that despite the name, any .25-caliber rifle works best with bullets no lighter than 100 grains.

Another .25-caliber that used to be quite popular was the .257 Roberts. This cartridge was originally made by necking down the 7mm Mauser cartridge to .25 caliber. Its promoter was the late Ned Roberts, an experimental rifleman whose career began before the turn of the century and lasted until about the 1940s. Remington embraced the Roberts cartridge as a commercial reality and Roberts and a man named Kimball started their own company and also produced rifles in this caliber. The .257 never lived up to its claims in my opinion. Roberts always claimed that Remington loused it up by loading the wrong weight bullets and by changing the shoulder angle and rifling twist rate, but this was probably sour grapes. Col. Townsend Whelen used to claim that a .257 ought to have a longer magazine and deeper throat in the chamber so that bullets could be seated out a little further, but I could never see how that would have significantly helped the .257. It was sort of an orphan among most (but not all) serious riflemen. Some, including myself, made special reamers and produced "improved" versions of it by fire-forming the case to a larger capacity. I called my version the Helldiver and at least it worked better than the original.

Another strange situation involves the .22/250. Remington adopted this cartridge a couple years ago and called it the .22/250 Remington. I guess they can call it whatever they want to but let's look at a little history and see if you think they had a right to stick their name on it. Back in the 1920s, a dedicated experimenter named Grove Wotkyns necked the .250/3000 Savage case down to .22 caliber. He called it Swift, and it became quite popular. A gunsmith by the name of Jerry Gebby, from Dayton, Ohio, made a lot of rifles in this chambering and called them the .22/250 Varminter, a name he copyrighted. Red Elliott, the chamber-reamer maker from California, always called the .22/250 the "Wotkyns Original Swift." When Winchester made their Swift they took a long look at the .22/250 and elected to use the 6mm Lee Navy case from the 1890s rather than the .250/3000 as Wotkyns had done. Over the years the .22/250, by whatever name you like, was one of the most popular wildcat cartridges ever made and for excellent reasons.

A similar situation exists with the .25/06, to which Remington has also added its name. This cartridge goes back to before World War I, when Charles Newton produced his .256 Newton (which was actually 6.5mm caliber in most versions) and A. O. Niedner produced rifles in .25/06 caliber. These early versions were not great successes simply because the powders used in those days could not achieve the velocities of modern propellants. It remained for today's slower burning powders to make the .25/06 the success it now is. In any event, the .25/06 is made by necking the .30/06 down to .25 caliber. It's that simple. And it was a famous wildcat cartridge for many years before being legitimized by Remington.

There is a recent trend to naming American cartridges in metric designations. It isn't universal, but it's happening just the same. A case in point is the 7mm Remington Magnum which could just as well have been called the .284 Remington Magnum. Introducing it at about the same time, Winchester named their .264 Winchester Magnum by our traditional decimal system; they could as well have named it the 6.5mm Winchester Magnum. Another instance is the 5.56mm, a military cartridge called the .223 Remington in commercial form.

NAMES, NUMBERS, AND ACTUAL SIZES

Every rifled barrel has two internal dimensions, bore diameter and groove diameter. Bore diameter is the size the barrel is reamed to before rifling, in the case of a .30-caliber rifle, .300 inch. The rifling is cut below that depth. In the case of a .30-caliber rifle the grooves are cut to a depth of .004 inch, making a groove diameter of .308 inch. A bullet must be made to groove diameter, .308 inch in this case, because it must be forced through the rifling and made to spin. It's legitimate to call a .30-caliber rifle either a .30 caliber or a .308, as you prefer.

But not every rifle is called by its precise bore measurements, which leads to confusion. This may not be of much importance to you. So long as you buy ammunition the same size as that marked on the barrel of your rifle, you're all right. If you're a reloader, it's another story.

All .22-caliber high-power rifles, with a few exceptions, actually have a .224-inch groove diameter and a bore diameter of about .219 inch. I say "about," because bore diameters vary, not because they're sloppy but because different rifling systems require different bore dimensions. The vital measurement is the groove diameter which must be at least as large as the bullet or a little larger, but never smaller.

Let's run through a few names and real measurements for the fun of it (skipping the .22s). All the 6mms are the same size even though they're called .243 (the real size), .244, and the .240 Weatherby. All the .25s measure .257 inch in the grooves regardless of the name; the .270 is really a .277 inch; the .280 Remington, .284 Winchester, 7mm Mauser, and 7mm Remington are all 7mms or .284 inch. All the .30s are .308 inch and so on all the way up to the .458 Winchester Magnum and .460 Weatherby, both of which shoot the same diameter bullet: .458 inch.

THE STRANGE CASE OF THE .220 SWIFT

In 1935, Winchester introduced the .220 Swift cartridge in their Model 54 rifle. The following year, when the Model 70 was announced, the cartridge was produced for that rifle. At the same time they changed the rate of rifling twist from 1 turn in 16 to 1 in 14 inches. The cartridge was pretty sensational, since it had an advertised muzzle velocity of 4,140 fps with a 48-grain bullet. All the promotional aspects of the Swift were involved with its sensational velocity and, of course, the 48-grain bullet.

Strange claims for its killing power came along, much as they had a generation earlier when the .22 Savage Hi-Power made its impact on the shooting world. Like the .22 Savage, the Swift killed by magic. By hydraulic shock. By some mysterious means that nobody could really understand. It was true that you could kill a deer with the Swift as if it had been struck by lightning — so long as you were close enough for the bullet to be still going very fast and hit it right. But if the range was a bit long, and the hit not quite right, you didn't get your deer at all. And sometimes that light bullet just broke up on impact and didn't penetrate. Other times the bullet struck a leaf, or maybe a blade of grass, near the muzzle, in which event it simply blew up right there due to its extreme velocity and rotational speed. So the Swift was condemned as well as praised. Those who reloaded for the Swift – bear in mind this was in the mid-30s, when the nation was in the grip of the Depression and the money-saving aspects of reloading were critical – also had strange tales to tell. They claimed the cases stretched and constantly had to be trimmed back. That the necks thickened up. That the Swift was fussy as to what loads you could use in it.

Actually, all these claims were false. The Swift is a fine cartridge that has seldom been understood. The real culprits in the game were Winchester – which should never have loaded the cartridge with the light 48-grain bullet at so high a speed – and the writers who seldom knew what they were talking about.

Winchester was plugging the velocity purely and simply. Instead, they should have loaded the Swift with a 55-grain bullet at a velocity level of about 3,700 fps. That might not have been so sensational, but it would have produced superior ballistics downrange where the targets were. Proof of this statement lies in the fact that every competent reloader who owned a Swift reloaded it with a 55-grain bullet and a load (either 37 grs 4064 or 33 grs 3031) that produced a velocity of about 3,700 fps. Its accuracy was superb and, if the day wasn't too windy, you could usually kill woodchucks out to 500 and 600 yards regularly. I have owned a few Swift rifles, all Model 70 Winchester, and they have always performed well. One was a standard-weight model that I used a 10X Unertl scope on. It was my favorite crow rifle for many years and was always handy to my shooting range in my Adirondack Mountain gunshop. There was a big elm tree about 250 yards from the shooting port and, when the crows returned in the spring, they used to like this tree. Just about every crow in this tree I ever shot I dropped with that Swift.

Alas, the misunderstood Swift was finally dropped by Winchester and was replaced by a strange number called the .225 Winchester. The .225 was loaded like the Swift should have been; with a 55-grain bullet at 3,066 fps, but the cartridge was a sort of semirimmed affair that just didn't ever get popular. That it came along when the Model 70 rifle was undergoing some changes didn't help it either because these changes left the shooting world pretty cold, and sales dropped. But now the situation has brightened, the Swift is back! As this is being written it's available in the Ruger Model 77 rifle and Savage Model 110. Should these rifles sell in volume you can bet it will appear in others as well. Now we can only hope the ammunition companies have the good sense to right that old wrong and load it correctly. I think they will today.

There was always a controversy between those who advocated the .22/250 and the Swift lovers. This was really a toss-up since there is no real advantage of one over the other. The only positive advantage I can cite for one over the other is that the Swift brass case is a little heavier and stronger at the base than the .22/250. That's a small point and need not be a consideration.

Two excellent cartridges that were early victims of the 6mms in the 1950s were the .250/3000 Savage and the .257 Roberts. The ancient .250, you will recall, was a development of Charles Newton for the Savage Model 99 lever-action rifle. It went on to become one of the favorite calibers in this fine rifle. The .257 Roberts was adapted to bolt-action rifles and, while it never achieved the popularity of the .250 Savage, it was a popular cartridge. But both were literally wiped out by the 6mms. A lot of shooters groaned a bit when the great old .250 Savage was erased, and they finally got their way. The cartridge is making a comeback and that's a good thing. It is doubtful that the .257 ever will and not too many tears were shed over its loss. Between the choices in 6mm and with two .25s today (the .250/3000 and .25/06) that particular ground is pretty well covered.

An interesting cartridge that never got off the ground in spite of its excellence is the .358 Winchester. This was introduced the same time as the .243, and it was made the same way – by necking the .308 Winchester cartridge up to .35 caliber (the .243 is the .308 necked down to 6mm). Now the .358 was far and away a better cartridge than the .35 Remington, which for many years has been one of the most popular cartridges for deep-woods hunting. This .35 Remington dates from the early 1900s and was popularized in the Models 8 and 81 autoloading Remingtons as well as the 14 and 141 pump-action Remington rifles. These models were dropped after World War II and the cartridge has since been kept alive by Marlin, which chambers

INTERCHANGEABILITY CHART

Cartridges in groups shown below will interchange.

RIMFIRE
.22 W.R.F.
.22 Remington Special
.22 Win. M/1890 in a .22 Win. Magnum Rimfire but not conversely

CENTER-FIRE
.25-20 Remington
.25-20 W.C.F.
.25-20 Win.
.25-20 Win. High Speed
.25-20 Marlin
.25 W.C.F.

6mm Rem. (80 & 90 Grain)
.244 Remington

.30-30 Sav.
.30-30 Win.
.30-30 Marlin
.30-30 Win. High Speed
.30 W.C.F.

.32 W.C.F.*
.32 Win.*
.32-20 Win. High Speed*
SEE NOTE A
.32-20 Colt L.M.R.
.32-20 W.C.F.
.32-20 Win. and Marlin
SEE NOTE B

.38 Marlin*
.38 Win.
SEE NOTE A
.38 Remington*
.38-40 Win.
.38 W.C.F.*
SEE NOTE A

.44 Marlin
.44 Win.
.44 Remington
.44-40 Win.
.44 W.C.F.

.45-70 Government
.45-70 Marlin, Win.
.45-70-405

NOTE A: *High-speed cartridges must not be used in revolvers. They should be used only in rifles made especially for them.

NOTE B: Not to be used in Win. M-66 and M-73.

Chart courtesy Remington Arms Co., Inc.

its fine little Model 336 for the .35 Remington. Unfortunately for the .358, it was too long for any existing lever action except the Savage 99, and that company didn't push the cartridge. But I wouldn't be too surprised to see this fine cartridge return one of these days in a good woods rifle and it would be better than the .35 Remington. (Savage has added the .358 to its 1977 line in the Model 99 rifle.)

To a large degree, the promotion behind a cartridge can make it popular or not. It's also a question of the particular rifle that is chambered for the cartridge, and the way the cartridge gets written up in the press that has a great deal to do with it. Just to cite one example of what can happen. In the mid-50s I was writing for the *American Rifleman* magazine and was asked by the editor, General Julian S. Hatcher, to review the Model 70 Winchester in .243 and the Model 722 Remington in .244 caliber. My tests and my writeup clearly showed that the .243 Winchester had an advantage, which was largely one of concept, since Remington had taken the varmint route.

Just as this book was about to go on press, word was received that Remington is now out with a new 8mm Magnum cartridge. Departing from the recent belted Magnum cartridges, Remington used the .375 H&H Magnum case full length and simply necked it down to 8mm. The size of an 8mm bullet is .323-inch, close to the .338 in bore diameter; indeed the closest thing to the new 8mm Remington is Weatherby's .340 Magnum, which uses the same long case and the .338 bullet. With the long .375 case, the new cartridge will not work in standard-length actions but will require the longer action, as does the .375 H&H. Winchester and Remington, among others; manufacture a long enough action for the .375.

Initially, this new cartridge will be loaded with 185- and 220-grain bullets, both of which have excellent ballistics and equally excellent downrange figures. Following are the figures supplied by Remington.

DOWNRANGE BALLISTICS OF 8 MM REMINGTON MAGNUM 185-GR. AND 220-GR. POINTED SOFT POINT "CORE-LOKT" BULLETS

Range (Yards)	*Velocity— 185 Gr.*	*Ft/Sec 220 Gr.*	*Energy— 185 Gr.*	*Ft.-Lbs. 220 Gr.*
0	3080	2830	3896	3912
100	2761	2581	3132	3255
200	2464	2346	2494	2688
300	2186	2123	1963	2201
400	1926	1913	1524	1787
500	1687	1716	1170	1439

SHORT-RANGE TRAJECTORY IN INCHES (SIGHTED IN AT 150 YARDS)

8mm Rem. Mag. Bullet Weight	*50 Yds.*	*100 Yds.*	*150 Yds.*	*200 Yds.*	*250 Yds.*	*300 Yds.*
185-Grain	+0.5	+0.8	0.0	−2.1	−5.6	−10.7
220-Grain	+0.6	+1.0	0.0	−2.4	−6.4	−12.1

LONG-RANGE TRAJECTORY IN INCHES (SIGHTED IN AT 200 YARDS)

	100	*150*	*200*	*250*	*300*	*400*	*500*
185 Grain	+1.8	+1.6	0.0	−3.0	−7.6	−22.5	−46.8
220 Grain	+2.2	+1.8	0.0	−3.4	−8.5	−24.7	−50.5

SOMETHING NEW

This something new is the practical application of an old device called a sabot (the t is silent), which is defined as a form of shoe used to surround a projectile and make it accept the rifling. Remington has just announced its adaptation in a .30/06 Accelerator cartridge.

This idea is simply a .22-caliber bullet weighing 55 grains, such as is used in the .22/250, wrapped in a sabot and loaded in the .30/06 cartridge. You shoot it in a .30/06 rifle. The sabot accepts the rifling and seals the bore, allowing the little bullet to exit from the muzzle with a velocity of 4,080 feet per second. That's the fastest muzzle velocity obtained by any commercially produced ammunition. It exceeds the .220 Swift's velocity by a small amount, but with its heavier bullet, it sustains the downrange velocity better than the Swift.

As soon as the Accelerator's bullet unit leaves the muzzle, it sheds the sabot quickly. The combination of extremely high rotational speed and air resistance snaps the sabot off quickly, as the pictures from Remington show.

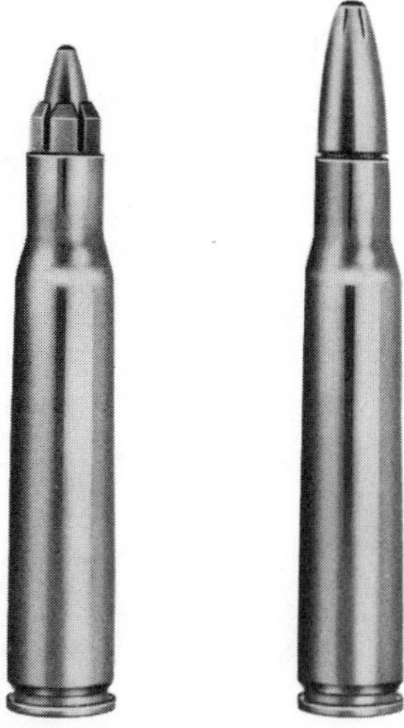

Here is Remington's new Accelerator (left) next to a standard .30/06 Springfield cartridge.

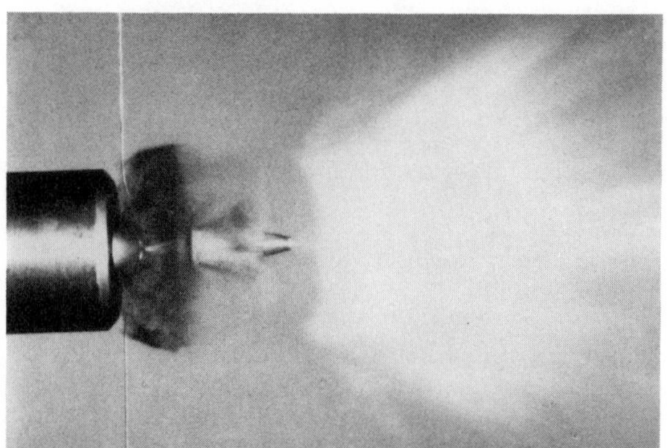

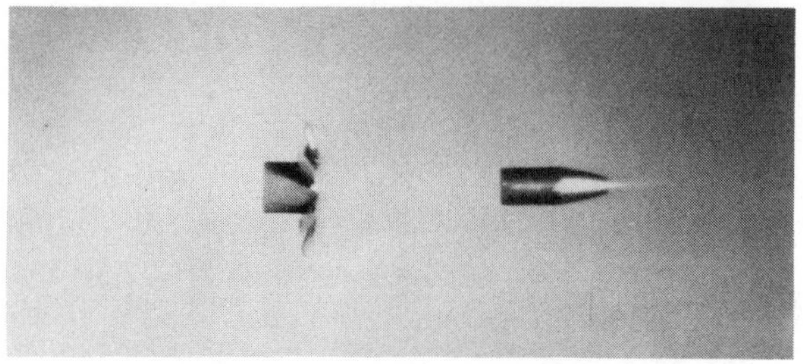

When the Accelerator bullet is ignited, it leaves the muzzle of the gun (right) at 4,080 feet per second. Eighteen inches from the gun muzzle (left) the bullet has fully separated from the sabot, which falls aside.

CHAPTER FOURTEEN

CASES AND PRIMERS

Cartridge cases are divided into two broad categories: metallics and shotgun. Metallics deal with both rimfire and center-fire numbers. While the rimfire cartridge is considerably softer than the center-fire, both are commonly made of brass. Its just that rimfire brass is softer. Any metal can be softened by annealing – in fact, that's what the word means. For example, steel is hardened by heating it and then quenching in water, oil, or air, depending on the properties of the particular alloy. Steel can be annealed by heating it to a specified temperature and then allowing it to cool slowly (often by placing it in the furnace and then turning off the furnace to let it cool overnight).

Brass works the opposite way; you heat and quench it to soften brass. Brass cartridge cases are made by a method known as "drawing"; you start by punching out a slug that resembles a coin of the proper thickness and diameter to finish up to the proper size. This coin or slug is then formed through a succession of die-and-punch operations which gradually form it into the elongated shape familiar to us as a cartridge. Each time the brass goes through an operation it is "work hardened," which is the same as when you bend a piece of metal back and forth until it breaks. You are work hardening that metal by the bending operation until it becomes crystalline and snaps apart. To avoid that, cartridge cases are annealed frequently during the forming operations so that the brass remains strong, tough, and elastic. It must be strong because the cartridge case is always the weakest part of the gun/ammunition combination; in some instances it must hold as much as 55,000 pounds-per-square-inch of chamber pressure. Naturally, the case is securely locked in place by the gun barrel and breech bolt. But any rupture of the brass case will result in the spilling of gas under very high pressure. Since that spilled gas can't go forward, because there's a bullet sealing the bore, it must go backwards or sideways.

A case must also be tough and elastic because it should not only hold those pressures, but ought to spring back a bit after the pressure has subsided, which will help ease extraction. Most of today's cartridge cases fit these requirements well. It wasn't always so, however, and in the early days of metallic cartridges there were numerous failures.

During World War II, when brass was in critical supply, many experiments were made with steel cases both in the Allied armies and on the German side. While these worked, and many millions of pistol and submachine-gun cartridges were made of steel, the practice was stopped as soon as enough brass became available. So far as I can recall, these experiments with rifle ammunition were never really practical.

It is critical that the base (rear) of the center-fire cartridge be as hard as possible. This is accomplished by the work-hardening principle already mentioned. Following the final drawing operation, which determines the final shape, the case has its primer pocket and flashhole punched into place. This serves to further harden the brass. Then the cartridge identification, manufacturer, and caliber is stamped, which further hardens the head. The hardness can be controlled by the amount of name and number stamping as well as its depth. The more and the deeper, the harder will be the brass at this critical point.

Details of case-head thickness are shown by this cutaway of a belted Magnum. This is one of the strongest case designs in use today.

Extracting grooves are machined after final shaping and, if additional annealing is required to soften the case mouth, the cases are placed standing in water to keep the bases cold and hard.

Since cases come in both straight and bottleneck versions it follows that some require more drawing than others. And it also follows that there are limits of shoulder beyond which ammunition makers do not like to go. The .30/06 has a shoulder angle of approximately 17°, and there was a period during which no ammunition manufacturer wanted to make cases with shoulders any steeper than that angle. But wildcat shooters were proving the point that steeper shoulders provided more powder capacity, so the factories gradually developed the capability of making steeper shoulders. The wildcatters also were claiming that steeper angles (30° was claimed to be the "ultimate" even though some wildcatters went to 45° shoulders) gave higher velocities with a given amount of powder. They claimed the steeper shoulder made the powder burn more efficiently. In fact there are some who still claim this, although, as far as I'm concerned, this claim is unsupported by any facts. Just to prove this point, there is often chatter in the pages of some gun magazine or another about which of the two popular 6mm cartridges is the better, the .243 Winchester or the 6mm Remington. The general claim is that the 6mm Remington is easier to reload. Some prefer it because it has a longer neck; it also has a slightly steeper shoulder angle than the .243. But, if you examine the ballistics with care, you conclude that with few exceptions, the .243 gets the same velocities as the 6mm Remington with a *grain or so less powder!* Which of these two cartridges you choose is of no real consequence, because the differences don't amount to enough to talk about. But it always annoys me to read that one is superior to the other for reasons that are unsupported.

One of the original bottleneck cartridges was the British .577/450 Martini-Henry. (The British label their cartridges the opposite of our way. For example, the .577/450 is the .577 cartridge necked down to .450 caliber. On the other hand, our .22/250 is a .22 caliber made by reducing the neck of the .250/3000 Savage case. We put the new caliber first; the British put the parent case first.) The bottleneck case permits more powder in a short, compact form. It also permits more powder than one could ever pack into any straight-sided case. For example, if you made a .30-caliber cartridge long and thin enough to be straight sided and hold as much powder as the .30/06, you'd have a long-as-a-pencil object that wouldn't perform worth beans because no matter what you did, you'd never get all the powder ignited properly.

During the late 1800s, the British concentrated on extremely large and powerful cartridges and rifles for the big game of Africa and Asia where their customers went hunting. On the other hand, the Germans, Swiss, and French worked at perfecting military cartridges. One of the greatest developments of this period was the 8mm French Lebel cartridge (and rifle) which was many years ahead of its time. (It has also been said that the French haven't done anything since in rifle or cartridge development.) In about 1885, the Europeans began using the new smokeless powder that had been made possible by Swedish chemist Alfred Nobel. Smokeless powder, with its much higher pressures, required much better cartridge cases than black powder, just as it required stronger rifle actions and better barrel steels.

In the meantime our cartridge development went along two broad lines. One was the whopping, fat, and long cartridge used in hunting heavy game, especially buffalo. Most of these cartridges were used in single-shot rifles, like the Sharps, Winchester, Ballard, and others (because magazine rifles were not made big enough for such cartridges). The giant of all these giants was what has become known as the Sharps "Big Fifty," a .50-caliber rifle shooting a cartridge 3¼ inches long. This remained a pretty rare rifle, although a few were used by buffalo hunters. Just the same it was pretty puny next to some of the English elephant rifles. The other line our cartridge development took was smaller cartridges for the popular magazine rifles, such as the Winchester and the Marlin. These cartridges included the .44/40 and .38/40. While they were much smaller, they had the advantage of being rapid-fire repeating rifles which meant a great many shots could be fired. They also often had the usefulness of being the same cartridge for the revolver that was packed on the hunter's hip.

"IMPROVED" CASES

For many years custom gunsmiths and experimental riflemen have sought to improve on the performance of existing cartridges by changing the shape and, usually, increasing capacity. This has sometimes actually improved performance, but more often has only resulted in more noise, more powder consumed, and faster barrel wear. One improvement that really worked was the Roy Weatherby improvement of the original .300 H&H Magnum. What Roy wrought was to expand the original case to larger dimension and load the resultant larger cartridge with a lot more powder. This was practical because it's a simple matter to "fire-form" the .300 H&H cartridge in the Weatherby chamber. (This is standard procedure in improved cases. The brass is usually sufficiently resilient to expand to fit the larger chamber without trouble. It may then be reloaded with a larger powder charge.)

The original .300 H&H case dates to 1912 and powders have improved a great deal since then. A .300 Weatherby would not have been practical in 1912 because the powders then available were not able to attain the velocities we can achieve today with such a case.

A colossal non-improvement is seen in the development by Holland & Holland itself when that staid old company took its .375 H&H Magnum case and necked it down to 6mm! This has to be one of the most drastic examples of too much powder capacity for too small a bore (commonly termed "overbore capacity") ever created. The big surprise is that it was a firm with the reputation of Holland & Holland – in this case they should have

Three 6mm cartridges: left to right, .243 Winchester; 6mm Remington (also known as .244 Rem.); and .244 H&H Magnum. This latter cartridge, made by reducing the .375 H&H Magnum cartridge to 6mm neck size, was one of the biggest "busts" of all time. It is a classic example of far too much powder capacity for the bore diameter and its performance was not significantly better than either the .243 or 6mm.

stuck to their shotguns. Needless to add, the .244 H&H never went very far because it couldn't live up to any promise. In 6mm caliber, it is futile to go any larger in capacity than the .240 Weatherby and you don't really have to go beyond the .243 Winchester or 6mm Remington.

SUB-CALIBER ADAPTORS

We used to call them auxiliary cartridges back in the old days. These are chamber-shaped steel units that will accept a lower-power cartridge for cheap practice shooting. An example would be any adaptor that is meant to be placed in the larger chamber and fire a small cartridge. One of the old favorites was one that you could chamber in the .220 Swift rifle that would fire a .22 Long Rifle cartridge. It consisted of a steel insert that nicely fitted the Swift chamber but was chambered for the .22 Long Rifle. To use it you simply put a .22 rimfire cartridge in the adaptor and chambered that in the rifle. It would give you roughly the same performance you'd expect from the smaller cartridge.

There are many other examples. The .32 Smith & Wesson cartridge in a .30/06, .30 Carbine in the .300 Winchester Magnum, and some others — most any others where the bullet size is compatible would work all right. No matter that the .32 Smith & Wesson lead bullet is a little oversize for the .30/06 bore, that's a strong action and the soft lead bullet will easily squeeze down to fit.

The accuracy of these adaptors isn't as good as full loads and they are just what they seem to be — but they will work and provide a certain kind of satisfaction to the guy who doesn't need too much or expect too much.

PRIMERS

The primer is a tiny pinch of violent chemical that explodes when hit or crushed. Its flame then saturates and ignites the main powder charge. The amount of priming compound necessary isn't any larger than the small amount you could get on the very end of a toothpick. If you placed this on a flat surface and hit it with a hammer it would explode. Essentially the same thing happens in your cartridge. In the rimfire the priming mixture is spread around the inside of the rim. The firing pin crushes any part of the rim between it and the breech end of the barrel and this explodes the mixture. A center-fire cartridge contains its own primer as a self-contained unit. The two common systems — the Boxer and the Berdan — are detailed in Chapter 12.

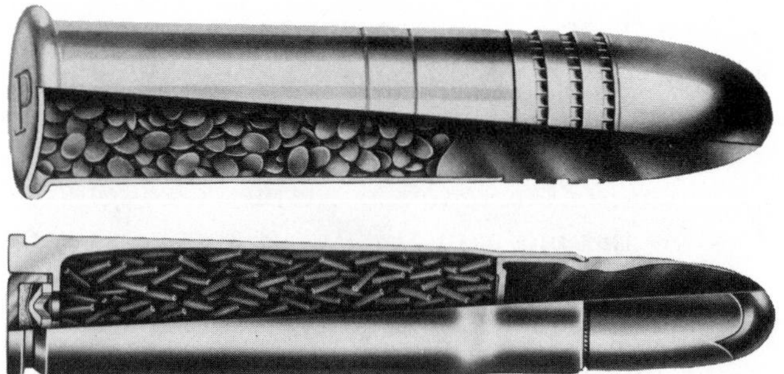

The differences between center-fire (above) and rimfire (below) ignition systems are shown by these cutaway sketches. Note that the rimfire priming compound is spread around the inside of the rim and that the rim metal is quite thin at this point. The center-fire primer consists of cup, priming compound, and anvil. Also shown is the flashhole leading from the primer pocket into the main body of the cartridge case. It can easily be seen that a center-fire cartridge is much stronger than a rimfire.

Primers are extremely violent and only a very small amount is required. In manufacture, the mix is handled wet (for safety) and in very small batches, for the same purpose. It is handled by workers from behind protective barriers and its storage facilities have roofs and walls that are easily blown away, with heavy earthen walls between them to confine any accidents to a localized area. The manufacture of primers is a thing not to be taken lightly.

Early primers were made of a material known as fulminate of mercury — one of the most violent chemical mixes known to man. I understand that fulminate of mercury is still used in such things as artillery shells, bombs, and the like but it's no longer used in small-arms primers because mercury residues attack brass and render the brass cartridge case weakened and not reloadable. Reloading is such a big business today that the market would not stand mercuric primers. Those primers that do not contain fulminate of mercury are known as "nonmercuric".

A later favored priming mix was potassium chlorate, which is just as violent but contains no mercury. But potassium chlorate did contain salt, very

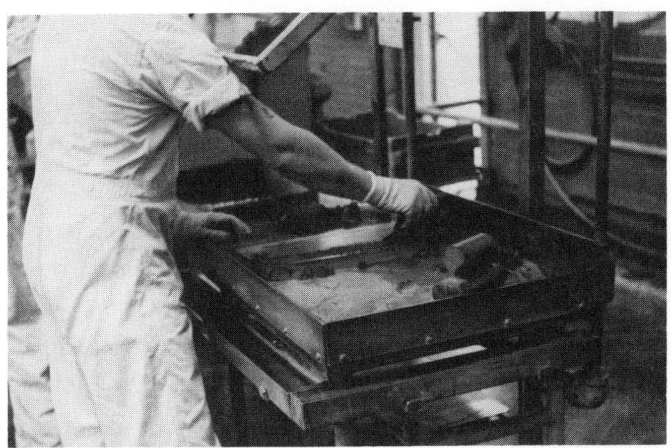

Handled moist because it is so sensitive, priming compound is placed into tiny holes in charge plates. At left an operator scrapes excess mixture off a charging plate for rimfire ammunition. At right, the operator is placing a loaded charge plate into the machine that will punch the mixture into rimfire cartridges.

similar to common table salt containing moreover all its moisture-collecting properties. That's why you had to clean a barrel after every firing; each shot would leave a salt residue which, if left, would collect water and rust the bore before too many hours passed. Since the only element that dissolves salt is water, water itself or a water-based cleaner had to be used. The GI army-issue rifle-bore cleaner was a whitish fluid commonly called "pigeon milk." For many years the famous Frankford Arsenal primer was potassium chlorate and government specifications for military ammunition called for the same primer. Frankford, in Philadelphia, was to small-arms ammunition what Springfield Armory was to small arms.

Even the army departed from the old chlorate (called corrosive) primer during the 1950s. All primers in use today, with a few rare exceptions, are nonmercuric and noncorrosive. The story of the noncorrosive primer began at the Remington plant in Bridgeport, Connecticut, in 1926 when a chemist named James E. Burns dropped in for a visit on his way to Florida. Burns had recently left the U.S. Cartridge Company and had a revolver in his pocket with six primed cartridge cases (no powder, no bullets) which he proceeded to fire six times making six loud snaps but causing no damage. He then told the Remington people to put the revolver, just as it was, in a very damp place and leave it there until he came back. They took him at his word and placed it where the entire outside of the gun became deeply rusted. A month later, when Burns returned, he wiped out the bore and charge holes and showed it to the Remington officials. The bores were as bright and shiny as new.

Burns had discovered a substitute priming mix for potassium chlorate. While it required another two years of experimenting before the primer was marketed, what Burns had done was eliminate fouling by primer residues by using lead styphnate, with tetrazene added as a sort of exciter for the styphnate. (Earlier primers contained about 20 percent ground glass to help ignite the priming mix.) Thus was born the first noncorrosive primer which Remington called Kleanbore.

(The reader is cautioned that my advice is to clean your guns just the same. My own practice is *never* to clean a .22 barrel, and to clean shotgun bores only after the season or after a rainy hunt or a day duck hunting in the salt marshes. High-power rifles I always clean after use, not because I don't trust the primers but because I've always believed the bore is too clean and dry after shooting, so a couple of patches with Hoppe's #9 followed by a lightly oiled patch does the job.)

Many years ago I picked up a pamphlet copyrighted in 1944 by M. J. Albert and H. F. Oelberg entitled *Primers* and it gives a wide variety of priming mixtures and tells you how to make your own. This is something I've never had the temerity to do (and never will). But you must remember that 1944 was wartime and there were no primers available for reloaders. It was make your own or not shoot. This booklet told you how to take a fired primer,

The only real difference between Winchester and Remington primers is that Winchester uses a three-legged anvil whereas the one Remington uses has two. Primers for reloading are packed in small boxes of 100 (cartons of 1,000) and are kept separated by partitions. These are older-style wooden boxes; today they are plastic. The primer elements are shown below. Reading from the center to both left and right are: top of primer cup, bottom of unfired primer, anvil, empty cup after firing.

straighten out the cup again with a small punch, carefully mix your priming (from materials apparently then available in drugstores), place a tiny bit in the inverted cup, cover with a tiny patch of newspaper, and reseat the anvil.

Every primer must contain elements that perform the following functions: a sensitizer to explode and start the procedure, a fuel, and an oxygen producer. The ideal primer is one that both ignites the powder charge and starts the bullet out of the case. (There is more power than you'd believe in that small primer.) And that should explain why there has recently been developed a primer called Magnum which is intended for the larger Magnum cartridges that hold a great deal more powder and have much more capacity than normal-sized cartridges. For example, a standard primer will work perfectly in the .30/06 cartridge. It will also work in the .300 Winchester Magnum but you will get better ignition in the latter by using a Magnum primer. There are two reasons for this: those given above relating to size and capacity, and the use of a slower-burning powder, which is a bit harder to ignite.

Primers come in two basic sizes for metallic cartridges, known as large rifle and small rifle. Manufacturers carefully list the uses for the primer sizes they make. Reloading manuals also tell what primers to use with specific loads they recommend. Reloaders should be careful to keep primers in their original boxes and to follow the recommendations exactly. Should any primers become strayed from their original boxes, it's better to discard them than to guess. Primers may be effectively "killed" by placing them in oil.

Primer pockets are usually sealed in manufacture against penetration by oil, or any other petroleum product. A bit of varnish provides satisfactory seal, although the military also insists on staking primers in place. (Staking consists of upsetting the brass around the primer pocket so that it flows toward the primer and prevents the primer cup from backing out. I've always felt this wasn't necessary but the military may have a logical reason for doing so.) Some years back someone recommended sealing primers in place with Loctite, which I advise against. Loctite is a sealant and perfect for holding screws in place, especially those that might vibrate

Primers used in military ammunition are usually staked by forcing the metal edge inward as shown on the case head at left. At right is a commercial case shown for comparison. The reloader should be cautioned against trying to remove any military primer live—that is unfired. For those unfamiliar with military designation, the "LC" refers to Lake City Ordnance plant, operated during World War II, and "43" the year of manufacture.

loose. You don't need the holding power of Loctite and it's better not to use it, because it could hold the primers too tightly for effective ejection during reloading. Moreover, all you need is a seal against oil. Most reloaders never seal; they simply keep their ammo clean and free of oil and that's as good a procedure as any to my way of thinking.

Primers must not only provide sure ignition, they also must provide consistent ignition; otherwise inaccuracy will be the result. There are a vast number of factors that affect rifle accuracy and ignition and consistency of ignition is one of them. As a result, there has been a great deal of effort expended in recent years to develop and produce consistent primers. Excellent primers are today produced by Winchester, Remington, Federal, Norma, CCI, and others. Remington, for example, lists seven different primers. These include, in addition to the four "basic" sizes (small rifle, small pistol, large rifle, large pistol) a special number for the .357 revolver cartridge, a large rifle primer for belted Magnum cartridges, and a special small rifle primer that is used in the .17 Remington, .221, .222, and .223 cartridges. This may seem like overduplication — after all there are only two basic sizes of primer — but the reason is that better and more consistent ignition is achieved by balancing primers to loads.

BLACK-POWDER GUNS

The increasing interest in black-powder firearms today indicates that we should talk about that kind of gun's ignition. There are two types of black-powder gun in general use today: the percussion-cap and the flintlock gun.

A percussion cap is much like the primer we have just discussed except it isn't nearly so sophisticated. It's simply a cup made of soft metal inside of which is the priming compound. This is placed over the nipple on the gun before you shoot and it should be a close fit over the nipple. The nipple acts as the anvil in a primer, the hammer of the gun having a deeply concave face so that it entirely embraces and covers the cap during firing. There is a small hole in the center of the nipple through which the flame of ignition reaches the main charge in the barrel. Be careful not to snap the hammer on a nipple without a cap in place, otherwise the nipple will be damaged.

A flintlock fires by a different means entirely. The lock contains a pan — which holds fine priming powder — and an upright steel piece against which the flint strikes to shower sparks into the pan. The flame then passes through a flashhole, or touchhole, into the main charge.

CHAPTER FIFTEEN

PROPELLANTS

When priming compound explodes, the result of that small explosion is to ignite the powder, which is the propellant. Powder burns. It does not explode. There are varying requirements for today's gunpowder. Different kinds of powder are required to drive a charge of shot, a large diameter pistol bullet at moderate speed, a small, high-velocity rifle bullet at tremendous speed, or a heavy artillery shell many miles. The same *basic* kind of propellant can be used for each, but many modifications must be made to provide powder suitable for each of these, and many more, specific uses.

The rifle barrel has often been compared to an internal-combustion engine, with the piston being replaced by a bullet (and with a new "piston" being required for each shot). The rifle barrel, however, more closely resembles a diesel engine, because the gasoline-operated engine is driven by a single explosion. A diesel, on the other hand, develops a relatively slow thrust throughout the piston stroke. So too does the gun, for the necessary chamber pressure cannot be generated with an explosion; rather we must make this pressure build slowly in order to accelerate the flight of the bullet down the barrel gradually, otherwise the result would be disaster. The pressures developed in the barrel would be beyond the ability of the barrel to contain them. Similarly, different situations occur in the many different types of guns. The propellant chosen for each individual cartridge and bullet weight must be compatible with those components, with the guns chambered for that particular cartridge, and for the uses to which such guns and ammunition will be employed.

BLACK POWDER

The first discovery of a fuel that would burn without atmospheric oxygen was the mixture of charcoal, sulphur, and saltpeter that was known as gunpowder. During that long period its composition changed little, although its appearance and methods of manufacture changed. Later it was formed into rough grains and graded by sifting; still later it was compacted by forming it into cakes under considerable pressure before being broken up for use. These efforts helped control combustion speed so that the pressures generated by combustion were distributed more evenly as the projectile traveled the length of the bore.

Black powder also has been widely used as an explosive in mining and quarrying and for blowing up enemy fortifications. Black powder is available today in granulations ranging from fine through coarse (FFFFG, known as 4FG, to FG); you use the coarser granulations with larger-bore rifles and heavier projectiles. The finer powders are for shotguns and for the pans of flintlocks.

SMOKELESS POWDER

It is generally claimed that the invention by a Frenchman named Pelouze in 1838 sealed the doom of black powder as a propellant. Pelouze discovered that an explosive could be made by "nitrating" cotton, which means treating cotton with nitric acid. That's an oversimplification of course, but the result is an explosive known as guncotton.

The active agent in any explosive of this type is the nitrogen atom in combination with two oxygen atoms (NO_2). Originally, the combination contained potassium, which fouled a gun barrel. Then the chemists found they could remove the potassium by means of sulphuric acid and add the residue to a simple hydrocarbon such as glycerin. The result is nitroglycerin. Uncertain and awkward to handle as a liquid, it was mixed with sawdust or some other porous substance, molded into sticks, and became dynamite.

Instead of glycerin we use cellulose in the form of wood pulp or cotton, treat it with nitric and sulphuric acids, and we get nitrocellulose, the chief ingredient of smokeless powder. But this material is too light and loose to pack into a cartridge so it is dissolved with ether and alcohol or acetone to make a plastic mass that can be molded into rods resembling spaghetti. This process was discovered by a French government chemist named Vieille in 1885.

That, basically, is how smokeless powder — the nitrocellulose variety which we also call a single-base powder — is made. There is also a double-base powder that came about in 1878, when Alfred Nobel thought of dissolving guncotton in nitroglycerin. Nobel made a huge fortune out of his discovery and, apparently appalled at the thought of what he had left behind, left his fortune to benefit mankind with what we know today as the Nobel Prizes. In any event, the Nobel invention is known as cordite and it is, for our purposes here, a smokeless powder containing both nitrocellulose and nitroglycerin, which is why we also call it a double-base powder. Some double-base powders are harder on a barrel than single-base powders, but this is more generally found with English cordite than with American double-base powders. For the record, the line of DuPont powders known as IMR (for Improved Military Rifle) are single-base powders. A few of the Hercules powders are double-base, otherwise most of the powders available to the American reloader are of the single-base variety (that is, nitrocellulose).

There is still another type of powder known as Ball Powder, an invention of Western Cartridge Company (now part of Winchester-Western) in the early 1930s. Ball Powder is made essentially the same as any other nitrocellulose powder except that it is made into an emulsion that forms small droplets on the surface that can be removed in that form. This procedure greatly reduces time and cost in the manufacturing process. Ball Powder is simply another form of nitrocellulose containing a small addition of nitroglycerin and is a double-base powder.

Although three types of smokeless powder have been mentioned, these three types can be manufactured in an endless variety of rates of burning. By this I mean that a much faster burning powder is needed for a shotgun or pistol cartridge as opposed to a Magnum rifle, which requires a slow-burning powder, comparatively speaking. Any of these types under discussion can be manufactured to deliver a desired burning rate.

Long ago it was discovered that, just like wood, small-size grains burned faster than larger grains. Take a piece of 2x4 pine 6 inches long and split it

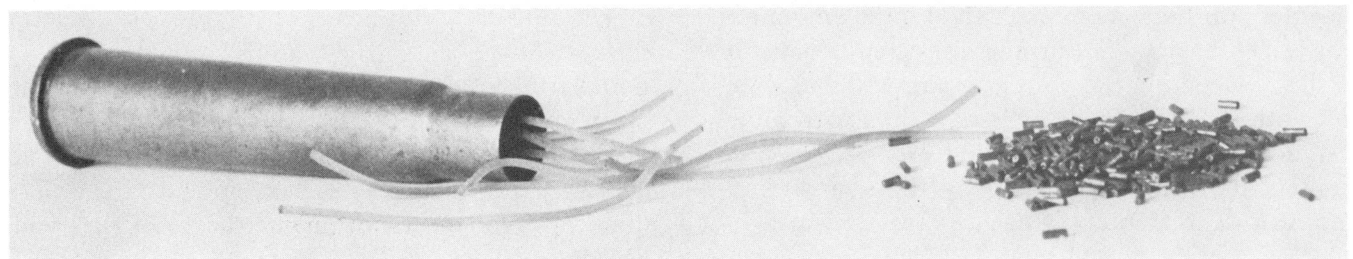

That stringy stuff that looks like spaghetti is cordite, an English propellant that is smokeless. It is what we call a double-base powder, meaning that it contains both nitrocellulose and nitroglycerin. Some American powders are double-base, but we do not use cordite. At the right is shown a typical American powder, one of the DuPont IMR powders.

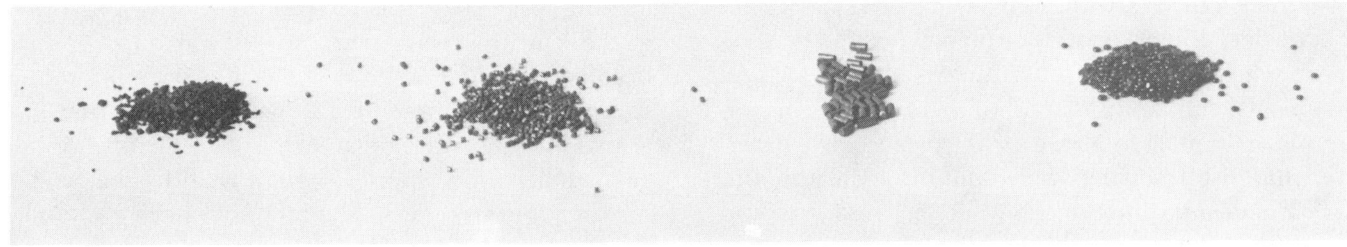

Left to right: Black powder, DuPont IMR 4227, IMR 4350, and Winchester-Western Ball Powder #785.

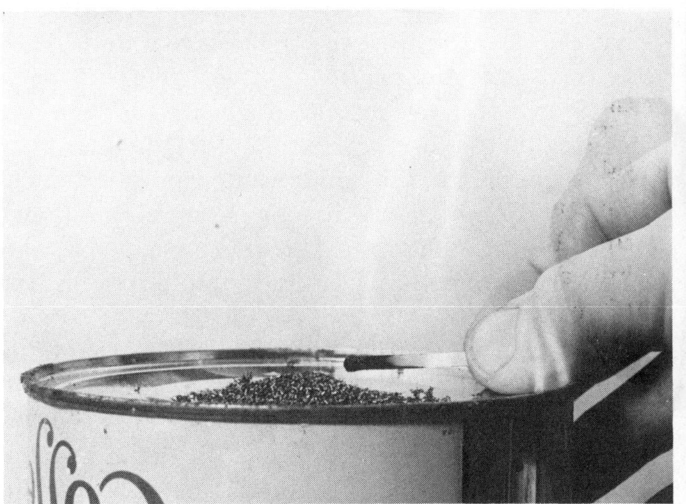

Smokeless powder, when lighted in the open as on this coffee can, burns comparatively slowly. It is not an explosive, but a flammable solid. Note that it is perfectly safe to light with a match held in the hand as at left. At right, the powder is burning. This is not to suggest the flame isn't a brisk one, but it's not an explosion. Under the confinement of a cartridge case, smokeless powder burns very much faster of course. Black powder, on the other hand, should never be lighted in this manner. It will go up with some violence and, indeed, can be used as a substitute for dynamite as an explosive.

into a couple of dozen pieces and it will burn a good deal faster than if left whole. The same exact thing happens with gunpowder because in both cases the exposed surface of a given amount of powder is increased. The greater that surface, the faster the rate of burning.

Col. Rodman of the U.S. Army discovered that you could perforate powder grains and thereby increase the rate of burning even further. Now you had an exposed area inside the grain of powder and burning was from both within and without.

Burning rate, then, is controlled by the size of

powder grains or, more precisely, by the amount of surface area exposed. Burning rates are further controlled by coating the powder grains with graphite. So, with nitrocellulose (single-base) and with nitrocellulose/nitroglycerin (double-base) powders we control the rates of burning by the size of their grains, by the amount of surface area, and by a retardant coating of graphite. Ball Powder, too, can be controlled. This control is exercised by rolling the spherical grains, while in plastic form, into flats like little pancakes. These can be rolled thick or thin or left in tiny spheres. Ball Powder also is coated to retard burning.

Powders must be mated to their loads with extreme care. It is easy to use the wrong powder and the results can be disastrous. (To use an extreme example, if you loaded an artillery piece with fast-burning pistol powder you would blow the gun and its crew clear to hell and beyond because it would develop pressure far too fast for the projectile to move before maximum pressure was achieved.) Powder is made in huge lots or batches and, while extreme control is exercised, any given lot may or may not turn out exactly as desired.

For example, let's say DuPont wishes to make a new lot of a powder for handloaders, say #3031 (these powders are called "canister lots"). Their supply of 3031 is low and must be replenished. So they manufacture a lot of powder with the hope that it will turn out to be 3031. It may or may not. DuPont won't know until the powder is manufactured and tested, re-tested, and tested some more. Should the lot fail to duplicate 3031 exactly it is given another number and will now be sold to one of the ammunition-loading companies which, in turn, will experiment with this powder to mate it to one of their own batches of ammunition. This particular lot of powder will be loaded to achieve specified pressures, velocity, and accuracy in a particular load.

This is one point the reloader must understand completely. Sometimes he will pull the bullet from a factory-loaded cartridge and examine the powder. It *looks* like 3031, so he thinks it is 3031. It is not and the wrong conclusion can lead to trouble. Reloaders should — indeed they must — stick to the canister lots of powders available to them and follow the guidelines given by the manufacturers. There have been times when a powder manufacturer manufactured a canister lot of powder and then could not duplicate it to restock dealers' shelves! That's one of the reasons a powder is occasionally taken off the market. There was not necessarily anything wrong with the powder, but it simply could not be duplicated with the precision necessary for a canister lot. The lot of 3031 you buy tomorrow will exactly duplicate the lot of 3031 you bought in 1948.

One of the problems with gunpowders is that they occupy a limited space in the cartridge case. When the powder is ignited it begins to generate gas, and the gas begins to move the bullet thereby leaving more space for the gas to occupy. Then the gas, filling this void, tends to lose pressure simply because the same amount of gas now occupies more space. The solution is in the perforation of powder grains. As a powder grain burns from the outside, it gets smaller and smaller, which reduces the burning area and so reduces the amount of gas given off. But by burning from within, the surface keeps expanding and more gas is given off. Thus the thrust against the bullet is maintained and, with the proper blend of powder, is actually increased so that the thrust against the bullet is maintained all the way to the muzzle.

The correct powder for a given load can be achieved by the size of the grain, including the size of the perforation. In some cannon powders, each grain sometimes has as many as seven perforations. When we use the term progressive powder, we mean a powder that will rapidly build its pressure (called the pressure curve) to start the bullet moving but which will then maintain that thrust all the way to the muzzle, at which point the pressure will have dropped substantially. A pressure curve builds steeply, then gradually tapers down as the bullet reaches the muzzle, but the push keeps pushing all the way down the barrel. Another advantage to progressive powders is that they develop maximum velocities without attaining extraordinarily high pressures. Such high pressures can be hard on a gun mechanism; they also are generally accompanied by high temperatures which tend to wear out a barrel by erosion faster than normal.

Burning rate is also a function of the heat within the cartridge case, which builds when a bullet is harder and slower to move. For example, it takes much longer to move the 180-grain bullet in a .300 Winchester Magnum than it does to move a pistol bullet, regardless of its weight and caliber. One

n Mag.

prime reason is that most pistol cartridges have straight cases, not bottle necked, which offers much more room for the gas to push against. When gas starts to build in the rifle cartridge, it turns back against itself and this hastens the rate of burning. The slower the bullet is to move, the more this gas feeds on itself, so to speak, and the more rapidly gas is created.

Often the rifleman who is a handloader will reload his cartridges with reduced loads which generally develop far lower velocity than do full loads. He may do this for target shooting, where his only interest is accuracy over a short range, where high velocity isn't necessary, and because the light load is easier on his barrel. He might also want to use such reduced loads for such small game as squirrels, where he doesn't want to destroy too much meat. In any event, he will use much less powder, usually of a faster burning rate than he will use in the full loads. This means the cartridge case will contain extra space because the lighter charge won't come anywhere near filling the case. Unless this space is filled by some other material, the powder will lie in different positions from shot to shot. It also will develop gas that must first fill the space before it can do any work. The usual solution is to fill the remaining space with a cereal grain such as Cream of Wheat. This cereal fills the space (the powder is loaded first) and either burns completely or is blown out of the barrel when the firearm is fired, offering a pleasing aroma.

BLANK POWDER

A blank cartridge has the sole function of making a loud noise. It is used in starter's pistols at track meets, in salute cannons by yachtsmen, in formal military formations as a salute over a grave, or as an honorary salute for dignitaries whose rank can be determined by the number of shots. This powder must burn with most extreme rapidity and must offer a suitable noise. It also must do this with no resistance from bullet or shot charge — nothing but a paper wad over the case muzzle to hold the powder in place. Blank powder must never be used in any loaded ammunition. It is the fastest-burning of all powders and a tiny pinch of it, if loaded behind any bullet, would cause the gun to blow up like a bomb. (In fact, hand grenades are loaded with a small amount of blank powder which will give some idea of its power.) Should you run across blank cartridges, as military surplus or whatever, use them as blanks if you wish but do not, under any circumstances, try to salvage the powder. (Also, do not reload blank military cartridges with full loads. Blanks are often loaded with cartridge cases that are not up to standard and are not suitable for full-load use.)

At one time, there was a powder widely used in .22 Long Rifle match ammunition called Lesmok powder. It was a mixture of guncotton and black powder, gave off more smoke than smokeless but less than black powder, and gave superb accuracy. Fortunately, it has now gone off the market; one of its other faults was that making it was extremely hazardous.

CORDITE

This is a British double-base powder with a rather high nitroglycerin content. It has been widely claimed that cordite is hard on gun barrels, that it erodes them quickly in comparison with most American powders. The point may be irrelevant since the British have been using cordite for both military and sporting purposes for many years in many parts of the world.

One of the most unusual things about cordite is the physical form in which it is loaded — long sections that resemble long, thin spaghetti. The "grains," unlike those in American powders, are usually as long as the length from the base of the cartridge case to the base of the bullet. This can be pretty startling when you first break down a British cartridge loaded with cordite. The method of loading cordite in manufacture also differs widely from our practices: The powder is inserted before the cartridge case is necked. That is, after all final case operations are completed, including primer seating, the strands of cordite are inserted, a glazed cardboard disc is inserted over the powder and then the case is necked. It would be impossible to get those long strands in place after necking. After necking, the bullet is seated and the round finished.

Cordite has another point that ought to be mentioned: its name seems magical to pulp fiction writers and newspaper scribes neither of whom understand anything about guns or ballistics. The "smell of cordite" is an ancient cliche that is often used, seldom understood.

CHAPTER SIXTEEN

BULLET DESIGN AND PERFORMANCE

Clearly the single most important part of all gundom is the bullet. Everything else is merely a vehicle to get that bullet precisely where it is wanted. And, once it arrives, it must do what it is expected to do. That sounds simple enough, but bullets are called upon to do many things, some of which are very different. So there are many kinds of bullets, some of which are multipurpose (or at least will serve several roles) and others that are of no earthly use save for their single special role. Bullet design, construction, and behavior are most interesting subjects, vastly more complicated than one might imagine, and one of the most important subjects this study will touch upon. However, before getting into the whys and wherefores of bullet design, how bullets are made and how they act or react when hitting the target, let's first define the word.

I think nothing infuriates a gun buff so much as to have people refer to ammunition as bullets. A bullet is a projectile. It is nothing else. It is not a shotgun slug, even though that slug somewhat resembles a bullet. It is a single projectile fired from either a rifle or pistol or revolver.

In today's scheme of firearms there are three common styles of bullet: jacketed, pure lead, and disintegrating. The jacketed bullet, the most common, is composed of lead core surrounded by a jacket either of a soft copper-nickel alloy or of mild steel. A pure lead bullet (which isn't usually pure because a little antimony is generally added to it) is most often found in .22 rimfire ammunition and revolver loads. Lead bullets are often equipped with a copper base called a gas check, which helps protect the soft lead from the hot propellant gas. And, finally, the disintegrating bullet, which is found in certain .22 Short cartridges, is composed of lead mixed with other elements that cause it to disintegrate instantly on impact. These cartridges are usually used in gallery shooting and are of little interest to the serious gunner. Their purpose is to permit close-range target shooting (often of the exhibition type) with the employment of a suitable steel backstop. The bullet breaks up into dust on impact and entails no danger whatever from a ricochet.

A bullet's weight, shape, and length control its air resistance and thus its length of flight when other things are the same. Its construction (including balance) controls its accuracy and ability to transmit its energy to the target; that is its "killing power." As to shape, bullets are either spherical or conical, there being many versions of the latter. Bullets may be further categorized by composition: lead, metal-cased, expanding, solid, armor-piercing, tracer, and incendiary, the latter three types being purely military.

Bullets are also often categorized by their construction. For example, full metal jacket, lead, lead with gas check, soft point, pointed soft point, wadcutter, metal piercing, jacketed hollow point, hollow point, sharp shoulder, metal cased (solid). In addition there are such proprietary types of construction as the Remington Bronze Point and Core-Lokt and Winchester-Western Silvertip. It would take too much space to detail them all.

LEAD BULLETS

Lead bullets, used almost entirely for .22 and pistol ammunition, are made either by casting molten metal in a special mold, many of which have as many as six cavities and will cast that number of bullets at a time, or by cold forming them from lead wire. The latter process is used by the larger plants, the former by most reloaders. Either way produces good bullets so long as proper procedures are used. At one time, all bullets were made of lead or a lead alloy, because it has been customary for years to add another metal to lead to increase its hardness slightly. In the early days this metal was often mercury (quicksilver); today it's tin or antimony or both.

Once cast or formed, the bullet is usually sized by running it through a sizing die which also inserts a lubricant into the grooves, or cannelures. Lead bullets, therefore, are often cast slightly oversize and sized down to exact bore size. It is important that lead bullets be lubricated or lead will strip off the bullet and adhere to the barrel. This is especially important with very high velocity ammunition.

Bullet diameter is also important. When a cartridge is first ignited, the brass case opens up to fill the chamber. This action releases the hold the case neck had on the bullet. Since the bullet hasn't yet moved, a little gas spurts past the bullet and into the barrel and the better the fit of bullet to bore the less gas will escape. (Such escaping gas has two effects: It wastes power and it causes "gas cutting" – or reduction in size – of the bullet, because the heat of the gas is higher than the melting point of the bullet.) In the days when the propellant was black powder, it was necessary to make bullets quite a bit smaller than barrel diameter. This was because the powder rapidly fouled the bore and bullets soon had to ride over this fouling, resulting in considerable loss of accuracy. This was especially true with breech-loading rifles (muzzle loaders tended to push the fouling back down the barrel during loading, behind the bullet).

Today's higher velocities call for rather hard bullets. It's probably safe to say that all bullets used these days, whether factory loaded or home cast, are hardened, usually with antimony. The harder bullet helps prevent skidding – that forward movement of the bullet before it begins to accept the rifling twist. A bullet, of course, will tend to want to move straight ahead down the gun barrel, but it must accept the rifling twist and begin to turn. The softer the metal the more the tendency to keep moving ahead. This undesirable characteristic is what the rifleman calls skidding. Another little trick helps prevent not only skidding, but the hot gases from melting the bases of lead bullets; at the same time, it helps prevent leading the barrel. This is to apply a gas check. A gas check is a small copper alloy cup that's fitted over the bullet's base (bullets must be specially cast for a gas check) and effectively seals the bullet base while extending up the side of the bullet about 1/16 inch.

The usual practice for lead-bullet mold identification is to list the style with a six-digit figure. For example, take a Lyman Ideal bullet #308245. The

Above Left: Cylindrical 100-pound lead billets moving along a conveyor to an extrusion press that will squeeze them into lead wire from which bullet cores will be made. Above Right: After leaving the extrusion press the lead wire is coiled in barrels. Left: The wire is then fed into a battery of machines that cut it into preformed sections of the exact weight required for the bullets being manufactured. Bullet cores are then placed into drawn jackets before final forming.

first three digits indicate the bullet diameter in thousandths of an inch. Thus this example would be a .308-inch bullet suitable for any .30-caliber rifle. The last three digits refer to a particular shape and weight configuration that would be found in the Lyman catalog. There are nearly as many styles and weights available as there are numbers and, if lead bullet shooting is your bag, you ought to get the Lyman, SAECO, and other bullet mold catalogs and study the listings.

.22 BULLETS

Bullets loaded for .22 firearms are generally of two basic types: hollow point and solid lead. Target .22 ammunition is loaded with much more carefully made bullets. One point about the .22-caliber bullet is that it's designed for subsonic flight, which means high-velocity loads will not shoot as accurately as standard velocity.

Most .22 ammo is greased in conventional fashion and you should keep it clean, usually by keeping it in the original container until ready to load. Putting a greased .22 cartridge in your pocket, or dropping it on the ground, means it will pick up dirt, which, if fired, will scratch the barrel. Because of this, some .22s are loaded with bullets clad with an alloy that doesn't require the lubricant in the ordinary sense. These cartridges can usually be carried loosely in your pocket and won't pick up anything of a foreign nature.

Early lead bullets were spherical, or as nearly as they could be made to it. The flight of a round ball is an interesting thing, because it involves some laws of physics that we don't ordinarily think about. A round ball is a miserable shape for the retention of velocity because the faster it is driven the sooner it slows down! That's because air resistance varies according to the square of the velocity. Double the velocity and you increase the air resistance by four times. Treble the velocity, air resistance increases nine times. As a result of this law of physics there are practical limits beyond which it simply makes no sense to increase the speed of a round ball.

It was discovered long ago that an elongated bullet — sometimes called a slug — produced better ballistic qualities than the sphere and that shape has been in common use ever since. Just about the only place you'll find spheres today is in shotgun pellets and muzzle-loading replicas.

METAL-CASED BULLETS

When smokeless powder came along, lead bullets were found unsatisfactory due to the higher temperatures and higher velocities obtainable with the new powders. The approximate date of this development was about 1885. There was, in fact, a UMC (Union Metallic Cartridge Co., the firm that later bought Remington Arms) bullet marketed in 1884 with a jacketed bullet for the .45/90 Winchester rifle. Smokeless powder and lead bullets didn't mix because the bases of the bullets melted and the bullets skidded in the rifling. Experiments with harder, solid materials were unsatisfactory because they were too light; it was evident that lead was necessary to provide the required density and weight to sustain velocity. The result was to use lead as a bullet core and provide a jacket to surround that core which would solve the problems.

One of the first metals used for jacket material was the so-called German silver, composed of copper and nickel. But this was expensive and was soon replaced by *gilding metal* (which is still used), a composition of copper with 5–10 percent zinc added. In Europe on the other hand, a mild steel was used for bullet-jacket material and still is by most European ammunition companies. Of course, a steel-jacketed bullet tends to rust, so it is lightly plated with a copper compound; thus the term steel jacket is accurately applied to some European ammunition. It is only accurately applied to a very few U.S. loads such as the .458 Winchester Magnum solid (Full Metal Case and labeled FMC) because this jacket toughness is required to get through the nearly 3 feet of bone structure in an elephant's head. The simple test for a steel jacket is to use a magnet. Mild steel jackets are no harder on rifle barrels than gilding metal jackets.

Bullet jackets are manufactured the same way that cartridge cases are, by punching out small discs from metal strips of the correct size and thickness. Then, through successive punch-press operations, these coinlike slugs are drawn and formed into bullet jackets.

A bullet may be formed one of two major ways: with open base, in which event the lead core is seated from the rear, or the other way around. Most hunting bullets have solid bases with the lead core seated from the front. In this event, the jacket material is always thinner at the nose end to facilitate its unrolling and to allow the bullet to expand on impact.

Full metal case bullets (those with a solid jacket at the nose end) are generally used for target shooting. They are also sometimes specially loaded for game such as squirrel and wild turkey, where it is desired not to spoil too much meat. They also are standard for military use since they conform to the terms of the Geneva Conventions.

Expanding, soft point or *hollow point* bullets are constructed along similar lines since they are all closed at the base and the lead cores inserted from the front. After core insertion, the front end of the jacket is closed in a die to the desired degree. For example, the major difference between a soft-point and a hollow-point bullet is in the amount of lead in the core. Less lead, not enough to fill the cavity, and you have a hollow-point bullet. Either bullet is of the expanding type so that word, in itself, is not really very descriptive. The important distinction of these types is that their jackets are closed at the rear, open at the front.

The first expanding bullets were jacketed. They were the typical bullets of the period in America: large caliber, slow moving. Spurred by the military developments in Europe, the next move was toward smaller bores and higher velocities. One of our early small-bore rifles was the .30/40 Krag rifle adopted by the U.S. in 1892. At the same approximate time, for there were many overlapping developments taking place during a short period of years, jacketed expanding bullets were made for various other small-bore cartridges such as the .25/35 and .30/30 WCF.

The rush toward higher and higher muzzle ve-

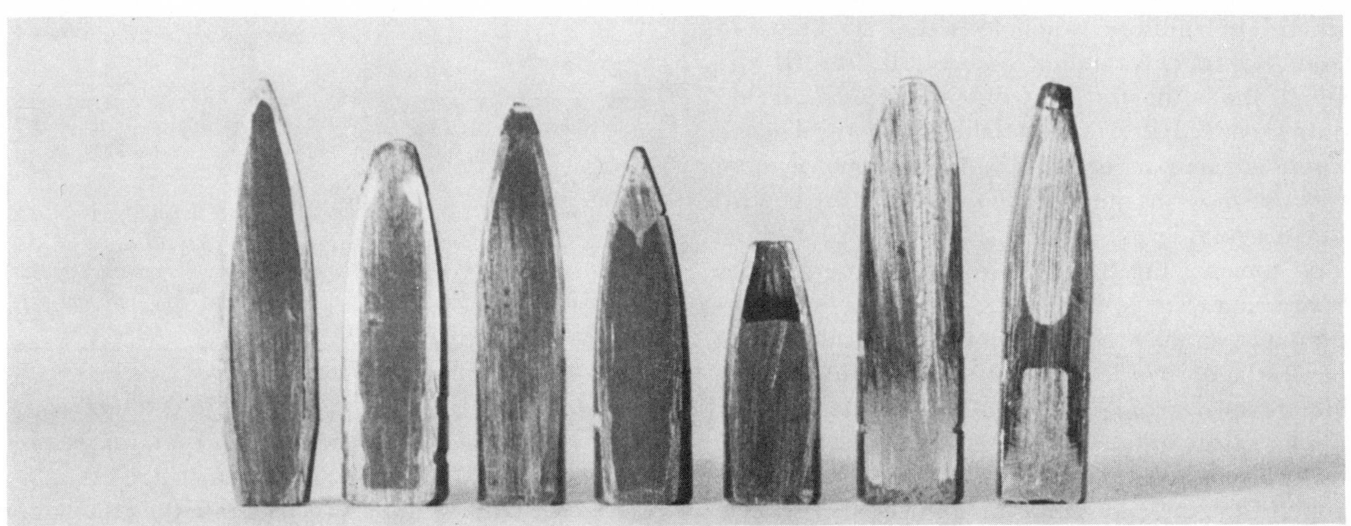

Left to right: Military boat-tail bullet with enclosed nose; Winchester-Western Power Point bullet, a soft-point design; Hornady spire point, a soft-point design; Remington Bronze Point; hollow point bullet with deep cavity; Winchester-Western Silvertip bullet — note that the tip jacket extends all the way down to the base; and Nosler partition jacket, a double-cored bullet for deep expansion.

locities was beginning and posed other problems that hadn't been considered before. One of the first problems noted was that the German silver jacket material used by the military through World War I, actually until about 1922, caused barrels to foul badly. Sometimes this happened at speeds about 2,700 fps; in other rifles and other calibers it occurred at lower velocities. In either event, the jackets caused thick metal fouling in the bore in the form of smears and lumps and usually on top of the lands, often to a depth of up to .004 inch. The fouling interfered with accuracy, raised pressures, and was hellish to remove. The same thing did not occur with gilding metal, which, in addition to the cost factor, soon replaced German silver.

If you examine the barrel of any rifle today, looking at the rifling at the muzzle, you will note a faint copperish color. This is called a copper wash and is a result of firing gilding-metal jackets; it causes no harm and does not build up. Once a new barrel has been fired it will have that copperish color forever.

THE ROUND-NOSE SOLID-JACKET BULLET

Round-nose bullets with solid jackets — called full patch by the military — were a military development and conformed to the Geneva Conventions. This was prior to the development of pointed bullets. As a military bullet, the round nose, such as was employed by our .30/40 Krag and the original .30/03 Springfield, both of which weighed 220 grains, was not a great success. Its weight was also against it, for muzzle velocities were relatively low, and the shape prevented good long-range ballistics.

This type of bullet tends to drill a straight hole when it reaches the target. It does not deflect easily, as does a pointed bullet, nor does it expand readily. In military use it was a success, except for the range limitations noted, and was a better wounder than

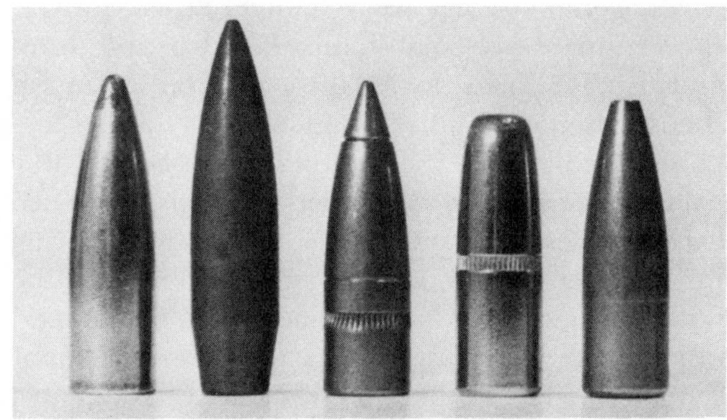

Several typical modern bullets for high-power rifles. Left to right: spitzer soft point; boat tail with solid nose; Remington's Bronze Point; soft-point, flat-nosed bullet for use in tubular-magazine rifles, like the Winchester 94 .30/30 carbine; open-point bullet. Each of these types has its own specific characteristics and is suitable for specific uses.

killer. The military rationale is that it's better to wound an enemy soldier than to kill him. (If he's killed, that's the end of it. But if wounded, he requires care that occupies other soldiers. Thus a wounded man, as opposed to a dead one, is more effective in terms of reducing the enemy's strength.) But the round-nose solid-jacket bullet wasn't much used for sporting purposes, for the same reasons. Sportsmen want to kill their game cleanly and outright and not have to follow it for miles until it bled to death, or if a dangerous species, turn on the hunter.

The extremely deep penetration of these bullets was soon noted, however, and they did become popular for the enormous, and dangerous, game of Africa. Such bullets, called solids, provided the necessary penetration to kill an elephant cleanly. The African elephant is huge and he's particularly dangerous when aroused. He can stomp you into the ground easily and he can fling you high in the air and then stomp you in the ground. When you hunt the African elephant you must kill him very dead, very quickly. There are two ways to do this, depending upon which part of the beast you are facing, or which is visible through the cover. He must be shot in either the brain or the heart. An elephant's brain is about the size and shape of a football and it's located behind nearly 3 feet of quite solid bone from the front. So, if it's a frontal shot you must take, your bullet must penetrate that bone and in a straight line. Otherwise you have a wounded animal on your hands and he's damned mad at you.

Many professional ivory hunters at the turn of the century used small-bore rifles (6.5 and 7mm and the .303 British) with these solid bullets to kill thousands of elephants. Extremely cool hunters, capable of stalking very close to the giant beasts, they could place these small bullets precisely and with excellent results. Today's elephant hunter favors much larger rifles and with good reason he's not the skilled professional that Karamojo Bell, Selous, and others were. The favorite cartridge for elephant shooting today is the .458 Winchester Magnum; Weatherby's bigger .460 Magnum is also popular, and a number of the older British double rifles in heavy calibers are still used, although their use is diminishing.

Both Winchester and Remington load the .458 with solid bullets and the ammunition is available on a worldwide basis, which is always an important consideration when choosing a cartridge. Weatherby's .460 is the same caliber despite the name and is loaded with the same bullet. It has a larger cartridge case and develops more velocity and energy.

Remington's Core-Lokt bullet, one of the more famous game bullets of all time. This development followed the Peters belted bullet of a generation ago. It features a thick, tough jacket toward the rear that resists expansion. Yet the bullet's nose is thin, soft and perforated to induce nose expansion.

POINTED MILITARY BULLETS

In about 1905 the German army reduced the weight of their 8mm service bullet from 236 to 154 grains and formed it with a sharp point instead of the older round nose. The result was that it could be driven at a muzzle velocity of 2,825 fps with a flat trajectory. When sighted to strike a mans belt at 500 yards, the bullet would not rise above his head at ranges up to 500 yards and would still strike him in the legs at 600 yards. This was an important consideration and it was not lost on other armies. The United States followed in 1906 with the 150-grain bullet and the new .30/06 cartridge (the .30/03 had used the older 220-grain round-nose bullet.) The Germans called this bullet a *spitzer,* meaning sharp point, and we still use the same word for any pointed bullet.

The military spitzer bullet was tried on game in the early days of its existence with mixed results. It would often — *usually* would be a better word — fail to follow a straight path, being deflected by nearly anything in its way — bone, flesh, tissue, or whatever. Often it turned sideways, in which case it inflicted some pretty serious damage indeed. I hunted with military ammunition just once, during World War II, in California for Columbian blacktail deer. There were several of us involved in the party and we had no other ammunition available but .30/06 military. We were lucky; two of us shot nice bucks and dropped both in their tracks. But because of its uncertain behavior, these bullets are undependable for hunting, should not be used, and are, fortunately, banned by many States. Naturally the same is true in warfare: sometimes these bullets kill cleanly, other times they wound terribly and still other times they pass through like a sword without hitting anything vital.

The correct use for any such bullet is either military, for which it was designed, or target shooting, where it winds up in an earth backstop. There is no other sporting use for such bullets except that a few of the semi-spitzer or semi-pointed variety are loaded for shooting squirrels and turkeys. These are generally in such calibers as the .222 Remington and the .22 Winchester Magnum Rimfire and are designed to kill cleanly without ruining meat as an expanding bullet would do on such game. You are well advised to use head shots on squirrels, in which event the style of bullet doesn't much matter. Turkey shooting is a toss-up between rifle or shotgun, but if a rifle is used, use one of the bullets just indicated and place the shot through the wing butts.

EXPANDING BULLETS

The first of this type of bullet made and used in the United States were made and loaded in cartridges like the .30/30 Winchester and .30/40 Krag, the latter then becoming popular as a game rifle. These early bullets had a metal jacket that was rather short and left a good amount of lead exposed at the tip. They were called soft-point bullets for that reason and were of flat-nose construction for the .30/30 (also .25/35 and other lever-action cartridges) and round nose for the .30/40. The flat noses, or at least a very blunt nose, were essential for the tubular magazines employed in Winchester and Marlin lever-action rifles. The .30/40 was available in the bolt-action Krag military rifle and the Winchester model 1895, which employed a box magazine so the cartridges were not lying in a row with bullet tip against primer, as in a tubular magazine.

These early bullets were intended for game of the deer class and worked very well on game of this size. The tips expanded — mushroomed — well and they were good at killing this sort of game cleanly and quickly. But when it came to larger game, such as moose or elk, or some of the more dangerous game, such as grizzly bears, these bullets did not penetrate sufficiently to kill well. The bullet expanded too quickly and expended all its energy on or just under the surface, or it broke apart on impact, especially if a bone were struck near the surface, and failed to kill.

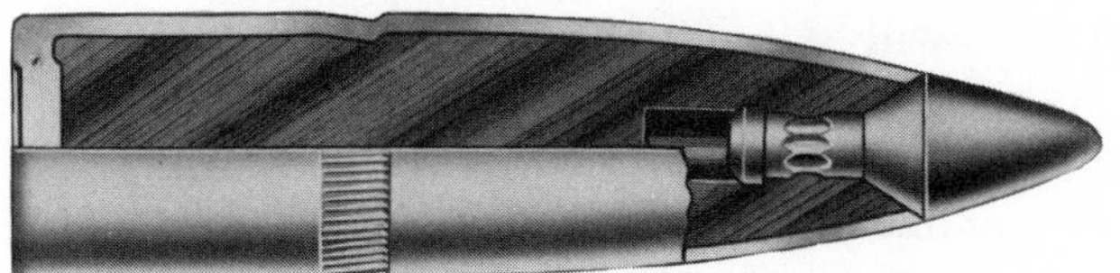

A cutaway view of the Remington Bronze Point bullet, which was popular some years back and is still offered in several loadings. This bullet is a typical hollow-point bullet with a solid bronze tip inserted into the cavity. The tip has two purposes: to prevent battering during recoil in the magazine, and to drive itself into the core upon impact and thus hasten expansion of the bullet's nose. Note that the cannelure (the knurned groove) is tapered; the purpose of that is to allow the cartridge-case mouth to be crimped into this groove, preventing the bullet from slipping down in the case.

The next step was to beef up the bullet jackets and leave a smaller amount of lead exposed at the tip. These bullets did a fine job of penetrating the heavier animals. They were excellent when you were shooting moose, elk, or grizzly. They could even smash through both shoulders of a large grizzly, for example. But when used on whitetail deer, they failed to expand at all and therefore failed to kill cleanly. True, they killed the deer, but you seldom got the animal because he was able to get away and die a lingering death.

Consequently, and for many years, the ammunition companies were forced to make ammunition that was right for deer and other ammunition that was right for larger game. The two didn't mix. Most hunters, being what they are, failed to realize that there was a difference. And sporting-goods store clerks, being what they are, weren't any smarter or better informed. And quite frankly, the ammunition companies didn't play it too smart either and didn't mark the boxes as well as they might have done. In any event, too many hunters got hold of the wrong ammunition and wounded game that got away. The result wasn't pleasant for anyone concerned. But the problem was a difficult one. It consisted not only of the varying game species likely to be hunted, but also the distances at which this game would be shot. A bullet with 2,700 fps of muzzle velocity has slowed to about 1,660 fps at 500 yards (180 grain .30/06). Clearly, a bullet will behave differently if it hits the animal at 2,700 fps than it will at 1,660 fps. Or anywhere in between. And the challenge was to produce bullets that would be effective at all reasonable ranges on any animal likely to be encountered.

There were, and there are, a number of solutions to this problem. An early solution, which is still with us, was the hollow-point bullet. The theory behind this bullet is pretty obvious. The cavity quickly becomes filled when the bullet hits an animal and this forces the jacket back and away from the core, allowing the bullet to mushroom to larger diameter. Hollow-point bullets work well; they expand consistently and with good reliability. They have just one failing — their velocity is not sustained nearly so well as an equivalent bullet with a spitzer point. Riflemen use the term "falls off" for the velocity loss suffered by a hollow-point bullet. Today, there are few hollow-point game bullets in any of the larger calibers; they're pretty much restricted either to lower-velocity cartridges or smaller-bore bullets used chiefly for varmint shooting. Even here, the hollow point is not so effective at longer ranges as the soft point and it has been learned that soft points expand just as well as hollow points in most situations.

In the mid-20s there arose a demand for a sharp-point expanding bullet. If it could be made in such a way that it would expand consistently and satisfactorily it would have all the answers, because its downrange ballistics would be so much superior to either the hollow point or flat point. But development of such a bullet posed problems. One of the big problems is that their points get battered and deformed so easily in handling and in recoil when they lie in the magazine. Another problem deals with the amount of lead that should be exposed. You can draw the jacket down so that only a pinpoint of lead is exposed, or you can use a shorter jacket and leave a lot of lead exposed. Obviously, these extremes will behave differently when they hit game. And they will behave differently at varying velocities.

The problem of deformity was solved first. It was solved by Winchester with their Pointed Expanding Bullet, in which the lead tip was enclosed with a very thin covering of gilding metal that extended inside the jacket itself. This was a forerunner of, and is not to be confused with, the present Silvertip bullet. And the problem was solved by Remington with their Bronze Point bullet, which was really a hollow-point bullet in most details with a small bronze tip stuck into the cavity. Both these bullets were excellent and performed their tasks well. In fact, the Remington Bronze Point is still with us in several loadings. The Winchester Silvertip of today is an improvement on the older bullet. Both these solutions, however, were then and are now reliable answers to a tough problem.

Concurrently, ammunition makers learned that they could control expansion by tapering the walls of the bullet jackets. So jackets are thin in front to permit expansion, and become thicker toward the rear to prevent it.

One of the more interesting (and more identifiable) developments during this period was the 1933 development by the Peters Cartridge Company (since bought by Remington) of the "belted" bullet. This bullet was made with a thin jacket, but about a fifth of an inch behind the point there was a belt of tough gilding metal a half inch wide. This had the effect of permitting rapid expansion of the tip but then the belt resisted further expansion and the bullet stayed in one piece. This was an excellent bullet and it performed well on game. There are still a few hunters around who think it among the best bullets ever produced. The message from the Peters belted bullet was not lost on others, however, and essentially the same thing has been accomplished by simply making the jacket heavier. The final result is just about the same and at far less cost, because the Peters bullet was costly to produce.

Shortly before World War II, Remington-Peters modified the belted concept by thickening the jacket at the same point as the belt occurred on the old belted slug. Additionally, they scalloped the front edges of the jacket, which tends to help the jacket roll back evenly all the way around and so promote expansion. This new bullet was called the Core-Lokt and it has proved one of the best game bullets ever developed.

Moreover, as mentioned, Remington's old Bronze Point bullet is still with us. This bullet is made simply by inserting a tip of bronze into what would otherwise be a hollow point bullet. Upon impact, the bronze is driven back into the cavity promoting expansion. Old as it is, the Bronze Point remains an excellent game bullet. Winchester-Western's answer to the controlled expansion problem was the company's Silvertip bullet, which is designed for deep penetration and controlled expansion regardless of range. This is achieved by a thin cupronickel jacket enclosing the nose and extending down nearly to the bottom of the jacket itself. In effect, the lead core is enclosed in a double jacket. This bullet has also proved itself in the world's hunting grounds and is a consistent performer on game for which each bullet is suited, and at varying distances.

The impetus behind all these developments was to produce a bullet that would expand enough (generally 2 to 2½ times the original diameter) and no more. This is achieved by making a soft expandable front end, combined with a tough rear end that will resist expanding. Another requirement of such bullets is that they stay in one piece rather than fly apart within the target. That's harder to achieve than it sounds, for it's easy for a lead core to completely leave the jacket in which case killing power can be reduced virtually to zero. One noteworthy solution to the problem years ago was a German development by the great firm of DWM (which, roughly translated, means German Ammunition Manufacturers) called the H-mantle. This bullet was something of a reverse of the Peters belted bullet in that there was a heavy, thick band of jacket metal inside the jacket.

DEVELOPMENTS SINCE WORLD WAR II

Most bullet development since World War II has been toward greater and greater accuracy, and the improvements have been incredible. It has been my privilege to have known those who own and manage the firms of Sierra, Hornady, and Speer (who make bullets for reloading, although Hornady has begun loading his own ammunition commercially and Speer — now part of Omark Industries — has begun a corporate expansion that now includes loaded ammunition, and both have expanded into reloading tools and diep) ever since the first days of benchrest shooting in 1947. Even though their most significant advances lie in accuracy, these firms have not ignored hunting. In fact, their bullets are just as fine and deadly as those produced by the giants. But it remained for one custom bullet maker in Oregon to pull a degree of one-upmanship by producing a hunting bullet that won't fly into pieces because it can't. A man named John Nosler began making bullets by drilling both ends of a solid piece of metal in a way that the two drilled holes didn't quite meet and the unit was left with a cavity in each end and a solid web of jacket material in the middle. He then put lead cores in each end and formed the result into a bullet. He calls this a partition-jacket bullet and it's one hell of a fine bullet indeed. I've killed some major North American game species with these bullets in .30 caliber from a .30/06 and in a .338 Winchester Magnum and their performance has been superb. It's exceedingly difficult to make a bullet such as the Nosler in perfect balance. He must have achieved this, however, because in every rifle I've tried his bullets they have performed with excellent accuracy.

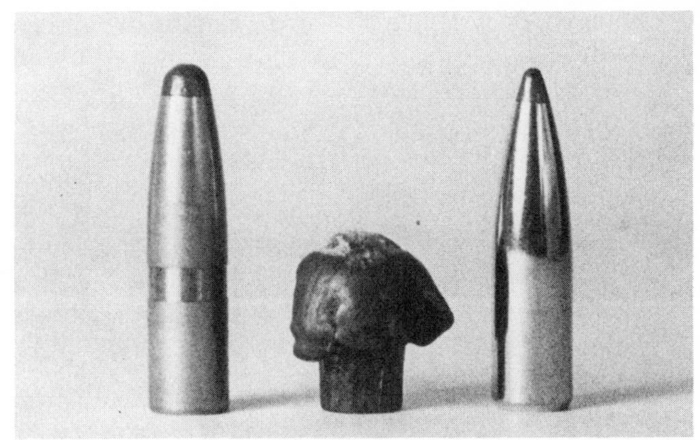

The old version (left), of Nosler's partition jacket bullet and the new. In between is a Nosler bullet recovered from a record-class caribou shot by the author in Quebec. Bullets shown are .30 caliber; the fired bullet was shot from a .30/06 rifle.

There really is no such thing as the perfect expanding bullet. If there were, everybody would use it, but everybody makes things just a little bit differently although the principles behind them are pretty much the same. Two schools of thought exist with regard to bullet behavior in game. One holds that the bullet must stay inside the animal and expend all its energy in the beast. They further claim that the ideal is the bullet that stops under the skin on the far side of the animal. The opposite school claims a bullet should expand nicely and plow a big hole right on through, exiting the animal and leaving a good blood trail that can be followed. Of course, there is now a third school that claims that extreme velocity causes a kind of hydraulic shock within the animal and that this is what does the instantaneous killing observed with certain high-velocity cartridges. Since all three versions have been voiced by hunters to whom we must listen, it follows that all three have some validity. Yet, they are so inconsistent that they can't be right for everyone. And they're not.

The most important thing to keep in mind is that you must place your bullet in a vital area. You can't kill a moose if you knock off a hoof with a 75mm artillery piece. On the other hand, if you carefully place a .243 bullet in the precise spot on a moose where it will do the most good, he will drop like a stone. That's the first basic lesson every hunter must learn. Then you must use the right bullet, which today means one of the better soft points, whether factory loaded or handloaded, on all thin-skinned game. If you're tackling Alaskan brown bears or if you're on an African safari you'll need tougher bullets, such as the solids that Winchester and Remington provide for their .458 Winchester Magnum loadings or one of the Weatherby Magnums.

VARMINT BULLETS

There are some bullets expressly made for varmint shooting and these are designed with thinner than usual jackets because they want to break up quickly on impact since they are used on small animals. Some of these bullets are loaded in the larger cartridges, like the 100-grain .270 and 110-grain .30/06, for example. These slugs start out at a high muzzle velocity but it doesn't last long because they haven't the weight to sustain that speed for more than a couple of hundred yards. (Actually a 180-grain bullet will pass the 110 grain at about 500 yards in a .30/06.) Varmint bullets are also supposed not to ricochet off into the next county. They won't if they impact at a close enough range while they're still steaming along at high speed, but they soon slow down and one must be sure of a safe backstop for any shot.

I think it's a mistake to shoot varmints with any rifle larger than, say, the .25/06. The heavier bores are better left for bigger game hunting. The hot .22s, such as the .220 Swift, .222 Remington, and .22/250, are ideal and for longer range shooting the 6mms are perfect. Varmint shooting takes extremely fine accuracy, a good, high-powered scope, and extremely lightly jacketed bullets. You want those little beasts to be killed humanely, which means the little bullets should blow up on impact.

Another cartridge employed just for varmints, though I've never used it, is the fairly new .17-caliber Remington. There's nothing new about .17-caliber rifles; they were used before World War II, but were then regarded as pretty freakish. The tiny bullets were only made by Sisk at that time and the barrels only by one or two barrel makers. Remington's .17 is based on their .223 basic cartridge, changing the body slightly and reducing the neck diameter to .17 caliber.

In rimfires the .22 WMR is a good cartridge to ranges of about 150 yards. Remington, for a brief period, made a 5mm rifle and cartridge for a tiny rimfire, but it never took hold and has been dropped. The .22 Long Rifle, in my opinion, is not a chuck rifle, although it serves to eliminate the pesky creatures from the lettuce patch so long as you get close enough. And hold for the head, will you?

I cannot emphasize too strongly that you must place your bullet properly for a good, clean kill on any sort of animal with any sort of rifle. The comparatively recent development of Magnum cartridges and excellent bullets have been tremendous strides forward, but they are no substitute for accuracy. The Magnums make it easier to hit because their trajectory is flatter and you need to make less allowance for distance than you did in the old days, when a bullet flew with a trajectory like a golf ball. And the modern bullet does a far finer job of transmitting its energy to the target than did the bullet of a short generation ago. But it is still vital to place that bullet in a vital spot.

ENERGY

Energy is one of the most misleading figures given in ballistics tables. It can be totally meaningless unless the construction of the bullet is such that it will transmit that energy to the animal. A 180-grain .30/06 bullet, for example, will be found in several bullet styles. Some of these are meant for hunting; others, intended solely for target shooting, have a closed nose or are of full-patch construction. While both will show the same theoretical energy in the ballistics tables, each will not deliver the same energy to the game.

Another excellent example is given when you compare the two loadings of the .458 Winchester Magnum. One is a 510-grain soft point, the other a

500-grain solid (with mild steel jacket). They have muzzle velocities of 2,110 and 2,120 fps respectively. You can regard that as a toss-up. Their respective muzzle energies are 5,041 and 4,989 foot pounds, also a toss-up. The important thing is that, even though these figures are identical for any practical purpose, the soft point .458 bullet will never penetrate into the brain of an elephant and the solid would slip through a charging lion like a sword. These figures are only meaningful if they are related to the bullet being used, as regards its construction and its capability of doing the job it is supposed to do.

BRUSH BUSTING

It is commonly believed that fat, long, heavy, round-nosed, rather slow-moving bullets have what is commonly called good brush-busting capabilities. That means, or is supposed to mean, that other things being equal, you are better off with one of these brush busters than something lighter if you hunt in a place like the wooded northeast or its equal. As an example, two of the more popular deer-hunting rifles in the northeast are the .30/30 and the .35 Remington. The .35 is said to be a much better brush buster. By extension of that philosophy, a .375 H&H Magnum or .458 Winchester Magnum would be even better.

Some writers have gone to the extreme of placing brush, twigs, branches, and the like in front of targets and then proceed to shoot through this Mickey Mouse jungle to prove — or disprove — their point. And that depends on just what point they're trying to make. We don't really know all that much about brush busting, except that it is overrated. Those tests that are made are worthless. You can't possibly duplicate a potential field condition by sticking branches in front of a paper target. We do know that a high-velocity bullet with a thin jacket can literally explode upon impacting something as trivial as a blade of grass. Indeed, some bullets self-destruct without hitting anything. This can be proved by taking one of the very lightly jacketed bullets meant for easy expansion in a .222 caliber and loading it to maximum velocity in a .220 Swift. It will never reach a target because its enormous velocity with corresponding rotational speed will cause it to fly into vapor shortly after leaving the muzzle. So, yes, there is something to this brush-busting theory — if you go to extremes.

However, I believe, and believe very strongly, in the theory expressed by my late good friend, Larry Koller. Larry used to say you'd best be able to see through the brush so you can see the animal and be able to slip your bullet through a hole in the brush rather than depending on its ability to penetrate or glance off any twigs, branches, or trees that happen to get in the way. This theory has another point to its credit: nobody has any business taking a shot where he can't see precisely what he's shooting at. If you can see the game on the far side of a blowdown, you can see it well enough to slip a bullet through the brush by finding a hole that will let your slug through without any chance of its being deflected.

VARIATIONS

During the many years since the transition from lead to jacketed bullets there have been hundreds of experimental bullets tried. Some of these were excellent but too costly to manufacture (bullets must be made by the millions to be economical), others were dismal flops. There is little to be gained from listing or discussing any of these, but should you have an idea you think would make a more perfect bullet, do some investigating before you spend any money on it. Chances are it's been tried and has failed for one reason or another.

CHAPTER SEVENTEEN

THE BULLET'S FLIGHT

There are two common misconceptions about shooting. The first is that the shooter is always to blame when he misses because the gun is never at fault. This is accepted as fact to the uninitiated who always think that, after all, what can be wrong with the rifle? This is silly just on the face of it, if only because there are errors galore in manufacture. And there are plenty of things that can happen to the flight of a bullet both inside and outside the barrel that some will never understand.

The second misconception is that a study of ballistics is dull and complicated. It can be both, and, indeed, often is, but it doesn't have to be. We'll just try to keep everything simple and easy.

INTERNAL

It's really not so long ago when the manufacturing rule of thumb was to assure easy and uncomplicated insertion of the cartridge into the chamber of the rifle barrel. This rule would probably still be followed were it not for the serious dedication to better accuracy that a few lone men set as a goal. They set out to look for answers to why a rifle wouldn't put every shot through the same hole every time it was fired.

One of the first of these experimenters was the late Dr. Franklin W. Mann, who experimented from about 1894 until about World War I and whose scholarly work *The Bullet's Flight from Powder to Target,* published in 1909, is a classic. Much of the basic research and findings of Dr. Mann are as true today as they were three quarters of a century ago. The next group of experimenters to make real progress was the modern benchrest shooters who got started in 1947. These men spent their own money seeking answers to accuracy problems that most others didn't care about. As recently as the 1930s and 40s, if you had a rifle — even one of those highly touted bolt-action rifles that were supposed to be so accurate — that would shoot groups at 100 yards of around 4 inches and if you wrote to the factory and complained, they'd reply: "That meets our standards of accuracy." That would be your answer and they would do nothing about it. Actually, they really didn't know how to correct it.

The benchrest shooters found out what made rifles shoot better and they set about making them shoot better. Much of the credit for publicizing what benchrest was doing was due to Warren Page's writing in *Field & Stream* over the years. Warren simply never let go of the objective. Other writers covered the subject on occasion, but Warren Page kept at it until things got done. It was this same group that gave birth to today's far finer accuracy, which is largely the result of better bullets. That same movement provided the climate and knowledge that led Sierra, Hornady, and Speer into better bullet manufacture, a move that was followed by Winchester and Remington. The first bullet I ever saw to come out of one of the big factories that was on a par with those custom bullets was the 80-grain .243 Winchester bullet made by Winchester and loaded in their first ammunition for that rifle. Today, everybody has learned how to make accurate bullets. They learned it, every one of them, from these experimental riflemen who discovered what happened inside a rifle barrel because they had a compelling interest in learning.

Dr. Mann, for example, was a physician when he patented and manufactured a machine for grinding the green bones in a slaughterhouse. There was, as it turned out, quite a market for such a machine and the doctor made a fortune, did not have to practice medicine, and spent the rest of his life seeking the secret of rifle accuracy. His first experiments dealt with the seating of a bullet in the rifled bore. Being unsatisfied with the misalignment of bore to bullet in conventional cartridges, he made a reamer to permit seating a perfectly tapered bullet (which had been made with the same reamer) directly into the bore ahead of the cartridge. This was a separately seated bullet. The charged cartridge case was then inserted behind the bullet. The doctor, of course, used cartridge cases that had been fired in the same rifle previously, thus they fitted the chamber perfectly.

That particular experiment was deemed useless because it opened up more problems than it solved. Just the same, note that a bullet must be seated accurately and uniformly in a way that it will enter the rifling with the axis of the bullet perfectly coinciding with the axis of the bore. While you ponder that for a moment, think about the millions of bullets being made every day. Not just by Winchester, Remington, and Federal. And not even just by Sierra, Hornady, Speer, Norma, and so on and on. The shooter has a right to expect that every one of those bullets will be seated just so in his own barrel, which might have been made by Winchester, Remington, Marlin, Colt, Harrington & Richardson, Savage, Champlin, Kleinguenther, Biesen, and who knows how many more custom gunsmiths let alone foreign makers.

Alignment depends upon the accuracy with which the chamber was cut and its alignment with the axis of the bore. It depends on the cartridge case, its fit in the chamber, and the bullet's seat in the cartridge-case neck. And it depends upon the throat (or leade as Col. Whelen used to call it), that short taper at the breech end of the rifling lands just ahead of the chamber. A bullet is of groove diameter (.308 inch in a .30-caliber rifle) while the tops of the lands are of bore diameter (.300 inch). The throat gives the lands a sloping surface which (1) permits you to seat the cartridge in the barrel and (2) allows the bullet to slowly ease its way into the rifling.

RELATIONSHIP OF BULLET TO BORE

The bullet must be of a size that it can be forced into the rifling and accept the rotation. The ideal size is generally considered to be exactly groove diameter or very slightly smaller. About .0005 inch smaller (one half of a thousandth of an inch) is ideal. In actual practice, bullets run smaller than that ideal and many groove diameters run large too. If you want a finely tuned target rifle you'll do well to get one to exact size and have your bullets as stated above for best results. But you'll pay well for this combination.

In the days of cut rifling (most barrels were cut-rifled up through World War II and for a few years

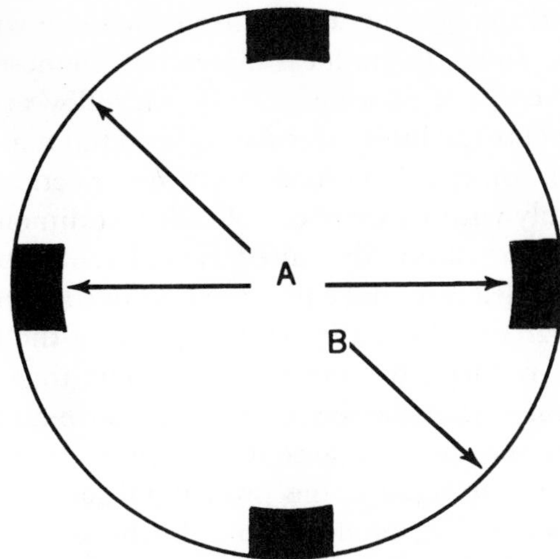

A rifled barrel is first bored to bore diameter, A, and after rifling it also has a groove diameter, B. Bullets are made to groove diameter so they can be forced into the rifling and accept its twist. In a typical .30-caliber rifle, the A dimension shown would be .300 inch and the B dimension would be .308 inch, meaning that each land *(shaded) would have a height of .004 inch. A .30-caliber bullet measures .308 inch.*

after that), barrels were far less uniform than they are today. What with the cold-forming process, as used by Winchester, and the button-rifling systems used by nearly everyone else in the industry, today's barrels are remarkably uniform.

By the same token, today's bullet dies are made of carbide, which can produce several million bullets before noticeable wear. In older days, before carbide bullet dies, it was the custom to make a bullet-forming die in .30 caliber to a diameter of .306 inch (this for .308-inch barrels remember). After running a few hundred thousand bullets the die would be worn to .308 or .3085 inch at which point it was scrapped. There can be vast differences in the performance of a bullet measuring .306 inch and one measuring .3085 inch.

For reasons that are unfathomable, some of these rules do not apply to every barrel. You can take one perfectly made rifle barrel, let's say it is a .22 caliber, and measures a perfect .2240 inch, which we can measure precisely today with an air gauge. This barrel might deliver its best accuracy with bullets measuring exactly .2240 inch, or it might do better with bullets .0001 inch smaller or .0002 inch smaller. You simply won't know until you try.

There is another system of rifling that presents a somewhat different ratio of bullet to bore. That's the multi-groove system, among the best known of which is Marlin's Micro-Groove. Marlin developed this and put it into production in about 1953, at which time they used varying numbers of lands and grooves depending upon the caliber. In .30 caliber they used about 16 lands and grooves — that's four times the norm — but I understand they have now reduced the number somewhat. In any event, the theory behind the Marlin system differs a little from that governing conventional rifling. Marlin figures that the greater number of grooves, which are shallower than is traditional, get a more firm but more gentle grip on the bullet. We'll get the theoretical advantage of that in a moment. First, though, remember that groove diameter must still be .308-inch minimum for a .30-caliber bullet, which means the Marlin system consists of shallower lands or it would displace too much metal and that would boost pressures too high. Instead of having a .300-inch bore diameter, Marlin's Micro-Groove system has a bore diameter of about .304 inch. While this is different, it is quite acceptable and, in fact, the Marlin brand has achieved quite a reputation for accuracy.

The reason for an advantage to a gentler, firmer grip on the bullet is that it tends to distort the bullet less. Imagine, if you will, that the bullet jacket is thicker on one side than the other. The gentle grip will tend to dig into the jacket more uniformly as against the conventional grip, which will force the bullet toward the jacket side of least resistance. Here's where we begin to get into something. A nonuniform bullet jacket means there's more lead

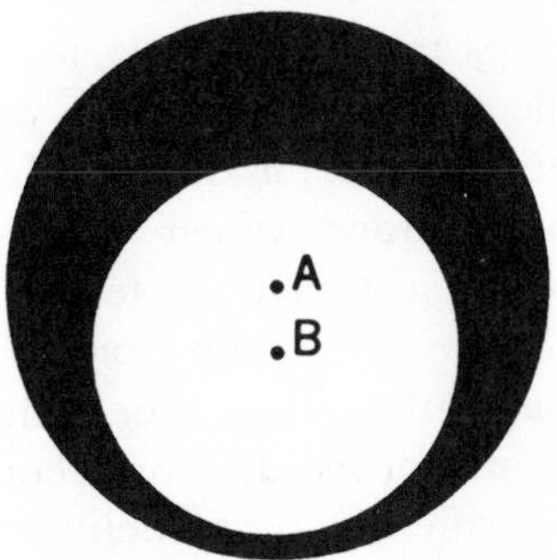

In this diagram of an unbalanced bullet, the shaded area represents the jacket. A is the center of form and B the center of gravity. When these centers do not exactly coincide, the bullet is forced to rotate around its center of form while in the barrel; once airborne, it will tend to revolve around its center of gravity. The result is an inaccurate (and unpredictable) flight.

on one side than the other. The lead is heavier than the jacket, thus the center of gravity doesn't coincide with the center of form. As this unbalanced bullet is forced through the barrel, its center of gravity is made to rotate around its center of form. There is nothing else the bullet can do, since it is confined by the rifle bore. Upon leaving the muzzle, however, the bullet tends to rotate around its center of gravity.

With conventional systems, the more pronounced this unbalancing, the more off-center the bullet will lie, while with the gentler grip of the multi-groove system the less off-center the bullet will tend to lie in the bore. That is the theory behind all the multi-groove systems and, while I've never made enough tests to offer convincing proof that it works, I have made some tests, none of them particularly scientific, but enough to make me believe there is something to it. For example I have a Marlin standard 20-inch barreled .30/30 carbine with a 4X scope mounted. This little gun has accounted for a number of deer in the Maine woods, but that's not unexpected. It also has been used to clip the heads off several partridges at distances ranging from 25 to 50 yards. All this with factory-loaded ammunition — and that is something worth noting. It's also very unscientific.

A little more scientific is my experimenting with a bull-barreled .30/30 on the 336 action that I had Marlin make me up some years ago using their standard Micro-Groove rifling. This rifle has a 30-inch barrel, straight, 1-5/16 inches in diameter. Using handloaded ammunition with 168-grain Sierra match bullets and a Lyman 20X Super-targetspot telescope, this rifle consistently gave me 100-yard groups ranging from ½ to ⅝ inch. Then the same rifle was turned over to the late Frank Jury, who then worked for Lyman. He reported the same kind of accuracy. When you've been in this rifle game as long as I have you learn that what can be done with one rifle doesn't prove anything except that a particular rifle will or will not shoot. So I make no claims for its superior accuracy. But it is a fact that this rifle and barrel delivered good accuracy, especially from a lever action, which "isn't supposed to do that."

BEARING AREA

That part of a bullet that is made to full diameter is called the bearing area. It isn't the same with all bullets. Since the bullet is tapered at the nose (and at the rear in a boat-tailed bullet) it follows that at some point the bullet is reduced from full diameter. Indeed, some bullets have been manufactured deliberately with two sections of different dimensions. These are commonly called two-diameter bullets and the idea is to make the rear part of these bullets to full groove diameter, while the rest of the bullet is then reduced to bore diameter. The theory behind this is that the section that is groove diameter will fill the grooves, accept the rifling twist, and seal the bore against the propellant gas. The forward section is intended to ride the tops of the lands and therefore provide more stability (and concentricity) without increasing the force necessary to drive the bullet into the lands. It will be obvious that the longer the bearing area, the more force will be required to drive the bullet through the barrel.

A parallel can be seen in artillery (artillery is basically a damned big rifle and many of the same things occur) where the shell itself, usually made of steel, is made to bore diameter. Thus the basic shell can slide down the barrel, riding on top of the lands. But an artillery shell is made with a big copper band around its middle called a rotating band. It's the function of this band to accept the rifling, giving the shell its spin, and seal the bore. Sealing the bore (which is technically called obturation) is essential if the gas is to thrust against the bullet. Otherwise gas pressure would be wasted and, in fact, gas squeezing past the bullet under intense pressure and white-hot heat will gas-cut both barrel and bullet, causing poor accuracy in addition to rapid barrel wear.

Most bullets are a bit smaller than groove diameter and you may well ask if gas isn't lost with each shot you fire. No, it isn't. That's because the bullet is hit so hard and fast by the intense blow of the propellant that it swells to fit the barrel. This is called upsetting — the same word that's used in forging when a red-hot piece of steel is whacked by the big drop-forge hammer and upset to a larger diameter. This is why, to offer a common explanation, you can shoot both .22 WMR and .22 Long Rifle cartridges in the same revolver barrel. A .22 WMR has a jacketed bullet measuring .224 inch, the .22 Long Rifle's lead bullet is .222 inch. By using different cylinders you can fire either cartridge through the same barrel because the soft lead .22 Long Rifle bullet will upset to fill the .224 grooves. In fact, many barrels for .22 rifles are all made to .224 inch.

In respect to bearing area, there is the matter of the boat-tailed bullet. It's a little harder for this bullet to upset to fill the grooves and it's a little harder for the gas to push against its base, because that base is smaller. There also is more of a tendency for the boat tail to allow gas cutting and more rapid barrel erosion than with a flat-base bullet. This need not be a concern to any hunter who doesn't use his gun that much. It is more of a factor with the target rifleman who shoots a good deal more.

Other factors that affect upsetting are thickness and hardness of bullet jacket, whether it's an open-point bullet with base closed (as are most hunting bullets) or a full-metal-cased bullet with lead exposed at the base. Rest assured that any bullet will upset, some more readily than others. This can be proved by the simple expedient of using a camera at the muzzle where a tiny puff of gas can be seen escaping from the muzzle before the bullet leaves. The high-speed motion-picture camera has done wonders for gun designers because it can capture things the eye can never see. However, we still have to theorize about what happens inside the barrel. There's no way to see what goes on in there.

The late Dr. Mann spent some forty years experimenting off and on to determine how quickly a bullet is upset in the bore. These tests were all made with lead bullets and the results were interesting. The experiments were made by using different barrel lengths and catching the bullets in oiled sawdust which recovered them in unmutilated condition. He found that, even when using a barrel as short as ¼ inch (which actually left most of the bullet out in the air before firing) the base of the bullet was found to be approximately double in size when recovered. As is normal when experimenting with something new, Dr. Mann soon learned that he was opening more questions than he was answering. He finally concluded, however, that the base of a lead bullet was actually upset *before* the bullet was in motion.

In 1906, Dr. Mann performed the same basic experiment to determine where a jacketed bullet upset using a .25-caliber Marlin barrel. An unfired bullet had a diameter of .258 inch and, after firing from a barrel only 1.32 inches long, had expanded to a diameter of .430 inch, or nearly double. It may be concluded from these tests that whether jacketed or lead, the bullet is upset to fill the grooves before that bullet is set in motion. The first action of the powder gas is to expand the brass cartridge case and release the bullet. It is at this point that a bit of gas squirts past the bullet. It is also true that no bullet completely fills the remote corners of the groove bottoms, so there's always a little leakage.

THE BALANCED BULLET

While its importance becomes more apparent after the bullet is airborne, the balanced bullet is also of importance internally because here is where it gets its thrust.

A bullet may be compared with a gyroscope, or a spinning top, because due to its rotation, that's precisely what it is. Most of us experimented with cheap, toy tops as youngsters and know that a cheap top will spin for a few moments or longer, depending on its quality. Precisely made tops have been made and spun in laboratories for hours. The ideal would be a top that would spin for days and, when it finally stopped rotating, would simply stand on its point. (That's as impossible as perpetual motion, but it would be the ultimate.) Just as a top must be perfectly balanced to spin a long time, so must a bullet be perfectly balanced to fly true. I believe the first person to discover this was Dr. Mann, who performed endless experiments with tops and who then deliberately unbalanced bullets and was able to predict their erratic flight. Not only does the unbalanced bullet not fly true; it sets up its erratic flight characteristics while still in the bore. For accurate rifle shooting, the bullet must be balanced and it must properly fit the bore it's shot out of.

TWIST

The rate of twist in a barrel must be fast enough to stabilize the bullet that will be used — or more accurately, the heaviest bullet in that particular caliber that is likely to be fired. Twist, which gives the bullet its rotation, is the same thing that makes a football forward pass fly true. Insufficient twist and the pass is a blooper; insufficient twist to a bullet and the bullet begins to tip and yaw and finally turn end-over-end and the result is not only erratic flight, but also short flight and no accuracy whatever.

Generally speaking, the longer a bullet, the faster must be the rate of twist. You can take two 100-grain 6mm bullets, one a round nose and one a spitzer (which will be a bit longer) and the shorter will be stabilized by a 12-inch twist while the longer one will not. In the early days of 6mm rifles there was some disagreement which twist should be used, 10 or 12 inch (meaning one complete turn in 10 or 12 inches of barrel length).

IGNITION

Smokeless powder is more difficult to ignite than black and requires a stronger primer, and the larger the powder charge the stronger must be the primer to achieve fast ignition. These are the reasons why there are many variations in modern primers. A powder charge must not just be ignited near the primer, the whole powder charge must be saturated with flame, a good indication of why a hotter primer is necessary to ignite the big charge behind a .264 Winchester Magnum as compared with the small charge contained in a .22 Hornet. Normal ignition takes place in about .0002 second.

The ignited gas builds what we call chamber pressure, which we can measure with the appropriate gauges, and it's of interest to note what a pressure curve looks like. It shows that the maximum pressure is achieved very rapidly and occurs while the bullet is approximately 2–3 inches into the barrel, at which point the bullet has only achieved about ⅓ its maximum or muzzle velocity. Naturally these figures will vary with caliber and bullet weight. The table shows a typical pressure curve using the 150-grain .30/06 military load as an example. Note that the pressure subsides rapidly and that the bullet's acceleration is fastest near the breech. Note too that time of travel, or barrel time, is about 1/10,000 second! This graph will show clearly why the breech end of a barrel must be the heaviest and it also shows why cutting a few inches off the muzzle doesn't reduce velocity too much. It also makes you realize the problems of a gun designer when he's trying to decide where to bleed a bit of gas for a gas-operated gun.

Pressure is measured by a complicated device that consists of drilling a hole into the barrel at the chamber and inserting a small steel plug on top of which is placed a small copper disc of known characteristics. Upon firing, the copper disc is crushed and the amount of crushing can be measured and computed into a factor. This used to be called pounds-per-square-inch (or psi) (the British used

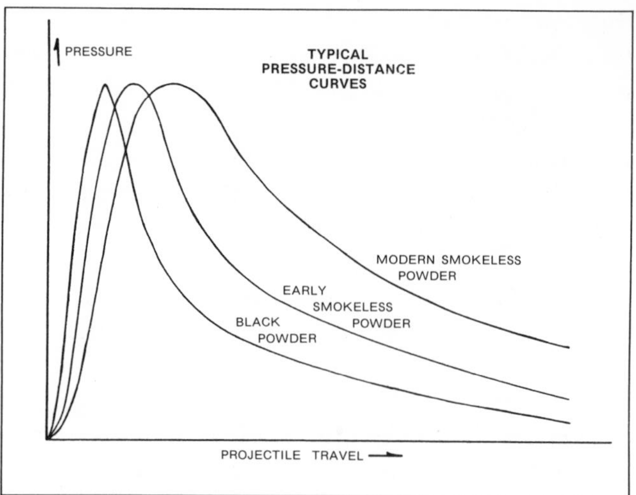

Typical pressure curves for propellant powders. Note that pressure builds rapidly at the breech end and then tails off toward the muzzle. This is why barrels must be larger at the breech end than at the muzzle. Note too that modern smokeless powders build their pressure more slowly (progressively) than earlier powders and that they sustain the delivery of propellant gas at a higher level all the way to the muzzle.

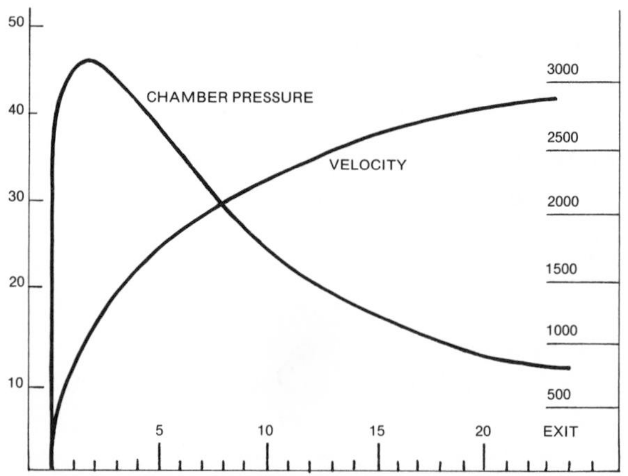

Bullet travel in barrel. Figures at the left indicate pressure in cup, those at right velocity in feet-per-second. This example is approximately correct for a 150-grain .30/06 with 24-inch barrel (bullet exits approximately 22½ inches from its position in the chamber).

tons rather than pounds, referring to the British long ton). However, the figure was not really pounds, or tons, or anything else save a measurement. It could be a comparative measurement; that is you could compare the figures for a .30/06 against a .222 for example. But to say the .30/06 developed 50,000 pounds-per-square-inch of chamber pressure was not necessarily correct.

Now the pressure designation has been changed to the mysterious designation cup, meaning copper units of pressure. Mysterious or not it's a good deal more descriptive — and more accurate — than the old psi. So far as I know the British still use tons of pressure, but that's not really of any importance since the figures are relative. You know for instance that a tough, strong, modern bolt-action rifle can safely be operated at a certain level of psi or cup or whatever you choose to call it. You also know that some of the older actions are not as strong and should be loaded with lesser pressure.

While copper discs are used for high-power rifles, lead discs are used for lower-pressure cartridges, such as shotgun and handgun. These are designated lup. Both cup and lup designations are interchangeable with the old psi term — it's simply a change in nomenclature. A rifle that used to develop 55,000 pounds-per-square-inch of breech pressure now develops 55,000 cup, or copper units of pressure.

The effect of heat on pressure must not be overlooked. It has been noted by many American riflemen that the English seemingly underload their ammunition and it is often wondered why. Similarly, our military ammunition is loaded a bit lighter than some think it can be. The reason is that heat has a serious effect on pressures and military ammunition must be capable of operating satisfactorily in any part of the world. British gunmakers customarily serve clients who traditionally hunt in the tropics — where the heat boosts pressures. Many American experimental riflemen have noted that, if they're shooting in the hot summer sun in the desert, and if they leave their ammunition exposed to the sun, it will generate fearful pressures. The reloader should always bear this in mind, for a handload near maximum that might be perfectly suitable in Quebec in the fall could be hot enough to cause trouble in the desert of Arizona in August.

BARREL TIME . . . TOTAL TIME

We have mentioned barrel time and earlier we mentioned lock time and ignition time. Note we can combine these various times and note that they accumulate and become more significant. They won't mean much to the average deer hunter, but they are of supreme importance to the target shooter. Let's take a look, and remember that there are big variations from gun to gun, and among cartridges, barrel lengths, powder used, etc. These time intervals from the moment the trigger releases the sear until the bullet leaves the muzzle look like this:

lock time	.002	to	.0057 second
ignition time	.0002	to	.0002
barrel time	.0007	to	.001
Total time	.0029	to	.0069

Pretty fast either way, yet the slowest total time is nearly three times as slow as the quickest. Enough to pull a 9 from a perfect 10-hold on the target!

VELOCITY VS TWIST

As said earlier, a fast twist is necessary for the longer, heavier bullets. Another factor in this relationship is velocity. For example, a .250/3000 Savage with a twist of 1 turn in 14 inches will not stabilize a 117-grain bullet. But the same barrel, if chambered to the .25/06, would stabilize the 117-grain bullet because the bullet would be driven faster. The higher the velocity the higher the rate of spin and so a faster cartridge can sometimes use a slower twist.

There isn't much you can do about the twist you have. You can measure what that twist is by using a close-fitting cleaning rod and measure the distance it takes for the rod to make a complete revolution. Or you can write and ask the manufacturer, giving the model and serial number. Sometimes twists are changed without notice; manufacturers make mistakes in twist too, and when this comes to light they simply change it without telling the public. When that happens nobody knows about it except a few reloaders who find out the hard way when a long bullet won't stabilize.

LOADING DENSITY

This refers to the amount of powder in a given case. If the case is full of powder, with the bullet seated to touch the powder, the density may be stated at 100 percent. Depending upon the size of the case, its wall thickness (which will be found to vary from one brand to another and among lots of the same brand), the weight of the bullet, and the powder used, the density may vary considerably. Consider, for example, a reloaded cartridge with a reduced load, say for small-game shooting. The loading density might be 50 percent or less. If the rifle were carried muzzle up, slung over the shoulder for instance, and then slowly brought into firing position the powder would lie near the primer. On the other hand if the rifle had been carried muzzle down, the reverse would occur and the result in terms of ignition and resultant performance would vary.

Cartridges work more efficiently when the loading density is at or near 100 percent because the ignition is more uniform. Still, no matter what is done to control uniformity in everything, results will vary. By this I mean that you can take the same barrel and same rifle, carefully select your components by weighing them and making every test you can determine so as to make everything absolutely alike. Then fire them and you will get variations in velocity that often amount to as much as 100 fps from shot to shot. Sometimes more. There is no explanation for such happenings that I know of. They occur, more with certain cartridges than with others. Nobody knows why.

Nor, as a matter of fact, does the rifle/cartridge combination that shows the most consistent velocity necessarily shoot with the most accuracy. These are among the many things about ballistics that cannot be explained.

Along similar lines of thought, it will be found that a given rifle barrel will usually show a preference for one kind of powder over another, other things being equal. Other barrels will digest just about any reasonable load regardless of the powder. To illustrate: most .220 Swift rifles will shoot with excellent accuracy with a good 55-grain bullet (Sierra, Hornady, Speer, etc.) and a load of *either* 37 grains 4064 or 33 grains 3031 powder. As a rule of thumb you can try any Swift rifle with either of these loads and it will probably do well with one of them. If it doesn't do well with either there's probably something wrong with the rifle and you'd be well advised not to buy it. Nobody can explain why this is so, but everybody who has had much experience with accurate rifles knows it to be true.

RECOIL, JUMP, AND VIBRATION

When a rifle is fired, the propellant gas expands in all directions shoving the case walls against the chamber walls. It shoves backwards against the case head, which in turn pushes against the bolt face. This rearward thrust extends throughout the entire rifle until it shoves against your shoulder. It also pushes against the bullet. And it shoves with the same force in all these directions at once. Naturally the bullet gets out of the barrel quickly because it's so light by comparison with the bulk of the rifle, but it's this same force that creates recoil.

When a shoulder arm is fired from the shoulder, the pressure or resistance on the butt is exerted below the line of recoil, which is a continuation of the axis of the bore. That makes the gun not only move to the rear but makes it pivot on the spot providing that resistance, so the gun tends to move not only backwards but upwards as well. This tendency is known as jump. Its degree or severity depends upon how far below the line of recoil that point lies, as well as on the configuration of the stock itself, and the caliber. That's a good point to keep in mind because it's an excellent argument in favor of the straight line of the classic stock.

There is some movement of the gun, any gun, before the projectile leaves the bore. This will vary to some very slight degree among the various cartridges, bullet weights, powder charges, barrel lengths, and so on, but *every* gun moves somewhat before the bullet leaves the muzzle. If you've ever observed a benchrest shooter in action, you will note that he takes extraordinary pains to place his rifle precisely the same each time he shoots. And he holds (or often doesn't hold at all) the rifle exactly the same each time. The same cheek pressure against the stock, the same part of the forearm resting, the same touch of the shooting hand against the stock and trigger guard. Everything. Everything the same. That's because the rifle, no matter the caliber, is going to be in motion as the bullet exits. And if there's something different about his hold, his touch, or anything, the result will show on the target.

At one time there used to be arguments about whether or not a gun moved before the bullet was on its way. All such chatter ceased long ago when the high-speed camera went to work and proved that it moved.

The third factor in gun movement before the

bullet leaves is vibration. There are two phases to vibration, the first is relatively minor and is caused by the movement of the firing mechanism itself. When the sear releases the firing pin or hammer, parts are set in motion and no matter how fast they move or how light they are they set up movement. A heavy hammer, for instance, flying up and hitting a firing pin sets up a vibration. But this minor vibration is quickly obliterated by the vibration caused by firing. This takes the form of many events which depend on differing factors including type of action, how the gun is constructed, how it is held by the shooter — the vibration possibilities are virtually infinite. But the most important vibration is the one set up by the barrel itself. Barrels come in varying lengths, dimensions, configurations, and bore diameters. They are chambered for a wide variety of cartridges, developing varying forces. And barrels are bedded in their stocks and held to their actions in varying ways.

As the gun tends to rotate around the center of its resistance — the butt — there is also a tendency for the barrel to flip down in a counterreaction. This downflip, which we usually simply call "vibration" while the British call it flip, is partly the result of the upward jump of the gun as a unit, mostly the result of the vibration of firing. Suffice it to say, for an explanation of this brief negative flip, that it resembles what happens when you suddenly move your hand up and back with a fly rod in your hand. The rod tip tends to stay where it is or to flip down in reaction. The gun barrel does the same thing to a far lesser degree and to a degree depending on the configuration of the barrel itself.

Firing a gun is akin to whacking a piece of pipe held in a vise with a big hammer. It shakes and vibrates. The way it shakes and vibrates depends on how it's held, how hard you hit it, the size of the hammer, the wall thickness of the pipe and many other factors. That's just what happens to a rifle barrel, which should help explain why it must be firmly screwed into its receiver, why the breeching must be tight, why the stock bedding must be right (and uniform), and why the whole thing must be tight enough to remain the same way for a long time, shot after shot.

They used to talk about nodes of vibration and how it was best if a bullet were to emerge at a certain point in the node. Some theorized how this could be determined by placing strings loosely over a barrel and whacking the tube with a hammer, to see where the strings gathered. Then, with some formula they wouldn't divulge, they'd say this barrel should be 27 and 15/16th inches long. It didn't mean a thing. They didn't know what the hell they were talking about and this node stuff finally went out the window. It had some validity though in that, depending on the load used, bullets emerged from the muzzle at different points in the vibration of the barrel. That explains why sometimes you can sight in with one weight of bullet, then switch to another weight and find your point of impact is off. It may be up, down, or to one side or the other, it simply means the barrel is in a different phase of its movement when this weight of bullet emerges. You might correct this with the cardboard shim mentioned earlier, or you might have to live with it. It also explains why the British spend so much time regulating a double rifle so it fires each barrel to the same point of impact with a certain weight bullet. It will rarely do the same with any load for which the rifle was not regulated.

Jump and vibration can seriously affect the shot. The amount they affect that shot depends, in addition to those things already mentioned, on the way the shooter handles his gun. Sling tension for example will drastically affect the outcome. And if you really want to have a shot go wild, just rest the barrel against a tree or fence post. It's perfectly OK to rest your *hand* on anything that's handy, and to rest the forearm on your hand, on your hat atop a rock, stump, or what have you. But don't let that barrel touch anything or you'll upset the vibration and your shot will miss by a country mile.

The rule then is to eliminate all the possible factors you can think of that will affect jump and vibration. You must get to the point where you do this automatically without thinking of it. And that means constant practice.

BULLET DEFORMATION IN THE BORE

In its work to determine ballistic coefficients for downrange ballistics, the Speer bullet technicians in Lewiston, Idaho, reasoned that actual firing tests were needed to prove — or disprove — their results. The reason was that too many factors occur *after* firing. To put that another way, it is unrealistic simply to inspect a bullet visually and calculate your ballistics from that shape. That may or may not be the shape in which the bullet leaves the muzzle.

Speer found that there was considerable deformation that took place in the bullet at the moment of firing, while the bullet was still in the bore. Most of this can be attributed to inertia slump or setback. They found, for example, that the base of the bullet began to move before the nose did, tending to make the bullet shorter and more cylindrical. They also found that the exposed lead nose of spitzer bullets flowed backwards, part of it into the expanded jacket and part of it being shorn off.

The leading factors influencing these results are the alloy of the lead core (i.e. its toughness), jacket strength and thickness, pressure of the lands being forced into the bullet (this may be one of the places where the shallow multi-groove system like Marlin's Micro-Groove is a big advantage), rifling shape and finish, and the "brisance" of the powder (which means the shattering effect of the propellant powder) or how sudden and sharp is the blow of the gases against the base of the bullet. These effects open up avenues for study that had not heretofore been considered. It must be admitted that, now we have the Speer data, the same thing could have been deduced from Dr. Mann's studies. But it wasn't until the advent of high-speed photography, which plainly shows a spitzer bullet entirely lacking its point and with a blunter shape than it had before firing, emerging from the muzzle of a high-power rifle.

I noted long ago that bullets with battered noses seemed to shoot as well as perfectly formed bullets from the same batch. But it never occurred to me to wonder why. The reason would now seem to be that any high-velocity rifle bullet with a lead-exposed tip is going to make its flight without that tip anyway.

MUZZLE VELOCITY VS BARREL LENGTH

There is a relationship between barrel length and muzzle velocity but it's usually far less than you might think. There was a time during which those companies who load ammunition would do all their testing for published ballistic tables in 26-inch barrels and list them accordingly. Since few rifles were turned out with barrels that long the point was rather silly. It was a compounded error too, because many of the claims for velocity were exaggerated even beyond what the added barrel length would achieve.

Actually the whole thing made no sense except to the promoter who had something to talk about. It means very little, if anything, to the hunter if his 180-grain .30/06 bullet is moving at 2,750 or 2,800 fps. And it doesn't matter much to the game either.

There are various rules of thumb. Remington offers one in their 1976 ballistics list, for example, which says that for every change in barrel length of 1 inch you gain or lose 10 fps if the muzzle velocity is in the 2,000–2,500 fps range, 20 fps if the range is between 2,500 and 3,000 fps, 30 if 3,000–3,500 and 40 if 3,500–4,000. That will be found to be reasonably close; close enough. In the first place those differences noted are within the tolerances between shots anyway. But it's really no big deal and you'll find the extra handiness of a 22-inch barreled sporter will more than offset the velocity of a full-length 24-inch barrel. Of course there are some rifles that do deliver a significantly faster speed with a barrel as long as 26 inches. And if you really want that kind of speed, you'll have to settle for a longer barrel. In my own opinion I'd as soon have a light, handy rifle with a barrel as short as 19 inches and take the velocity I get, which will be plenty.

The hotter the cartridge as a rule, the more velocity you'll lose by trimming it's length. And the higher the velocity, the faster you'll wear out the barrel, too. Quite possibly the worst offender in today's cartridge lineup is the .264 Winchester Magnum. You can prolong barrel life considerably, however, if you shoot slowly, letting the barrel cool as much as you can between shots. Overheating, through firing, is the biggest cause of barrel erosion.

MUZZLE BLAST

We all recognize muzzle blast as the nasty, sharp, piercing noise that bellows from a gun's muzzle. And we also know that the more powerful the cartridge and the shorter the barrel, the worse the blast effect. It is for this reason that everyone who shoots should always wear ear protection, except while hunting. The blast is a useless by-product of firing and has no desirable effects whatever. It does not help propel the projectile and it represents wasted power. A bit of this power is utilized in gas-operated guns but, aside from a couple of the very earliest gas guns, the gas is bled from a point behind the muzzle so it has nothing to do with muzzle blast. Contrary to some beliefs, bleeding a bit of gas to make a gas gun work does not rob the bullet of enough propelling force to amount to anything at all. It may be stated categorically that a gas gun develops just as much velocity as does any other gun.

As a matter of fact, in one very short experiment, a ballistics laboratory drilled a ¼-inch hole in a .22 rifle barrel only 1 inch from the breech. That meant it was just barely in front of the .22 Long Rifle bullet as it lay in the chamber. The velocity loss in a 20-inch barrel was approximately 40 percent – a significant amount, but quite a bit less than you'd expect with a hole of that size, that close to the chamber. The experiment was deemed too short to be reliable. Nevertheless, it shows that you can bleed an awful lot of gas off at a critical point and it will have far less effect than you'd expect.

EFFICIENCY

The rifle (or any firearm for that matter) is not a very efficient "engine," but we can draw some conclusions with regard to its efficiency that are proportionate to bore diameter. For instance, a .22-caliber rifle is about 22 percent efficient while a .45-caliber rifle is about 45 percent efficient. In fact, as a rule of thumb the efficiency percentage roughly equals the bore size. I've used .22 and .45 caliber as the approximate limits on either end, .22 caliber being approximately as small as is practical and .45 caliber is just about as large as you want to go without having undue recoil. These figures are empirical and were derived from an examination of many center-fire cartridges. They are by no means meant to be anything more than a general rule of thumb. Efficiency rises as caliber gets larger because the projectile's base area increases with the square of the caliber.

EXTERNAL

The subject of external ballistics deals with the bullet's flight after it leaves the muzzle. The path of this flight is called the "trajectory" and it's a parabolic curve, which means it flies in a curve but that the curve decreases faster at the latter part of its flight than it ascends at the beginning. You could compare this curve to the throw to home plate by an outfielder; the ball starts out at high speed and moves relatively straight, but the farther it goes the slower it goes and it falls faster and faster. The same thing happens to a golf ball.

No bullet goes in a straight line. That's an impossibility because there's a phenomenon called gravity that makes its presence known on the bullet the moment it is out of the bore and thus unsupported. If we want the bullet to go farther, we must raise the muzzle of the rifle, which is accomplished by raising the rear sight, which, in effect, depresses the butt (or raises the muzzle).

The other major factor that influences the flight of a bullet is air resistance. If you fired a rifle in a vacuum the maximum velocity achieved would continue until the bullet hit the ground, pulled down to earth by gravity. Shooting a rifle on the moon, for example, where the force of gravity is far less than on earth, would mean the bullet would travel an enormous distance. I suppose that could be computed, but I don't know what purpose the calculation would serve. One of the moon-walking astronauts whacked a golf ball as a stunt. As far as I know that ball may still be flying. These things may not be important except to serve to illustrate how important air resistance is to the flight of a rifle bullet (or golf ball).

There was a time, before the U.S. Space Program began, when many of these things were hard to understand, because most of us were not exposed to speeds in excess of the speed of sound, zero gravity, and the lack of atmosphere. The space talk during the years since this program began has made it easier to understand the flight of a bullet and its problems. Let's first point out that a bullet is not self-propelled like a rocket or an airplane. The initial thrust it gets inside the barrel is all the propulsion it will receive. It also travels in the earth's atmosphere, which means it must contend with both air resistance and gravity – and these forces are something to consider. From the space program we got an idea of air resistance, from the knowledge that a space vehicle will burn up from air resistance even at extremely high altitudes (where the air is very thin). Moreover supersonic aircraft make a sound wave, or sonic boom. So does any bullet that flies faster than the speed of sound (which is virtually every bullet in existence except a few slow-moving pistol bullets and the standard-velocity .22 Long Rifle). Consequently you can't silence any gun except one that shoots a slug moving below the speed of sound — another fact that's constantly abused by newspaper and other fiction writers. You can silence the muzzle blast and the report of the gun's firing won't be heard, but you cannot silence the flight of the projectile because it will make the sonic boom, the sharp "crack" you hear when a bullet goes overhead. Anyone who has ever been in the target pits has heard this crack with every shot fired.

AIR RESISTANCE

Air resistance is a powerful force as all of us who have experienced strong winds know. On a still, quiet day you can walk slowly along and give no thought to air resistance at all, but on a windy day it's a totally different matter. Given a strong enough wind you have to lean into the wind making walking against it more and more difficult as wind velocity increases. Anyone who has experienced winds of hurricane force are aware that it can blow houses down, barns away, and has even been known to drive a straw into the side of a wooden building. Consider then just what happens when you fire a bullet on a still day!

A .22 Long Rifle bullet leaves the muzzle at about 1,100 fps. That velocity can be translated into a wind of 752 miles an hour. (Keep in mind that winds of hurricane force are those in excess of 75 mph.) Applying the same thinking to a .30-caliber bullet leaving the muzzle at 2,700 fps, it strikes a wind force of 1,841 miles per hour! That's enough to slow the bullet down to a speed of 2,460 fps at 100 yards and only 1,068 fps at 1,000 yards.

Bullets travel through the air with varying degrees of efficiency, depending on their shape, weight, and diameter. It takes no imagination to know that the .45/70 bullet used today, which is as flat on the front end as a barn door, is going to meet severe air resistance. On the other hand, a spitzer-pointed, boat-tailed bullet will have considerably better ballistics because it will slip through the air better. You can also use the analogy of aircraft frame design, noting that planes designed for supersonic flight are very streamlined. Another point of comparison is found in the racing sailboat, which has a sharp bow to slice through the water and a tapered stern to allow the water to return to its previous position easily and without "tail-dragging." Water and air are two very different things and present varying problems, but the resistance to penetration is fairly similar. If you push a trim, slim sailboat and stop the power, it will glide a long distance in the water. Do the same with a flat-ended barge and it won't go far. Bullets behave in exactly the same way.

The sketch shows five general forms of bullet, from left to right they range from terrible to excellent in ability to retain velocity. A round ball is next to useless. Bullet number 2, a short, blunt form, is better than a round ball but not suitable for long-range shooting. A longer round-nose bullet, as represented by bullet number 3, is better; its point is not so blunt and its length is longer. The longer length provides better ballistics and we use the term sectional density to indicate this. Bullets with high sectional density, that is a long weight to length ratio, perform better at longer ranges than bullets with low sectional density. Bullet 4, with its sharp point, will penetrate the air better than any of the shapes to its left. It represents the most common type of high-power rifle bullet in use in the world today. But the boat-tailed bullet, number 5, is the best shape of all in terms of velocity retention and long-range performance.

Bullet cores are made of lead, the best metal for the purpose to provide a relatively cheap core material that will produce high sectional density. Any lighter metal would fail to meet that goal. You can readily appreciate this if you throw a golf ball and

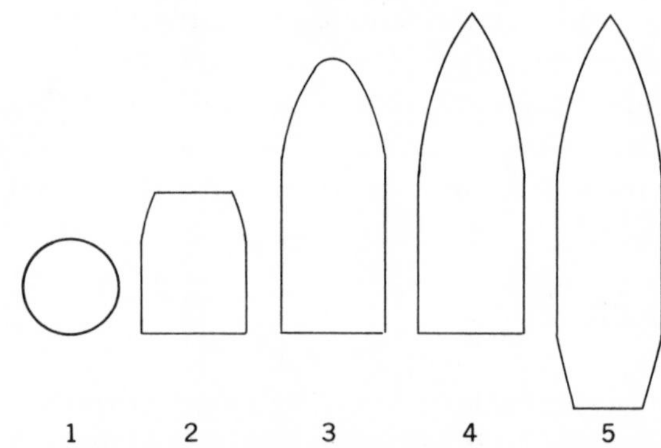

From left to right are shown projectiles with poor-to-excellent flight characteristics. The round ball is the worst possible shape because its air resistance increases in proportion to the square of its velocity. Figure 2 is a typical pistol bullet shape, suitable for short-range shooting. Figure 3 is a blunt-nosed, elongated projectile approximately similar to those used in rifles of the .30/30 class. Figure 4 is the most common shape employed, the flat-based spitzer bullet and Figure 5 is the same basic shape as No. 4, but with a boat tail to reduce tail drag.

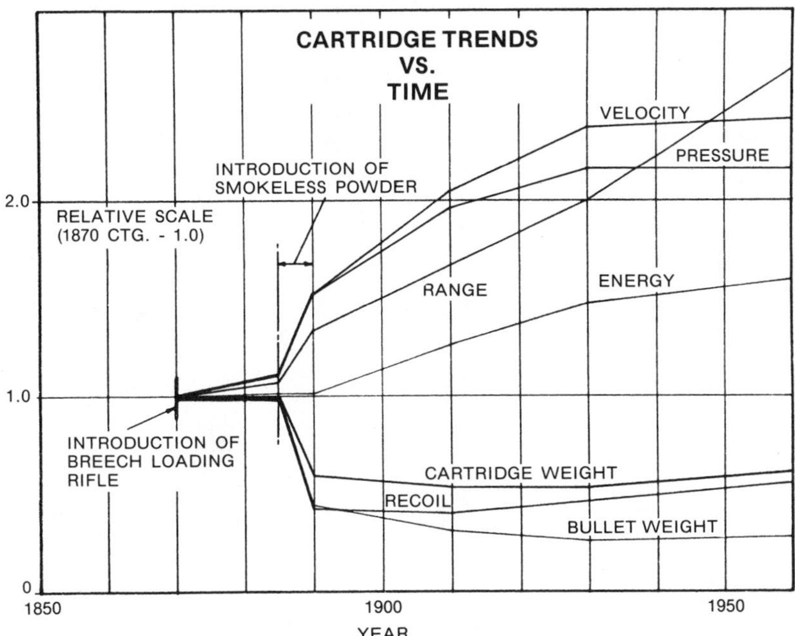

This chart plots trends over the years since the introduction of the breech-loading rifle, arbitrarily given here as 1870. Note that once smokeless powder was marketed in about 1885, cartridge weights, recoil, and bullet weight were all reduced sharply while velocity, pressure, range, and energy all increased significantly. The most impressive figure given on this chart is the increase of range, which is a function of accuracy and bullet shape in addition to the other factors given. I would tend to question the range graph, but the other figures given on this scale are accurate. (Chart courtesy of Winchester-Western.)

Ping-Pong ball with as much force as you can. Both balls are roughly similar in size and you know without trying it which will fly the farthest. Similarly, you can look at two bullets of different shape and tell at a glance which bullet will be able to sustain its velocity best.

By taking a bullet's weight, diameter, shape, and material into consideration we can establish an index which ballisticians call a ballistic coefficient which they define as the index of a bullet's ability to overcome resistance in flight relative to the performance of a standard projectile used to compute ballistic tables.

GRAVITY

Gravity pulls everything toward the earth as soon as it is unsupported, as in the case of a projectile, by the gun barrel. The moment a bullet leaves the muzzle it begins to drop and it continues to drop at an accelerated rate. It should be noted that the bullet drops from the line that is a continuation of the axis of the bore. (In the case of a long-range shot, when the rifle barrel is elevated slightly, the bullet will rise. But it will fall from the continuation of that line, and that's what we're talking about.) That line, by the way, is what riflemen call the angle of departure or line of departure.

If you were to hold a rifle perfectly level and fire it, and at the same precise moment drop a bullet of the same size and weight from the same height, both bullets would strike the ground (assuming a level surface such as water) at the same instant. The reason is that the pull of gravity is the same, even though one bullet has forward momentum that will not affect the pull of gravity at all, other things being the same. When any body falls from gravity its velocity accelerates at a constant rate until air resistance finally prevents it from falling any faster. In the first second of a bullet's flight it will drop 16.1 feet below the line of departure. To cite one simple example, with a 150-grain bullet from the .30/06 at a muzzle velocity of 2,700 fps, its time of flight for the first 100 yards is .116 second; in that length of time the bullet will drop 2.4 inches. This means that if we aimed the rifle so the bore axis were exactly in line with the target at 100 yards and we fired the rifle, the bullet would hit 2.4 inches below that line.

Gravity and air resistance are the two major factors affecting the flight of a bullet, but they are by no means the only things. But before going further, let's digress and discuss a few basics about the flight of a projectile.

Our interest lies primarily along two lines: the actual line of sight, which can be defined as the straight line from sight to target and the line the

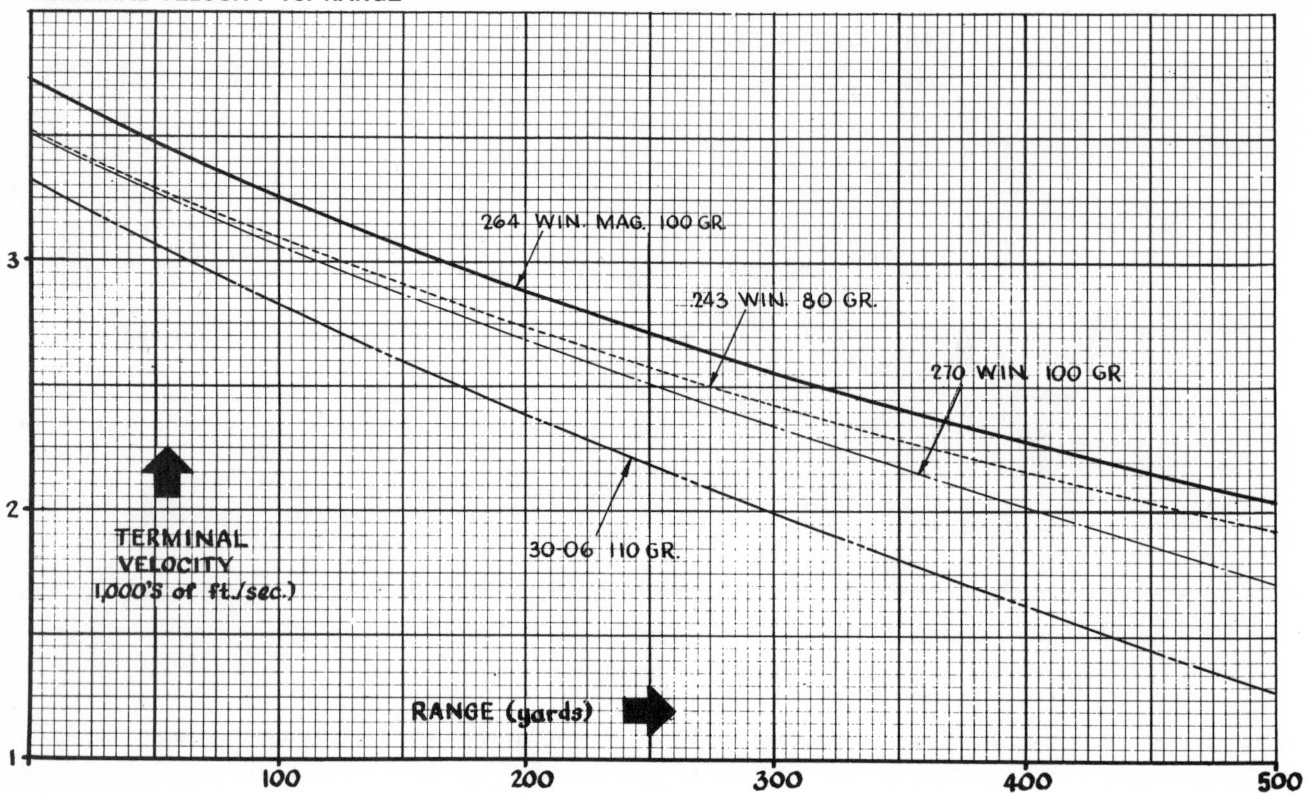

This chart shows how the more efficient bullets retain their velocity over long range. Note that the 80-grain .243 Winchester bullet retains almost as much velocity at 500 yards as the 100-grain .264 Magnum. And note how the 110-grain .30/06 bullet falls off quickly. Interestingly, the 80-grain .243 has exactly the same 500-yard energy as the 100-grain .270 bullet. The chart helps support what many shooters already know: that the .243 is one of the finest long-range varmint cartridges ever developed. (Chart courtesy of Winchester-Western.)

bullet actually travels. As bullets do not travel in a straight line the second path is the line we are most interested in. Our concern is to make the bullet pass through the line of sight *at* the target. This is called sighting in, or zeroing in, and is accomplished by moving the barrel's muzzle up or down (by moving the sight the opposite way) until the path of the bullet exactly coincides with the line of sight at the range we wish to sight in for. Let's say our distance is 200 yards, and we're using a .30/06 with 180-grain bullet at 2,700 fps of muzzle velocity with a scope-sighted rifle. By checking ballistic tables (in this case from *Hornady Handbook*, which has worked out these computations for us) we note that when our rifle is sighted in at exactly 200 yards, the bullet is 1.5 inches low at the muzzle (because the scope itself is 1.5 inches above the bore); at 100 yards the bullet is 2.2 inches above the line of sight, at 200 yards it is exactly on the line of sight and at 300 yards it has fallen to 9.3 inches below that line. To carry this two steps farther it has dropped 27.6 and 57.6 inches at 300 and 400 yards respectively.

Trajectories are usually plotted by quoting midrange trajectory, meaning that the bullet is so many inches above the line of sight at midrange. That really doesn't tell you very much and the ballistic tables now are coming around to the information as I have just expressed it. This is a meaningful way to advise the rifleman what to expect from a given bullet at a given velocity at whatever range he chooses. It permits him to sight in at a range that will be useful for the particular country he will be hunting. Once that has been determined he will have a pretty good idea of exactly where his bullet will be at varying ranges. However, remember that all rifles do not shoot alike and not all velocities are identical. This won't mean much at 100 yards or even at 200 yards, but when you begin to get farther from the muzzle it will be an important factor. You are advised then to sight in at your predetermined distance, say 200 yards. Then you must target your rifle at other distances in order to compute exactly where your bullet will be at those distances instead of relying on any table. The tables are only a guide; your own rifle is the only thing that really counts.

Of course things do not always turn out as planned. A few years ago I was on a mule-deer hunt in New Mexico and made my plans very carefully. My rifle, a .30/06, was accurately sighted in for exactly 200 yards and I knew precisely where the bullet was at distances to 500 yards. While working through some heavy timber and brush I surprised a magnificent mule deer buck in the tangle and shot him at a range of no more than ten yards. I could as easily have bagged him with a handgun.

Once you have gotten your rifle sighted in, and checked at the other distances, you can simply hold over (or under) the right amount if your game animal stands at a range other than that for which you are exactly sighted in. (Or you can employ one of those new scopes that you simply dial for the distance.) But you'd better be right in your range estimation or all these calculations are for nothing. If you estimate your game at 500 yards and he's really only 350, you're going to miss.

Ballistics tables must of necessity be accepted as a guide. They are quite accurate, as the ballisticians have gone to great length to compute (and I mean the word literally because they have fed into computers all the necessary data) the trajectory of an ideal bullet of the particular shape under discussion. These calculations take into effect the velocity, gravity, rate of rotation, barometric pressure, temperature, humidity, altitude, size, and shape of the bullet. Firing tests determined the drag characteristics, which is defined as the rate at which a bullet decelerates. The drag function usually employed is either that determined by Col. Ingalls, a set of figures that is compatible with a mathematical model built by Mayevski and used in Krupp test firings in 1881 for a projectile with the same approximate shape as a modern bullet. Tests have indicated that the Mayevski findings (as used by Hornady in his reloading handbook) are compatible with Ingalls as used by the late Gen. Julian Hatcher in his ballistic work. Indeed, most ballisticians have apparently used the Ingalls tables. The reason one or another of these standards is used is that otherwise empirical findings would have to be learned for each and every bullet shape and the job would hardly be worth the tremendous time expended. By plugging in one of the standards, the computer can tell us, in a matter of moments, all we need to know. Let's take a look at some of the other things that can affect the bullet's flight, which can make all calculations more or less useless.

WIND DEFLECTION

It isn't going to do us much good if we accurately estimate the range of a deer standing at exactly 300 yards and we know exactly where our bullet will be at that distance, but there's a gale blowing and our perfect neck shot hold allows the bullet to be blown to the side far enough to miss. The wind can blow a bullet a vast distance, depending on the range over which the bullet flies, its velocity, its weight, and its shape. Similarly, a tail wind will slightly accelerate a bullet and a head wind will slow it a bit.

The wind, as a matter of fact, is one of the most perplexing and damnable things the rifleman has to contend with. It usually comes in gusts and can come from any direction, and these directions often change as you pull the trigger. It may not exist where you are standing but be blowing a gale where the target is. Experienced riflemen often can "dope" the wind pretty well, but it's all guesswork born of experience and a lot of shooting. Many rifle ranges have flags set down the range so the riflemen can keep an eye on the flags and hope to shoot when the air is still, or at least when conditions are similar to when the last shot was fired. Generally speaking, sharp-pointed bullets will provide less wind deflection than a blunt pointed bullet. There are two reasons for this: (1) they go faster and so the wind has less time to blow against them and (2) they encounter less air resistance. For example, it has been proven that the standard velocity .22 Long Rifle needs less wind allowance than the .22 LR high speed. Since both bullet shapes are the same, how can this be? It is because of the higher air resistance built by the high-speed bullet. One theory says that the wind not only affects the bullet itself, but also the wall of massed air surrounding the bullet that's been built up by air resistance.

The big, fat .45/70 bullet, weighing 405 grains,

really should not be affected too much by the wind. That's a lot of weight and despite its slow travel you wouldn't think it could be blown off course easily. Wrong. It will be blown exactly 2 inches at 300 yards from a crosswind of only 15 mph – not much of a breeze. A few other computations are for a crosswind of only 10 mph at a range of 100 yards.

Cartridge	Bullet Weight in grains	Muzzle Velocity in fps	Wind Deflection in inches
.22 Long Rifle	40	1,070	3.29
.270 Winchester	130	3,160	.32
.30/06	150	2,910	1.05
.35 Remington	200	2,080	1.74

As you can see, the wind, besides being unpredictable, can throw all your best laid plans out the window when it comes to hitting that nice buck across a canyon. A rifleman has to compute for wind allowance and he has to do it purely by a gut feeling born of experience on the range and over varying terrain. That's one of the reasons varmint hunting is so valuable. You get to learn, on small targets, how far to hold into the wind just by its feel and the way it bends the grasses between you and the target. There are even times when the wind blows one way for part of the range and the other way over the rest. Under certain situations it can cancel itself out. But don't count on it.

DRIFT

Another word sometimes used is crawl and I like it better for the word means the very slight sideways movement of a bullet due to its rotational speed. To explain this I think it is simplest to build a picture of spinning a perfectly round object, say a baseball bat, and then carefully dropping it in still water. As soon as the splash subsides and so long as the bat is still rotating, it will begin to crawl sideways in the direction in which it is turning. While the effect is much, much less, a rifle bullet does the same thing in flight. Assuming a right-hand twist of rifling, thus a right-hand rotation, the bullet will crawl slightly to the right. This isn't a big deal. A 150-grain .30/06 drifts just 13 inches to the right at a range of 1,000 yards.

YAW, TIP, AIR SPIRAL

While there is no such thing as a perfect bullet, today's bullets are remarkably close to that ideal – a good deal closer than they were prior to World War II for example. Nonetheless, bullets can make strange motions as they fly downrange.

It was previously stated that every bullet is unbalanced to some degree, simply because we can't make things absolutely perfect. Bullet imbalance occurs when a gilding metal jacket is thicker on one side than the other, meaning that there will be more lead on the thin side. That means, in turn, that the bullet's center of gravity will not coincide with its center of form. As this bullet goes down the barrel it is made to rotate around its center of form simply because the barrel holds it there. But once the bullet leaves the barrel, it tends to rotate around the center of gravity. Eventually, the bullet will be rotating around its center of gravity rather than its center of form but its flight will be unpredictable. It will not print on the same place at the target as will a more nearly perfect bullet. This is called the center of gravity spiral, because the bullet flies in a spiral the diameter of which is very small and whose pitch is the same as the pitch of rifling. Dr. F.W. Mann proved this long, long ago by deliberately unbalancing bullets by drilling holes in their bases and then placing them in the chamber so as to emerge from the muzzle with the light side up. By such placement, he could predict the flight. But you can't do that because you don't know where the bullet is unbalanced.

Dr. Mann called this the X error and he spent a long time solving and explaining it. He then found another error (which he dubbed Y) and discovered that it was due to a tipping bullet. A tipping bullet may be said to wobble as it passes through the air. Such a bullet is also imperfect, though it may not necessarily be unbalanced. Like the unbalanced bullet though, it will have an error which is due to air resistance to the tipping – or yawing – of the bullet. The extent of this error is dependent upon the shape of the bullet and the amount of tipping, its speed, and the number of gyrations per second. Sometimes these two errors can cancel each other and the shot will print dead center.

A tipping bullet can occur from a number of sources. There can be damage to the muzzle of the rifle, a bullet's base may have been deformed, it may not have been seated concentrically in the cartridge case, or it may have become a bit bent in the case by rough handling. However, and fortunately, we have at last learned how to make bullets that are close to perfection, even though there are still more worlds to conquer in ballistics.

ALTITUDE AND TEMPERATURE

Any rise in temperature will increase velocity, since it increases pressure. If you're hunting in the desert in hot weather, it will pay you to sight in again under those conditions. Similarly, the higher the elevation the less air resistance. This may not sound like much but if you have sighted in your rifle at or near sea level and then hunt in the high Rockies, you will find things quite different – especially over longer ranges.

The main lesson to be learned from this is that you must make the proper allowances, check your sighting, and beware of the changes that can take place. Some of the extremes really can make a vast difference.

UP AND DOWN SHOOTING

It's an old rule of thumb that one tends to shoot too high when shooting at sharp angles either up or down. And it's a fact. The reason is simple, applies only to extremes, and only at distances of 200 yards or more; otherwise the effect is minimal.

For example, if you are shooting at an angle of 45° (either up or down it makes no difference), you're forming an equilateral right triangle. In this triangle the actual distance from you to the target is, say, 150 yards but the level distance is only 100 yards. And it's over the level distance that the force of gravity applies. If you hold for a 150-yard shot, your bullet will be high (not so high as to cause a miss at that short distance, but you can easily see that a 300-yard shot would be a miss).

To carry this example to an extreme, you might be shooting almost vertically downward, as at a deer at the bottom of a deep canyon. In this case your range – as far as gravity is concerned – would be virtually zero and if you held for the exact distance you'd shoot far over his back.

VELOCITY

The speed of bullets is measured by instruments called chronographs. In use, the rifle is fired so the bullet breaks two screens set at a predetermined distance from one another. Passing through the first screen starts an electrical circuit; passing the second one stops it. The time is recorded in milliseconds and these can be translated into feet-per-second. The usual rule is to fire a minimum of ten shots and average the results, because there will always be a variation between shots.

ENERGY

Energy is a unit of work and it is expressed in foot-pounds, which is defined as the energy required to lift one pound a distance of one foot. You can compute a bullet's energy by squaring its velocity, multiplying that by the bullet's weight in grains, and dividing the result by 450,250. It's a lot easier to read it out of a catalog since the ammunition makers have done all the work for you. However, it is very important to consider the ability of certain bullets to *transmit* their energy to the target.

SECTIONAL DENSITY AND BALLISTIC COEFFICIENT

These are terms employed by the ballistician and, aside from a brief definition, we aren't going to spend much time with them. Sectional density is the relationship of a bullet's weight to its diameter. Bullets with higher sectional density, which means long in relation to their diameter, hold their velocity better than short, blunt bullets with low sectional density.

Ballistic coefficient is a figure used to determine ballistics by computer. Expressed mathematically, it is the ratio of a bullet's weight to the product of the square of its diameter and its form factor.

A typical example of velocity retention can be had by comparing the 110-grain .30/06 bullet with the 180-grain from the same cartridge. The 110-grain slug leaves the muzzle at the flashy speed of 3,420 fps, but at 300 yards it has slowed down to 1,970 fps. On the other hand, the 180-grain slug leaves the muzzle at a less sensational speed of 2,700 fps and at 300 yards it's still moving smartly at 2,190 fps, or 220 fps faster than the 110-grain slug. Assuming both were fired at the same identical moment, somewhere between 300 and 500 yards the 180-grain would overtake and pass the 110-grain bullet. There are countless other examples. Study ballistics beyond the first column and pick a load that is delivering energy, with a bullet capable of transmitting that energy out where the game is.

CHAPTER EIGHTEEN

WHIMS, ENGRAVING, CRAFTSMAN-SHIP

Two of these subjects are delicate. The things one likes or dislikes in guns are purely personal and any appraisal of craftsmanship can be a grimly serious business. A long time ago the late Captain Crossman, who wrote for *Outdoor Life* for many years, had a pat answer when people said to him that a pretty gun (meaning a fine, nicely engraved gun) never shot any better or any harder than a plain one. Crossman's reply to that was "a necktie doesn't keep you warm, either."

Guns are many things to many people. Some are the tool of their owners; I would include the shotgun a farmer keeps near the henhouse, the .22 a trapper carries on his trapline and guns intended for similar routine, functional uses. These are purely tools; no romance, no soul. Just a bang and another fox won't raid a henhouse, another trapped animal is ready for the stretching board. This doesn't necessarily mean that the people who use guns as a tool don't also own fine guns which they respect and admire. Indeed, many do. Moreover many owners of fine guns have guns for loaning — for rainy days and other occasions when they don't want to risk one of their favorite guns.

I've always felt that the reasoning that one can't afford a fine gun was stupid. Elsewhere in this book I have mentioned that I've had many opportunities to buy fine guns but didn't have the money. So I've been stupid. And that's true because I've blown enough money in other ways that would have gotten me a gun collection worth a fortune today. All you have to do is look at the stock market situation from about 1970 through 1976 and you'll get an idea of what I mean. So if you truly like fine guns, invest in them. They're well worth buying. Then take care of them properly. That means you should use your guns and give them the proper care and respect to which they're entitled.

It's a whim of mine that the only rifles I want in my rack are those that shoot with good accuracy. And I make no exceptions to that. If a rifle won't deliver excellent accuracy I won't keep it around. There is not, at this moment, in my personal collection any rifle that won't shoot within 1 inch at 100 yards, and most of them do quite a bit better than that. I recall an experience at my local gun club not so long ago when I sighted two rifles for a hunting trip. One was a prototype .30/06 bolt action, stocked by Al Biesen. This rifle shoots in less than an inch and I've bagged caribou, wolves, and deer with it. The second rifle was a .338 Winchester Magnum, Model 70. It also shoots under an inch; in fact, it usually shoots closer to ⅝-inch groups. (I only shoot three shot groups when targeting a hunting rifle.)

When I got to the range, a group of local cops were there and one of them had just bought one of those horrible 7mm ancient Mausers that I believe he bought at Woolworth's for about $10. (Considering where that gun was shooting, he overpaid.) He was shooting it at about 30 yards and it was printing about 3 feet low and his shots were scattered so badly you couldn't call it a group anyway. Finally they had enough and I set up my gear at the 100-yard bench. It was a case of "they all laughed when I sat down at the bench," because even though neither rifle had been fired since the last hunting season, one of them printed exactly where I wanted it (2 inches high) and the other only needed two clicks to get it sighted.

These cops simply had never before seen a good rifle shoot. It's not their fault — more people have never seen what a good rifle can do than the other way around. If you tell the average guy, even the average hunter, that rifles exist that can consistently hit a common house fly on a 100-yard target, they'll think you're nuts. But it can be done.

Recoil is something that a lot of people fear. And the fear of it causes them to flinch, which means a missed target. Back in his outfitting days, Les Bowman used to make each of his hunters sight in before they left for the hunting camp. Shooting under Les' critical eye, they'd often flinch when shooting the heavy Magnum rifle they'd brought along. Les was watching for this and he'd begin to work with them by starting with a lighter rifle, like a .243. If they could handle the .243 Les would then bring them back up to their Magnum. Maybe by now they'd been cured but, if not, Les would make them hunt with the .243, simply because they could put their bullet where it should be. And a 6mm bullet in the vitals is going to kill an elk quicker than a .300 Weatherby Magnum that hits nothing but dirt and rocks. And there's no doubt that recoil can hurt you. If a rifle is badly stocked, a mild cartridge can be punishing. A heavy rifle, like a .375 H&H or .458 Winchester Magnum, for example, is really no fun to shoot. But, once you have the rifle sighted, and you know you can shoot it and you know where your bullet is hitting, then you can hunt with it competently because you know you won't feel the recoil when shooting at game.

Recoil also brings up the matter of gun weight as against caliber, as against weight of the shooter. Heavy recoiling guns should be heavy — as heavy as the type of hunting they're built for will permit. This is because the weight will soak up a lot of the recoil and you won't feel it as much. Those big British double rifles for elephant, buffalo, and rhino often weigh 11–12 pounds and up. That's a lot of weight to carry, but these rifles are usually toted by a gun bearer and the only time the hunter has to handle them is when the game is sighted. Winchester's .458 Magnum Model 70 weighs 8½ pounds (without scope) and that's as light as I think that big gun ought to go for any comfort in shooting. Actually a little more weight wouldn't hurt it a bit. Naturally a lighter recoiling rifle can, and should, be made lighter. I'm a strong believer in light-weight hunting rifles so long as they still shoot with good accuracy. I've had many a 19-inch barreled sporter that shot like a dream and handled beautifully.

Weight of the shooter also becomes a factor in recoil. A light person tends to feel recoil less than a heavy hulk. I'm a 200-pounder and I feel recoil more than some lightweights simply because the recoil moves them quicker and is therefore less punishing. Some years ago there was a little flyweight of a woman who shot big game all over the world. She shot a .375 H&H Magnum and it didn't hurt her a bit. A fat man would have been hurt a good deal more than she was. This may not sound real,

There are still a few independent engravers plying the trade. Among the best is John Warren of Eastham, Massachusetts. John used to handle the complete gunsmithing job, but his engraving got in such demand that he had to give up everything else. Here are both sides of a Model 92 Winchester showing his delicate touch.

but it is a fact that the lighter the person, the heavier recoiling gun he can handle without feeling it so much. If you don't believe me, stand with your shoulder against a tree some day and shoot a powerful rifle!

I think it should be a rule that you should never buy a gun unless it has a makers name on it. Most guns are produced by the major factories who stamp their names, but I don't mean those. Some imports have no names; some products of gunsmiths are produced without name. These should be shunned, I believe, for the simple reason that if a maker didn't think enough of his product to stamp his name on, it should be avoided. But there are also some unscrupulous characters around who will do their own work on a barrel that already has another's name on it, and others who will stamp their name on the work of other, and better, workmen. I know of a man, now dead, who had no compunction about stamping his name on any decent-looking barrel that came into his shop. And I've run across others who have taken barrels made and produced by reputable gunsmiths and gunmakers and then rebored and/or rechambered these barrels while leaving the original name intact. How to avoid these? I don't know, for I've been the victim myself of more than one of the examples I've just related. The best advice I can give is only to deal with someone who is honest enough to guarantee that he'll give you your money back if you find the merchandise isn't what it was supposed to be.

As anyone who has read the chapter on stocks realizes, I believe the shape of a stock is important. It is just as easy to manufacture a stock that's shaped like a stock should be than to make a monstrosity. The same amount of work is involved. Yet, some factories turn out stocks that are supremely ugly. Whether it's because they don't know any

A Winchester Model 94 by John Warren that incorporates Winchester's trademarked Pony Express rider along with some fine English scroll.

better, whether their designers are purely mechanical engineers, whether their machinery has limitations, or just what I don't know. But, since some companies can make a decent stock, it follows that the job can be done in volume production and there's no excuse for ugliness. As I've said before, you spend a great deal more time looking at your gun than you do shooting it. You may as well have something nice to look at.

I realize everyone doesn't like what I do, and this can have a lot to do with what I'm saying here. But then, you can apply exactly what I'm saying to the other guns if you don't agree with me. Nevertheless, there are some basics which shouldn't be broken, but which are broken every day. I'd rather have just one fine gun than a half dozen so-so guns, the total dollars being about the same. You could easily make this same comparison with cars. A Ford Pinto, or Chevy Vega, will get you where you're going the same as a Rolls or Mercedes. Which would you rather own? Which would you rather drive? Which is the best buy? Well, a Model 70 Winchester bought some years ago (it was one of those vaunted pre-64 models) is worth four to five times its purchase price. But there aren't that many examples of ordinary run-of-the-mill guns that are worth anywhere near that today. What's a ten-year-old car worth? If it's a Rolls or Mercedes it's still worth a bundle, but not a Ford or Chevy (except for the antiques and genuine classics, which is another story).

You don't really need a "best" gun. There are a lot of guns around that will do the same thing – shoot as well, last as long. But it's still not the same. I remember a long time ago with the late Lucian Cary talking about the niceties of a well-made well-finished gun. The point came up that it really didn't matter what the insides of a gun looked like and Lucian, who violently disagreed with the point, said "*you* know what it's like." And that's really the crux of the thing.

I hate to see the glossy, shiny finishes that most stocks come with today. They can be seen a couple of miles away on a sunny day, and that is ridiculous. This is the result of market testing – makers put them on the racks in gun stores side by side with nice, dull, oil-finished stocks and the result was that consumers picked up the flossy stuff and that's what they bought. That's why most stocks are so glossy today. It's a mistake, but the market supported it. Of course, if they'd never have made the experiments in the first place who knows what might have happened. Another market test showed that people picked up rifles with longer barrels quicker than they did those of conventional length. Place several guns in a store rack, one of them a couple inches longer than the rest. That's the gun that'll be picked up.

The choice of a scope and mount also gets into personal whims. How do you choose among the several makes of excellent scopes available on today's market? It's hard and I don't know the answer. It would take an optical engineer to know how to pick which is the best optically. Some look a little better, but that's just a matter of cosmetics and, aside from what I've said about some other parts like bolt handles and the like, the appearance between scopes doesn't matter too much. Some have more accurate adjustments, but scopes of high quality and high price are pretty much alike. So I can't honestly tell you which is the best. Moreover, quality sometimes changes and what's really best today may not be all that good tomorrow. Mounts are getting easier to choose all the time. There was a time when every gunsmith plying the trade got an idea for a new mount and so did every manufacturer and importer of scopes. Now it's settled down pretty well to the two that have been the best right along anyway — Redfield and Weaver. This isn't to say the others are no good, not by a long shot; but these two are the simplest, most rugged, and have been around a long, long time and given excellent service all that time.

Speaking of whims I'd like to offer a suggestion of a gun battery, but that would be just one man's opinion. It would get into brand recommendations, would eliminate some excellent guns that might well suit you better than me, and, in general, would be a waste of paper. However, if you're starting out I would recommend the first purchase should be a .22 rifle. Let me again emphasize that I wish some manufacturer would market a good single-shot bolt-action .22 rifle. This is just about the safest kind of rifle to get a kid started out right. But sales of these are so slow that nobody gives a damn about making them. This is where the public is at fault and I don't know if the basic blame is with manufacturers who have been advertising the wrong products, ammunition makers who simply want to sell more ammunition (auto guns use more of it than single shots), or whether it's that same old American tradition that has built more and more power into cars until we reached a crisis a year or so back with the oil situation. I don't know where the blame lies. But I suspect we all share in it somehow.

Following the .22, you can then move up to a deer rifle the caliber of which will depend on where

Presentation-grade guns are also turned out by Savage; shown are Models 110 bolt action and 99 lever action with good wood and fancy engraving. Years ago, Savage made a Model 99-K, which was quite richly engraved and brings fancy prices on the collector's market today.

you hunt. The honorable .30/30 and similarly trusty .35 Remington are a couple of fine choices. If it's a bit bigger game you're after, the .30/06 can never be the wrong choice and will handle anything on this continent.

ENGRAVING AND OTHER DECORATIONS

There's no question that engraving adds class to a gun and that it adds value as well. It ought to add value — good engraving is expensive. There was a time in the late 1800s and early 1900s when a number of fine engravers plied their trade in the New Haven area. One of these was the great Rudolph Kornbrath, still spoken of as "the immortal Kornbrath." Kornbrath worked for Winchester although some say he moonlighted for Marlin on occasion and it's quite possible that he did. Then there was the Ullrich family, a whole family of engravers of whom, it has been claimed, August Ullrich was the best. The Ullrichs too worked for Winchester, but it is known that some of them also worked for and moonlighted for Marlin as well. Some of the guns of the period, both Winchester and Marlin, are engraved with a truly masterful touch. And make no mistake about it, an engraver is an artist of the highest order.

There are more engraved guns coming out of Europe and Japan today than are being made here. Not too many Americans have picked up the art, the prime reason being money. Engraving is costly and the wage scale here is still higher than in some other parts of the world. You can get picky, though, about the animal forms you see on some examples of imported engraving. My own favorite engraving is the small English scroll with no dogs, no birds, no game of any sort. Just scrolls. To my eye this adds up to sheer delight. Many engravers add gold, silver, and ivory inlays, which are then carved in relief. The inlays can take the form of animals, or initials, or whatever you want.

I've shown some of the work of two of this country's best engravers practicing today: Alvin White and John Warren. This is not meant to slight others because there are other excellent men practicing the art. It's just to give an idea what is being done here today. Also shown are some jobs turned out by some of our major factories — all high-class stuff indeed, and a great adjunct to a fine firearm. Even if you can't have a good engraver do the whole job for you, it's a touch of class to have the gunsmith's name and the caliber engraved rather than stamped in the steel. Engraving is expensive. Good engraving is even more expensive and its cost is something you'll have to evaluate for yourself. It takes an estimated 25–30 years for a man to become a "master engraver"; depending upon the amount and intricacy of the engraving to be done, the work itself can take from several hours (for initials for example) to a hundred hours or more. Convert those hours into dollars and you will quickly run up a big bill.

The reader who has a more than casual interest in engraving should read a book by E. C. Prudhomme, himself an engraver, entitled *Gun Engraving Review*, published by Gun Engraving Review Publishing Company, Ward Building, Shreveport, Louisiana, in 1961. The book contains many pictures, some in color, by many of the world's best engravers and is well worth studying.

Another form of decorative work on guns is etching, a process where the work is covered with wax, then the design is traced into the wax down to the bare steel. Acid is then applied and eats the design into the steel. Etching can be very attractive when correctly done. In fact the etching process can produce an interesting finish not unlike fine sandblasting when acid is evenly applied to whole surfaces. Like engraving, it calls for careful work; the result is considerably different but to some eyes it can be most attractive.

Here (and on the facing page) is a collector's item for you: Winchester Model 94, serial number 2,500,000. As you can see, the custom shop wouldn't let it out the door without doing some elaborate work on it.

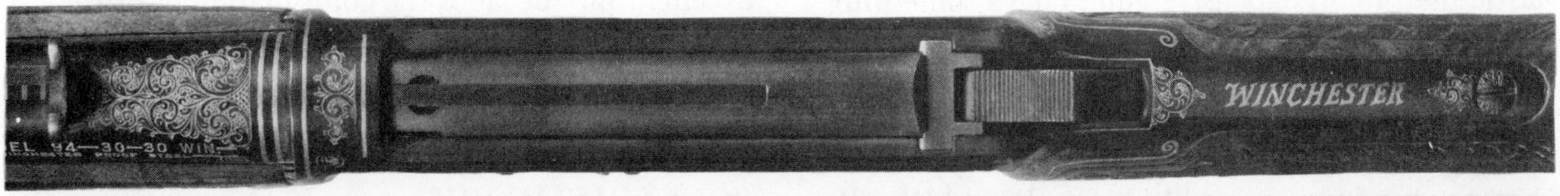

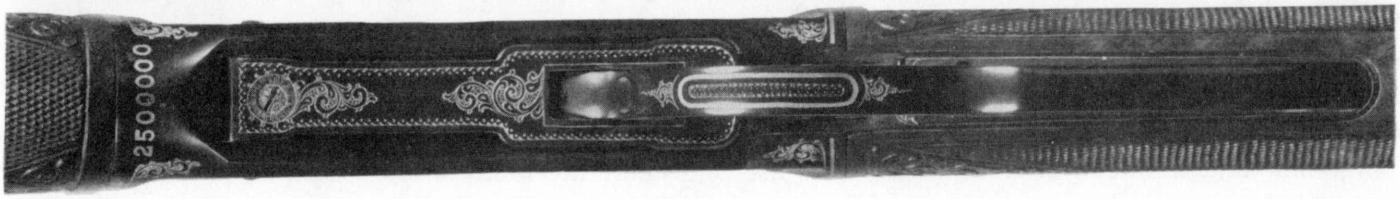

AN APPRAISAL OF CRAFTSMANSHIP

I hate to have to say this, but it's true and it must be said: Many, but by no means all, of the guns turned out today are not as well made as their counterparts were a few years ago. The same thing may be said of cars (where a certain "planned obsolescence" philosophy has long been part of the business) and many other products as well. The external appearance of any gun can be misleading. Some perfectly decent looking guns are positively rotten when you view the inside. And there are a number of imports that are fairly handsome outside but terrible underneath. It's been an old European custom for years to slap some pretty shoddy merchandise together, polish it neatly on the outside, add a few lines of engraving (by an apprentice), and ship it to the States for some rich American to be fooled.

The looks and appearance of a gun are largely matters of personal preference and you alone must be the judge of what you like. Now, having picked up a gun that appeals to you, study it carefully. First, if it is a well-known American brand — or an import made for a well-known American company — you know that you have recourse to the maker, although that sometimes takes a bit of doing to get satisfaction. Still it's better than getting stuck with something unknown made by an unfamiliar name.

Study the outside carefully. A fine external finish usually means careful attention to detail inside as well. Work the action; it's usually a little stiff in a new gun, but note how it works and look at the parts while you're working the mechanism. In today's production there are many stamped parts, many plastic parts — perfectly all right if the gun is priced accordingly. But you may not want to see plastic used in an expensive gun. That's something youll have to judge for yourself.

I have discussed the matter of today's gun production with a lot of people in many phases of the industry. Most of us are old enough to remember what gun production was like before World War II. We admit that guns cannot be made today like they were in the 30s — nobody could pay for them. Moreover, the advances in machine tools and other manufacturing techniques have been enormous. These new machines can produce better parts faster, and therefore at less cost, than could ever be done before the War. They also can produce more accurate parts with better machining. And the advent of precision casting, usually called investment casting, is an excellent development that produces parts to exacting tolerances requiring little in the way of finishing. I feel that, because of these advances, many of today's guns can and should be made better than they are. But I think one of the reasons they are not is that the public has become brainwashed. They are told, by advertising, by many gun writers, and by reading catalogs, that this is what guns should be like. How does a young fellow who's just getting an interest in guns, who has no one to turn to for an opinion, know what a gun ought to be? How does he define quality? He reads the Spritz catalog; he likes the looks of the Spritz Model 100; he believes what the copy tells him. Now he visits a gun store where he's confronted by a clerk who doesn't know a Spritz from a Winchester from a Remington from a Simson Mauser. He takes the Model 100 Spritz in his hands and he thinks it's great, because he's been led to believe it's all the catalog says it is. If you multiply this lad by all those in his position you begin to get a picture of hundreds of thousands of new gun buyers who just plain don't know what a gun ought to be. So the crap sells and keeps selling.

In many cases you've got to look deeper than the exterior, something you can't do very well in the gun store. I could tell stories about what's under the exterior in some pretty fancy name guns at pretty fancy prices. On the other hand, there are some excellent guns for the price on the American market today. Some of these are absolutely top-quality guns at absolutely top dollar. They're well worth the money and if you can swing it you'll get a good buy. There are also some excellent quality guns available at quite low cost. These represent an excellent buy because the combination of price and quality is right. You can't expect to get a Rolls-Royce for the price of a Ford Pinto, but you should expect to get your money's worth from either one.

"CUSTOM" WORK

By all odds some of the very best — and some of the very worst — examples of gun work are turned out by shops calling themselves custom gun shops. There are today a few examples of small shops — some one-man shops, others employing a handful of dedicated craftsmen — that are turning out abso-

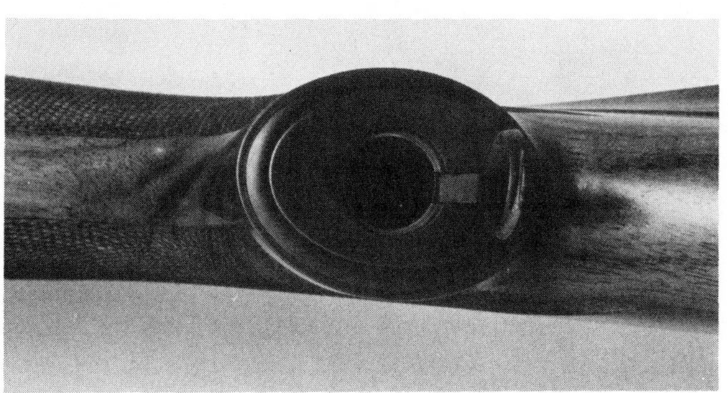

A trap-door pistol-grip cap can't hold much in the way of useful material. The British used to install them to carry an extra front sight, but that's hardly practical in these days of scopes. Nevertheless if you want this sort of added touch, it can be supplied by such as Champlin on this .458 Winchester Magnum.

lutely superb examples of gun work. However I think the most abused word in all gundom is "custom." It ought to refer to a firearm that is produced to order exactly as the customer wants it and/or what is decided by the maker and his customer (the maker adding his expertise). And in many cases that is precisely what it does mean. In other cases, custom is applied to any product that isn't turned out by a major arms factory and such output can range from hideous to dangerous.

This also is the area in which many other abuses occur, such as failing to stamp the caliber on the barrel, reboring and rechambering without changing the original maker's identification, and similar shenanigans. Bad as the metal aspects of these guns are, however, it must be said that the stocking is even worse. If you order a custom gun, or a custom stock, you should insist that it be what you ordered. And you should not tolerate any violations of either the agreed-upon specifications or workmanship. The inletting of this stock should be such that you should not be able to insert a piece of ordinary writing paper anywhere. When you dismount the metal from the stock (and you should make this inspection before accepting the work) the inside should be neat, clean, and tidy, and an exact mirror image of the metal parts (with proper allowance for movement). There simply is no excuse for any other kind of work and you should not tolerate it. This doesn't mean that you shouldn't allow the gunmaker some leeway in his own ideas. But these things should be discussed and agreed upon in advance. There are some gunmakers, for example, who will not make anything except a classic stock. If you learn this in advance, and if classic isn't your choice, then this isn't your man. By all means, get these matters squared away so there will be no surprises for either party when the work is done.

Similarly, if you are offered a second-hand custom gun be critical in your examination of it. Under no circumstances should you buy it if the stock has gaps that indicate bad work. If it looks clean and neat, examine the inside to make sure that's the same. If the maker's name is on the barrel, assuming a custom barrel, attempt to find out if he's still in business. If the rifle is one of the hot .22s or a hot Magnum, the barrel may well be shot out. The barrel may also have been rebored and/or chambered. You should be skeptical of these products unless they are identified as the product of a well-known maker and can be proven original.

Another point to look for is to make sure the stock's pores are filled. Wood is porous, and part of the finishing operation is to fill these pores. This is done in many ways, but a brief description of one of the old, tried and true methods will serve to explain it. I've always used GB Linseed oil, a carefully nurtured secret formula put up by a man named George Brothers who has now sold the product and process to Harrington & Richardson. You simply apply a coat of GB, preferably right after the final sanding of the stock with the finest finishing paper you can buy and while the sanded dust is still on the stock. This will mix with the finish and fill the pores. Let it dry thoroughly and then sand again right down to the bare wood. Some say you can do this with a single application, but it's always taken me several. What you're doing is filling the pores with finish and the result will be perfectly smooth. Every stock should be perfectly smooth with every pore perfectly filled.

CHAPTER NINETEEN

ACCURACY

The story of modern rifle accuracy is the story of benchrest shooting and that story has been told by Warren Page in a book entitled *The Accurate Rifle* also published by Winchester Press. We started the game of modern benchrest shooting in a big way over Labor Day weekend in 1947 in Johnstown, New York. Actually, the first man long ago who laid down behind a log and rested his rifle over that log was the first benchrest shooter. There was a flurry of that sort of shooting in the days when Harry Pope and George Schoyen and others made those wonderful barrels back in the 1890s and early 1900s. But, by and large, the game was ignored until the late Harvey Donaldson invited a number of shooters to a match that Labor Day weekend. I was one of those honored by the invitation and the late Al Marciante and Nick Papernek accompanied me.

We learned a lot that first year, and we shared it with others. We fired 3-shot groups at 100 yards and I won a match, which thrilled the hell out of me. As I remember it was a group measuring 5/16th inch, center to center of the widest shots. And it was with a rifle I'd built myself! One of the things we learned quickly was that you had to make your own bullets to win. An outfit called RCBS was making bullet swages, a die that fitted a conventional loading press of the C type into which you placed the bullet jacket with a snipped-off piece of lead wire for the core. Raising the handle swaged (rhymes with sage) or formed the bullet into the shape of the die and, presto, you had your bullet.

Some of us make our own bullet-making dies. I

From left to right; Ray Biehler, Walt Astles, Harvey Donaldson, and the author. Biehler and Astles made the dramatic improvement in bullet manufacture by developing the expanding-up principle. Harvey Donaldson was a cartridge designer, experimenter, and noted raconteur.

shot a 200-yard world record in 1948 with bullets I'd made myself in swages I'd made myself right there on the range (we mounted the loading tools on the rear deck of our cars). That target was published in Warren Page's book. Soon, a couple of savvy lads from Rochester, New York, named Ray Biehler and Walt Astles, worked some miracles with new bullet swages based on a basic idea presented by a man named Jonas Hallgrimsson from Brookline, Massachusetts (but originally from Iceland). Ray Biehler was a professor from Rochester Institute of Technology and Astles was a toolmaker.

Between the basic ideas and the skills of the men involved, they worked out what they termed the expanding-up method of making bullets. The process is now universally followed. Briefly, this means that every succeeding operation in bullet manufacture makes the bullet a little bigger. To properly understand this you have to let me digress to the older methods. Bullet makers used to think it was all right to take a bullet jacket exactly .224 inch in diameter, insert a core, and swage the bullet. Sometimes, with certain bullet-making dies, because the dies were two piece, the bullets came out with a little ridge around the middle. These bullets were then "ironed" by passing them through a finishing die that actually reduced their diameter a little.

What was learned was that when you made a bullet slightly smaller, or even kept it the same size, there was a certain amount of expansion of the jacket that took place after leaving the die. The result was a loose core. Maybe only a tenth of a thousandth of an inch — or less — but a loose core just the same, and the result was an unbalanced bullet the flight of which was unpredictable. On top of that, it was soon learned that lead wasn't quite the dead metal everybody thought it was. Lead didn't necessarily remain exactly as it was after forming. And, of course, jackets that were absolutely concentric were demanded.

Finally Biehler and Astles found sources of concentric jackets. These had a slight taper to their inside walls and an outside diameter a little smaller than the finished bullet would be. They made a precise core swage — a beautifully made die that swaged a piece of lead wire to precise weight and dimensions that would exactly fit the taper of the bullet jacket's inside. Now the core was seated in the jacket in a special die that seated it firmly enough to expel all air and thoroughly filled the bottom of the jacket. This die was of a size to allow very slightly expansion of the jacket. Next, the jacket with seated core was swaged into the bullet-shaping die, which was the finish die, and produced the ogive (nose curve) and brought the bullet to a point. The result of this procedure was to produce much more perfect bullets than had ever been made before and a corresponding increase in accuracy was seen instantly. Within a short time everybody shooting benchrest either had a set of B&A dies or bought bullets from someone who made them in B&A dies.

It didn't take very long for the word to spread. I remember one match because Clair Taylor and Don Robbins, who made some of the finest rifles during that period, showed up using Sierra bullets. And damned if those Sierra bullets didn't shoot along with the home-produced product from B&A dies. This was almost sacrilege. Benchresters had believed nobody could do anything as well as they could, but in another year or so the same procedure was followed by both Hornady and Speer. This information wasn't lost on the major firms, either. One of the early benchrest shooters was Mike Walker, of Remington's design staff, who was responsible for the 721, 722, 725 and today's 700 actions as well as the .222 cartridge. Wayne Leek, another Remington designer with imposing credentials, also shot in some of these early matches. But it took quite a long time before the

In the center stands a .30/30 cartridge, just as you buy it over the counter. At right is a reloaded .30/30 using the Sierra 180-grain boat-tailed bullet. A sample bullet is seen at left. Note that only about 1/8-inch of the cartridge's neck has been resized to hold the new bullet; the remainder of the case was not touched by the sizing die. This permits the case to assume the exact shape of the rifle's chamber and assures concentric loading.

major ammunition makers realized they'd better make a better bullet than they were turning out, for the magazines were playing up accuracy and shooters were starting to demand better products.

It may not have been the very first, but the first of the really fine bullets produced by one of the majors that I ever used was the 80-grain .243 Winchester bullet. In those days I was writing for *The American Rifleman* and I tested the new .243 Model 70 for that magazine. Its accuracy was incredibly fine . . . so good I couldn't believe it. This was with the ammo that came along with the rifle . . . factory loaded. I soon obtained a supply of the bullets from Winchester, a set of reloading dies from RCBS and proved to myself that Winchester had learned to make bullets.

That's where it all began. The bullet was the key, and, had anybody really studied it sooner, it was all right there in the writings of Dr. F. W. Mann published in 1909.

The benchrest lessons didn't just apply to bullets. They applied to other components of the ammunition and they applied to rifles too. But we learned that some of the older rifles would shoot much better with the new bullets, too, and in my opinion at least, the improved bullets resulting from benchrest shooting was the most significant improvement in the story of today's better accuracy.

Many experiments were made with rifle actions. The early favorite was the Mauser military, probably because there were so many of them available. Another favorite was the Winchester Model 70, but it was much more expensive than the Mauser so

An early benchrest shooter using a Mauser action with custom barrel and stock with amply wide forearm to better sit on the rest. Note that his shoulder is not touching the butt and that he's squeezing the trigger with thumb behind trigger guard and forefinger on the trigger. His scope is the big Unertl.

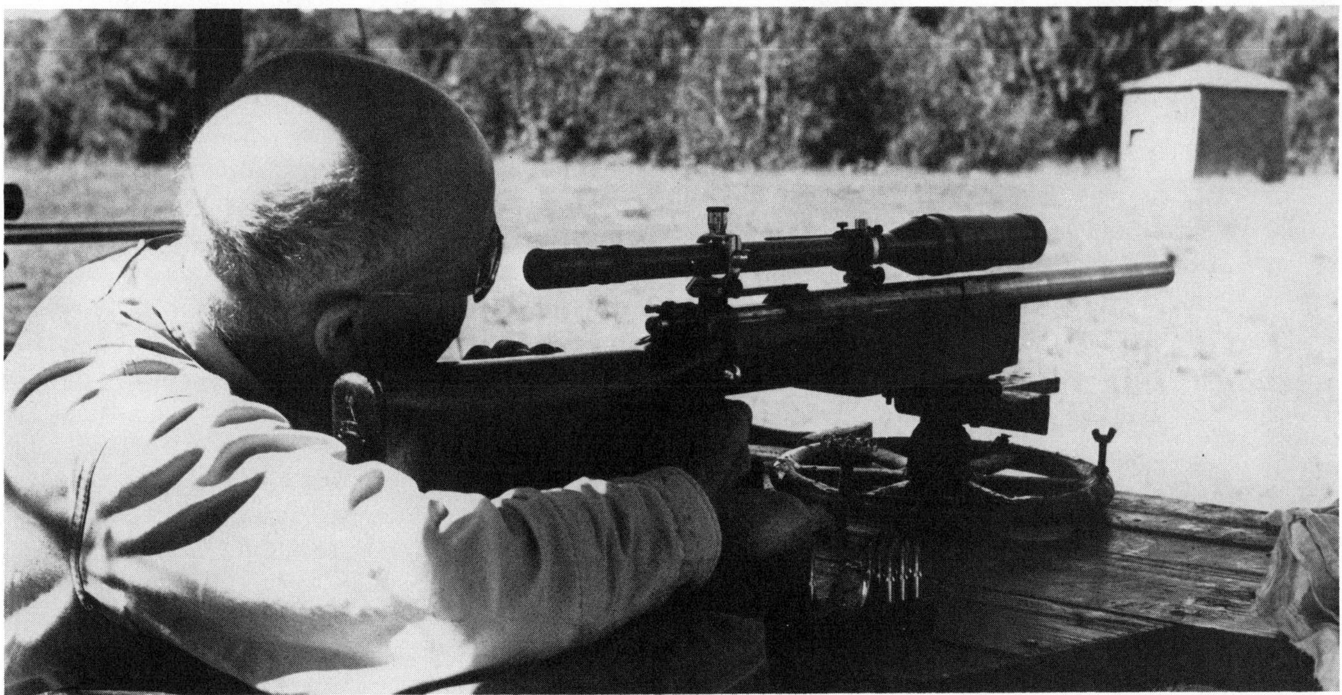

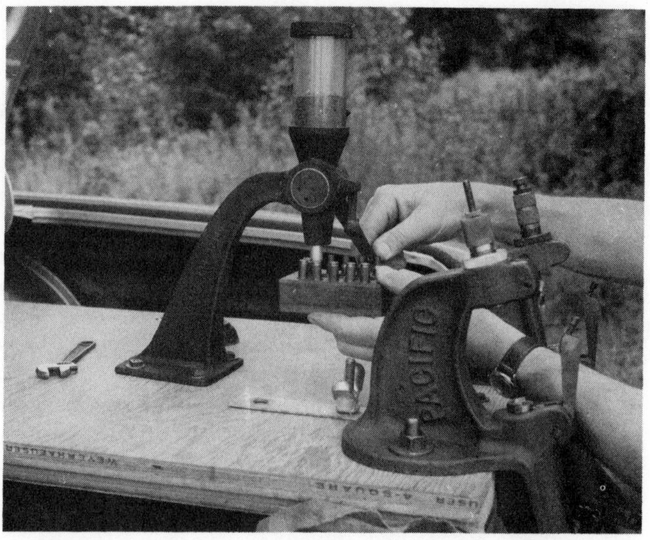

"Working up a load" is handloader's language for finding the best combination of primer, powder, and bullet for a particular rifle. The simplest and fastest way to accomplish this is to mount the loading gear on your car trunk. This shooter has resizing die in one tool, bullet seater in another, and is metering powder into primed cases prior to seating bullets.

you didn't see so many of those. Then came the 722 and that's been the benchrester's action almost ever since. The trend today is toward custom actions, although many shooters still use the 722 and sleeve the action with a long, round metal sleeve that stiffens the action and also permits mounting the scope entirely on the sleeve (instead of partly on the receiver, partly on the barrel). These sleeves are secured to the round Remington receiver with a Devcon epoxy.

Today's barrels are better than those we started with in 1947. Back then we had only a few choices of custom barrels and a few shooters used factory products. Al Marciante showed up at that 1947 match with a Model 70 Winchester varmint model in .220 Swift, a hot rifle for its day.

The process of button rifling didn't originate with the bench shooter but he adopted it quickly. Today's benchrest barrels are mostly made of stainless steel and are rifled by the button method. Some of the finest barrels are air gauged to check uniformity, and I suspect some of them are carefully hand lapped slightly after rifling. Fortunately, the benchrest shooter talks a lot. He doesn't keep his secrets, and as a result, everyone soon knows what he's done to make his rifle shoot more accurately. That's one of the big lessons learned. That's one of the most important contributions made by a bunch of individual riflemen to gundom. Just as the Kentucky rifle evolved from the German Jaeger rifle, and as the Plains Rifle evolved from the Kentucky, so has the modern, accurate sporting rifle evolved from the demands of use.

HOW CAN ALL THIS BENEFIT YOU?

It already has, if only because the rifle and ammunition you buy today will shoot much better than that you bought 20 years ago. Often, you can make it shoot better than it will right out of the box.

You'll need a nice, light, crisp trigger pull. You'll need a properly bedded action and barrel. You can do a certain amount of correcting if some of these things aren't up to snuff on the rifle you bought. But, rather than fiddle with them yourself, find out who's a good gunsmith and ask his advice. Make sure he knows what it's about before you trust your rifle to him though. Then you'll need a good scope, mounted properly and tightly (many scopes loosen in recoil; when they're fitted you should use that little tube of Loctite that comes with nearly all scope mounts today). A scope will reduce your error of aim. Lastly you'll need a good sturdy shooting bench, from which to shoot so you can eliminate the human element as much as you can. That's what rifle testing is all about — eliminating all the errors possible.

Let me tell about one example of the joys of owning and shooting a super-accurate rifle: This refers to my Model 70 Winchester .338 Magnum. I use a handload of the 210-grain Nosler bullet with a charge of 68 grains Re21 powder and a CCI Magnum primer. (Unfortunately, Hercules has taken this excellent powder off the market.) This rifle, with this load, shoots groups of ⅝ inch at 100 yards and I sight it to hit about 2½ inches high at 100 yards. A couple of years ago I was hunting deer in New Mexico with Bob Behn, Marlin's advertising manager at the time. We were up in a canyon and spotted a pair of deer way across the canyon at a slight elevation, but no more than about 20° uphill. We figured the deer were a solid 500 yards away, and we studied them for a full 20 minutes before Bob decided to shoot the buck. By this time I had persuaded him to use my .338 (I'd already shot my deer) and told him just where to hold.

Here is a bench all rigged up for the experimental rifleman to develop a load for his rifle. Loading tool, powder measure, powder scale, bullets, and powder are all evident. This is a handy setup that avoids wasted time.

Ordinarily you shouldn't shoot at a deer that far away and I wouldn't have recommended it under any ordinary circumstances. But Bob Behn is a cool shot and I knew pretty well where this rifle would shoot. The only guessing was the exact range. We were with an experienced guide who agreed with us on the distance so I had no real fears about the bullet connecting. Bob fired and the rest of us watched in our binoculars. Never in my life have I seen a deer drop so fast. And lie so still. He never twitched, laying with all four feet in the air. When Bob and the guide finally arrived at the scene, it was observed that the bullet had caught the deer low in the neck, forward of the brisket and had completely torn out the throat.

The pleasures of a good shooting rifle are many, and as I've said, that's the only kind I will tolerate in my rack.

been continual, although gradual, improvements in almost all cartridge-performance characteristics, without sacrificing compactness.

It is of interest to determine how these significant performance advances and size reductions have been obtained. These are the result of several factors, of which perhaps the most important is improved propellants, which feature precise control of rates of gas generation, and of course, higher potential.

Also important factors in cartridge-performance improvements are higher strength materials — which permit operation at higher and more efficient pressure levels — greater uniformity of materials — which permit reductions in component weight without sacrifice of strength and safety margins — and last but far from least, very careful design to achieve the desired ballistic levels.

It is interesting to trace the steps in the design and development of a high-performance Center-Fire cartridge to illustrate how the characteristics of a new entry to the Winchester-Western line are defined. As an example, we will follow the development of the .264 Winchester Magnum, an outstanding cartridge that was added to the line in 1960.

The .264 was conceived in answer to the need for a high-intensity cartridge that would be capable of safely outperforming certain "wildcat" cartridges. (Many of these cartridges have considerably over-advertised performance, which is often attained at dangerous pressure levels.)

First, it was determined that Winchester-Western needed a cartridge with the following performance characteristics:

- a. Flat Trajectory.
- b. High Retained Energy.
- c. Low Wind Drift.
- d. Moderate Recoil.
- e. High Initial Velocity (if compatible with the first four requirements).

The first three requirements are characteristic of two ballistic properties: a good ballistic coefficient for the bullet, and a high initial velocity.

To determine how these characteristics were designed into the cartridge, a very limited excursion into the field of ballistic design is desirable. First in order to obtain long-range performance, it is essential that the bullet have an excellent ballistic coefficient.

The ballistic coefficient is the measure of a projectile's performance in flight; the higher the value of the ballistic coefficient, the better the bullet's ability to resist the decelerating force of air resistance, and to retain its velocity. Thus with a good ballistic coefficient, projectile drop, wind drift, and velocity loss are decreased.

The equation for ballistic coefficient is:

$$C = \frac{W}{id^{2}}$$

where

C = ballistic coefficient

W = bullet weight, pounds

i = coefficient of form, numeric

d = bullet diameter, inches

Also, bullet weight is proportional to the cube of the diameter.

Thus, in order to obtain the maximum ballistic coefficient, it would appear to be desirable to use the largest caliber possible.

However, there are definite limitations on increasing caliber to attain good long-range performance; in effect, it is necessary to make a compromise between ballistic coefficient, muzzle velocity, and recoil, in order to attain the overall performance desired.

For example, with modern propellants, which must be burned in conventional-length barrels and within certain pressure levels, there are limitations on the amount of propellant that can be efficiently consumed, and on the efficiency with which potential energy of the propellant can be converted into projectile kinetic energy.

In general, these follow certain relationships, as shown in Figures 1 to 3 (see next page).

Figure 1 indicates the heaviest propellant charges that normally can be used effectively in various calibers. You will note that the maximum practical propellant charge is proportional to caliber.

For example, about 37 grains of powder is the maximum practical charge in Caliber .20, while Caliber .40 can use up to about 74 grains of powder. Figure 2 indicates the usual efficiency with which propellant potential energy is converted into projectile kinetic energy for various calibers. It is strictly empirical, and has been derived from examination of many conventional Center-Fire calibers. Note that in Caliber .20 the efficiency is about 22 percent, and increases to about 40 percent at Cali-

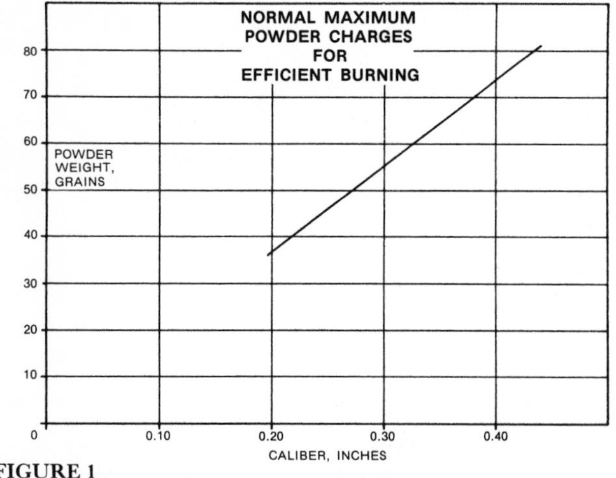

FIGURE 1

ber .40. The slight curvature is a result of the effect of propellant gas generating rate characteristics and the projectile's base area, which increases with the square of the caliber.

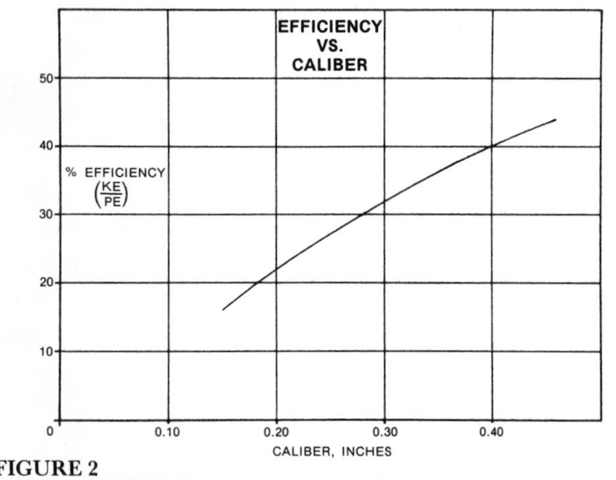

FIGURE 2

By combining the efficiency and maximum charge curves, it is possible to plot the maximum predictable kinetic energy directly as a function of caliber, as shown in Figure 3.

It is obvious that for maximum projectile energy, the largest caliber possible should be selected.

While it is obvious that the largest bores deliver the most kinetic energy to the projectile, we must remember that for good long-range performance with a given ballistic coefficient, high muzzle velocity is the prime parameter required.

Another important factor that must be considered is bullet stability. In order to stabilize projectiles by rotation, or to cause them to fly "point on," it is essential that certain weight limitations be observed for each caliber. In general, it can be stated that the ratio of bullet weight to the square of the caliber (or sectional density) must be between the limits 0.15 and 0.35. Lower values are impractical, as the projectile becomes too short for effective shape, and higher values cannot be stabilized by the spin imparted by the rifling.

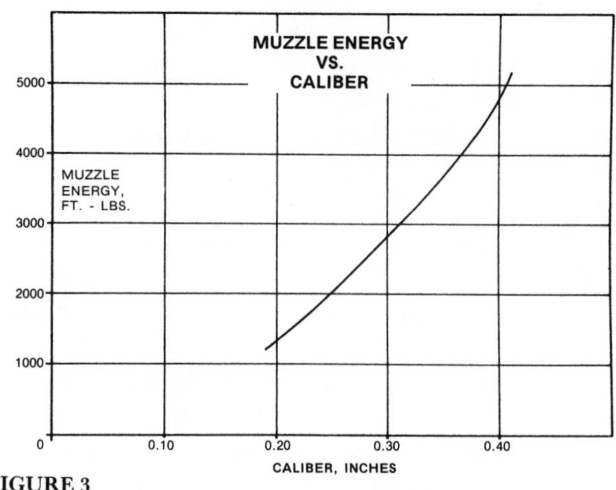

FIGURE 3

At this point we should recall the basic rule that bullets with equal ballistic coefficients, launched at the same velocity, will have exactly the same trajectories.

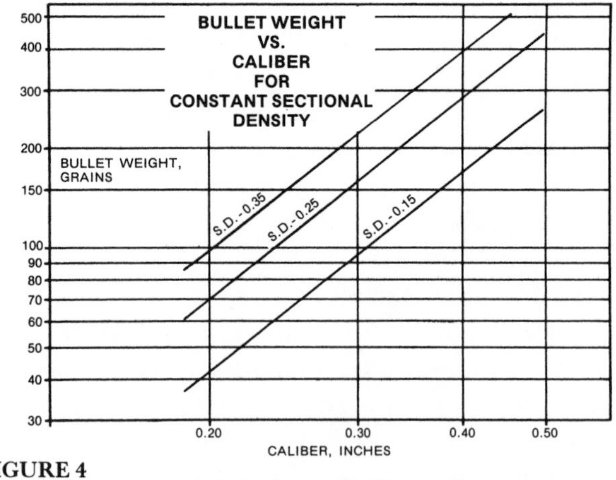

FIGURE 4

In effect, the lines on the graph on Figure 4 are lines of constant ballistic coefficient for bullets with similar point shapes, and a Caliber .20 projectile weighing 70 grains will give the same trajectory as a Caliber .40 projectile weighing 280 grains, or four times as much, if they are both launched at the same velocity.

With this fact, plus the maximum predictable muzzle energy expected from various calibers from Figure 3, we can calculate the attainable muzzle velocities for three bullets of equal ballistic coefficient, but different calibers.

VELOCITY AND RECOIL VS CALIBER			
Caliber	.20	.30	.40
$\frac{W}{7000d^2}$	0.25	0.25	0.25
Bullet Weight, Grains	70	158	280
Max. Eff. Pdr. Wt., Grs.	37	55	74
Efficiency, percent	22	31	40
Kinetic Energy, Ft-lb	1,345	2,815	4,885
Muzzle Velocity, ft/sec	2,940	2,830	2,800
Recoil Velocity, ft/sec (8-lb. gun)	6.96	12.16	19.56
Recoil Energy, Ft-lbs. (8-lb. gun)	6.02	18.4	47.6

FIGURE 5

In Figure 5, the net effect for bullets of equal ballistic coefficient is a slight improvement in muzzle velocity as caliber is reduced, combined with greatly reduced recoil (Caliber .20 recoil is about ⅛ Caliber .40 recoil). This indicates that for minimum drop and wind drift at long range, it is advisable to use the largest powder charge permissible, with the smallest possible bore, and bullets of optimum point shape.

It was with these basic factors in mind that preliminary design of the .264 Winchester Magnum was initiated. It was decided that the basic case used in the 458–338 series, with its 75-grain powder capacity, would be used with the smallest practical bore that could utilize this extremely large charge. This case also permitted cartridge design that was compatible with the existing M-70 rifle. It was recognized that utilization of this high charge in such a small bore would present difficult, although challenging, development problems.

From experience gained in the design and development of many small arms, aircraft ordnance, and other high-performance cartridges, the conclusion was reached that about .26 caliber was the minimum bore practical, and .264 (or 6.5mm) was selected, since bullets for preliminary tests were available in large quantity and varied style, without incurring fabrication expense for experimental samples.

With bore size and case capacity selected, only the choice of bullet weight was left for prediction of performance.

With a charge of 75 grains of propellant (over 50 percent more than had ever been used successfully in bores this small), and an assumed efficiency of 25 percent (to allow for the slightly decreased efficiency of the slow powders that would be required) a muzzle energy of 3,100 foot-pounds was calculated, as follows:

The direct equation for the conversion of propellant potential energy into projectile kinetic energy is:

(1) $KE = \%E \times PE$

where

KE = kinetic energy, ft-lbs.

$\%E$ = efficiency of gun cartridge.

PE = potential energy in propellant, ft-lbs.

The equation for potential energy is:

(2) $PE = W_p \times PE_g$

where

PE = potential energy in propellant, ft-lbs.

W_p = powder weight, grains.

PE_g = potential energy per grain of powder.

(PE_g can be assumed at approximately 165 ft-lbs./grain for estimating purposes).

Substituting, we derive:

(3) $KE = \%E \times W_p \times PE_g$, or for the example in question.

$KE = 0.25 \times 75 \times 165$

KE = 3,100 ft-lbs. (approx).

Based on this value, and an assumed coefficient of form of 0.70 (which reflects good point shape), velocities, drops, and remaining energies were estimated for varying projectile weights, using standard procedures for calculation of exterior ballistic data. These are tabulated in Figure 6 (next page).

Figure 6 shows that the light bullets have the highest muzzle velocities (as expected) and the flattest trajectories, but also the lowest remaining energies, while the heavy bullets have almost the

CALCULATED PERFORMANCE
.264 WINCHESTER MAGNUM
ME = 3,100 ft-lbs.
i = 0.70

Bullet Weight (Grains)	Muzzle Velocity (ft/sec)	Sect. Dens. $\frac{W}{7{,}000d^2}$ (lb/in²)	Ball. Coef. $\frac{W}{7{,}000id^2}$ (lb/in²)	Recoil, 8-lb. Gun (ft-lb)	500 Yard Velocity (ft/sec)	500 Yard Energy (ft-lb)	500 Yard Drop (inches)
80*	4,180	0.164	0.235	20.5	2,070	760	41
00	3,740	0.205	0.293	20.1	2,110	990	47
120	3,410	0.246	0.352	20.0	2,110	1,180	52
140	3,160	0.287	0.411	20.2	2,080	1,350	58
160*	2,950	0.328	0.469	20.5	2,030	1,460	65

*80- and 160-grain bullets may not attain coefficient of form of 0.70, due to extreme shortness and length, respectively.

FIGURE 6

same 500-yard velocities and about 40 percent higher energy.

From these characteristics, two bullet weights were selected for final development; a 100-grain bullet for high-velocity use on small game and varmints, and a 140-grain bullet for long-range use on medium game.

The 100-grain bullet was selected to obtain high initial velocity and flat trajectory, while the 140-grain bullet was selected to deliver reasonably flat trajectory, high remaining energy, and low wind drift.

The major component development phases in a new cartridge development are of interest. Briefly these are:

a. Bullet
b. Case
c. Propellant

The bullet is perhaps the most important cartridge component. Its performance is easily evaluated by the consumer without complicated ballistic test equipment, for accuracy and upset are easily checked. In addition, projectile shape must be optimum for velocity retention, and the materials of construction must not foul the bore.

The second major item is the cartridge case. The case must have sufficient strength to withstand the high pressures necessary for high performance levels, yet the case walls must not be so thick that interior volume is decreased to the point where an adequate quantity of propellant cannot be carried. (Incidentally, contrary to popular opinion, thick case walls do not in themselves guarantee strength.)

The third major item is the propellant; it must have a high potential energy, and the correct burning rate to release this energy before the bullet emerges from the bore, yet at the same time it must not exceed the pressure limitations for the cartridge.

Related requirements for the powder are low bore erosion, reduced flash and smoke, and uniform ballistic performance at the extremes of climatic conditions and after long-range storage under adverse conditions.

Some of these characteristics are not always immediately compatible, and as a result, the development of components that meet all specifications is an empirical problem, not capable of direct solution by theory, but requiring experimentation.

As an indication of the development effort required for one component, it is interesting to examine the samples of bullets that were fabricated and evaluated before acceptable 100- and 140-grain bullets were available for the .264. All these bullets were tested for ballistic level, accuracy, upset, and many other performance objectives. The number of bullets (sixteen 100-grain and twenty-four 140-grain) is indicative of the difficult ballistic problems attendant upon this development.

After a rather brief coverage of the ballistic prob-

ANTICIPATED VS ACTUAL BALLISTICS
.264 WINCHESTER MAGNUM

	100 Grain Bullet		140 Grain Bullet	
	Est.	Act.	Est.	Act.
Muzzle Velocity, ft/sec	3,740	3,700	3,160	3,200
500 Yard Velocity, ft/sec	2,110	2,030	2,080	2,100
Muzzle Energy, ft-lb	3,100	3,040	3,100	3,180
500 Yard Energy, ft-lb	990	915	1,350	1,370
500 Yard Drop, inches	47	49	58	57

Note: Actual velocities and drops agree with predicted values within 4%!

FIGURE 7

lems involved in the development, it may be enlightening to compare ballistic predictions with actually attained performance levels for the .264. These are shown in Figure 7.

A comparison of actual and predicted velocities and trajectories shows agreement within 4 percent.

This close match between predicted and actual performance levels is indicative that with careful calculation of ballistic performance, the most modern and extensive types of ballistic test equipment, engineers skilled in ballistic testing, and diligent experimentation, the desired performance levels can be attained in the development of a new high-performance cartridge.

That's the story of the .264 Winchester Magnum cartridge, directly from the lips of Winchester. As we've already indicated this cartridge has not been an over-riding success and I predict that it never will be. But the thought processes and rationale behind such a development are interesting.

INDEX

Boldface numbers refer to illustrations

Accelerator cartridges, 137-138, **138**
Accuracy, in rifles, 196-197, **196, 197;**
  barrels, 196;
  making bullets, 193-195, **194, 195**
Accurate Rifle, The (Page), 193
Actions, bolt, 7-18, **9, 10, 12, 14, 16, 17;**
  double barrel, 18-19;
  lever, 21-25, **22, 23, 24;**
  pump, 27-28, **27;**
  rimfire lever, 25-26;
  single shot, 19-21, **20, 21;**
  see also specific makes
Ajax Model 100, 92
Albert, M. J. *Primers,* 143-144
Allin Conversion, **21**
American Civil War, and firearms, 3
Ammunition, 123-130;
  cartridges:
    center-fire, 127-128, **128,**
    rim-fire, 126-127, 128,
    wildcat, 128-129;
  metrics, 129;
  sub-caliber adaptor, 129
Anschutz, **106**
Appel, Dr., 77-78
Appel, barrel, 79; process, 78-80, **80**
Astles, Walt, 194, **194**
Automatic gun, 4;
  see also specific makes

BAR, *see* Browning firearms
BB caps, 126
Balickie, Joe, **97**
Ballard rifle, 20, 141
Ballistics, 123
Barrel, 71-88, 147, 196;
  double rifle, 82-83;
  early, 71-72;
  fastening, 84-85, **84;**
  gun "blueing," **87,**
  headspace, 86;
  interchangeable, 84;
  length, 87-88;
  life, 83;
  liners, 83-84;
  making, 77-80, **78, 79, 80, 81;**
  name stamp, **88;**
  proofing, 84;
  recoil compensators, 87;
  ribs, 86-87;
  rifle chambers, 85-86;
  rifling, 72-76, **75, 76**
Bausch & Lomb scopes, **115**
Bee cartridge .218, 132, 133, 200
Berdan, Hiram, 128
Biehler, Ray, 194, **194**
Biesen, Al, **14, 96, 104,** 107
Biesen grip, **97**
Biesen stock, **99**
Blackburn trigger guard, **97**
Black powder guns, 145
Blowback, 30-32, **31**
Bolt actions, 4, 7-18, 19, 24;
  gas escape, 12-13;
  guard screws, 13;
  innovations, 15-17, **16;**
  left-handed shooter, 17, **17;**
  Mauser, 8-9;
  safeties, 13;
  short and long, 13-15;
  sporters, 10-12, **9, 10, 12, 14;**
  straight pull, 17-18
Boxer, Edward M., 128
Boxer Rebellion, 33
Breech action, *see* Actions
Breech-action locking systems, 37-44;
  direct-lever, 42-43, **43;**
  hump, 43-44;
  inertia, 44;
  sliding wedge, 42;
  toggle, 44;
  turn bolts and adaptations, 38-42, **38, 39, 40;**
  underlocks, 44
British .303, 132; .577/45, 140, 141
Brownell, Len, 102
Browning firearms, auto-5 shotgun, 32, 67;
  autoloading and lever rifles, 46, 49;
  BAR (automatic rifle), 33, 35, 98;
  BLR, 22, **24,** 25, 26;
  disconnector, 61;
  machine guns, 42;
  Model 1885, **18**
Browning, John M., **18,** 20, 25, 27, 30, 32, **43,** 54, 85
Bullard rifle, 25
Bullets, 153-182;
  brush busting, 163; developed since World War II, 161-162;
  energy, 162-163;
  expanding, 159-161;
  flight of, 165-182, 167, **170, 176,** 177, 178, 180;
  lead, 153-155;
  making of, 193-195, **194**
  metal cased, 156;
  pointed military, 158-159;
  round-nose solid jacket, 157-158, **157;**
  .22, 155-156, **155**
  varmint, 162;
  see also specific makes
Burgess, Tom, **97**

Burns, James E., 143
Bushnell, Dave, 114, 116, 121

CB caps, 126
Caliber, 123, 131, 135
"California School" of gun design, 89, **90,** 102
Canadian Rose, 18
Canjar, M. H. trigger, 62-63, **62**
Carbine, 4; U.S., 34-35
Cartridge, 12-15, 123, 125-126, 131-132;
center-fire, 127-128, **128;**
feeding, 45-50, **46, 48, 49;**
how named, 133-134;
interchangeability chart, 137;
developed before war and still standard, 199-200,
developed for war and obsolete, 200,
developed since war, 201-202;
rimfire, 126-127, 128; .22, 126, 199; .30/06, 132; .30/30, **195;** .32/20, 134; .44/40, 134; .45/70, 131-132;
see also specific makes
Cartridge cases, 139-142; **140, 141**
Cary, Lucian, 75, 102
Center-fires, 127-128, **128,** 133
Centurion Model 10, 92
Chambers, 85-86
Champlin Arms Co., **16, 111**
Champlin rifle, 15, **16,** 17, **105**
Charter Arms "Explorer" Model, .22, **31**
"Cheekpiece," 102, 103
Civil War Guns, 114
Cocking, 6
Colonial days and firearms, 5
Colt .45, 67; Model 1895, 33
Colt-Sauer rifle, 15, **15,** 41, **41,** 64
Comfort, Ben, 14
Cordite, 151
Core-Lokt Bullet, 160
Craftsmanship, 190-191, **191**
Crossman, Captain, 183
Custom work, 190-191, **191**

Direct Lever locks, 42-43, **43**
Donaldson, Harvey, **194, 200**
Donaldson, .219, **200**
Double barrel rifles, 18-19
Dovetail sights, **110,** 111, 114
DuPont, 93; powders, 148, **149,** 150

Ejection, 6, 53-55, **54, 55**
Elliott, F. K. "Red," **129,** 134

Enfield action, 1917, **97**
Enfield rifle, 10, 11, 49, **75,** 76-77
Engraving guns, **185-188,** 188
European bolt action sporter, 11
Extraction, 6, 51-53, **51**

Farquharson, 20, **20,** 68-69, **68, 97**
Fastex, camera, 55
Fecker, J. W., 118
Feeding, 6; systems, 45-50, **46, 48, 49**
Firearms, *see* specific kinds and makes
Firing, 5-6; systems, 65-70, **68, 69**
Flintlock gun, 145
Flobert, Louis, 126
Franks, John, 93

Garand, John, 33, 54
Garand, M1, 33-34, 49-50, 67
Gas escape, 12-13
Gas operated firearms, 29, 32-35, **32, 33, 35,** 85
Gatling gun, 4
Gebby, Jerry, 134
Gipson, Vernor, **200**
Greener, W. W., 39-40
Griffin & Howe, side mount, 114
Guard screws, 13
"Guardians of the Birmingham Proof House," 84
Gun Engraving Review (Prudhomme), 188
"Gunmakers Company" (London), 84
Gun powder, *see* Propellants
Gun stock, 89-107;
butt plates, 106-107;
checkering, 104-106, **104, 105;**
designing, **90, 94;**
inletting, 94-99, **95, 96, 97;**
laminations, 93-94;
materials, 90-92, 91;
nylon, 66, 93;
rifle and shotgun stock, 94;
shape, 101-104, **101**
"Gun that Won the West, the," **18**

H & H, *see* Holland & Holland
H & R Ultra 360 autoloader, 43
Hageman, Wray, 118
Hallgrimsson, Jonas, 194
Hatcher, General Julian, 138, 179
Henry, .44, 126
Hensoldt scope, 114
High Power, .22, 200; *see also* specific makes

Holland & Holland, 18;
Apex, .240, **129;**
cartridges, 13-15, 128;
Magnum, .244, **129, 141,** 142;
Magnum, .300, 141, 200;
Magnum, .375, **97,** 129, **133,** 141, 163, 199
Hornady spire point bullet, **157**
Hornet, cartridge, .22, **84,** 132, 133, 199, **200;**
Model 70 rifle, 15
Howe, Jim, 10
Hump locks, 43-44
Huntington, Fred, **129**

Inertia-locking systems, 44
Ingalls, Col., 179
Ithaca, 25; Model 51 shotgun, 42

Jaeger, Paul, 114
Jaeger, rifles, 5;
side mount, **103,** 114, **115**
James Woodward .303 British double rifle, 82
Jet, .22, **202**
Jury, Frank, 168

K-14, 15, 16
Kentucky rifle, 5, 92
Kleinguenther rifles, 15-17, **40, 63**
Kollmorgen scope, **115,** 116, 120
Kornbrath, Rudolph, 188
Krag, cartridge, 132, 134, 200;
rifle, 12, 156, 159
Krag-Jorgensen rifle, 9

Lancaster-oval bore (rifling system), **75,** 77
Landis, Charley, 202
Le Faucheux, 127
Lee, T. K., 120-121
Leek, Wayne, 194
Left-handed shooter, 17, **17**
Lens, *see* Scopes
Leupold scope, **114, 117,** 118, 122
Lever-action repeating rifles, 21-25, **22, 23, 24**
Lever-locks, 42
Locking, 6; systems (breech-action), *see* Breech-action locking systems
Loctite, 122
Lovell, **200**
Luger pistol, 44
Lyman, 111-112, 116